THE EPIC OF GOD

A GUIDE TO GENESIS

Revised Edition

Michael Whitworth

START2FINISH

ISBN-10: 0988512181
ISBN-13: 978-0988512184

Library of Congress Control Number: 2014935923

Published by Start2Finish Books
PO Box 680, Bowie, Texas 76230
www.start2finish.org

Printed in the United States of America

Cover Design: Josh Feit, Evangela.com

To the love of my life

Sara Anne

who gives me another reason to fall in
love with her every moment of the day.

She is a Godsend (Gen 2:18).

CONTENTS

Foreword   11

Introduction   13

Genesis Q&A   15

1 In the Beginning   21

Genesis 1:1–2   22
Genesis 1:3–2:3   26
Genesis 2:4–25   29
Talking Points   33

2 Paradise Lost   35

Genesis 3:1–19   36
Genesis 3:20–24   44
Genesis 4:1–16   45
Genesis 4:17–26   49
Genesis 5   50
Talking Points   53

3 Deliverance   57

Genesis 6:1–8   58
Genesis 6:9–22   61
Genesis 7–8   63

Genesis 9:1–19   67
Genesis 9:20–29   69
Talking Points   72

4   Cradle of Civilization   75

Genesis 10   76
Genesis 11:1–9   79
Genesis 11:10–32   82
Talking Points   85

5   Two Steps Back   87

Genesis 12:1–3   88
Genesis 12:4–9   93
Genesis 12:10–20   94
Genesis 20   96
Talking Points   99

6   The Fog of War   101

Genesis 13   102
Genesis 14   105
Talking Points   110

7   In Between   113

Genesis 15   114
Genesis 16   119
Genesis 17:1–14   124
Genesis 17:15–27   129
Talking Points   132

8   Judgment Call   135

Genesis 18:1–15   136
Genesis 18:16–33   139
Genesis 19:1–29   144
Genesis 19:30–38   152
Talking Points   154

9   A Faith Odyssey   **157**

    Genesis 21:1–21   158
    Genesis 21:22–34   161
    Genesis 22   164
    Genesis 23   172
    Talking Points   175

10   To Be Continued ...   **177**

    Genesis 24   178
    Genesis 25:1–11   183
    Genesis 25:12–18   186
    Genesis 25:19–34   187
    Genesis 26   191
    Talking Points   196

11   He's the Cheatin' Kind   **199**

    Genesis 27:1–28:9   200
    Genesis 28:10–22   204
    Genesis 29:1–30   207
    Genesis 29:31–30:24   209
    Genesis 30:25–43   212
    Genesis 31   214
    Talking Points   220

12   Family Matters   **223**

    Genesis 32:1–21   224
    Genesis 32:22–32   227
    Genesis 33   229
    Genesis 34   231
    Genesis 35   234
    Genesis 36   237
    Talking Points   240

13   O Brother, Where Art Thou?   **243**

    Genesis 37   244

Genesis 38   250
Genesis 39   255
Genesis 40   257
Talking Points   259

14   **Brave New World**   **263**
Genesis 41   264
Genesis 42–45   268
Genesis 46–47   274
Talking Points   278

15   **For Your Family's Sake**   **281**
Genesis 48:1–49:28   282
Genesis 49:29–50:26   293
Talking Points   299

Epilogue   301
Abbreviations   303
Acknowledgments   307
Bibliography   309

FOREWORD

We live in a world where books abound. Our homes, our offices, and now our eReaders are filled with books. Yet in this cluttered world, there is still a need for good books. In the church, there is a special need for books that will help us have a better understanding of the Old Testament.

The book you hold in your hand is a good book. It is a book about the Book of Origins, "The Book of Genesis." It is a good book written by a good man. Michael Whitworth has provided a tremendous resource for anyone who wants to have a deeper understanding of the beginning of all things. Although Michael is a young man, his study of God's Word, as well as his ability to communicate it, whether in preaching or writing, places him in a unique position.

This is not a shallow book. It is a book with great depth. Michael has done his homework. His research is thorough and his conclusions are most helpful. It has been a joy for me to read this book, and it has been especially helpful to me during a time when I have been preaching through the Book of Genesis. Michael's insights have been a great help to me, as well as to the church during our study of Genesis.

Some might ask, "Why Genesis?" The answers to this good question are numerous. Through a study of Genesis, we learn about creation, we learn about our first parents, we learn how sin entered the world, we learn about God's amazing grace in dealing with sin, and we learn so much more.

The Apostle Paul reminded us, "For whatever was written in earlier times was written for our instruction, so that through perseverance and the encouragement of the Scriptures we might have hope" (Rom 15:4 NASU). There is so much to learn about our Great God by studying this book. Just one small example—the first words of Gen 8 read, "But God remembered Noah…" What a wonderful blessing! What a wonderful lesson! We have a loving Father in Heaven who does not forget His people. Praise God!

I am thrilled to recommend this book to you. It should be read by every preacher, by every church leader, by every Bible class teacher, and by every Christian. Your heart will be thrilled as you read this book and study the great Book of Beginnings. May God bless you richly as you study His Word.

— Jeff A. Jenkins
Flower Mound, Texas

INTRODUCTION

In college, I took what I thought would be a cupcake course to fulfill my P.E. requirement: swimming. Embarrassing as it is to admit, I drastically underestimated how difficult—how physically taxing—it would be. The class final required us to swim forty laps in an Olympic-sized pool.

I almost passed out after ten.

But I learned in that course that swimming is an excellent cardio workout because it utilizes several muscles in the human body, and that translates into gains in other health pursuits. Swimming helps me lift more and run farther. It better conditions me for all other physical activities. Can a person get in shape without swimming? Maybe. But it's much harder.

Genesis is a book of beginnings. It speaks of the origins of man, Israel, sin, and redemption. It introduces us to several biblical themes, the most important of which is God's sovereign authorship of life. In Genesis, the Almighty is depicted as Creator, Sustainer, and Judge of all things. He creates man from the ground and breathes life into his inanimate body. He provides the first couple with a home, a mission, and a blessing. Even after he judges their sin, the Lord remains a part of his people's lives. Cain rebels, Abraham haggles, and Jacob deceives. Yet they individually discover that God is the One authoring the script, directing the play, guiding their steps. The paradox of divine sovereignty and free will is one of life's great mysteries, and Genesis introduces us to its enigmatic tension.

This project has been over four years in the making. In that time, I have come to love the book of Genesis for so many reasons, all of which I hope to share with you in what follows. The greatest reason I love this book is also why I love all of the Old Testament: it's like swimming for my spiritual health, a great exercise in godliness (1 Tim 4:8). Can a person grow spiritually without reading the OT? Maybe. But it's much harder.

I realize that some object to *any* in-depth study of the OT, using the argument, "We no longer live under the Law, so why should we study what it says?" But realize that this was *never* the opinion of New Testament writers! Paul argued in Rom 15:4, "Whatever was written in former days was written for our instruction, that through endurance and through the encouragement of the Scriptures we might have hope." He later reminded Timothy that the young evangelist had known the Scriptures (i.e. the OT) from childhood, and that they could make him "wise for salvation through faith in Christ Jesus." It was then that Paul declared *all* Scripture to be useful for "training in righteousness" because it equips us "for every good work" (2 Tim 3:15–17).

In other words, Paul believed that OT books like Genesis could still be instrumental in saving, sanctifying, and equipping the people of God.

I thus consider Genesis to be of grave importance. In a world that blames God for disasters, yet credits luck or karma for life's blessings, we need reminding that the Lord alone is the universal Maestro. Evil and suffering are not from his hand, yet he is mighty enough to work the worst of circumstances for our ultimate good and his own exalted glory. It is ours to choose whether we will cooperate with his unfolding redemptive drama—whether we will submit our lives to his will. Each step taken and word spoken should be a confession of just who is crafting our life's story. In Genesis, we are confronted with the lives of the faithful and faithless, and are challenged to emulate the former, so that we might thereby please God (Heb 11:6) and not remain in abject darkness (John 12:46).

If we truly want to draw closer to God's heart, we will allow our faith to be tested and refined in the fire of trial (1 Pet 1:6–7). In Genesis, we see that process played out in an up-close and uncomfortably familiar way. But the book also gives us a glimpse of God's matchless love, of his concern for the welfare of his people, and of his plan to redeem a fallen, wretched world. Like swimming, Genesis can strengthen our spiritual muscles; it can clarify our faulty vision and transform our nagging deficiencies.

Embark with me on an amazing journey through this "book of beginnings" to when the world was an infant and our common ancestors were learning to walk with the Lord. Listen to their stories. Celebrate their victories. Agonize their failures. And may your faith in the God of Abraham, Isaac, and Jacob deepen as he equips you for every good work.

GENESIS Q&A

In a recent interview with myself, I asked a few questions about this guide to Genesis. I hope that the answers will orient you both to Genesis and to this guide.

Q: Who wrote Genesis?

A: Moses. An editor later added the occasional comment, but Moses wrote the bulk of the book. If you want to get technical, God authored it because his Spirit inspired Moses (2 Pet 1:21).

Q: When was Genesis written?

A: About 3,500 years ago.

Q: How do you know?

A: Israel's exodus from Egypt occurred around 1446 B.C. During the next forty years, as Israel wandered in the desert, I imagine Moses had a lot of free time on his hands to write stuff. Like Genesis.

Q: Why do you believe Genesis was written?

A: I explained that in the *Introduction*.

Q: So I should read the *Introduction* if I haven't already?

A: Yes.

Q: Do I have to read the *Introduction* to go to heaven?

A: Yes.

Q: Seriously?

A: No.

Q: Can I understand the rest of Scripture without studying Genesis?

A: I don't think so.

Q: Why?

A: It's like trying to understand Tolkien's *The Two Towers* or *The Return of the King* without *The Fellowship of the Ring*. The middle and end just won't make much sense unless you know about the beginning.

Q: It's that hard?

A: Sort of. But then again, I tend to exaggerate a lot.

Q: Are you always like this?

A: Only if I haven't had coffee in a really, really long time.

Q: What would be the best way to use this guide?

A: If you ever needed to start a fire…

Q: Seriously?

A: Well, if you were desperate, I guess so. But I think the answer you're looking for is this: I recommend a four-pass system of studying Scripture. Let's take Gen 6:1–8 as an example. It always helps to first read the broad context of a passage. Gen 6–9 comprises the entire Flood narrative, including a prologue explaining the reason for the Flood, and an epilogue that relates an embarrassing, though relevant, story from Noah's latter years. If you wanted to study the Flood's prologue, then I would recommend that you read 1.) Gen 6–9, 2.) Gen 6:1–8, 3.) that passage's section in this guide (e.g. pages 58–61), and 4.) Gen 6:1–8 again. Reading through the passage several times, plus studying it in this guide, will hopefully cement it in your mind.

Q: Similar to how watching a good movie a second or third time enables you to "catch" things you missed the first time?

A: Precisely!

Q: What can you tell us about how this guide came together?

A: I struggled with what to include and what to leave out. I didn't necessarily want to discuss everything there is to know about a given passage, nor did I want this to become a survey of everything scholars have said without throwing in my own two cents. But I want the reader to understand God's word, so I tried to answer common questions that arise from the text. Please don't expect me to deal with every issue, and I don't always expect you to agree with my conclusions. Study and reflect on your own and then make an informed decision; don't take my word for it. My goal was to present this material in a format that would resemble a friendly conversation, albeit a one-sided one. Each chapter ends with a few "Talking Points," truths that will hopefully provide good material for lessons or sermons and spark positive discussion in a class or small-group setting. At the end of the day, I want each person who reads this guide to have a better grasp on what Genesis is saying, and consequently to draw closer to God's heart. Ultimately, only the reader can judge for himself whether I have succeeded.

Q: Do you recommend a specific Bible translation?

A: Not really. This guide primarily uses the English Standard Version (ESV), but it always helps to read the Bible in more than one translation. I do recommend a good Study Bible with a wide selection of maps to aid you in study.

Q: Would you like to add anything else before we conclude?

A: Did you read the *Introduction*?

Q: Only I'm allowed to ask questions around here. But yes, I did.

A: Then the only other thing I would add is an encouragement to meditate on what God has to say in Genesis. I hope that you are given a vision of God's greatness and grace, and that you respond by exchanging your fear for faith. Again, I pray that studying this book of beginnings draws you closer to the heart of your Creator.

For there is another history that a people makes besides the externals of wars, victories, migrations, and political catastrophes. It is an inner history, one that takes place on a different level, a story of inner events, experiences, and singular guidance, of working and becoming mature in life's mysteries; and for Israel that meant a history with God.

GERHARD VON RAD

1

IN THE BEGINNING

I wish I could write like Moses. His inspired account of creation is both majestic and restrained; he leaves us awe-struck, yet craving more at the same time. Admittedly, a few not-so-basic questions about life go unanswered—we have no idea whether Adam and Eve had belly buttons, and Gen 1–2 says nothing about where darkness originated (though Isa 45:7 does). But in the opening pages of Genesis, you and I are told enough to conclude that everything originated from the heart and hand of God.

This bold proclamation on Moses' part, that one deity is the Creator of all things, stood opposed to the pagan propaganda that God's people had been exposed to through the centuries. Israel needed to know that there was no uncontrollable chaos or warfare in the beginning, only authoritative words from the Alpha and Omega, the Ancient of Days.

A word of caution: God's people today sometimes make the critical mistake of combing Genesis (especially the first two chapters) for answers to scientific questions, and that bothers me. The original purpose of Genesis was not to answer our 21st century inquiries, and we shouldn't read it like a science textbook. When we talk about creation, we are dealing with events no person witnessed. They are beyond the human experience. They are the majestic works of God. It is unfair to expect the Bible to be a scientific textbook. If it were, it would be cost-prohibitive for the masses to own—have you seen what a biology textbook costs these days?

With that said, however, I want to make one thing very clear. Scripture and science need not live in enmity with one another as we pretend that they do, and should science ever disagree with Scripture, then the Bible is to be our ultimate authority. It is, after all, the revealed Word of God. It saddens me that those who claim the atonement of Christ feel the need to subject his words to science's claims, or to expect every phenomenon in Scripture to have a scientific explanation. Science *might* be able to explain the Flood or the destruction of Sodom, but it will never be able to explain a virgin birth or an empty tomb. Science never died for my sins, and when the Son of Man returns in his unparalleled glory to be marveled at by all the nations and take his bride home, to what will science attribute that great day? Solar flares?

In short, you and I have no biblical reason *not* to take Moses literally in this chapter when he claims that God created the universe in six days and then rested. Nor do I have any biblical reason to doubt the historicity of Adam and Eve or the Fall. We cannot be dogmatic when divine revelation does not permit us to be so, yet just as Moses wrote to combat the lies of ancient paganism, he also left evidence to expose Darwin's deception.

But can I let you in on a secret? In writing Gen 1–2, Moses wanted to refute error, but this was not his primary purpose. More than anything, Moses wanted Israel's God to be exalted as Lord of all. That is what these first two chapters of Genesis are all about. This is what the Bible is all about! This is what we should be about! All things were created by God's word, are sustained by his power, and work to his glory (Rom 11:36). We need God as a play needs a playwright, or a masterpiece needs a master craftsman. To those who live within his boundaries, the Lord provides blessing and life, but to those who do not, curses and death. More than a science lecture or a polemic against paganism, Gen 1–2 was meant to publicize the majesty and mercy of God. So let's take a peek behind the curtain at the beginning of time!

GENESIS 1:1–2

"In the beginning, God created the heavens and the earth." Of all the words in Scripture, few are more famous than these. As an exceptional wordsmith, Moses chose his words with exact precision. In this, the very first mention of God in Scripture, Moses selected the Hebrew noun *elohim*, a generic term that can mean both the true God (over 2,000 occurrences in the OT) and false gods, such as Dagon (1 Sam 5:7) and Baal (1 Kgs 18:24). Meanwhile, the personal name of God, *yhwh* (i.e. Yahweh), is not used until 2:4.

So why did Moses use Elohim in the first chapter, yet switch to Yahweh in the second? It's because Yahweh highlights God's relational nature, while Elohim calls attention to his immense majesty and universal sovereignty, themes that are quite appropriate for their respective chapters.[1] In other words, Moses wanted readers of Gen 1 to envision Creator God as grander than our collective imaginations.

Even in his sentence structure, we see traces of Moses' intent to exalt God. The awkward Hebrew word-order of Gen 1:1 spotlights God as One without beginning or origin and unbound by time or space, religious ideas that were totally unprecedented in ancient times.[2] Inspired by God's Spirit, Moses was thus determined to correct the error of his day.

In antiquity, people used mythology to explain the world and how it functioned, similar to how we today turn to science for our answers. If you had asked an Egyptian or Canaanite, "Where does rain come from?" the response would have been a dramatic and elaborate tale about the rain god, not a physical science lecture. Since the dawn of time, every society has had its own cosmology—a creation story explaining the earth's origins—that served as the incubator for that society's world-view. In short, people tend to speak and act out of their answer to the question, "Where did I come from?" or "How was the world created?"

Ancient cosmologies experienced wide circulation in their day, and Israel was likely exposed to some during her sojourn in Egypt. At the least, Moses had to have been familiar with them, because he was an adopted member of Pharaoh's household and a product of Egypt's finest schools. But later in life, God inspired him to pen the truth about the beginning of time.[3] A sampling of these creation myths from three of Israel's neighbors can help us understand the significance of Moses' words.

EGYPT

According to the Egyptians, there were no gods "in the beginning"—just primordial waters or a cosmic bowl of soup. One creation account says that the god Amon-Re (i.e. Amun-Ra) emerged from these waters and created the lesser deities of the pantheon through sneezing and masturbation. This

1.   Victor P. Hamilton, *The Book of Genesis: Chapters 1–17* (Grand Rapids: Eerdmans, 1990), 153.

2.   Nahum M. Sarna, *Genesis* (Philadelphia: Jewish Publication Society, 1989), 5.

3.   Gordon Wenham calls Gen 1 "a polemical repudiation of [Babylonian and Egyptian] myths," (*Genesis 1–15* [Dallas: Word, 1987], 9). Gerhard Hasel sees in Gen 1 how "Israel has forcefully rejected and fought off that which it felt irreconcilable with its faith and understanding of reality," ("The Polemic Nature of the Genesis Cosmology," *EQ* 46 [1974]: 82).

tradition comes from a papyrus with the heading "The beginning of the book of overthrowing Apophis, the enemy of Re and the enemy of King Wen-nofer—life, prosperity, health!—the justified, performed in the course of every day in the Temple of Amon-Re, Lord of the Thrones of the Two Lands, Presiding over Karnak." Apparently, the Egyptians were really good at building pyramids but terrible at titles.

A rival cosmology in Egyptian lore, written on what is called the Shabaka Stone, asserted that Ptah created Amon-Re, meaning Ptah was the true creator-god. Ironically, the myth later says that Ptah created all things "through what the heart thought and the tongue commanded." That sounds very similar to the recurring phrase in Gen 1, "God said…"

But don't be misled—there is a significant difference between "creation by word" in Egyptian mythology and in Genesis' theology. Ptah created the cosmos by uttering magical spells; he had to manipulate a power greater than himself in order to effect creation. On the other hand, "The first chapter of the Bible knows only of creation by an effortless, omnipotent, and unchallengeable divine word."[4] In other words, God is powerful enough to speak plainly, and it is done (Heb 11:3). He is not subject to the intricacies of magic, forced to utter an exact formula. Rather, all things are subject to him!

MESOPOTAMIA

Much of what we know about the creation myths of the Fertile Crescent comes from an ancient story known as *Enuma Elish*. Apsu and Tiamat, god and goddess of the sea, were angered by the noise created by other deities. Apsu wanted to kill them, but Tiamat was not so willing. She warned Ea, god of wisdom, of Apsu's plan, and Ea used his magical powers to murder Apsu. Ea then became the most powerful god. Meanwhile, he and his consort Damkina conceived a child named Marduk, who became even more powerful than his father. He was a constant source of aggravation to Tiamat (baseballs through the windows, loud parties late at night—the usual). Distraught over the murder of her husband, and angered by Marduk's disruptive ways, Tiamat fought Marduk and was defeated. Marduk thus became the chief god and, after killing Tiamat, created the world by tearing her corpse in half. "Then the lord [Marduk] paused to view her [Tiamat's] dead body, That he might divide the monster and do artful

---

4. Hasel, "Polemic Nature," 90.

works. He split her like a shellfish into two parts: Half of her he set up and ceiled it as sky..."[5] Later, Marduk created man from the blood of the slain god Kingu.

In another story from Mesopotamia, *Atrahasis*, humans were created as an afterthought when the gods demanded that the god Enki relieve them from their forty-year-long drudgery of menial tasks, such as gathering food and digging irrigation ditches.

CANAAN

In Canaanite lore, the chief god Baal was presented with two war-clubs and subsequently battled Yam, god of the sea. Baal was victorious, but the end of the battle account is unknown; the stone tablet on which it is inscribed is broken just when it gets to the good part. The remainder is thought by scholars to have been the Canaanite creation story, but this isn't certain.[6]

These creation myths speak volumes about the values of Egypt, Mesopotamia, and Canaan, particularly their low view of deity.[7] These nations wanted their gods to be just as arrogant, moody, and unmerciful as themselves. Their gods weren't morally superior, only more powerful. Stronger, but not holier. Paganism has always attempted to bring the divine down to our level.

Almost as bad is the low view of humanity held by these pagan cosmologies. If human beings were really created as an afterthought to do the gods' dirty work, then this explains why ancient cultures placed so little value on the sanctity of human life.

The most popular cosmology today, evolution, claims all things were created by chance. Human beings evolved over hundreds of thousands of years from tiny atoms swimming around in primordial waters—we seemingly can't escape the cosmic-bowl-of-soup motif! Consequently, the impersonal forces of luck, fate, and karma govern the world, not God. Evolution, the new paganism, is a product of man's desire to eliminate accountability to anything divine. If life is an accident of cosmic proportions, then we can all resort to a dog-eat-dog mentality—survival

---

5. ANET 67.

6. Lucas, "Cosmology," DOTP 133–34.

7. Kenneth Mathews notes that those in antiquity perceived the world "as a playground for capricious deities," (*Genesis 1–11:26* [Nashville: Broadman, 1996], 118).

of the fittest—without any consequences. Evolution's low view of humanity is surely responsible for the abject despair so epidemic in our world.

We may scoff at these absurd creation myths from yesteryear, but they are scarcely more ridiculous than evolution. The ancients imagined their gods as being bound by time and space; evolution completely ignores any notion of the divine. The goal of ancient pagans was to bring God down to their level. Now, it is to make God irrelevant entirely, to "banish him to the hidden corners of our lives."[8] And both systems of thought degrade the value of human beings. If the gods are violent, or if God is irrelevant, then racism, genocide, and abortion become morally palatable. If we are the fruit of afterthought or accident, then human life is not sacred.

But in Gen 1:1–2, Moses rescues us from these damning, destructive lies. He declares emphatically that the universe is not a result of chaos or warfare, but of God's orderly and peaceful design. Creation did not spring from a cosmic bowl of soup, but was conceived in God's heart. Human beings were not an afterthought, but a purposeful part of his plan. We were not created to provide God with food; it was God who gave man food in the beginning (1:29). The Creator is not bound by time and space, nor is he subject to the same whims and emotional immaturity as we are. He instead transcends all things.

Far from being irrelevant, it is in God that "all things hold together" (Col 1:17).[9]

GENESIS 1:3–2:3

In the ANE, bestowing a name implied ownership and rule. Several biblical persons had their names changed by a superior (e.g. 2:20; 17:5; 32:28; 2 Kgs 23:34; 24:17). In the same way, God's sovereignty over all the earth, a prominent biblical theme (Pss 24:1; 95:3–5), is underscored by his bestowing names like "day," "night," "sky," "land," and "seas." But conspicuously missing in Gen 1 are the Hebrew words *shemesh* and *yareah*, "sun" and "moon." The author preferred the generic phrases "greater light" and "lesser light." The ancients notoriously worshiped the sun, moon, and stars (Deut 4:19; Jer 10:2). But by withholding

---

8. John H. Walton, *Genesis* (Grand Rapids: Zondervan, 2001), 66.

9. It is significant that ANE cosmologies explain the origins of deities, while Genesis presupposes God's eternality (Sarna, *Genesis*, 5). "God's existence is not explained but is axiomatic and self-evident," (Bruce K. Waltke and Cathi J. Fredricks, *Genesis* [Grand Rapids: Zondervan, 2005], 68).

their names (the stars being almost an afterthought), the heavenly bodies are robbed of any claim to divinity.[10]

From the creation of light, the narrative quickly moves through each successive day. Moses is like a tour guide at a museum; he shuffles us through each "exhibit," allowing just enough time to stand in awe of the display before moving on to something more wondrous. He thereby keeps our focus on the Craftsman, rather than the masterpiece.[11] Days one and four deal with light and the heavenly bodies; two and five detail the creation of the sky, sea, and their creatures; three and six the formation of dry land and its creatures.

The story climaxes with the creation of man and woman. That this event is so prominent starkly contrasts with pagan cosmologies, particularly those of Mesopotamia. Those stories portrayed man's creation as an afterthought. But in Genesis, God calls the attention of his heavenly court to what he is about to do (cf. Job 38:7).[12] While he had created everything by divine fiat up to that point, God formed man with his own hands. "Let there be…" gave way to "Let us make…" God deemed his creation "good" six times (1:4, 10, 12, 18, 21, 25); only after the creation of man did he call it "very good" (1:31). God gave to Adam alone dominion over the earth and its inhabitants. Unlike the animals, mankind is the only creature that bears God's image.

This concept is a heavy one to consider, and its implications are equally profound. In ancient times, rulers were thought to be the "image of the gods" (i.e. the gods' representatives on earth). However, this designation was never extended to the average Joe, so when Moses applied this it to all humanity, the Genesis cosmology became all the more radical compared to its contemporaries.[13] Everyone was created in God's image and thus has intrinsic value. It also means that everyone represents God's presence on earth. Such an

---

10. Hamilton, *The Book of Genesis: Chapters 1–17*, 127–28.

11. "[God] distributed the creation of the world into successive portions, that he might fix our attention, and compel us, as if he had laid his hand upon us, to pause and to reflect," (John Calvin, *Commentaries on the First Book of Moses Called Genesis*, trans. John King [Grand Rapids: Eerdmans, 1948], 1:78).

12. There are sound arguments for and against identifying "us" (1:26) as a Trinitarian reference. The Trinity is certainly a biblical concept (if not a biblical term), but "us" may refer here to God's heavenly court (1 Kgs 22:19–22). For more on this interpretation, see Walton, *Genesis*, 128–30; for a survey of all the interpretive options, see Wenham, *Genesis 1–15*, 27–28.

13. Hamilton, *The Book of Genesis: Chapters 1–17*, 135.

awesome, even frightening, concept makes the biblical call to godly living all the more crucial: if we fail to reflect God's nature on earth, no other created thing is left to answer that call.

Only after his creation was "very good" did God rest from his work (2:2), though "rested" is a poor translation. The nuance of the verb *shabat* is one of ceasing and stopping, not relaxing and rejuvenating (cf. Josh 5:12; Ezek 16:41). Here, the seventh day is blessed and hallowed, but it would not become a mandatory day of "ceasing" until Sinai (Exod 20:8–11).

Christians no longer observe the Sabbath as Israel once did. Even Sunday, sometimes considered the Christian Sabbath, is not shackled by the same rules. "These things were like a shadow of what was to come. But what is true and real has come and is found in Christ" (Col 2:17 NCV). This means the Sabbath principle still holds great importance for God's people. Reality is indeed found in Jesus, one who regularly escaped the routine so that he might partake of the holy (Mark 1:35).

Following his example, every Christian should find ways to pause the weekly grind and commune with the Father. God prohibited Israel from working on the Sabbath to remind them that he was really in charge. If the world survived when God rested, things wouldn't fall apart when Israel did the same. Christians also need a reminder that all things are held together by God. This is our Father's world, rather than our own.

A common question raised in studying Gen 1 is this: How long was each "day"? Some argue that the term must be understood as a literal 24-hour period. Others reject this in favor of the "day-age" theory, meaning that each "day" was really an era of time, perhaps thousands or millions of years. The Hebrew *yom* is consistently translated as "day" throughout the OT, but admittedly with a wide variety of meanings. I personally believe the days of Gen 1 were 24 hours in length because other passages consistently allude to six days of creation and a seventh day of rest as if they constituted one week in the natural way a "week" is understood (Exod 20:11; 31:17).[14]

Those who believe in a "day-age" interpretation point out that "day" can

---

14. For more arguments in favor of this view, see Terence Fretheim's affirmative response to the question "Were the Days of Creation Twenty-Four Hours Long?" in *The Genesis Debate*, ed. Ronald Youngblood (Grand Rapids: Baker, 1990), 12–35.

refer to an era of time, such as a millennium (Ps 90:4). But this alternative is more in line with modern science, and the conclusions of science are always changing—raise your hand if you were taught in grade school that Pluto was a planet. I concede that there may not be a 100% decisive answer to this question, but an unbiased reading of the text does leave the impression that God created the universe in six 24-hour periods.

GENESIS 2:4–25

Sprinkled throughout Genesis is a particular expression that lends structure to the book. Eleven times (2:4; 5:1; 6:9; 10:1; 11:10, 27; 25:12, 19; 36:1, 9; 37:2.), Moses uses the phrase "these are the generations of" (i.e. "this is the history of") to introduce a new section of material, particularly the stories of a new family unit. It occurs in Gen 2:4 for the first time.

The theme of Gen 2 may seem like a mere repetition of Gen 1. But the creation account given here focuses on how God created a one-of-a-kind garden-home for Adam. As we noted already, the creation of man is without equal, and a fresh trail of grammatical breadcrumbs leads us to this discovery:

1. A double name for the Creator, LORD God (Yahweh Elohim), is used in 2:7 to communicate both God's sovereignty over, and his intimacy with, the human race. That expression never occurred in Gen 1.

2. Adam received from God himself the breath of life, something no other creature obtained.

3. Adam is also created from mere clay or dirt, a detail that "simultaneously expresses both the glory and the insignificance of man."[15]

I would prefer "frailty" to "insignificance," but his point is that, well, we're made from dirt! In a culture where the material of something designates its value (diamond jewelry, solid-wood furniture, leather interior), our being made from dirt should give us pause (cf. 18:27). But being made from dirt also expresses our glory because we are never told what material was used to fashion fauna, fish, and fowl. When it came to his crowning achievement, God decided to roll

---

15. Sarna, *Genesis*, 17.

up his sleeves and actually get his hands dirty; he took what was insignificant
and made life. And Scripture considers our being made from dirt as a sign of our
dependence on God (Ps 103:14), not just our relative insignificance.

Kings of antiquity often built magnificent gardens and temples adjacent to
their palaces as monuments to their unsurpassed wealth[16] (e.g. Nebuchadnezzar's
hanging gardens of Babylon). Eden is likewise depicted as God's garden-temple,
filled with rich spices and precious stones (2:11–12; cf. Ezek 28:13), an earthly
monument to his unsurpassed majesty. For "garden," LXX translators used the
Greek *paradeisos*, a word borrowed from the Persians, and no greater ideal of
paradise exists than the one depicted in Gen 2, one of God and his children
dwelling in perfect harmony with one another.

A river flowed from Eden that later separated into four. The Tigris and
Euphrates were important rivers in the Fertile Crescent, but the exact identity of
the Pishon and Gihon are unknown. The Pishon has been speculated to be the
Indus or the Ganges, while the Gihon is thought to have been the Persian Gulf or
Red Sea. However, these rivers are not identified so that Eden's geographic location
can be determined. Rather, just as the non-literal phrase "All roads lead to Rome"
signified that city's importance in its time, Eden's "location is not given so that it
can be found but so that its strategic role can be appreciated."[17] In this sense, the
garden's river symbolized God's life-giving presence flowing forth to all the earth.

Two of Eden's trees are singled out. The first made perpetual life possible
for all who ate its fruit, and God never restricted access to it until after the Fall.
The second was rendered off-limits, however. What exactly was imparted by
eating its fruit is still debated, but that is a discussion for the next chapter. What
must be noted here, however, is that God gave to man the autonomous freedom
to make his own decisions, and he did so presumably to discover what was in
Adam's heart (cf. Deut 8:2).

After Adam was created and placed in Eden, he was given the task of
working and keeping the garden. Work is often thought to be a consequence of
the Fall, but notice that in the perfect world that God created, man was created to
work as a means of glorifying the Lord. Moses would later use the same Hebrew
verb translated "work" to describe the Levites' service in the Tabernacle (Num
3:7–8), and the service of all Israel to her God (Deut 6:13; 10:12). We may

---

16. Walton, *Genesis*, 166–67.

17. Ibid., 169–70. Wenham adds, "Maybe the insoluble geography is a way of saying that
it is now inaccessible to, even unlocatable by, later man (cf. 3:24)," (*Genesis 1–15*, 66–67).

suppress or neglect it, but the need to serve our Creator has been fundamental to our existence since the beginning (Eph 2:10). It's embedded in our DNA!

It is only then that God called something "not good" in his creation. He noticed Adam's loneliness and brought to him the animals he had created. Adam gave names to each, but he did not find a suitable companion to aid him in fulfilling God's purposes. So God blessed his life with Eve, a woman formed from his ribs. Reflecting on the significance of being created from the rib, Matthew Henry eloquently observed that the woman was

> Not made out of his head to rule over him, nor out of his feet to be trampled upon by him, but out of his side to be equal with him, under his arm to be protected, and near his heart to be beloved.[18]

Adam's response to the creation of Eve, "This at last is bone of my bones and flesh of my flesh" (2:23), highlights their equality and his feelings of incompleteness without her. Moses then draws out a principle applicable for all time: there comes a point in every man's life when he must leave his family behind and search for a woman to be his helper and partner in fulfilling God's purposes.[19] He and his wife are united in a unique covenant-bond of emotional and sexual intimacy, something the Scriptures call "one flesh." It is no coincidence that woman was to be a "help" to the man, a word mostly used in the OT for divine aid (cf. Exod 18:4; Deut 33:26; Ps 124:8). Eve was, as is every godly wife, a true Godsend. And in that relationship of "one flesh" so unique to marriage, a man and woman can experience a hint of Eden's by-gone splendor.

B efore we rush to the remainder of Genesis, it would do us good to pause and reflect. It is here, in the first words of Scripture, that God is exalted to the highest of places: sovereign Creator, supreme Ruler, and compassionate Father. The majestic God of Gen 1 who transcends time and space is the same relational God of Gen 2 who is intimately involved in the lives of his people.

18. Matthew Henry, *Commentary on the Whole Bible* (New York: Revell, 1970), 1:20.

19. "[The statement], 'a man forsakes his father and mother and sticks to his wife,' [is] an astounding declaration in a world where filial duty was the most sacred obligation next to loyalty to God," (Wenham, *Genesis 1–15*, 88).

Moses' comment, "The man and the woman were both naked, but they were not embarrassed" (2:25 GNT), draws the curtain on a universe as God intended it, and underscores the sad reality that things have shifted violently off course since then. The evil that plagues the human condition is conspicuously absent "in the beginning." There was a time when everything was in total subjection to God's will. But in light of the Fall, we can only look forward to the day when God will restore "unity to all things in heaven and on earth under Christ" (Eph 1:10 NIV).

What a day, glorious day, that will be.

TALKING POINTS

T he creation myths of Egypt, Mesopotamia, and Canaan, especially how they depicted their respective gods, betrayed the values of those cultures. Israel's cosmology, detailed in Gen 1–2, also said a lot about their God. For example, in these chapters we learn that Yahweh is a God who loves order and structure. He created all things in perfect sequence and ordained that all things reproduce after their kind. He is also sovereign over all created things, and all things came into being through divine fiat, i.e. his spoken word. God does not have to manipulate or strive—only to speak—in order for his will to be accomplished. The apostle Paul later claimed that God's eternal power and divine nature are witnessed in the natural world (Rom 1:20; cf. Ps 19:1). Thus these two opening chapters are of profound importance in our quest to better understand the nature of our heavenly Father.

I t was not unusual for ANE civilizations to claim that their regent bore the image of the gods. What was unusual (even unheard of) was for anyone to claim that all people were made in God's image, but this is exactly Genesis' claim (1:26–27). More than that, all of us have in ourselves the breath of life put there by the Lord (2:7). In Gen 1–2, Moses has very much democratized the concept of *imago Dei*. These chapters are the bedrock of the human rights movement. It is illogical to say that all human life is sacred, that all are created equal, and that all are endowed with certain inalienable rights unless we also affirm the other truths of Gen 1–2, namely that there is a Creator who values every life as masterpieces borne of his heart (Eph 2:10). Most everyone has heard the title of Charles Darwin's famous work *Origin of the Species*, but few know the complete, original title: *On the Origin of Species by Means of Natural Selection, or the Preservation of Favoured Races in the Struggle for Life*. From its inception, the theory of evolution has been consistent with a world-view that favors one group of people over another: rich vs. poor, educated vs. uneducated, bourgeois vs. proletariat. Just as ancient cosmologies fostered moral decay, modern evolution has corrupted the value of human life, most notably the lives of the "least of these." Any appeal to human rights apart from a confession of the imago Dei doctrine is wholly inconsistent and built upon a foundation worse than sand.

W hen it was instituted as a holy day at Sinai, the Sabbath became a weekly mechanism that helped Israel move from a self-centered to a God-centered perspective. By spending time on the Sabbath reflecting on the way of the Lord vs. the folly of one's own way, Israel was promised to prosper (Isa 58:13–14). The 92nd psalm was often read on the Sabbath. It opens by praising Yahweh's covenant faithfulness; it later exalts him for causing the righteous to flourish, and for destroying the enemies of his people. By reading this psalm on the Sabbath, Israel had a weekly reminder that, for all her work and worry, God was the One writing the story. He was in control. And though we are no longer subject to Sabbath regulations (Col 2:16), the NT nonetheless teaches that remembering the Lord on the Lord's Day is to be our greatest priority. Investing in the assembly of the saints over many years fortifies us for the day when our faith will be supremely tested (Heb 10:25). For all of our work and worry, a weekly Sabbath reminds us that God is the One writing the story.

S cripture nowhere teaches that women are inferior to men (cf. Gal 3:28). However, there are indeed gender-specific roles ordained by God in family and ecclesiastical life. A man is primarily responsible for work (1 Tim 5:8) and woman for the home (Tit 2:5); this does not mean men have no domestic responsibilities (Eph 6:4), or that women have nothing to contribute in the marketplace (Prov 31:18). In the life of the church, gender roles are being redefined in a way that does not please the Lord (cf. 1 Cor 14:34; 1 Tim 2:11–14). To say that man is the head of woman (1 Cor 11:3) does not mean that man is superior to woman; it is a confession of the God-ordained created order, a celebration of biblical manhood and womanhood. Paul claimed that God pours out his wrath against those who depart from the created order, including those preferring homosexual desires over heterosexual ones (Rom 1:26–27). If we dare think his wrath will be any different toward those who have forsaken the divine order concerning gender roles in the church or in the home, we may prove sadly mistaken.

2

PARADISE LOST

As a book of origins, Genesis tells us all about the existence of evil, and Moses' audience was no stranger to such. For centuries, Israel had endured the torturous realities of slavery, religious persecution, and infanticide in Egypt. And as the rest of the OT details, untold hardship awaited them in the Promised Land. Little has changed since then. If any are acquainted with evil and suffering, it is the people of God. Israel must have wondered, "Have things always been this way? If not, when did evil enter the world? Is God responsible?" The resounding chorus of "good" and "very good" in Gen 1 teaches us that the world as God created it was perfect, so something dreadful must have occurred after the fact.

The amount of time that passed between Gen 2 and Gen 3 is unknown, but if the world was "very good" at the close of Gen 1–2, it is emphatically clear that God is *not* the origin of evil and death; these entered the world because Adam and Eve rebelled against the provision, authority, and love of Yahweh—"sin came into the world through one man, and death through sin" (Rom 5:12). Anytime we reject the lordship of our Creator, we too invite evil and suffering to reign in our personal lives, if not on a cosmic scale, and thereby bring upon ourselves the sentence of death, "for the wages of sin is death" (Rom 6:23).

With their rebellion, Adam and Eve levied unspeakable hardship upon this small planet. The earliest chapters of Genesis testify to this. Their oldest son murdered his brother in cold blood and appeared to exhibit no remorse. His descendants grew even more depraved, with one murdering a mere lad for a small slight. The fifth chapter of Genesis highlights the scourge of death on the human race with the refrain "and he died."

But even in the midst of so much evil, the light of grace kept shining.

Rumors of an old rugged cross first appear in 3:15. And though God granted free will to his people, he did not allow wickedness to hold hostage his plan for reconciliation. In spite of a paradise lost, the Epic of God continued to unfold undeterred on the stage of history.

As you read these chapters, attempt to see things through God's eyes. We normally perceive sin from our own perspective—how it makes us feel guilty, depraved, or inadequate. We think of sin as destroying our mind, demonizing our hands, and darkening our heart (cf. Ps 51), and all of these things are true. But by instituting a sacrificial system to atone for sin, God taught Israel that sin most of all destroyed their relationship with him.[1] "Against you, you only, have I sinned and done what is evil in your sight" (Ps 51:4). The Lord hates how sin inhibits his people's ability to live life to the full (John 10:10), but it is the loss of relationship he mourns the most, for he is too holy to be in the presence of sin (Hab 1:13). As you read these chapters, imagine the Creator's grief as his beloved children reject him. Empathize with the wounded lover who is Yahweh, and you will glimpse just how awful the events of Gen 3 really were.

GENESIS 3:1-19

The myths and legends of the ANE had intriguing ways of explaining man's loss of immortality. In the *Epic of Gilgamesh*, the hero acquired a magical plant that would have given him immortality, only for it to be stolen and swallowed by a snake. In the *Tale of Adapa*, the god Ea deceived the man Adapa into refusing food offered to him by the god Anu, food that would have granted him eternal life. His consolation prize was a garment to wear while leaving Anu's presence. In both of these stories, man lost his access to immortality through no fault of his own. But that is a picture wholly inconsistent with the one painted by inspired Scripture. According to Genesis, death is a product of our own rebellion against the Creator and Lover of our souls.

The serpent of Gen 3 is a bit of a mystery. As an animal, Moses stresses that God created it (3:1), but we don't know how exactly it fell under Satan's influence. Ancient Israel likely did *not* identify the serpent with Satan *per se*, though this identification is later made in the OT Apocrypha (Wisdom of Solomon 2:24; Sirach 21:2; 4 Maccabees 18:8) and confirmed in the NT (John

---

1. Walton, *Genesis*, 231.

8:44; Rom 16:20; Rev 12:9; 20:2).[2] However, in ANE cultures, the serpent symbolized chaos, magic, power, and wisdom—all of a demonic nature. The OT itself depicts the serpent as an enemy of Israel (Num 21:4–9) and of God (Isa 27:1), a concept that is very close to the one behind the Hebrew *satan*, meaning "adversary." So if Israel did not equate the serpent to be Satan as we now understand him, they would have at least considered it to have been a creature at odds with God's rule.[3]

The serpent's strategy in deceiving Eve is one that bears inspection (cf. 2 Cor 2:11), for these are the same tactics Satan uses today. The serpent:

1. Misrepresented the words and heart of God; it focused on God's prohibition without a single mention of Yahweh's lavish provision.

2. Smuggled "in the assumption that God's word is subject to our judgment,"[4] but such is not the case. If the revelation of God can be obeyed at our whim, then he is no longer Lord of all—the patients are running the asylum.

3. Created a false distance between the first couple and their heavenly Father. Notice that it neglected to use the title "LORD God" (Yahweh Elohim), preferring instead the impersonal "God." Later in the conversation, the serpent falsely questioned God's motive for placing a prohibition on the one tree. Satan would have us believe that the Lord of heaven does not desire intimacy with his covenant people, nor is he concerned for our welfare.[5]

The serpent/Satan also had help. Notice that Eve corrected the first question, admitting that they could eat of any tree except one. But then she added that they were not allowed to "touch" the forbidden tree, thereby introducing

---

2. Walton concludes, "We can be comfortable with that identification [i.e. of the serpent as Satan] from a theological standpoint, even if the association was not recognized by Old Testament Israel," (Ibid., 210).

3. Wenham points out that, per Israel's kosher laws, only a dead animal corpse would have been considered more unclean than a snake (*Genesis 1–15*, 73).

4. Derek Kidner, *Genesis* (Downers Grove, IL: Inter-Varsity Press, 1967), 67.

5. "Satan teaches men first to doubt and then to deny," (Henry, *Commentary on the Whole Bible*, 1:23).

"into her own mind the suggestion of an unreasonably strict God."[6] In response, the serpent went beyond misrepresentation; it now directly contradicted God's Word: "You will not surely die" (3:4; cf. 2:17). Satan has been a liar since the beginning (John 8:44), for God's Word is fixed firmly (Ps 119:89) and will never pass away (Matt 24:35).

What is arguably most disturbing about this story is that Adam was with his wife the entire time; plural pronouns are used consistently throughout this section. This means that Adam at least heard the conversation and could have prevented his wife from yielding to temptation, but he just stood there and ate the fruit Eve handed him. In Adam's weakness is a condemnation of any man who does not spiritually lead his family. If a man's love for his wife and children truly knows no limits, he will be their spiritual leader, nurturer, and guardian— roles at which Adam failed miserably with disastrous consequences.

So what exactly was obtained when one ate of the tree of knowledge of good and evil? Here is what we know for sure about this tree:

1.   Eating the tree's fruit was forbidden (2:17).

2.   Eating its fruit "opened the eyes," making one like God, knowing good and evil (cf. 3:5, 22).

Various suggestions have been put forward for what exactly this tree imparted, including omniscience, moral discernment, and sexual awareness. But all of these options have their difficulties. The tree could not have granted omniscience, for Adam and Eve don't "know all" at the end of the story. If the tree bestowed moral discernment, then why did God consider them capable of choosing right over wrong when he gave the prohibitive command (2:17)? Neither do I believe eating of this tree brought on sexual awareness—as will be noted later, the Hebrew of 4:1 suggests Adam and Eve were sexually intimate before the Fall.

The Hebrew concept of "knowledge" also has to do with experience; e.g. to experience someone sexually is "to know" that person (4:1, 17; 24:16; 38:26). The idea of "knowledge of good and evil," therefore, may mean "experience with good and evil." In other words, by eating this tree's fruit, Adam and Eve would begin to experience good things and bad things: love and hate, peace and war,

---

6. Sarna, *Genesis*, 24. "This is so typical of us sons and daughters of Eve. ... When we don't like a prohibition or a warning, we magnify its strictness. The suggestion that our superior is unjust mitigates our culpability," (R. Kent Hughes, *Genesis* [Wheaton, IL: Crossway, 2004], 68).

health and disease, life and death. Before Gen 3, they had only known love, peace, health, and life. Eating of this tree exposed them to the other side of the coin, the very thing from which God had wanted to protect them.

In the end, however, I think it matters less what was imparted by this tree, and more what this tree represented. To partake of its fruit was to violate God's authoritative word, and this point cannot be overstated. "In all this the tree plays its part in the opportunity it offers, rather than the qualities it possesses; like a door whose name announces only what lies beyond it."[7] The tree gave the first couple an opportunity to rebel against their benevolent Creator and heavenly Father.

And what happened next absolutely opened their eyes. The fruit made Adam and Eve wise, but it was more wisdom than they bargained for. Embarrassed, they donned makeshift clothes and hid from God's presence. The Hebrew word translated "naked" ('erom) usually describes someone stripped of protective clothing and consequently feeling defenseless, weak, or humiliated (Deut 28:48; Job 1:21; Isa 58:7).

As he regularly did, God arrived to walk with the first couple in the evening breeze.[8] He asked where they were hiding,[9] which is ironic because he had to have known the answer already. Throughout Genesis (4:9; 16:8; 18:9; 32:27), God asked questions of people, the answer to which he already knew. He often did so as a way of inviting voluntary confession of sin.[10] Here, God gave Adam and Eve the opportunity to own up to their sin—which they eventually did, but not before engaging in a pass-the-buck form of protest (cf. 1 Sam 15:24). Neither took any real responsibility. Adam's response is arguably the most pathetic; he coldly calls Eve "the woman you put here with me" (3:12 NIV), rather than "my wife," again rejecting the roles of spiritual leader, nurturer, and guardian commissioned him by his Creator.

For the first time in its brief history, something in God's creation was cursed, and sadly it was by God himself. The biblical concept of "curse" has nothing

---

7. Kidner, Genesis, 63.

8. Hamilton notes that the verb "walking" (3:8) is in a particular form "that suggests iterative and habitual aspects," (The Book of Genesis: Chapters 1–17, 192).

9. "What a pathetic delusion for anyone, then or today, to imagine that it is possible to hide from God," (Hughes, Genesis, 77); cf. Ps 139:7–12.

10. "God is encouraging introspection; why exactly are they just there, beyond those trees, hiding from the Lord who has provided all their needs and blessed them abundantly?" (Bill T. Arnold, Genesis [Cambridge: Cambridge Univ. Press, 2009], 67).

to do with hexes or magical incantations. Rather, "to curse is to remove from God's protection and favor,"[11] and starting here, we can identify with what we read about in Genesis: evil, guilt, and pain. In a scene reminiscent of a criminal trial, God stood before the serpent, the woman, and the man and assumed his rightful role as Judge. Make no mistake: to be judged by God is a terrible thing. John witnessed as much in his Apocalypse; he saw everyone from the least to the greatest "calling out to mountains and rocks, 'Refuge! Hide us from the One Seated on the Throne and the wrath of the Lamb! The great Day of their wrath has come—who can stand it?'" (Rev 6:16–17 Msg).

THE SERPENT

If surviving artwork is any indication, it was commonly believed in the ANE that the serpent once walked on two legs like a human,[12] a belief echoed by Josephus (*Antiquities* 1.50). But this is not enough for us to say that snakes once had legs. Biblically, it is irresponsible to interpret one phrase literally ("on your belly you shall go") and the other figuratively ("dust you shall eat"); snakes do not literally eat dust. But literal vs. figurative aside, God clearly condemned the serpent to "a status associated with docility (crawling on the belly) and death (eating dust)."[13] In the OT, "dust" is often emblematic of humiliation and defeat (18:27; Josh 7:6; Pss 7:5; 44:25; 72:9; Isa 25:12; 49:23; Mic 7:17). Indeed, Satan and all his dark forces received an everlasting humiliation when they were defeated at the cross (1 John 3:8), and are thus destined on the final day for torment in a lake of fire "day and night forever and ever" (Rev 20:10). "Amen. Come, Lord Jesus!" (Rev 22:20).

Beginning with the early Christian writers Justin Martyr and Irenaeus, the promise of 3:15 has been known as the *protoevangelium*, the first announcement of good news. It is prophesied here that the "offspring" or seed of woman would be at eternal odds with the serpent (i.e. Satan or the forces of evil). The two verbs "crush" and "strike" are actually from the same Hebrew verb meaning "bruise." The idea implicit in the curse is that the offspring of the serpent and the woman will exchange blows until the serpent's head is eventually crushed.

---

11. Walton, *Genesis*, 229. He suggests that, to avoid confusion, the best English translation is "damn" because "it wishes for a person to be eternally removed from God's protection, favor, and presence." Perhaps we need just such a term for so dreadful a concept.

12. Sarna, *Genesis*, 27.

13. Walton, *Genesis*, 225.

Whether Moses knew the full force of this curse/prophecy when he recorded it, the protoevangelium refers to the decisive victory over Satan won by Jesus via his atoning death and resurrection: "God stripped the spiritual rulers and powers of their authority. With the cross, he won the victory and showed the world that they were powerless" (Col 2:15 NCV; cf. Heb 2:14).

That there is now enmity between Satan's forces and the children of Eve cannot be understated. You don't need me to tell you that we live in a world filled to the brim with human suffering. Plague and disease. Crime and war. Famine and drought. Earthquakes and tsunamis. Divorce, recession, unemployment, slavery, injustice, abuse… Need I go on? In light of Gen 3, it is undeniable that Satan is the source of all these things, and it has been allotted to us to suffer in this life because of the Fall. This means that, for all the cures we invent for disease, for all the policing and international diplomacy we engage in, for all the technological advances we achieve, and for all the politicians we elect, movements we support, and self-help books we read, our deepest problems are rooted in sin and thus require a Savior.[14]

And not just any savior, but One who will do more for us than set a cosmic "reset" button and let us try again. We need a Savior who will save us from both our sins and ourselves. We need a Savior who will turn our affections upward to the greatness of God (Col 3:2). The promise of 3:15, the promise of hope and redemption, is more about the glorification of Yahweh's great name than it is the expunction of our sins. "It is not for your sake, people of Israel, that I am going to do these things, but for the sake of my holy name" (Ezek 36:22 NIV). This is his story, not ours.

THE WOMAN

I have never given birth to a child, and barring a future medical miracle, I don't plan on ever doing so. So I want to defer here to Bill Cosby, one of the greatest theologians of our time. He reminisces about his wife's first pregnancy

---

14. "All the ideologies, all the utopian promises that have marked this century have proven utterly bankrupt. Americans have achieved what modernism presented as life's great shining purpose: individual autonomy, the right to do what one chooses. Yet this has not produced the promised freedom; instead, it has led to the loss of community and civility, to kids shooting kids in schoolyards, to citizens huddling in gated communities for protection. We have discovered that we cannot live with the chaos that inevitably results from choice divorced from morality," (Chuck Colson and Nancy Pearcey, *How Now Shall We Live?* [Carol Stream, IL: Tyndale House, 1999], xi).

in the bit "Natural Childbirth"—how they attended prenatal classes, mastered breathing techniques, etc. But when labor pains hit at the hospital, his wife abandoned all desire for a natural childbirth. Cosby quotes Carol Burnett, who famously once compared labor pains to taking your bottom lip and pulling it over your head. Cosby said that on the second major contraction, his wife stood up in the "stirrups," grabbed his bottom lip, and violently demanded morphine. She then screamed at her husband: "*You* did this to me!"

Such are the consequences of the Fall. Whereas procreation had previously been a blessing (1:28), God informed Eve that, at least as a process,[15] it would now be fraught with suffering, especially in the form of labor pains.[16] Scripture considers labor pains to be the worst form of suffering (Isa 13:8; 21:3; Mic 4:9–10), and in spite of all the medical advances made in recent times, there remain many reasons to be concerned about the birthing process. A woman holds an immense emotional investment in her children, but God cursed this relationship by increasing her birth pains.

A woman's relationship with her husband was also cursed. "Desire" is not indicative here of a romantic or sexual desire (though this is certainly its meaning in Song 7:10), but the desire to subdue, rule, or control—"the desire to defeat a foe."[17] The same term with an identical meaning will appear in 4:7, thus "the woman has the same sort of desire for her husband that sin has for Cain, a desire to possess or control him ... Sin has corrupted both the willing submission of the wife and the loving headship of the husband."[18] In the NT, it is clear that life in the Spirit requires the woman to submit to her husband as Christ submits to God (1 Cor 11:3).

THE MAN

The last to be addressed is the man. Most of God's wrath and words are reserved for him. Adam's eagerness to shift the blame to Eve, his listening to her instead of God, and his negligence in protecting her from the serpent, are

---

15. The *process* of procreation is cursed, but its *end* (children) remains a blessing (Ps 127:3).

16. It's possible to understand the woman's curse to apply more broadly to the entire period of conception to birth, instead of narrowly to that of labor pains; cf. Tzvi Novick, "Pain and Production in Eden: Some Philological Reflections on Genesis iii 16," *VT* 58 (2008): 235–44.

17. NIDOTTE 4:341.

18. Susan T. Foh, "What Is the Woman's Desire?" *WTJ* 37 (1975): 381.

deplorable. Adam's curse was not work *per se*, for he had been created to work in Eden (2:15) as a way of glorifying Yahweh; Adam's curse was that his work would no longer cooperate and yield great results with such little labor as had been the case prior. His work would be frustrated, refusing to provide the fulfillment it once did. It is a curse that still haunts the careers of every son of Adam alive today. The next time you have a terrible case of the Mondays, blame yourself and Adam, and then seek hope and inspiration in the Second Adam (Rom 5:15)!

Also leveled on Adam's head was the curse of death. It has been suggested by some that death existed before the Fall. To what extent cannot be ascertained, but some familiarity arguably had to exist, or the threat of 2:17 would have been incomprehensible to Adam. In the end, however, conjecture on whether death existed before the Fall matters little. The reality is that this story blindsides us with a cold hard reality: there is something worse than no longer having a pulse, and that is alienation from our Creator.[19] To know the Lord is to know life (Ps 36:9; John 14:6; 17:3). As for physical death, it remains to this day a great curse on the human race and symbolizes both our frailty and our separation from God. Only in Jesus is the tyranny of death (spiritual and physical) defeated, a truth joyfully heralded by Paul: "[Christ] abolished death and brought life and immortality to light through the gospel" (2 Tim 1:10).

There is a trend, even in some "Christian" circles, to regard this story as a partial or complete fable. But if Adam and Eve were not historical figures, if there was never a "Fall" as described in Gen 3, then what are we to make of the multitude of times the NT broaches this chapter? The historian Luke traced Jesus' genealogy all the way back to Adam (Luke 3:38), and Jude reckoned Enoch as "the seventh from Adam" (Jude 14), which would have been a challenge if Adam was not a historical person. In two different letters, the apostle Paul used the Gen 3 narrative to engage in a compare/contrast between the first and Second Adam (Rom 5:12–21; 1 Cor 15:22, 42–49). He would also mention the serpent deceiving Eve in two other epistles (2 Cor 11:3; 1 Tim 2:14).

I do not intend to slight the other passages mentioned, but I consider Luke 3:38 to be the most troublesome for those contending that Adam was a mythical character. What does it do to our faith in Jesus Christ, the Son of God,

---

19. Wenham points out that, in the OT, "To be expelled from the camp of Israel or to be rejected by God was to experience a living death," (*Genesis 1–15*, 90).

if we say that his ancestor Adam wasn't real? When we start talking about what is ancient myth vs. historical reality in Scripture, we can't order *à la carte* off the menu. Doesn't it stand to reason that, if we saw certain members of Jesus' lineage were mythical, we are eventually forced to concede Jesus of Nazareth, the son of Adam, to be an equal figment of our collective imaginations?

GENESIS 3:20-24

God provided garments of animal skins for Adam and Eve to cover their now-shameful nudity (their self-made fig leaves had been little more than loincloths). The Hebrew noun translated "garments" (*kuttonet*) meant clothing that reached the knees or even ankles.[20] God gave these garments to the first couple as an act of grace; he did for them what they could not do for themselves.

But as long as Adam and Eve remained in Eden, they had unrestricted access to the tree of life, which could still bring them immortality. God could not allow this, so he expelled them from the garden. We are intended to perceive this as an abrupt, harsh scene. The verb translated "drove out" (Hebrew *garas*) is a violent putting away, such as Moses and Aaron being expelled from Pharaoh's court (Exod 10:11), God driving the nations out of Canaan (Exod 34:11) and evildoers from his Temple (Hos 9:15), or David being driven into the wilderness by Saul (1 Sam 26:19).

The Lord also stationed at Eden's entrance cherubim wielding a frightening sword of fire to prevent their return to God's presence. In the OT, cherubim are always depicted as guardians of the holy. They were cast in gold above the Ark of the Covenant, their wings serving as God's footstool (Exod 37:7-9); their image was also woven into the curtain separating the Holy from the Most Holy Place (Exod 36:35). When Jesus died, this same curtain was torn in two from top to bottom (Matt 27:51), restoring man's access to God's presence (John 14:6; Heb 10:19-22).

A ll too often, the story of the Fall becomes our own life's narrative. As young children, we are like Adam and Eve; we are pure and innocent in God's eyes. But the tempter comes and convinces us through lies and subtleties that God's provision is not sufficient, that his Word is not authoritative, or that his love

---

20. Sarna, *Genesis*, 29.

is not immense. We are persuaded to believe that we know best, but anything that separates us from God cannot be "best" (cf. Prov 14:12). We partake of the world's forbidden fruit, and a great gulf is created between the Father and us. Embarrassed, we hide from him, using every type of fig leaf to pretend that we are not really naked in his presence, but "all our righteous acts are like filthy rags" (Isa 64:6 NIV). The sentence of death is great and terrible, but deserved, for our sin is an abomination to him.

But God is also merciful. In baptism, the garments of a sacrificial Lamb are given to us (Gal 3:27) that we might return to the presence of the Holy (Heb 4:16). The loss of immortality? I consider that an act of grace as well; living forever in a fallen world is a punishment too great to bear. Instead, God has prepared a place for us greater than our collective imaginations (1 Cor 2:9). Beginning in Gen 3, we learn something interesting about God: his wrath over sin is great, but his mercy is greater. "Where sin increased, grace abounded all the more" (Rom 5:20 NASU).

To our knowledge, Eden passed into oblivion, never to be seen again. It makes occasional appearance in the rest of Scripture, emblematic of God's blessing and presence. Images of the Tabernacle and Temple are both rooted in scenes from Eden, and the apostle John "saw a new heaven and a new earth" (Rev 21:1) which bore a striking resemblance to the garden of God. In other words, the Bible often utilizes memories of Eden when it discusses our eternal reconciliation with God in that land beyond the river. On that not-so-distant day, when faith becomes sight, we shall see it and him with our own eyes, and nothing will ever separate us from presence of the Lord again. Not sin. Not death. Not the serpent. Not Satan. Nothing.

What a day, glorious day, that will be.

GENESIS 4:1-16

The phrase "Adam knew Eve his wife" (4:1 NKJV) is a Hebrew euphemism often used in Genesis to describe marital intercourse (4:17; 24:16). But this statement doesn't necessarily mean that sexual intimacy first took place outside of Eden.[21] From sexual union with her husband, Eve became pregnant and

---

21. Believe it or not, this very point was debated between Chrysostom and Augustine. Hamilton (*The Book of Genesis: Chapters 1–17*, 164) claims that the Hebrew grammar here suggests that the first couple knew each other sexually "before they ate from the forbidden tree," while Wenham maintains the evidence is inconclusive (*Genesis 1–15*, 100).

named her firstborn son "Cain," from a Hebrew verb *qanah* meaning to acquire or possess (cf. Ruth 4:5; Prov 4:5; 8:22). She named her second son "Abel" (*hebel*, "breath, nothingness," cf. Ps 144:4; Eccl 6:12), perhaps an unintended auspice of just how brief a life her younger son would live.

We are not told why the two brothers offered sacrifices to God, or even how they learned proper worship protocol. In fact, the text sheds little light on why Cain's offering was unacceptable, save the insinuation that he did not "do what is right" (4:7 NIV). In the NT, Abel's sacrifice is commended for being "by faith" and "more acceptable" than Cain's (Heb 11:4). The apostle John notes that Cain's actions were "evil" and Abel's "righteous" (1 John 3:12). It has been suggested that Cain's offering was rejected because he offered plants instead of animals (i.e. his sacrifice was bloodless).[22] But the Law of Moses later deemed acceptable these same sacrifices (Deut 26:1–11); it's hard to imagine Cain's offering being rejected for this reason. So why did it prove unacceptable to the Lord?

The answer lies in the *quality* of the offerings. It is said that Abel's offering was "from the firstborn animals of his herd, choice cuts of meat" (4:4 Msg),[23] but Cain's was evidently not of his firstfruits (Lev 2:14). The attitude of the worshiper as reflected in the quality of the offering seems to have been the issue (cf. Lev 22:20–22; 2 Sam 24:24; Mal 1:6–14). God's reprimand of Cain is a warning to any who would worship with a heart void of reverence and sacrificial gratitude.

The significance of 4:7 cannot be overstated. For one thing, this is the very first mention of sin in the entire Bible (search for it in Gen 3; it's not there). But it is the imagery that is most striking. Sin is vividly personified as a monster of the darkness, a predator (1 Pet 5:8) waiting to ambush Cain and devour him. A word from 3:16 is repeated here; it is said that sin *desires* Cain, i.e. it desires to subdue and devour him. But it is also very much within Cain to defeat sin as a man would defeat a wild animal. Disaster may have lurked around the corner, but Cain was responsible for his own behavior, and it was imperative that he subdue his passions by God's help (Ps 19:13).[24]

---

22. Gerhard von Rad, *Genesis*, rev. ed. (Philadelphia: Westminster, 1972), 104.

23. Under the Law of Moses, an animal's fat portions carried great significance. When a peace or fellowship offering was sacrificed (which may have been what Cain and Abel were offering), most of the meat was salvaged and eaten as a meal, but the fat was the Lord's (Lev 3:16). Eli's sons would later profane this sacrifice by seizing more than their allotment (1 Sam 2:16).

24. Hamilton (*The Book of Genesis: Chapters 1–17*, 228) notes, "The text makes Cain's personal responsibility even more focused by its use of the initial emphatic pronoun: "*you*, you

Cain ignored the Lord's warning (never a good idea), and instead arranged a rendezvous with Abel in the fields and murdered him. Though the narrator describes the scene with unexpected brevity, two details that we learn elsewhere add significantly to the picture. First, the Law of Moses later stipulated that a crime committed out in the fields was proof that the offense was premeditated (Deut 22:25–27). What Cain did was not a momentary lapse in judgment; it was calculated murder.

Second, the Hebrew *harag* ("killed") specifically meant "ruthless violence by private persons."[25] In 1 John 3:12, the apostle rejected the conventional Greek verb *apokteino*, meaning "to murder," and opted for another verb that described an especially brutal act. The verb *sphazo* means "to slaughter or butcher." Rather than a simple knock on the head, we are to imagine an enraged Cain hacking his brother to pieces with merciless brutality.

After the murder, God mercifully invited Cain to confess his actions with the question, "Where is Abel your brother?" (4:9). But Cain coldly shrugged off any responsibility for his brother, his spiritual heart being more calloused than his parents' had been in Eden. Only then did God transform into the divine Prosecutor and Judge; he called Cain to "Listen! Your brother's blood cries out to me from the ground" (4:10 NIV).

In those words, an important pillar of biblical theology is established: innocent bloodshed must be atoned lest it corrupt the ground and disperse the divine presence.[26] This story, along with the legislation of the Law, warned Israel that "the life of the flesh is in the blood" (Lev 17:11), and when that blood was spilt unjustly, the soil of the Promised Land became stained, poisoned (cf. Num 35:33–34). Even when a murder could not be solved, the Law mandated some measure of atonement (Deut 21:1–9).

Innocent bloodshed was so much against God's created order, it was said to make the ground cry out (cf. Rev 6:10). In Scripture, the idea of a "cry" going up to God is indicative of persecution and suffering, a plea to answer the prayer of one in dire straits (e.g. 18:20; Exod 2:23; Judg 3:9). It is used for the cry of those without food (41:55), the wail of those expecting to die (Exod 14:10), or the scream of a rape victim (Deut 22:27). Maximus, the 5th century Bishop of

---

are to master it," (emphasis his).

25. Wenham, *Genesis 1–15*, 106.

26. Ibid., 107.

Turin, said, "Blood, to be sure, has no voice, but innocent blood that has been spilled is said to cry out not by words but by its very existence and to make demands of the Lord not with eloquent discourse but with anger over the crime committed," (*Sermons* 88.1).

Here, Abel's blood cried out for justice, and because his blood polluted the ground, Cain could no longer enjoy the fruit of his labor. Adam's curse was that the ground would not make his labor easy; Cain's was that it would not cooperate at all. In response, an unremorseful Cain whined that his punishment was unreasonable. He was frightened at the prospect of leaving his family behind and facing would-be assassins (most likely Abel's descendants) seeking to avenge his brother's murder (cf. Num 35:19).

Whether this paranoia was warranted we cannot know, but we do know that alienation from God produces fear (Job 15:20–25).[27] It is also clear that Cain's heart was completely cold and hard, for he was concerned more with his punishment than his crime. Yet in an act of grace[28] similar to the garments given to Adam and Eve (3:21), God promised Cain protection (cf. 2 Sam 14:14), symbolized by a "mark." We are not told exactly how God marked Cain,[29] so we must conclude that it is immaterial to the story. The Lord subsequently banished Cain from his presence, and Cain journeyed east—a direction that has become, and will continue to be, an ominous one in Genesis (cf. 3:24; 11:2; 13:11).

As readers, we are understandably frustrated that the text does not answer some of our questions. Though we may know *why*, we don't know *how* God approved Abel's sacrifice and not Cain's.[30] How did God mark Cain? If Adam's family was the extent of the world's population, why was Cain afraid for his life? And for the love of wedding cake, whom did he marry? For whatever reason,

---

27. Ibid., 109.

28. "God's concern for the innocent is matched only by His care for the sinner," (Kidner, *Genesis*, 76).

29. But it is fun to speculate! Conjectures have ranged from paralysis, to a particular hairstyle, to (more plausibly) a tattoo of some sort (cf. Ezek 9:4). Jewish rabbis (Gen Rab 22:12) speculated that the mark was a dog to serve as both a reminder of God's protection and to scare potential assassins, or that Cain himself was a sign (i.e. a warning).

30. The long-standing belief is that fire from heaven consumed Abel's sacrifice, but not Cain's (cf. Lev 9:24; 1 Kgs 18:38; 2 Chr 7:1). Walton goes so far as to suggest, not implausibly, that God continued to meet after the Fall with the first family at the edge of Eden, where he "may have personally conveyed his pleasure or displeasure," (*Genesis*, 263).

such questions are not answered explicitly by the text, either because the original audience already knew the answers, or the Spirit of God judged them to be unnecessary to the narrative.

What can be safely assumed, however, is that the story of Cain and Abel is more than an official police report of the first murder. Considering that he enjoyed God's favor, "there are hints that Abel is the elect younger brother."[31] And though the oldest son was favored in ancient times, it is a trend in Genesis for the younger to be favored over the older. As we will see, Abraham is favored over his brothers, Isaac over Ishmael, Jacob over Esau, and Judah and Joseph over the other sons of Israel. This preference or "election" has nothing to do with eternal salvation, but it does mean that God chose to fulfill his scheme of redemption through one over the other. When Cain killed his brother in jealousy, he perhaps unwittingly killed the one chosen by God to continue the promise of Gen 3:15. Satan had crushed the head of the one who was supposed to crush his own. Surely God's plan had now been thwarted.

But that's just it. It may *seem* as if Satan had produced an insurmountable roadblock, the perfect foil to Yahweh's plan. But the ways of the Lord are infinitely higher. He blessed Adam and Eve with another son, Seth, whose name means "appointed." Cain, therefore, is merely the first of many in Scripture who made the regrettable choice to rebel against God's will and suffer the consequences (cf. Jude 11), without any damage done to the scheme of redemption.

GENESIS 4:17–26

It is assumed that Cain married a sister or other close relative. He was blessed with a son, Enoch, and Cain named the city that he founded after him,[32] though Cain's city-building endeavor was a clear violation of his sentence to be "a wanderer on the earth" (4:14). In the subsequent genealogy, Cain's family is traced all the way to Lamech, the first bigamist,[33] and his three sons.

---

31. Wenham, *Genesis 1–15*, 102.

32. There is some textual ambiguity about who exactly built the first city. It is odd that Cain built a city after being condemned to a vagabond life. Scholars speculate that it was really Enoch who built the first city, naming it after his first son Irad, and that the text attributes this milestone to Cain due to a scribal error or gloss. Mesopotamian tradition does state that the first city was known as "Eridu," a word very similar to the name "Irad," (Ibid., 111).

33. While it is true that polygamy was never condemned explicitly in the OT, it was never condoned either. Hamilton argues, "Nearly every polygamous househould [*sic*] in the OT

An unfortunate incident is recorded about Lamech, after which he bragged to his wives that he killed "a young man" who simply wounded him. By exhibiting such vindictive arrogance and excessive brutality (not to mention disrespect for monogamy in marriage), Lamech proved that Cain's descendants had become increasingly depraved. It's worth noting that Cain's lineage is not listed past the eighth generation; Lamech and his family presumably perished in the Flood.

In ancient times, people believed the gods were responsible for the advancement of civilization, such as teaching people how to build cities, domesticate animals, play music, work with metal, and tailgate at sporting events. But Moses claims that Cain's descendants were responsible for these advances (4:20–22), an acknowledgment that God blessed Cain's family in spite of their wickedness. It is also a reminder that social and technological advancement does not necessarily equate to spiritual maturity or moral superiority.[34] In our own world, the most innovative minds sometimes seem to be the most hostile to faith and godliness.

The chapter's concluding statement, that in the days of Seth and Enoch "people began to call upon the name of the LORD" (4:26), indicates that worship (i.e. prayer and sacrifice) of Yahweh as the true God of heaven was not totally abandoned during this morally dark time. There were still those who sought an intensive and intimate relationship with the Creator.

GENESIS 5

By listing the generations connecting Adam and Noah, this chapter bridges their stories. The author follows a particular template in recording the biography of each patriarch, and with only a few exceptions, the formula is the same:

1. Father's age at first son's birth
2. Years lived after birth of first son
3. Notice of other children
4. Sum total of years lived
5. Notice of death.

---

suffers most unpleasant and shattering experiences precisely because of this ad hoc relationship. The domestic struggles that ensue are devastating," (*The Book of Genesis: Chapters 1–17*, 238).

34. "The Bible nowhere teaches that the godly should have all the gifts. At the same time we are saved from over-valuing these skills: the family of Lamech could handle its environment but not itself," (Kidner, *Genesis*, 78).

The genealogy begins with Adam, who was made "in the likeness of God" (5:1); it is then said of Seth that he was born to Adam "in his own likeness, after his image" (5:3; cf. 1:26–27). So that we do not mistakenly think that Adam was the only one to carry the *imago Dei*, we are told that procreation hurled it forward into Seth's DNA. The serpent's deception had not stripped it from mankind. Every offspring of Adam, from this point forward, would inherit the image of God!

We are also immediately impressed with the incredible length of human life in the pre-Flood world. Jared, Methuselah, and Noah all lived more than 950 years; only Mahalalel and Lamech failed to reach 900 years. But these lengthy lifespans are significantly muted by the refrain "and he died," a harsh, poignant phrase that reminds us of the judgment under which we all live. But ironically, the eight-fold reminder of this curse in this chapter can be seen as an act of grace on God's part. Calvin commented:

> It is useful, in a picture of so many ages, to behold, at one glance, the continual course and tenor of divine vengeance; because, otherwise, we imagine that God is in some way forgetful; and to nothing are we more prone than to dream of immortality on earth, unless death is frequently brought before our eyes.[35]

In other words, testaments to God's punishment remind us that he is faithful and consistent in all things, for good and bad, and that wisdom is to be gained by contemplating our own certain mortality (Eccl 7:2). Or as Moses would later put it in the only psalm attributed to him, "Teach us how short our lives really are so that we may be wise" (Ps 90:12 NCV).

Enoch and Noah are the only ones in this genealogy to receive special attention from the author, and Enoch's biography is the most unique. He is the seventh (a significant biblical number) generation listed from Adam. It is twice mentioned that Enoch "walked with God" (5:22, 24), a phrase indicative of a life lived in harmony with God and his will (cf. 6:9; Mic 6:8; Mal 2:6; Col 2:6; Rev 3:4). Though very similar, "walk with" is different from "walk before" (17:1; 24:40; 2 Kgs 20:3). The former means an "intimate relationship;"[36] the latter,

---

35. Calvin, *Genesis*, 1:229–30.

36. TDOT 3:394. On this point, Arnold notes an important distinction; "The faithful devotion of this simple 'walk with God' is precisely the piety fostered by the Old Testament, in

"obedience and subordination."[37]

The phrase "walked with God" is repeated emphatically to clarify that Enoch's short life was not due to sin, which would have been an easy assumption for ANE readers (cf. Deut 5:16). The normal refrain of the chapter, "and he died," is conspicuously absent from the account of Enoch's life. Instead, the text includes the twin phrases "he was not" and "God took him" (5:24),[38] meaning that Enoch was raptured to heaven without dying, as was Elijah (2 Kgs 2:11–12). In this way, walking with God is presented as our only means of escape from the cyclical plague of death. "Death's authority is not absolute; it can be overruled by God,"[39] a hope still held today by children of the King (1 Cor 15:51–52).

The final significant note of the chapter is Lamech naming his son. The patriarch looked back to the agony that had afflicted man's work since the Fall and longed for God to bring relief from the curse. The word translated "painful" (Hebrew *issabon*) is used only three times in the OT, and all in Genesis (3:16, 17; 5:29). It might be that Noah, whose name means "rest" or "comfort," was thought to be the one who would bring fulfillment to the promise of 3:15. And relief would indeed come in Noah's lifetime via a global Flood and a cleansed earth.

But relief from the curse of death would not come through Noah; that would have to wait until the dawn of Easter morning. By virtue of the resurrection, we have the unfailing hope that we will one day have access to the tree of life (Rev 22:14) and live forever in God's glorious presence.

What a day, glorious day, that will be.

---

contrast to the harsh legalism so often associated with it," (*Genesis*, 88).

37. Hamilton, *The Book of Genesis: Chapters 1–17*, 258.

38. These two phrases are used elsewhere as euphemisms for death (42:13; Job 7:21; 8:22; Pss 37:10; 39:13; Ezek 24:16, 18; Jonah 4:3), but Enoch's deathless departure from earth is corroborated by the author of Hebrews: "By faith Enoch was taken up so that he would not see death" (Heb 11:5 NASU).

39. Allen Ross, "Genesis" in *Cornerstone Biblical Commentary: Genesis, Exodus* (Carol Stream, IL: Tyndale House, 2008), 66.

TALKING POINTS

In November 2011, I along with many others in the world read with horror about the crimes of Jerry Sandusky at Penn State University. The scandal that ensued after he was indicted by a grand jury eventually cost Penn State's legendary head football coach Joe Paterno and university president Graham Spanier their respective jobs. What I found tragically ironic about the affair is that many people rightly condemned Paterno and Spanier for not doing the "right thing," i.e. reporting Sandusky's crimes to the proper authorities. Yet many of these same people would deny that man is created in the image of God as opposed to being products of an evolutionary process begun millions of years ago. So this leads me to ask: if we are the results of evolution, where does our inherent sense of morality originate? Why is it plain to almost everyone that Paterno and Spanier failed to do their "moral duty"? It is because, as creatures crafted in God's image, we have inherited an innate sense of right and wrong. When we see genocide in Darfur, planes flying into the Twin Towers and the Pentagon, or hear of the sexual abuse of children, we know that those deeds are evil. Passion wells up inside of us, crying, "These things should not be!" If evolution is true, we have no business accusing Mr. Paterno or Mr. Spanier of abandoning their obligation to a higher morality, nor do we have the right to judge Mr. Sandusky for his hideous crimes, for these themes cannot coexist. But if evolution is false and the events of Gen 1–3 are true, we are forced to admit that there is an objective right and wrong, a standard by which we can discern good from evil.

The gift of garments to the first couple (3:21) was certainly an act of grace on God's part. But could it be that banning their access to the tree of life (3:22) was also an act of grace? With sin having now invaded the world, perhaps it behooved a merciful God to make immortality an impossible achievement. One can imagine the horror of someone like Herod, Hitler, or Hussein living forever; their reign of terror would know no end. Human suffering would be even more enormous than it already is. In the past few years, my generation has observed the fall of dictators such as Saddam Hussein, Kim Jong Il, and Muammar Gaddafi, not to mention terrorists like Osama bin Laden. Their deaths remind us that no matter the severity of the suffering, there comes a time when it will end.[40] A bad king cannot live forever; there is always hope that tomorrow's regent will be better (e.g. "The king is dead; long live the king"). In America, we have shortened that time considerably; we theoretically have the ability to overthrow the government every four years at the ballot box. Barring the way to the tree of life seems to us as punishment, but it could also be affirmation of a God who graciously gives us what we need: an anticipated finality to the misery of our sin and its consequences in the world.[41]

The narrative accounts of the Fall and Cain's murder of Abel bear many similarities, not the least of which being God holding the offenders accountable for their actions. It must be conceded that there is within us all not just the desire to sin, but also the tendency not to own our sins. Some do this by practicing a robust self-righteousness, but this makes us no friend of God. The Lord swore that the offspring of the serpent and of the woman would be at enmity with one another (3:15), and since Jesus accused the religious leaders of his day of being children of the devil (John 8:44), that should give us pause. Yet others avoid owning their sins by making excuses. Someone once told me that excuses are like armpits: everyone has them and they all stink! By listening to our excuses, one would think that our sins are always someone else's fault. But maintaining a biblical view of sin requires us to confess our culpability. Reconciliation with the Father is impossible as long as we deny ownership of our transgressions—"If we say we have no sin, we deceive ourselves, and the truth is not in us. If we confess our sins, he is faithful and just to forgive us our sins and to cleanse us from all unrighteousness" (1 John 1:8–9). A confessed sin, no matter how terrible, is never beyond the forgiveness and redemption our Creator offers.

We shouldn't ignore the fact that the second-oldest story in the Bible is a cautionary tale about worship attitudes. Abel stood justified before God because he gave to God out of the best that he had. His attitude was characterized

---

40. C.S. Lewis wrote, "Death is, in fact, what some modern people call 'ambivalent'. It is Satan's great weapon and also God's great weapon: it is holy and unholy; our supreme disgrace and our only hope; the thing Christ came to conquer and the means by which He conquered … [Death] is a safety-device because, once Man has fallen, natural immortality would be the one utterly hopeless destiny for him," (*Miracles* [New York: Macmillan, 1947], 151, 156).

41. "There is wisdom in restricting the tenure of power. There is grace and hope in new beginnings. Thus, death holds out to us the promise of new beginnings," (Walton, *Genesis*, 303).

by humility and trust, and he thus offered his sacrifice "by faith" (Heb 11:4). On the other hand, Cain's sacrifice seems to have been rejected because, for him, it wasn't much of a *sacrifice*—it cost him hardly anything. Thousands of years later, God remains very concerned with the attitudes of his people when they worship him. Awe, gratitude, and surrender should characterize our approach, not dismissiveness, greed, and self-absorption. If we give God the leftovers of our time and attention, we can hardly expect better treatment than Cain. Does worship steal your breath away? Has it cost you something? Does it leave you feeling small? These are important questions.

That Enoch was the only one in Gen 5 to escape the plague of death should not escape our notice, reflection, or comment. It certainly did not elude the author of Hebrews (11:5–6), who eloquently noted that Enoch's faith made him pleasing to God. In our present culture, people will flock to athletic clubs, avoid food preservatives no one can pronounce, and obsess over their caloric intake in an effort to cheat death as long as possible. But "while bodily training is of some value," faith and godliness are the only true ways by which we can escape this world and inherit the one to come (1 Tim 4:8; 1 John 5:4). Our faith is to be in Jesus, who violently destroyed death at the cross (2 Tim 1:10); as was modeled by Enoch, godliness is to be expressed by an intimate walk with the Lord. "Where communion with God has been restored, there deliverance from death is bound to follow."[42]

---

42. Geerhardus Vos, *Biblical Theology* (Grand Rapids: Eerdmans, 1948), 47.

3

DELIVERANCE

The story of Noah's ark is among the most well known in Scripture. Regardless of whether one accepts as fact all biblical claims concerning the Deluge, it's pointless for anyone to deny that there was an unprecedented flood many, many years ago—a litany of flood stories have been preserved from civilizations in Europe, Asia, and even North America.[1]

If you think that any account of the Flood is a ridiculous notion in our modern world, consider this plotline: Scientists receive warning three years in advance that a global flood will wipe out all civilization. International heads-of-state begin secret preparations to build seven massive state-of-the-art ships deep within the mountains of Asia. Passage on these ships is sold to a select group of people, international *crème de la crème*, who must pay a fare of one billion euros per ticket. In addition to human occupants, various animals and treasures of the world (e.g. the Mona Lisa) are loaded as cargo onto these ships. After many days at sea, the ships spot land on South Africa's Cape of Good Hope and the human race is perpetuated. This is the plot of Roland Emmerich's blockbuster film *2012*.

That the story of Noah's ark has become such a favorite for young children is quite puzzling to me. Its artwork adorns nurseries and Sunday school classrooms; its figurines make for great fun at bath time. And even I have to admit that I adored it as a little kid. In fact, my first sermon was on Noah's ark. At the end of the message, I imitated my favorite preacher (my dad) by telling a joke: "One day, Noah went out looking for his ark. He asked the lion, 'Lion, have

---

1. Kidner, *Genesis*, 95. Ronald Youngblood claims there are about 150 of these stories, "and they come from nearly every part of the world," (*The Book of Genesis*, 2nd ed. [Grand Rapids: Baker, 1991], 113).

you seen my ark?' The lion said, 'No.' Noah asked the bear, 'Bear, have you seen my ark?' The bear said no also. Finally, Noah came across a great big termite. 'Termite, have you seen my ark?' And the termite said"—in the lowest octave my four-year-old self could muster—"'I can't believe I ate the whole thing!'"

All that aside, I wonder if we, by making Noah's ark so popular with kids, also confer on this narrative too much cuteness or innocence. After all, what we really have is "a horror story in which human beings — men women, and children — and innocent animals are swept away by merciless floodwaters."[2] In this light, Noah's ark seems quite inappropriate as baby-room décor. So what are we to make of this story?

It is true that the early chapters of Genesis describe how sin spread at a break-neck pace: first the Fall in Eden, then Cain murdered his brother in cold blood. In the Flood narrative, sin seems to have broken new barriers; we learn here of fallen angels "who did not stay within the limits of authority God gave them but left the place where they belonged" (Jude 6 NLT). Sin became so universal and horrible that God was forced to cleanse the earth.

Yet even in his justified wrath, God could not bring himself to destroy *all* of creation, so he commissioned Noah to build an ark, more or less an oversized barge, and Noah's family survived the Deluge. In the text, we discover that the preservation of those eight souls aboard the ark was 100% God's work of grace. In his wrath, he also remembered mercy.

GENESIS 6:1–8

The beginning of this chapter is a prologue of sorts explaining why God decided to destroy the world. The corruption and violence on earth had become greater than he could tolerate, and he was forced to execute judgment. Noah and his family would be delivered from the impending destruction, but only because Noah found grace in God's eyes (6:8) and was obedient (6:22).

Yet two very strange phrases appear in the Flood prologue. First, who are "the sons of God" and "the daughters of man" (6:2)? Second, who are "the Nephilim" (6:4)? Suffice it to say that the answers to these two questions have been intensely debated through the centuries with three alternatives emerging. One commentator admits that "this issue is one of the thorniest in Old

---

2. James McKeown, *Genesis* (Grand Rapids: Eerdmans, 2008), 58.

Testament interpretation,"[3] and another concedes, "It is so full of difficulties as to defy certainty of interpretation."[4]

Until the 2nd century A.D., the dominant interpretation was that "the sons of God" referred to angels, based primarily on the use of the phrase in Job 1:6; 2:1; 38:7.[5] As the interpretation claimed, the sin of the angels was a transgression of boundaries. The human race was also culpable because nowhere is the implication given that these sexual relationships were forced; rather, fathers willingly consented to give their daughters away in unholy unions. This is also the understanding advanced in the NT (1 Pet 3:19–20; 2 Pet 2:4; Jude 6; 1 Cor 11:10?), in Philo (*Giants* 2.6–8), Josephus (*Antiquities* 3.1), other non-inspired works of Jewish literature (1 Enoch 6:1–2; Jubilees 5:1), and the works of early Christian writers such as Irenaeus (*Against Heresies* 4.36.4) and Tertullian (*Idolatry* 9, *Prayer* 22).[6]

But beginning in the 2nd century, Jewish and Christian commentators each adopted different perspectives. Starting with Julius Africanus, many Christian interpreters (including Augustine, Calvin, and Luther) have identified the sons of God with the line of Seth and the daughters of men with the family of Cain. In this case, the wickedness in question was inter-marriage between a righteous (Seth) and wicked (Cain) family (cf. Deut 7:3). But in spite of the fact that Moses elsewhere calls God's chosen people his children (Deut 14:1; 32:5–6), the problems with this view are:

1. It forces two different meanings on "man" in 6:1–2.

2. It does not account for the lineages of Adam's other children (5:4).

3. Scripture nowhere else calls Seth's lineage "sons of God."

Meanwhile, Jewish scholars from the 2nd century onward argued that the sons of God were ancient rulers who practiced polygamy and promiscuity with

---

3. Walton, *Genesis*, 291.

4. Sarna, *Genesis*, 45.

5. The phrase is also "a common expression for the council of the gods in Canaanite usage," (Mathews, *Genesis 1–11:26*, 324).

6. It is possible for Matt 22:30 and parallel passages to coexist with this interpretation. Jesus' statement could represent a post-Flood reality, he may have meant that angels cannot marry one another, or not had rebellious angels in mind at all—"in heaven" being the key phrase.

the women of their kingdoms, i.e. the daughters of men, though the text never even hints at polygamy. Appeal was made to those passages (e.g. 2 Sam 7:14; Pss 2:7; 82:6) where the king is considered to be God's son. However, while it is true that individual kings often claimed divine parentage in order to legitimize their authority, "there is no evidence that groups of kings were so styled."[7]

My personal view is that "sons of God" equates to angels, but this view is not without reservations. It's impossible to be certain enough on this issue to warrant dogmatism. I admit that this theory better resembles something from *The Lord of the Rings* than sacred Scripture; Calvin in fact claimed that the view can be "refuted by its own absurdity."[8] But the notion isn't so far-fetched if we remember that these same fallen angels inhabited human bodies as demons during Jesus' ministry. Besides, and with all due respect to Calvin and others, objectors who think this view is too outlandish to possibly be true must also admit that it is no more sensational than 900-year-old men and a global Flood, to say nothing of the virgin birth and the resurrection of Christ.

As for the Nephilim ("fallen ones"), these seem to have been ancient warrior-heroes, offspring of the angel-human union. The LXX translates the term with *gigantes*, creatures in Greek mythology descended from a god(des) and a human. Jewish literature claimed that these Nephilim stood as tall as 450 feet (1 Enoch 7:2), but the ANE literary hero Gilgamesh (more on him later) is said to have been a much-more-modest sixteen feet tall with a nine-foot stride. Whoever the Nephilim were, the term cannot be an ethnic designation since they would have all died out in the Flood, yet they are mentioned again in Moses' writings (Num 13:33).

Despite all the mystery surrounding this passage, one thing that is abundantly clear is the world's corruption had reached such a critical mass that God was forced to act. He limited the days of humanity to 120 years, i.e. he declared a 120-year grace period between the Flood's announcement and advent (1 Pet 3:20). To interpret this statement as God shortening the human lifespan is also a possibility,[9] but this does not seem to have been the consensus of the rabbis or of early Christian writers. For one thing, life spans after the Flood didn't immediately drop to under 120 years. In fact, for all we are told, Joseph

---

7.   Hamilton, *The Book of Genesis: Chapters 1–17*, 264.

8.   Calvin, *Genesis*, 1:238.

9.   As Walton notes, commentators are equally divided on this issue (*Genesis*, 296, n. 10).

is the first person in Genesis not to reach the six-score threshold (50:26). And what are we to make of Ps 90:10?

It's at this point that I feel the need to offer this warning: don't become so enamored with interpreting the sons of God, the Nephilim, or the 120-year-sentence that you neglect 6:5–8, a paragraph that poignantly and vividly conveys just how heart-sick God was over the wickedness of the pre-Flood world. God "regretted" (Hebrew *naham*) creating mankind (cf. 1 Sam 15:11), a complicated[10] word that can mean "repent" or "change one's mind" in certain contexts (Exod 13:17). But here, it conveys shock and sorrow over a corrupted creation God had once declared to be "very good." It's not that God believed he had made a mistake in making us; he was disheartened that it had come to this. The grief that God felt is that of brothers learning their sister has been raped (34:7), of a father learning his son is dead (2 Sam 19:1–2), or of a wife abandoned by her husband (Isa 54:6). God was so overwhelmed with sorrow that he destined the entire globe for destruction.

But in an act of sheer grace, he singled out Noah, a man through whom the entire human race would be preserved.

GENESIS 6:9–22

The suspense of the prologue intensifies with 6:8, a verse that perfectly transitions into Noah's story. The patriarch is characterized as "righteous" and "blameless" in both his human and divine relationships. The latter word, as it is used in the OT, seems to carry the concept of unimpeachable integrity (Prov 2:21; 28:18); it appears dozens of times to describe a sacrificial animal that is "without blemish" (e.g. Lev 1:3). The former term is "the most general Hebrew term to describe good people."[11] In sum, Noah's "contemporaries [have] no excuse to criticize his conduct;"[12] he "stands alone 'in his generations' like some single tree, green and erect, in a forest of blasted and fallen pines."[13] Like his great-grandfather Enoch, it is even said that Noah "walked with God." While Noah's

---

10. Both the LXX and NIV each use ten different words to translate this one Hebrew term in various places (Ibid., 309).

11. Wenham, *Genesis 1–15*, 170.

12. Youngblood, *The Book of Genesis*, 89.

13. Alexander Maclaren, *Expositions of Holy Scripture: Genesis* (Grand Rapids: Baker, 1978), 48–49.

virtue did not make him worthy of deliverance,[14] the reader is led to believe that
it played some part in his divine selection (cf. Ps 25:14).

The Flood prologue had generically condemned "the wickedness of man"
(6:5). But here, the crime is further specified: the earth was full of "violence"
(6:13). That word is especially telling—God had intended for man and animals
to fill the earth, i.e. to reproduce. Instead, the created world has become filled
with "violence." The Hebrew *hamas* means "cold-blooded and unscrupulous
infringement of the personal rights of others, motivated by greed and hate and
often making use of physical violence and brutality."[15] We are dealing here with
the darkest shades of human sinfulness—dark because violence is always of
personal insult to God since each one of us bears his image.[16]

God instructed Noah to build an ark,[17] a box-shaped barge without rudder
or sails. It was constructed out of "gopher wood," possibly an ancient term for
cypress (cf. NIV, NRSV), which "was widely used in shipbuilding in ancient times,
due to its resistance to rot."[18] But this is nothing more than an educated guess; we
really have no idea what gopher wood was.

The unit of measurement given is a "cubit," a term mentioned over 100
times in Scripture and normally considered to be the distance between one's
elbow and the tip of the middle finger, or approximately eighteen inches. This
would then render the ark as measuring 450 feet long, 75 feet wide, 45 feet
high, with a total deck area of about 95,700 square feet.[19] By comparison, an
American football field is 360 feet long (including the end zones), and about 160
feet wide. A cubit's-width opening or gap was left at the top of the ark (common
to some ANE buildings,[20] probably for ventilation), and a door was added.
Conspicuously missing is any mention of a rudder or sails: the fate of all aboard

14. "The salvation of the most righteous men must be attributed to God's mercy, not to
their own merit," (Henry, *Commentary on the Whole Bible*, 1:124).

15. TDOT 4:482.

16. Calvin said that, because we all carry the *imago Dei*, "no one can be injurious to his
brother without wounding God himself," (*Genesis*, 1:295–96).

17. This word in Hebrew (*tebah*) is different from that used for the Ark (*'aron*) of the
Covenant. A *tebah* will be what the infant Moses is placed in by his mother Jochebed (Exod 2:3),
making this the first of many parallels between Noah's and Moses' story.

18. Sarna, *Genesis*, 52.

19. Hamilton, *The Book of Genesis: Chapters 1–17*, 282.

20. Kidner, *Genesis*, 89.

would be solely in God's hands.

The immense size of this vessel may be difficult for us to appreciate since we live in an age of aircraft carriers and cruise ships. But for purposes of comparisons, note that the ark had a carrying capacity in excess of 15,000 tons. By comparison, the largest ships of antiquity maxed out at 4,000 tons and were considered "wonders of the classical world and testimony to their technological advancement."[21] For much of the OT period, ships were no more than 170 feet in length, so the size of Noah's ark was unprecedented in the ancient world.

Noah was also instructed to take a pair of every unclean animal and seven pairs of every clean animal (7:2),[22] enough food for the voyage, and place all these in the ark. The comment, "So Noah did everything exactly as God had commanded him" (6:22 NLT; cf. 7:5, 9, 16), highlights the fact that Noah was an individual determined to do his Creator's will; the story of his life had been surrendered to the pen of the divine Author.

GENESIS 7-8

Several attempts have been made to unearth significance in the date-stamps that appear in these two chapters (7:4, 6, 10–12, 17, 24; 8:3–6, 10, 12–14). It is thought that the numbers must hold some special symbolism that is foreign to us. But Moses' chronological precision, one that is unprecedented in the rest of Genesis, may only be intended to emphasize the legitimate historicity of the Deluge. In other words, outlining an event's precise timeline distances it from the genre of "Once upon a time..." (cf. Luke 3:1–2). Brueggemann disagrees: "Our interpretation will be distracted if there is insistence on finding data to prove that this is a 'historical' narrative."[23] But a plain reading of the text makes it seem as if the narrator wishes to slap us in the face with this very data so that we cannot miss it.

To our knowledge, the ancient world had never seen rain until this time (cf. 2:5; Heb 11:7)—at least rain in this volume. Moses takes great pains to emphasize that the impending disaster was a result of God's righteous condemnation of the world. The survival of Noah's family was not an accident, but an intentional act of divine providence. God had warned Noah of the Flood, commissioned the ark

---

21. ZIBBCOT 1:45.

22. Since mankind was vegetarian at this point (cf. 9:2–3), the classification of "clean" and "unclean" in Noah's day likely had to do with sacrifice, not diet (Walton, *Genesis*, 313).

23. Walter Brueggemann, *Genesis* (Louisville: John Knox, 1982), 74.

for the salvation of his family, led the family into the ark, sent rain upon the earth, and then caused the floodwaters to recede. So overwhelming was this Deluge that even the tallest mountain rested under more than twenty feet of water (7:20).

I am convinced that we are intended to see in the Flood a reversal of the Creation story—think of it as God's global renovation project. Whereas in Gen 1 "God saw everything that he had made, and behold, it was very good" (1:31), now "God saw the earth, and behold, it was corrupt" (6:12). The Lord brought the animals to Noah (6:19–20; 7:2–3) as he had for Adam (2:19). The expanse separating "waters from the waters" (1:6) was removed, and "all the fountains of the great deep burst forth, and the windows of the heavens were opened" (7:11).

Four times (7:18, 19, 20, 24), the Hebrew *gabar* is used, meaning "prevailed." It is used elsewhere in the OT as a military term (e.g. Exod 17:11; 2 Sam 11:23; Lam 1:16). Here, the floodwaters acted as the army of the Lord, dispensing his justice and punishment on a corrupted planet. All life was extinguished—God had given the breath of life to his creation (2:7); it was now taken away (7:22). In his wrath, God reversed the work of his hands because of its wickedness. But in his mercy, God restored his creation because of his great love. The first act of Creation had been God's Spirit moving on the water's surface (1:2). The first act of restoration after the Flood was God's Spirit moving on the water's surface (8:1).

But before the Spirit moved, "God remembered Noah" (8:1). This doesn't mean that God remembered the patriarch in the same way you or I remember where we last left our car keys. He isn't recalling something previously forgotten. For God to "remember" someone indicates that he is about to take action for that person's welfare, that he is about to deliver in a mighty way (cf. 9:15; 19:29; 30:22; Exod 2:24; 32:13; Pss 25:6–7; 74:2).[24] Simply put, God remembered Noah in the sense that he gave him favorable consideration and did something grand on his behalf.

When the ark finally came to rest on dry ground, it had been six months since raindrops first began to fall. Noah's family waited an additional 75 days before the peaks of surrounding mountains were visible (8:4–5). Forty days later, Noah sent out a raven, a dove, a second dove, and then a third dove to discern whether the waters had receded; this was actually a common method

---

24. "Revolutionary acts of salvation and deliverance often ensue when God remembers someone in the midst of their pain or crisis," (Arnold, *Genesis*, 104). "His remembering ... asserts that God is not preoccupied with himself but with his covenant partner, creation," (Brueggemann, *Genesis*, 85).

used by ancient seamen in order to find land.[25] When the second dove returned with a fresh olive branch in its beak, Noah knew that his time on the ark was coming to an end. The third dove failed to return at all. So it was that, almost a year after Noah's family had entered the ark, God beckoned them to exit onto dry ground.[26]

In gratitude for his family's survival, Noah offered sacrifices. God swore to himself that he would never allow the preceding disaster to repeat itself, though the human heart was in the same evil state as it had been before the Flood (6:5; 8:21). That last point is an important one. Though nothing had changed in the human heart, it's not as if the Flood was for naught. God had both cleansed the earth and served notice of the massive consequences our sins incur.

NOAH & GILGAMESH

As noted before, several accounts of a massive flood can be found in the surviving literature of various ancient civilizations. But the one most comparable to the Genesis account is found in what is known as the *Epic of Gilgamesh*, a story uncovered by George Smith in 1872. The comparisons between this piece of ancient literature and the biblical account are intriguing. In *Gilgamesh*, the gods decide to flood the world and kill everyone. The god Ea warns the hero Utnapishtim of the impending deluge and orders him to build a boat. Completing the vessel in seven days, Utnapishtim loaded it with his family and animals and thus survived the flood. After the storm, he sent out birds to discern when it would be best to disembark the vessel, and after disembarking, he offered sacrifices to the gods. In response, the goddess Ishtar gave a jeweled necklace to Utnapishtim as a pledge that she would never forget the flood's devastation.

As you can see, there are several points of comparison between Genesis and *Gilgamesh*, but it is the points of *contrast* that are the most revealing. In *Gilgamesh*, overpopulation and noise pollution are the reasons for the flood. In Scripture, it is the moral depravity of mankind (6:13).

In Gilgamesh, Utnapishtim's vessel is square, measuring 120 cubits on all sides. It has seven decks, and he loads it with not only his family and animals, but also gold, his extended kin, and even the craftsmen who had helped him build

---

25. Sarna, *Genesis*, 57.

26. "Consider how great must have been the fortitude of the man, who, after the incredible weariness of a whole year, when the deluge has ceased, and new life has shone forth, does not yet move a foot out of his sepulchre, without the command of God," (Calvin, *Genesis*, 1:280).

the vessel. Utnapishtim closes the door to his own vessel when the flood comes. In Genesis, God closed the door (7:16). Utnapishtim's vessel is outfitted with sails and a rudder. In Genesis, the ark was rudderless with no sails, completely dependent upon the providence of God. Salvation and redemption are always and forever God's work.[27]

In *Gilgamesh*, the gods cower against the wall like scared dogs when the deluge becomes too much for them to handle. In Noah's case, God was at all times in complete control of the circumstances. "God's actions are measured and just, never reckless or unmerited, and God's punishment does not go beyond the ability of God's grace to restore."[28] The Lord foretold the Flood's duration (7:4) and was true to his word (7:12). Utnapishtim's storm lasted six days and nights; Noah's lasted forty.

In *Gilgamesh*, Utnapishtim offers sacrifices to the gods after the floodwaters recede, and the text says that when they "smelled the sweet savor, the gods crowded like flies about the sacrificer."[29] Noah offered sacrifices to God out of gratitude, and "the LORD smelled the pleasing aroma" (8:21), meaning he accepted with favor Noah's offering. If we dare to see Noah's sacrifice as being food for the Lord, the book of Psalms is quick to correct our misguided theology: "If I were hungry, I would not tell you, for the world and its fullness are mine. Do I eat the flesh of bulls or drink the blood of goats?" (Ps 50:12–13). The answer is a deafening "No!"

In other ANE literature, since overpopulation had caused the flood, the gods subsequently set in place sterility and infant mortality to keep man in check.[30] In Genesis, God again commands his creation to "have many children; grow in number and fill the earth" (9:1 NCV). Overpopulation is not something that anyone should fear since it is God's prerogative to open and close the womb (I'm talking to you, People's Republic of China).

Some scholars allege that the biblical Flood story borrows from the one preserved in *Gilgamesh*, yet they cannot marshal a single shred of evidence to support such a position. If anything, the flood story in *Gilgamesh* preserved some

---

27. "If Noah is to emerge alive from the ark, it will be because of the grace and protecting presence of Yahweh—divine mercy rather than human skill will be the determining factor," (Hamilton, *The Book of Genesis: Chapters 1–17*, 296).

28. Arnold, *Genesis*, 99.

29. ANET 95.

30. Hamilton, *The Book of Genesis: Chapters 1–17*, 313.

of the truth, but as it was passed down orally in pagan societies, it was inevitable that it would be corrupted by pagan theology. The people of God should be thankful that, by virtue of the Spirit who inspired the pen of Moses, we have a reliable and true account of what really took place. "The biblical story of the Flood has been made a witness to the judgment and grace of living God."[31] It asserts, not surprisingly, that God was sovereign over the Flood's devastation and Noah's salvation, and that same God holds watch over the course of our lives as well.

GENESIS 9:1-19

For the first eight chapters of Genesis, mankind had been vegetarians, but this exclusive practice came to an end when God gave Noah and his family permission to eat meat, though the blood had to be properly drained first (9:3–4). To insure that the sanctity of life was not devalued in the process, capital punishment was ordained for those who shed innocent blood (cf. Num 35:31), and not even animals were exempt (Exod 21:28). Murder's hideous nature is underscored by the phrase "his fellow man" (9:5), or literally in the Hebrew, "his brother." All of us are connected as bearers of a singular divine image, as children of one man, and are ruled by one God. Murder blasphemes this doctrine.

God blessed Noah and his family, commanding them to spread out and repopulate the earth (9:1, 7). He also made a covenant with Noah, revealing his previous oath to never again destroy the world with a flood (8:21). As a reminder of the covenant, God placed a rainbow in the sky. The Hebrew word translated "rainbow" (qeshet) can also refer to the warrior's weapon (e.g., 21:16; 27:3; 48:22). It was not uncommon in the ANE to depict deity as holding a warrior's bow[32]—Hebrew poetry does it (Ps 7:12; Lam 2:4; Hab 3:9). In both the prophecies of Ezekiel and the Apocalypse of John, the rainbow symbolizes God's glory (Ezek 1:28; Rev 4:3; 10:1). In Genesis, God placed a warrior's bow in the heavens with an arrow symbolically pointing towards himself, and he entered into a contract with Noah on pain of death. "Of course, God can't die, and that is precisely the point. He can't break the covenant either."[33]

---

31. Von Rad, *Genesis*, 124.

32. Assyrian artwork from the 11th century B.C. depicts two hands coming out of clouds, one offering a blessing, and the other clutching a warrior's bow (Walton, *Genesis*, 345).

33. Tremper Longman III, *How to Read Genesis* (Downers Grove, IL: InterVarsity Press, 2005), 119.

Questions linger about the Flood. Was it global? The rabbis claimed proudly "that the Land of Israel was exempt from the Flood," and there is no evidence of the Flood at Jericho, a site that appears to exhibit occupation going back 9,000 years.[34] Yet the phrase "all flesh ... under heaven" seems plain (6:17). I concede that this phrase is often used euphemistically in Scripture for the whole *known* world (cf. 41:57; Deut 2:25; 2 Chr 36:23; Luke 2:1). But it also carries a global meaning in other passages (Deut 4:19; Job 28:24; 37:3; 41:11; Dan 9:12),[35] and the NT seems settled on the fact that the Flood was as global as the Second Coming will be universal (cf. Luke 17:26; 2 Pet 3:5–7).

Looking strictly at the text of Gen 6–9, it seems plain that the Flood was global. It is said that "all the high mountains under the whole heaven were covered" (7:19), and even after the rain ceased, "the waters were still on *the face of the whole earth*" (8:9), a phrase that most interpret in a global sense when it appears in 1:29 and 11:9. In addition, if the Flood was local and not global, then God's promise (9:11) is worthless—there have been countless local floods since then.[36]

From my perspective, it seems that all objections to the Flood being a global incident eventually boil down to a one's inability to believe in the validity or historicity of such a massive and miraculous event. But if this is too fantastic to be believed, I return to the same question I raised in the first chapter: what of the virgin birth and resurrection of Christ? Either we believe in a God for whom nothing is impossible, or we don't.

One last question: What happened to the ark? Despite what you may have been told in an e-mail forward or on a special episode airing on *The History Channel*, we don't know. Looking for the remains of the ark on Mt. Ararat in Turkey is misguided since the text only mentions the "mountains of Ararat" (8:4), i.e. the mountainous region of Ararat. The specific Mt. Ararat has only been identified with the Flood narrative for about the last one thousand years.[37]

Josephus quoted Berossus, the 3rd century B.C. Babylonian priest, who claimed, "It is said there is still some part of this ship in Armenia, at the mountain of the Cordyaeans; and that some people carry off pieces of the

---

34. Sarna, *Genesis*, 48.

35. "The God of the Old Testament does not see and own only what resides within the boundary of the nation of Israel; he sees the whole earth and owns all of it," (Steven A. Austin, "Did Noah's Flood Cover the Entire World?" in *The Genesis Debate*, 212).

36. Warren W. Wiersbe, *Be Basic* (Colorado Springs: Cook Communications, 1998), 100.

37. Arnold, *Genesis*, 105.

bitumen, which they take away, and use chiefly as amulets for the averting of mischiefs," (*Antiquities* 1.3.6). But the likelihood of the ark surviving to this day is incredibly remote. As with the Ark of the Covenant, the NT autographs, Ezekiel's Jerusalem diorama, and other biblical relics, Noah's big boat seems lost to history, which may be a good thing.

GENESIS 9:20–29

Noah had been given a name that meant "rest" or "comfort" because his father believed "He will comfort us in the labor and painful toil of our hands caused by the ground the LORD has cursed" (5:29 NIV). Out of this passage grew a tradition claiming Noah was the inventor of the plow, and thereby brought relief to the difficult work of tilling the ground with a hoe.[38] Regardless of whether this is true, Noah is described here as "a man of the soil" (9:20) who planted a vineyard. He then made wine[39] and became intoxicated, arguably the first person to ever suffer the effects of alcohol, which may explain why he is not censured for his act.

While Noah lay nude in his inebriation, Ham dishonored his father by leering at him (cf. Hab 2:15) and then telling his brothers. The Hebrew verb *ra'ah* means to look at in a searching way—certainly not innocuously or unintentionally (cf. Song 1:6; 6:11).[40] In contrast to Ham's deplorable actions, Shem and Japheth honored their father by covering him.[41]

Some have a hard time believing that Ham's sole sin was voyeurism, that the phrase "saw the nakedness of his father" (9:22) must be "a euphemism for a more serious offense."[42] It has been variously suggested that Ham castrated Noah (Gen Rab 36:7), sodomized him,[43] or committed incest with Noah's wife.[44] But

---

38. Sarna, *Genesis*, 44.

39. "It is interesting that the vine comes originally from Armenia, which is where the biblical ark landed," (Wenham, *Genesis 1–15*, 198).

40. HALOT 3:1159.

41. Ham's vs. Shem's & Japheth's actions are further polarized by a parallel in ANE literature. The *Tale of Aqht* commends any son "who takes [his father] by the hand when he's drunk, carries him when he's sated with wine," (ANET 150).

42. Wenham, *Genesis 1–15*, 199.

43. Sarna, *Genesis*, 66.

44. Frederick W. Bassett, "Noah's Nakedness and the Curse of Canaan: A Case of Incest?"

realize that these options necessitate details the Bible never provides.

At this point, I should note that patriarchal blessings and curses are a regular feature in Genesis. Isaac and Jacob would go on to bless their sons, and Abraham assuredly did the same. Understand that the father's words had a lot to do with the destiny of the son and his posterity. They are not to be necessarily considered pronouncements from God, but they nonetheless held prophetic sway over future events, and were considered irrevocable (27:37). That's why these occasions are treated with such gravity by the author.

Another lingering question is why Canaan was cursed when his father Ham was the culprit? Some speculate that Canaan was somehow culpable in his father's act, and that the details are omitted for whatever reason. But a more probable explanation is that this is among the earliest occasions in Scripture where the son suffers for the father's crime (cf. Exod 34:7; Deut 5:9; Lam 5:7). "Hebrew theology recognized that due to parental influence future generations usually committed the same acts as their fathers whether for ill or good."[45]

By the way, attempts to demonstrate how this story was fulfilled in history are too numerous to recount, but each option proves variously problematic upon inspection. The most viable interpretation is that Noah's curse looked forward to the day when the Israelites (descended from Shem) and Philistines (Japheth) subjugated and enslaved the Canaanites (Josh 9:23; 1 Kgs 9:21).[46] That Noah's blessing/curse has so many potential fulfillments may underscore just how far-reaching it was.

A final question is why Moses would include such a bizarre story in the Genesis narrative? It must have been to explain the moral depravity of Ham's lineage. In the Law, God would condemn the sexual promiscuity of Egypt and Canaan, both of whom descended from Ham (10:6)—"Do not act like the people in Egypt, where you used to live, or like the people of Canaan, where I

VT 21 (1971): 232–37. A rebuttal to this view can be found in Brad Embry's "The 'Naked Narrative' from Noah to Leviticus: Reassessing Voyeurism in the Account of Noah's Nakedness in Genesis 9:22–24," JSOT 35 (2011): 417–33.

45. Mathews, Genesis 1–11:26, 421.

46. One widely held view of yesteryear can certainly be dismissed. Noah's curse in no way justified the enslavement of African-Americans (descendants of Ham) in the Old South. "Since [the text] confines the curse to this one branch within the Hamites, those who reckon the Hamitic peoples in general to be doomed to inferiority have therefore misread the Old Testament as well as the New," (Kidner, Genesis, 104).

am taking you. You must not imitate their way of life" (Lev 18:3 NLT). Following that mandate in Leviticus is a list of sexual taboos of which both nations were guilty, expressed more than a dozen times in terms of uncovering a relative's nakedness. So this disturbing story explains how Ham's descendants tragically lost their moral compass.

TALKING POINTS

At its root, sin is a transgression of God's boundaries, but we must never view God's judgment of sin as being without an emotional element. For example, in the state of Texas, it's illegal to carry a pair of wire cutters in your back pocket. If I were to do so, I would technically be violating a legal code, but would anyone really be upset over my "crime"? Sin is more than a violation of God's legal code; it breaks his heart. The wickedness of Noah's day made God "deeply troubled" (6:6 NIV), and our sin affects God in the same way. Sin is not a sickness that needs to be medicated, or a personality disorder that needs to be treated. Sin is not a blunder we can flippantly dismiss with "Everyone makes mistakes." A mistake is wearing two socks that don't match; *sin* is an offense and abomination against a holy God. Our sins cost God the life of his Son. "[Sin] is against God, against his nature and his dominion, against his love and his design. Those that love God do for this reason hate sin."[47] More than a cute children's story, may the story of Noah's Flood impress upon us the high cost of sin and the great severity of God's righteous judgment. "Unless we wish to provoke God, and to put him to grief, let us learn to abhor and to flee from sin."[48] Flee indeed! Flee into the arms of the One who wants to be your Savior before he becomes your Judge! Flee to the Author and Sustainer of life!

We can't help but wonder if the Flood could have been avoided had the wicked responded to Noah's preaching (2 Pet 2:5) with repentance. In Genesis, the pattern has been for God to announce judgment and punishment before dispensing it, as if giving his people a chance to repent and avert disaster. We never learn whether Adam, Eve, or Cain repented of sin. On the other hand, when God commissioned Jonah to preach a message of judgment and doom, nothing was ever said about God relenting on his decision if Nineveh repented. But that is exactly what they did, and God spared them (Jonah 3:6–10; cf. Jer 18:7–10). We can only wonder what could have happened in Noah's day. But for us, even though God has already announced judgment for the wicked (1 Cor 6:9–10; Rev 21:8), "if we confess our sins, he is faithful and just to forgive us our sins and to cleanse us from all unrighteousness" (1 John 1:9). Scripture urges us to act promptly since "today" is the day of salvation (2 Cor 6:2), and we have

---

47. Henry, *Commentary on the Whole Bible,* 1:222.

48. Calvin, *Genesis,* 1:249.

no promise of tomorrow. "Just as it was in the days of Noah, so it will be in the days of the Son of Man: People went on eating, drinking, marrying and giving in marriage until the day Noah boarded the ark, and the flood came and destroyed them all" (Luke 17:26–27 HCSB).

Proponents of global warming claim the melting polar ice caps will flood the globe and wreak havoc on the planet. Hollywood has lent its weight to this theory with such blockbusters as *2012*, a film that bears a striking resemblance to the Flood narrative. However, God has stated that such will never again happen, and we know that God's Word never fails (Isa 55:11), nor can he lie (Heb 6:18). Scripture calls us to steward this third rock from the sun if for no other reason than it is God's possession (Ps 24:1), and some of us could show greater appreciation for the natural resources the Creator has given us. But Christians are also assured that the business of the world will go on until God's people hear a trumpet and a loud voice in the sky. Everything will once again be destroyed as it was in Noah's day (2 Pet 3:10), but it won't be of concern for the people of God; at that point, "we will be with the Lord forever" (1 Thess 4:17 NIV). So the next time you read about the polar ice caps melting, chill out.

4

CRADLE OF CIVILIZATION

As we have already seen with Gen 5, a common interruption in the narrative flow of Genesis is the genealogical lists of the patriarchs. The majority of these names disappear from the inspired record as quickly as they are introduced, but they are invaluable since they link the stories of Genesis' families together: Adam to Noah, Noah to Abraham, and Abraham to Joseph. These lists are a reminder that everyone shares a common ancestry in Adam and Noah.

Following the Flood account, and before the spotlight narrows to Abraham, a table of seventy nations is listed in Gen 10. In the next chapter, the story of the Tower of Babel explains how languages originated. The author thereby provides us with a subtle reminder that the world was created as a united whole, connected by one language and purpose, and ruled by the sovereign hand of one God. Any disharmony that now exists is therefore a result of man's stubborn determination to rebel.

Our corrupted, fallen world loves drawing distinct lines of demarcation based on race or ethnicity, education level or socio-economic status, language or dialect. Regrettably, the Lord's church has not been immune to this; where there are multiple congregations in one city, they are sometimes divided along some of these lines (e.g. "rich" churches, "black" churches). But our differences shouldn't necessitate division, for we "are all one in Christ Jesus" (Gal 3:28).

Indeed, Gen 10–11 prove that God faithfully works out his redemptive plan through multiple generations and across countless centuries, and that he cares intimately for those of every skin-color, language, and nationality. In Gen 10, seventy nations are listed, but all of them have both a common father and a common Creator. In Gen 11, those nations were scattered by God across the face of the planet due to linguistic differences brought on by their pride and arrogance. At that point, it seemed as if the world was destined again for total destruction, just as it was in the days of Noah. But as it turned out, God had other ideas.

One could almost be forgiven for believing that God cared only for Israel as his chosen people, but that is simply not true. God loves every tribe and tongue. The call of Abram and the establishment of Israel as a nation was a part of his grander scheme. The Babel narrative may have ended with terrible consequences, but Gen 11 doesn't end without signaling the beginning of a new chapter in God's Epic: the call of Abram—the call to be a blessing to the nations—would climax in the salvation of the Gentiles (Gal 3:8).

GENESIS 10

Seventy different nations are listed here, making it easy to understand why this chapter is so often called the "Table of Nations." Because we are dealing with a very ancient list, identifying and locating all of these nations is impossible; for some of them, scholars can only make semi-educated guesses. But generally speaking, Japheth's family settled in Europe and Asia Minor, Ham's family in Palestine and Africa, and Shem's in what is now considered to have been the Fertile Crescent. We are wrong if we assume that this list is comprehensive; the number of nations has arguably been whittled down to seventy "to convey the notion of the totality of the human race."[1]

One important disclaimer: Moses' grouping of these nations is not always a clear indication from which son of Noah a particular nation descended. These nations are categorized as much by land and language as clan and nation (10:5, 20, 31). In other words, geography, linguistics, and even political alliances play as much a part in the grouping as shared DNA.

The list begins with the descendants of Japheth who settled the farthest away from Israel and had contact with them the least (Ezek 38:6 describes some of them as being "from the uttermost parts of the north"). Some of Japheth's children spread out between the Aegean and Caspian Seas (i.e. modern-day Georgia, Armenia, and Azerbaijan). Others settled along the northern coast of the Mediterranean, perhaps as far as the Iberian Peninsula (Tarshish), and also populated the Mediterranean's numerous islands. Of particular interest is Javan, ancestor of the Greeks, as well as Madai ("Medes" NJB), whose descendants

---

1. Sarna, *Genesis*, 69.

formed with Persia the daunting Medo-Persian Empire.

The lineage of Ham populated much of Africa and Palestine. "Cush" is most often identified with Ethiopia (Jer 13:23), and "Put" with Libya; the OT considers both nations to be Egypt's allies (2 Chr 12:3). Some translations render "Egypt" as "Mizraim," a Hebrew word that means "two lands" and is most likely a carryover from when Egypt was comprised of a North and South Kingdom. Egypt's children (10:13–14) settled in various places along the Nile.

Of specific interest to Israel would have been the descendants of Ham's youngest son, Canaan. Sidon was the oldest Phoenician city, located on the Mediterranean coast north of Tyre. Heth was the father of the Hittites, who must be distinguished from the empire of the same name that once existed in modern-day Turkey. The Hittites of the OT dwelt in Canaan's hill country, and it's probable that these are the people Moses had in mind. The Jebusites, Amorites, Girgashites, and Hivites are all known to have lived in Canaan (Deut 7:1). The other nations mentioned were located in Palestine or were Phoenician colonies scattered throughout the Mediterranean world.

Those from Shem settled in an area stretching from the Arabian Peninsula to the Black and Caspian Seas, but mostly along the Tigris and Euphrates; generally speaking, they were the ancestors of those who later spread to the remainder of Asia. The nation of Elam was located north of the Persian Gulf where the Iranian province of Khuzestan is now. Descendants of Asshur (Assyria) and Aram would form nations that would persecute Israel for many years. The name Eber became the origin for the term *Hebrew*[2] His son's name, Peleg, means "to divide," which explains the editorial note that "in his days the earth was divided" (10:25). It's likely that it was during Peleg's life that the Tower of Babel was built, and God subsequently introduced linguistic divisions on the earth.[3]

With the mention of Peleg and Joktan, the narrator does for the first time something he will do often in Genesis. He gives the genealogy of the non-elect brother (e.g. Joktan, Ishmael, Esau) before continuing with the story of the elect brother (e.g. Peleg, Isaac, Jacob). Comments on Joktan's descendants are concluded with a mention of the extent of their territory (10:30); unfortunately, "Mesha," "Sephar," and "the hill country of the east" are locations that have proven impossible to identify.

You also should know about the textual ambiguity in 10:21 that different

2. Kidner, *Genesis*, 109.

3. Wenham, *Genesis 1–15*, 231.

versions translate it different ways. Was Shem (ESV, NASU) or Japheth (NIV, NKJV) the oldest son of Noah? The former is, in the words of Wenham, "the modern consensus translation."[4]

One particular person of interest in this chapter is Nimrod (10:8–9). Reference is made to an early Hebrew legend (cf. Mic 5:6) about this man's exploits that has since been lost to us, but it appears Nimrod was an ancient version of Chuck Norris.[5] Nimrod's name can mean "we shall rebel," and Jewish tradition considered Nimrod to be the inventor of idolatry and the leader of those who built the Tower of Babel.[6]

There have been attempts to identify the Nimrod of Genesis with various historical figures, including Naram-Sin, an Akkadian king who reigned for several decades around 2250 B.C. One of the titles for Naram-Sin was "Strong Male" (cf. 10:8), and archaeologists have uncovered several commemorations of his exploits.[7] Another scholar makes an intriguing case for identifying Nimrod with Hammurabi, the famed Babylonian king and lawgiver,[8] though the date of Hammurabi's reign (early 18th century) makes this improbable. A likelier suggestion than the previous two is Sargon I of Akkad (2350–2295 B.C.), Naram-Sin's grandfather.[9] Other candidates include Amenhotep III of Egypt[10] and Tukulti-Ninurta I of Assyria.[11] Regardless of his identity, Nimrod was credited with establishing some of the greatest cities of the ancient world, including Babylon and Nineveh (10:10–12).

---

4. Ibid., 228. "Because an adjective does not usually modify a proper name in biblical Hebrew, this is the natural meaning required by the syntax," (Sarna, *Genesis*, 78).

5. "There is no theory of evolution, just a list of creatures Nimrod allowed to live." "When the Boogeyman goes to sleep every night, he checks his closet for Nimrod." "Nimrod is the reason Waldo is hiding." I could go on and on.

6. Yigal Levin, "Nimrod the Mighty, King of Kish, King of Sumer and Akkad," *VT* 52 (2002): 366.

7. Sarna, *Genesis*, 73.

8. Walton, *Genesis*, 369–71.

9. Arnold (*Genesis*, 116) believes Nimrod to have been a composite of Sargon I and Naram-Sin. See also Levin, "Nimrod the Mighty," 350–66.

10. Von Rad, *Genesis*, 146.

11. E. A. Speiser, "In Search of Nimrod," in *Oriental and Biblical Studies*, eds. J. J. Finkelstein and Moshe Greenberg (Philadelphia: Univ. of Pennsylvania Press, 1967), 41–52.

GENESIS 11:1-9

Any hope that the world would be a better place after the Flood is dashed with the Babel narrative. The previous chapter illustrated where the various nations ended up; this story tells how they got there. Attention shifts to "a plain in the land of Shinar" (called "Sumer" in ANE texts), also known as Babylon (10:10). Noah's descendants left Ararat and journeyed east, which in Genesis is often indicative of a separation from God (cf. 3:24; 4:16; 13:11). At that time, the people of "the whole earth had one language" (11:1).[12] Imagine that, a world without pocket translators, *Rosetta Stone*, or surly high school French teachers!

As a little kid in Bible class, I was left with the distinct impression that the Tower of Babel resembled a spiraling tower such as the one depicted in Gustave Doré's 1865 engraving *The Confusion of Tongues*. But the tower probably resembled the ziggurats discovered by archaeologists in modern-day Iraq. The square base of these ziggurats (from the Akkadian verb *zaqaru*, meaning "to build high") varied at 20–90 meters on each side, and about thirty of these ziggurats have been discovered.[13] They were built to resemble large mountains and were centers of religious activity for ancient Mesopotamian cultures. At Babylon, Nebuchadnezzar built a seven-story ziggurat to the god Marduk much later than the Tower of Babel (he actually rebuilt the ruins of an older ziggurat), but it still carried the name *Etemenanki*, "house of the foundations of heaven and earth"[14] (cf. 11:4). Unlike the pyramids of Egypt, ziggurats in Mesopotamia were completely filled with dirt and had a façade of kiln-fired brick (cf. 11:3). Each one had a stairway or ramp that led to the summit where a little room had been constructed with a bed and table. This was where the gods would lodge as they made the journey from heaven to earth—think of it as an ancient Motel 6 where the light was always left on.

The narrator notes that the building materials used to construct the tower were very different from those traditionally used elsewhere in the ANE. Whereas a structure in Palestine had a stone foundation and mud-brick walls (not until the

---

12. The concept of one original language has gained increasing acceptance among linguists (William F. Allman, "The Mother Tongue," *U.S. News & World Report*, November 5, 1990, 60–70).

13. John H. Walton, "The Mesopotamian Background of the Tower of Babel Account and Its Implications," *BBR* 5 (1995): 156.

14. Hamilton, *The Book of Genesis: Chapters 1–17*, 352, n. 11. Other ziggurats of Mesopotamia carried the names "Temple of the Stairway to Pure Heaven" (at Sippar) and "Temple which Links Heaven and Earth" (at Larsa).

time of Christ were bricks used there in construction), a building in Mesopotamia had kiln-fired brick and bitumen for mortar (and then, only for very important buildings due to the expense), and that is what the builders of the tower used.

The pivotal moment is when God arrived on the scene (11:5). Perhaps tongue-in-cheek, the narrator writes that God had to come *down* to see what was being done, despite the fact that the tower was supposed to stretch *up* to the sky. "God sits high above the round ball of earth. The people look like mere ants" (Isa 40:22 Msg). The construction project was clearly a human initiative, and a puny, pathetic one at that. The Lord issued a summons to the angels to join him in spreading confusion (cf. Deut 32:8–9). He injected disunity into the builders' midst by confusing their language. No longer would one person find it easy to understand another.

As a consequence, the building project fell off for a time, and the citizens of Babel went their separate ways, clustering into clans based on language. The narrator ends with another tongue-in-cheek reference to the etymology of "Babel." Whereas the citizens of Babylon claimed that the name of their great city meant "the gate of the gods," Moses says it derived from the Hebrew *balal* meaning "he confused."[15]

One question that arises from the text is this: what exactly was Babel's sin? In Sunday School, I was always told that it was their disobedience of God's command to fill the earth (1:28; 9:1). Their fear was that they might "be dispersed over the face of the whole earth" (11:4).[16] But it has been argued that when God said to multiply and fill the earth, he meant it as a blessing, not a command; the Hebrew can certainly be translated this way (cf. 2 Sam 18:23).[17]

Was Babel's pretension and hubris their sin? Possibly. They certainly congregated in a large group to accomplish a very ambitious goal. In the text, Yahweh muses that in light of the people's great numbers and unity, "this is only the beginning of what they will do. And nothing that they propose to do will now be impossible for them" (11:6). So God subsequently divided them into separate nations and languages to limit the grave impact of consolidated wickedness. "God knew that the consequent nationalism and warfare were lesser

---

15. Kidner, *Genesis*, 110.

16. "Instead of trusting in God's command to fill the earth, they insist on going their own way which could only lead to disaster," (P. J. Harland, "Vertical or Horizontal: The Sin of Babel," *VT* 48 [1998]: 528).

17. Walton, "Mesopotamian Background," 166.

problems than that of collective apostasy."[18]

I think there is truth in both of these suggestions. If the punishment was dispersion, it seems disingenuous to argue that their sin had nothing to do with disobeying the command to "fill the earth." But given the great wickedness that God observed before the Flood, it seems justified to assume that Babel's threat was too much evil in one place.

Yet there is one more aspect to Babel's sin than these options provide. Scripture says that these people settled at the site of Babylon to "make a name" for themselves, something only the Lord is allowed to do (Neh 9:10; Isa 63:12; Jer 32:20). The citizens of Babel sought to bring glory to themselves at God's expense, and that is a big no-no. "I am the LORD; that is my name; my glory I give to no other" (Isa 42:8). Babel's choice to congregate in evil, rather than fill the earth in righteousness, was symptomatic of their refusal to make Yahweh the reigning king of their lives and give him praise. When we seek our own agendas instead of God's, we share in Babel's folly.

There may be one final principle worth noting: God hates division, but he is not above dividing us in order to teach us to rely more fully on him. There is no denying that the Bible is in favor of unity (Ps 133:1), something for which Jesus specifically prayed on the eve of his crucifixion (John 17:21). But note that Jesus qualified that request with, "May they also be one in Us" (HCSB). Unity at any cost is not God-honoring unity. Walter Brueggemann writes:

> This text suggests a different kind of unity sought by fearful humanity organized against the purposes of God. This unity attempts to establish a cultural, human oneness without reference to the threats, promises, or mandates of God. This is a self-made unity in which humanity has a "fortress mentality." It seeks to survive by its own resources. It seeks to construct a world free of the danger of the holy and immune from the terrors of God in history. It is a unity grounded in fear and characterized by coercion. A human unity without the vision of God's will is likely to be ordered in oppressive conformity. And it will finally be "in vain" (Pss 49:10–20; 127:1–2).[19]

---

18. Ross, "Genesis," 92.

19. Brueggemann, Genesis, 100.

To be sure, the citizens of Babel were united, but it was a unity opposed to (rather than working for) the will of God. Attempts to maintain the unity of Jesus' body at the expense of truth or righteousness will always be frustrated by a holy God intent on purifying his Son's bride.[20]

This is his story, not ours.

GENESIS 11:10-32

This final section of Gen 1–11 is quite similar to the genealogy given in Gen 5, though the sum total of years lived for each person is omitted here. Another notable omission from the genealogy is Arphaxad's son Cainan (Luke 3:35–36). The Masoretic Text (the basis for most translations of the OT) omits any mention of him, but Luke's genealogy is based on the LXX version of Gen 11:12–13, which reads:

> Arphaxad lived 135 years and fathered Cainan. Arphaxad lived 430 years after he had fathered Cainan, fathered sons and daughters, and died. Cainan lived 130 years and fathered Shelah. Cainan lived 330 years after he had fathered Shelah, fathered sons and daughters, and died.

With the close of this chapter, the patriarch Abra(ha)m enters the biblical spotlight. His father Terah was an idolater and pagan (Josh 24:2, 15), which should come as no surprise since his home was Ur of the Chaldeans,[21] a major center of moon-worship in ancient times. In addition, the names Terah, Milcah, and Sarai are all related to worship of the moon god Sin.

In Abram's day, Ur would have been a once-grand cultural center now declining due to economic hardship and overpopulation.[22] Its remains reveal that it had several important structures, including lavish royal tombs and a massive ziggurat measuring 205 feet by 141 feet.[23] Its close proximity to the Persian Gulf

---

20. "It is wisdom to leave off that which we see God fights against," (Henry, *Commentary on the Whole Bible*, 1:81).

21. It has long been argued that the phrase "of the Chaldeans" is an anachronism, proof that the Genesis text was updated after Moses. But this is not necessarily so. See William D. Barrick's "'Ur of the Chaldeans' (Gen 11:28–31): A Model for Dealing with Difficult Texts," *MSJ* 20 (2009): 7–18.

22. Sarna, *Genesis*, 88.

23. Osborne, "Ur," DOTP, 875.

likely means the city's wealth derived somewhat from maritime trade.

It is not clear why Terah migrated to Haran,[24] an important commercial center on a major trade route 550 miles NW of Ur, and (like Ur) a center for worship of the moon-god Sin. Terah's original destination was Canaan (11:31), and Acts 7:2–4 indicates that Abram received the call to depart for Canaan while still in Ur. Did Terah's family leave Ur because God called Abram, only to lose zeal for the expedition when they reached Haran? Another possibility springs from the fact that the Elamites destroyed Ur in 1950 B.C. Did Terah's departure have more to do with these circumstances than divine call? In either event, it seems Abram was reluctant to completely obey God's command until his father had died. Such is often the case when called to do something bold; we are reluctant to leave our world of security for the wild frontier of faith.

Whenever the flow of a genealogy is interrupted, we should pay attention, and the detail of Sarai's barrenness is an important one to future narratives. Barrenness was a grave condition in ancient times (cf. Ps 127:3–5). No heir meant no one to care for you in your old age, and no means by which to perpetuate the family line and bring prestige to your name. In fact, "life after death" for the ancients took the form of living on through your descendants. No descendants? No life after death! Barrenness was synonymous with abject hopelessness. But in what would become a recurring theme of Scripture, God was prepared to deliver hope to his people in the midst of their despair.

One last detail about Terah before our attention turns to his famous son: there is a discrepancy as to how long Terah lived. He was 70 when Abram was born (11:26), it says he lived to be 205 (11:32), and it is certain that he died before Abram left for Canaan (Acts 7:4), though Abram was 75 when he left for Canaan, not 135. Two solutions have been put forth:

1. Abram was not the oldest, but was born 60 years after Terah's first child, making him only 75 when his father died.

2. An ancient version, one known as the Samaritan Pentateuch, has Terah dying at age 145, not 205. "This [solution] seems preferable, if only because Abram would scarcely have made the exclamation of 17:17 had his own father begotten him at 130."[25]

---

24. There exists no linguistic similarity in Hebrew between *Haran* the person and *Haran* the city. The similarity only exists in English.

25. Kidner, *Genesis*, 112.

These two chapters concerning the post-Flood world carry a stark reminder that God cares about all nations. The migration of Noah's children to their various locations across the globe was God's plan; Moses would remind Israel on the banks of the Jordan, "When the Most High gave the nations each their heritage, when he partitioned out the human race, he assigned the boundaries of nations" (Deut 32:8 NJB). It would appear to anyone that the earth was populated by means of happenstance wandering, but it was in fact the product of God's design. What he had once done for the oceans (Job 38:10–11), God also did for the nations.

Centuries later, exiled Israel would discover comfort in passages like Gen 10–11. If God was truly sovereign over the nations, including those founded by Nimrod, then they had to believe by faith that such was specifically true of Assyria and Babylon. If the God of their fathers had dispersed the builders of Babylon in lingual confusion; if he had established the nations and assigned them all their boundaries, then surely he had power to debase one and exalt another. "Though Babylon reaches as high as the heavens and makes her fortifications incredibly strong, I will still send enemies to plunder her. I, the LORD, have spoken!" (Jer 51:53 HCSB). Yahweh had most assuredly not abandoned his people. Israel had only to wait for him to further unfold his redemptive plan to unite all nations and peoples under the reign of his Holy One, a plan that would culminate in "every tongue [acknowledging] that Jesus Christ is Lord" (Phil 2:11 NIV).

A plan that commenced with the call for Abram to leave his father's house.

TALKING POINTS

The Table of Seventy Nations seems to have been of particular interest to Luke, the sole Gentile author of the NT. Jesus commissioned seventy disciples[26] in Luke 10 to go and preach the coming of God's Kingdom, a mission that looked forward to the day when the Gospel would be taken to the Gentiles, ("the world he [Christ] created he must also redeem").[27] That process receives significant attention in the sequel to Luke's Gospel, the Acts of the Apostles. Jesus gave a final commission to the apostles to be his witnesses "to the ends of the earth" (Acts 1:8 HCSB). That process began on Pentecost when there were assembled "in Jerusalem God-fearing Jews from every nation under heaven" (Acts 2:5 NIV). It may be that we are supposed to see at Pentecost a reversal of Babel—the multi-lingual crowd heard the gospel preached in their native language (Acts 2:8–11). Later, Paul would proclaim on Mars Hill that God had made "from one man every nation" (17:26), a fact that Gen 10 illustrates well. Such is a reminder to Christians that nationalism, racism, xenophobia, and segregation have no place in the Kingdom of God. We should be the first to eagerly anticipate the day when all nations flow into the house of Yahweh (Isa 2:2), a day that will see innumerable hosts "from every nation, from all tribes and peoples and languages, standing before the throne and before the Lamb … crying out with a loud voice, 'Salvation belongs to our God who sits on the throne, and to the Lamb!'" (Rev 7:9–10). What a day, glorious day, that will be.

We sometimes treat strangers in ways we would never treat family or close friends—with rudeness, arrogance, or cruelty. But as Gen 10 demonstrates, the entire world is one big family with a common father in the first man, and a common Creator in the God of heaven. The late evangelist Marshall Keeble was famous for commenting on the brotherhood of man by quipping, "If I miss him in Christ, I'll hit him in Adam." Indeed, Jesus' Golden Rule is illogical apart from the claim of Genesis that every human being shares a common ancestry in Adam and Noah. This alone should inspire all Christians to reevaluate their treatment of others. Our call is to exercise acceptance, patience, forgiveness, submission, and love—not only because that is what God did for us in Christ, but also because that's just how you should treat family.

---

26. Due to a textual variant, it is uncertain whether Jesus sent out 70 (HCSB, NASU, NRSV) or 72 (ESV, NIV). Bruce Metzger concluded that the evidence for both is "evenly divided" (*A Textual Commentary on the Greek New Testament*, 2nd ed. [Stuttgart: United Bible Societies, 1994], 126).

27. Hamilton, *The Book of Genesis: Chapters 1–17*, 348.

A mong the neatest experiences of my life is an occasion when my wife and I were privileged to host a meal in our home for a foreign missionary and his family. Though we confessed the same Lord and anticipated the same eternal hope, we spoke different languages and were from separate races. Needless to say, it was quite a challenge to communicate with them when the interpreter was unavailable. The experience reminded me that, in a fallen world, we continue to deal with the consequences of Babel's sin. Through the prophet Zephaniah, the Lord promised a day was coming when there would be "no more haughtiness on my holy mountain" (Zeph 3:11 NLT), a day when "the speech of the peoples" would be changed (3:9). I guess it is natural for us, when we hear the language or accent of another nationality, to grow frustrated, and for ethnocentric arrogance to rear its ugly head. But instead of getting all in a bind, perhaps it would do us good to pause and consider why linguistic differences exist in the first place (sin), and how they point to our need for a Savior who, at the end of time, will hear "every tongue confess" him to be Master (Phil 2:11). That same Savior, so I've been told, loves all the little children of the world—red and yellow, black and white. We should endeavor to do no less, regardless of our differences, for we are all precious in his sight.

5

TWO STEPS BACK

S ome of my earliest memories are of dad reading stories to me every night. Being the master storyteller that he was, my dad always had a yarn to spin at bedtime. Sometimes they were embellished accounts of childhood exploits; others, it was Bill Cosby's stand-up comedy bits. The Berenstain Bears and Curious George would appear from time to time, as did dad's memories of Tom Landry's Dallas Cowboys. But most often, it was tales of those heroes of faith found in the Scriptures. He told me of Noah's ark, David vs. Goliath, and the three Hebrew children being cast into the fiery furnace (dad always called them "Shadrach, Meshach, and Under-the-bed-we-go"). These individuals were spoken of in reverent tones. As I drifted off to sleep each night, visions of Moses at Sinai or Elijah at Carmel would dance in my head.

Abraham, as one can imagine, was a staple in my regular, not-so-fictional diet of "Once upon a time…" The patriarch indeed casts an impressive shadow over Scripture's pages: Israel's religious heritage (Exod 3:6), material inheritance (Deut 1:8), and ethnic identity (Matt 3:9) were all associated with Abraham. At times, it was for Abraham's sake that God chose not to destroy Israel (2 Kgs 13:23). Ultimately, Abraham was remembered as God's friend (2 Chr 20:7).

In the NT, inspired writers consistently point to Abraham as the ultimate example of one who is faith-full. When Paul discussed justification by faith in Rom 4 and Gal 3, Abraham was his go-to argument. In Heb 11, the patriarch's faith is offered as an example to emulate. In another letter, James argues that, as was the case with Abraham, true faith is always validated by obedience (Jas 2:17–18). It is easy to see how Abraham's name became synonymous with faith itself.

But therein lies the problem. Abraham's faith, long acclaimed as the ultimate model to emulate, had as many hiccups as highlights. His relationship with God was peppered with doubt and failure. No sooner did he load a U-Haul and leave his homeland on blind faith, than he forgot God's promise of protection and lied about his relationship with his wife. Inexplicably, after several years of spiritual maturation, he did it again.

In the past, I always approached Abraham's life as I would a star athlete—with awe, reverence, and a "Please, sir, can I have your autograph?" Upon deeper study, however, I discovered a life of faith with a haunting familiarity to it. Abraham's faith certainly had its unparalleled moments (when anyone leaves their homeland simply because God said so, it's noteworthy). But it was Abraham's *failures* that made him relatable for me. In short, I discovered in Abraham's life more of myself than I expected.

The reality is that all of us approach the lives of biblical heroes in this way. We stand in awe of Noah and his ark, Moses at the Red Sea, or David before Goliath. "My faith could never be that great," we think to ourselves. But when we actually read the stories of these heroes in the text, we are caught off guard by their human frailty, and that should encourage those of us whose walk of faith often seems like "one step forward, two steps back." What we forget is that greatness is never achieved overnight. Every one of God's faithful servants overcame multiple obstacles and recurring failures in order to fulfill God's purposes for life. Abraham was no exception. If the father of the fearful faithful learned to trust over time, then there remains hope for us as well, the many children of father Abraham.

GENESIS 12:1–3

The call of Abram (as he is known in the text until Gen 17) is a dramatic one in Scripture, widely acknowledged as a turning point in the biblical story. It is a new beginning, a new genesis in the Epic of God.[1] In one sense, the story that began here would not culminate for another two millennia on a Roman cross. Yet in another sense, that narrative is still unfolding in the lives of all God's people.

Abram received a call to leave Ur (Acts 7:2–4), but for whatever reason had

---

1. "In [Gen 1–11] the downward spiral of divine-human relations is marked by a series of curses and punishments in which God is mainly reactive as he punishes and curtails the activity of his recalcitrant subjects. In contrast, ch. 12 opens with a new divine initiative introduced by God in a speech. Creation had come into being through divine speech, and now at this strategic turning point in the history of the created order God speaks again," (McKeown, *Genesis*, 73).

not made it any farther than Haran. After the death of his father, Abram received God's call once again. It was the call to pick up and move to a new land, the land of Canaan. The command to "Go" meant that Abram needed to "determinedly [dissociate] himself from his familiar surrounding,"[2] (cf. Exod 18:27; Josh 22:4), or as Calvin paraphrased the command: "I command thee to go forth with closed eyes, and forbid thee to inquire whither I am about to lead thee, until, having renounced thy country, thou shalt have given thyself wholly to me."[3]

That Abram did so was a dramatic move on his part. In the ancient world, to leave your father's house was to forfeit one's inheritance and claims to family property. More than that, Abram was being asked to forsake the gods of his father's household (Josh 24:2) and worship Yahweh alone. To be asked to surrender home, family, and faith—things so fundamental to a person's identity—was a tall order. But coupled with the command to "Go" came some very special promises.

These verses constitute the beginning of God's promises to the patriarch. While they might have been rather vague at the outset, God spent the next century fulfilling these promises in Abram's life, one way or the other. It is important that we delineate these promises here and now, for they are collectively the lens through which we must view all of Abram's life. These four promises were of:

PROPERTY

"Go from your country … to the land that I will show you" (12:1). For all we're told, Abram set out from his homeland in a general direction, but was ignorant of just where exactly he was going. I've moved a few times in my life, but I always had a clear destination in mind—the patriarch had none. The promise of land, of property, drives the narrative of Abram's life beginning in Gen 12. He arrives in the land, only for it to be plagued with famine. He returns to Canaan in Gen 13, only for it to appear insufficient for both his and Lot's herds. In Gen 14, foreign militaries threaten Abram's peaceful existence in the land. Throughout, God kept promising that all of Canaan would be given to the patriarch and his descendants (12:7; 13:15, 17; 15:18–21), culminating in the oath, "I will give to you and to your offspring after you the land of your sojournings, all the land of Canaan, for an everlasting possession, and I will be their God" (17:8). But

---

2.   T. Muraoka, "On the So-Called *Dativus Ethicus* in Hebrew," *JTS* 29 (1978): 497.

3.   Calvin, *Genesis*, 1:344.

Abram himself would never legally own a single divot of sod in Canaan except for his own grave (23:17–18; 25:9).

And his descendants wouldn't possess Canaan until after suffering four centuries "in a land that is not theirs" (15:13). But that simply means that this promise became a profoundly important one for Abram's descendants. God's promise to give Canaan to the Israelites is a prominent feature of Moses' speeches in Deuteronomy, and the tension of dwelling in the land of promise vs. being expelled from it saturates the entire OT.

> See, I have set the land before you. Go in and take possession of the land that the LORD swore to your fathers, to Abraham, to Isaac, and to Jacob, to give to them and to their offspring after them.
>
> Deut 1:8

> You shall walk in all the way that the LORD your God has commanded you, that you may live, and that it may go well with you, and that you may live long in the land that you shall possess.
>
> Deut 5:33

> Those blessed by the LORD shall inherit the land, but those cursed by him shall be cut off … The righteous shall inherit the land and dwell upon it forever.
>
> Ps 37:22, 29

> For the upright will inhabit the land, and those with integrity will remain in it, but the wicked will be cut off from the land, and the treacherous will be rooted out of it.
>
> Prov 2:21–22

Israel's disobedience eventually brought destruction and expulsion:

> Behold, the day of the LORD comes, cruel, with wrath and fierce anger, to make the land a desolation and to destroy its sinners from it.
>
> Isa 13:9

> Therefore I will hurl you out of this land into a land that neither
> you nor your fathers have known, and there you shall serve
> other gods day and night, for I will show you no favor.
>
> Jer 16:13

And as he gazed upon the destruction that had taken place, Jeremiah lamented, "Our inheritance has been turned over to strangers, our homes to foreigners" (Lam 5:2). Being exiled to another land other than the one of promise was disorienting for Israel: "How shall we sing the LORD's song in a foreign land? If I forget you, O Jerusalem, let my right hand forget its skill! Let my tongue stick to the roof of my mouth, if I do not remember you, if I do not set Jerusalem above my highest joy!" (Ps 137:4–6). Even today, those of the Zionist movement (including notables such as Glenn Beck, Tom DeLay, Jerry Falwell, John Hagee, Hal Lindsey, and Pat Robertson) place great importance on Palestine as being the land of Israel's inheritance, the land sworn by God to the patriarch—making the words of 12:1, the promise of property, all the more weighty (if not misunderstood).

POSTERITY

"I will make of you a great nation" (12:2; cf. 18:18). God later added that Abram's descendants would become a nation as innumerable as sand and stars (13:16; 15:5; 22:17). Implicit in this was also the promise of a son (15:4), though Abram and Sarai had no biological children at the time (11:30).

But if the promise of property drives the narrative of Gen 12–15, the promise of a child drives it beginning in Gen 15 until the birth of Isaac. Abram's and Sarai's frustrations over being childless is palpable and a regular source of conflict. Abram arguably thought that Lot would be his heir until the latter moved away in Gen 13. In Gen 15, Abram seems indignant that the replacement heir is a servant in his household. In Gen 16, Abram thinks the tension to have been resolved with the birth of Ishmael: he goes thirteen years considering the promise fulfilled until he learns otherwise—"Why not let Ishmael inherit what you have promised me?" (17:18 CEV). Even after Isaac was born, this promise continued to drive the narrative as the patriarch was called to offer this unique, special son as a sacrifice back to God. This is the promise with which the patriarch arguably struggled the most. But it was a promise worth pursuing—such an offer by God to man was unprecedented in the ANE world.[4]

PROSPERITY

"I will bless you and make your name great" (12:2; cf. Deut 7:13). Abram enjoyed a measure of economic prosperity before this promise, but certainly went on to profit materially by God's grace. He would receive from foreign kings gifts of silver, gold, and large flocks of animals. He would enjoy possession of certain "status symbols" such as camels. As we will see, he was even able to afford a 318-man private security force.

In ancient times, however, possessing a great name also had to do with achieving prestige and fame that would outlive the individual, something that is certainly true of Abram's legacy four thousand years after his death. The reason for this particular promise was "so that you will be a blessing" (12:2). In his lifetime, Abram would indeed be a blessing to many. Those who treated the patriarch favorably found themselves blessed, but Abram was a channel of blessing to every nation by virtue of the incarnation and atonement of Christ (Gal 3:14).

PROTECTION

"I will bless those who bless you, and him who dishonors you I will curse" (12:3; cf. 15:1). Though the ESV distinguishes between the two, most English translations of 12:3 disguise the difference between the first and second use of "curse"—e.g. "whoever curses you I will curse" (NIV). The words are different in Hebrew. The first meant to disdain or despise and refers to verbal harassment (cf. Exod 21:17; 2 Sam 16:5–13); the latter "curse" signifies a formal legal conviction of sin similar to God's curses on the serpent, Eve, Adam, and Cain. In other words, if someone so much as slandered Abram on Facebook or looked at him cross-eyed, then that person would be placed under God's ban and experience divine damnation. And we know, "It is a fearful thing to fall into the hands of the living God" (Heb 10:31).

The use of the plural vs. singular, "those who bless" vs. "him who dishonors," indicates that more people will bless Abram than will curse him. God not only promised Abram protection, but also assured that Abram's need for such protection would be rare.

4. ZIBBCOT 1:69.

GENESIS 12:4–9

With little more than his family and God's promises, Abram embarked from Haran on a month-long journey of over 500 miles. Once in Canaan, he first stopped in Shechem (generally regarded as the geographical center of the Promised Land), and camped near a distinct oak tree in that region. This tree seems to have become quite a landmark, turning up several more times in the OT (35:4; Josh 24:26; Judg 9:6, 37). God's reaffirmation of his promises of posterity and property led Abram to commemorate the occasion by building an altar.

But one wonders what Abram must have thought when he heard "To your offspring..." (12:7) instead of "To you..." Were he and his family now permanently dispossessed? Had he unwittingly left the comforts of Ur and Haran only to face a nomadic future? In so many ways, embarking on a life of faith requires us to eschew a comfortable, stationary existence for a challenging, uncertain one (Heb 11:13–16).

Some consider the note, "At that time the Canaanites were in the land," to be an addition by a later editor. When Moses wrote these words, of course the Canaanites were still there; they wouldn't be expelled until Joshua's campaign! On the one hand, I don't think it's a threat to inspiration to suggest that an editor after Moses inserted this statement. But Hezekiah ben Manoah, a Jewish rabbi from the 13th century A.D., believed the statement to be original to Moses, and that it was "written from the perspective of the future,"[5] meaning the statement functions as a promise that the Canaanites were in the land, but would not be so *forever*. If so, it illustrates how God's promises and life's reality can collide so violently in the land of faith. Archaeology has shown that places like Shechem and Bethel were thriving settlements in Abram's day. The Canaanites were in the land, and only by faith could God's promise be trusted.

After staying in Shechem for a time, Abram journeyed 23 miles south to Bethel, a place that housed a shrine to the Canaanite god El. The patriarch spurned the thought of showing customary honor to this false god and instead worshiped the true God at this place.[6] The phrase "called upon the name of the LORD" (12:8) "implies more than simple prayer: it suggests that Abram worshiped in a regular formal way (cf. 4:26; 21:33; 26:25; Zeph 3:9)."[7] With

---

5. Sarna, *Genesis*, 91.

6. Ibid., 92.

7. Wenham, *Genesis 1–15*, 281.

Abram's later movement into the Negeb (the arid land SW of the Dead Sea), he completed a tour of the whole Promised Land from north to south.

GENESIS 12:10-20

Famine came to Canaan, so Abram sought refuge in Egypt, though the thought that he would stay only until the famine abated seems suspect. The text says that he intended to "sojourn" or "live there for a while" (NIV). The same word (Hebrew *gur*) is used elsewhere of a stay of several years in length (2 Kgs 8:2), if not a permanent residence (19:9; 2 Sam 4:3; Ps 61:4). This is our first clue that Abram has exchanged altars of faith for webs of deceit. Seeking refuge in Egypt may or may not have been wrong,[8] but his apparent desire to tarry there long-term, rather than return to Canaan at the earliest opportunity, wasn't motivated by faith. We are thereby presented with a mirror image of our own faith-journey, an example "of the sudden transition that can be made from the plane of faith to that of fear."[9]

Several scholars have noted the frequency of famine in Palestine if seasonal rainfall does not fall in necessary volume,[10] and average annual rainfall in the Negeb is only 4–12 inches anyway.[11] Contrast Palestine and its fickle seasonal rainfall, with Egypt where the land is fertilized each year by the much-more-reliable Nile floodwaters. Consequently, Egypt was noted in Scripture for its relatively stable food supply (Deut. 11:10). It was a place of refuge for neighboring countries in times of famine (cf. 41:57), a fact corroborated by an inscription in the Egyptian tomb of Hor-em-heb.[12]

---

8. Note that Abram went to Egypt without God's consent (cf. 26:2–6; 46:2–3). Maclaren asks, "Was Abram right in so soon leaving the land to which God had led him, and going down to Egypt? Was that not taking the bit between his teeth?" (*Genesis*, 85). And Waltke concludes, "Since he receives no revelation to sojourn in Egypt (cf. 12:1; 26:2–6; 46:2–3), he is stepping out of the stones in God's will to find bread," (*Genesis*, 213).

9. Kidner, *Genesis*, 116.

10. Sarna, *Genesis*, 93; Walton, *Genesis*, 395; Wenham, *Genesis 1–15*, 287. It is interesting that "modern archeologists and geologists have found evidence of a massive three-hundred-year drought cycle" in Canaan that is dated to the period of Abram (Walton, *Genesis*, 395; cf. John Noble Wilford, "Collapse of Earliest Known Empire Is Linked to Long, Harsh Drought," *New York Times*, August 24, 1993).

11. ZIBBCOT 1:73.

12. "Certain of the foreigners who know not how they may live have come ... Their

In spite of her 65 years of age, Abram considered Sarai's striking appearance a liability while living in a foreign land. When they had left Haran, they had agreed to deceive when necessary in order to protect Abram's life (20:13). His plan seems to have been to pose as the brother in order to intercept any marriage plans (cf. 24:55; 34:13–17). Sarna mentions an ANE institution known as "fratriarchy" in which a woman without a father was protected by her brother who negotiated marriage with interested parties.[13]

Sarai's beauty at an age when a woman has normally surpassed society's definition of "beautiful" could be due to any number of factors. Ancient cultures had very different standards for beauty than our modern superficial ones. Also, the patriarchs and their families lived much longer lives than anyone today. Abram eventually lived 175 years (25:7) and Sarai 127 years (23:1)—for all we know, her physical appearance at the middle age of 65 was the same as today's woman at 35 or 40.

In any event, when the Egyptians noticed Sarai's striking beauty, she "was taken" to Pharaoh. We are not told if this was with or without Abram's permission. But since it was Pharaoh doing the taking, Abram's opinion likely wasn't much of a priority. The text is unclear whether sexual intercourse actually took place. It says Sarai "was taken," but that phrase is too ambiguous to know what exactly happened. It seems she was added to Pharaoh's harem, one way or another, and Pharaoh awarded Abram with a substantial bride price of livestock and servants. The gift of female donkeys (Job 1:3; 42:3) and camels were particularly valuable.

But I doubt that we are intended to see in this detail God's implicit approval of Abram's actions. There is a sharp distinction between wealth that is received from evil doings vs. from God (Prov 10:2, 22). In addition, we should bear in mind that these treasures from Pharaoh would bring with them a high cost, for they turned out to be "the seeds of further crises;"[14] the great number of livestock would create conflict between Abram's and Lot's herdsmen (13:7), and one of the female slaves would cause a rift between Abram and Sarai (16:1). Sin's reward always proves to be our undoing (Rom 6:23).

No sooner had Sarai been taken than God cursed Pharaoh and his house with "great plagues"—the same word used to describe the ten plagues God

countries are starving," (ANET 251).

13. Sarna, *Genesis*, 95.

14. Ross, "Genesis," 99.

brought on Egypt through Moses (Exod 11:1), and it is also used specifically of skin diseases (Lev 13) such as leprosy (2 Kgs 15:5). The king was understandably upset with Abram, who had put him at risk by deceiving him. It is a foreign, pagan monarch who is concerned with this breach of morality, not Abram![15] His silence during the interrogation effectively betrays his guilt. In his justified anger, Pharaoh could have just as well had Abram executed for his deceit. As it was, however, Pharaoh expelled him from Egypt in a manner similar to God's exile of Adam and Eve from Eden (3:23). In a desperate attempt to save his own life in a foreign land, Abram almost lost it. Ironic, no?

GENESIS 20

Twenty-five years later, Abraham found himself in a similar situation. For much of that time, he had been living near Hebron (13:18), but he now moved on, journeying as far as the Sinai Peninsula before doubling back to Gerar, an area eight miles south of Gaza (cf. 10:19). We aren't told why Abraham moved; Arnold assumes "another famine is the reason."[16] At Gerar, the ruler Abimelech[17] noticed Sarah and took her as his wife just as Pharaoh had done, but this time the text is explicit that intercourse did not take place (20:4).

In a dream, God condemned Abimelech for taking Sarah, though Abimelech had done so "with a clear conscience" (20:6 HCSB). God made clear that, if Sarah were not returned to her husband, severe punishment would be imminent. As it was, the Lord had already struck Abimelech's harem with barrenness, and had afflicted Abimelech himself with some sort of sexual dysfunction (20:17–18).[18]

However, I can't help but find interest in the phrasing of Abimelech's protest: "Lord, will you kill an innocent people?" (20:4). Recall that this story comes on the heels of the destruction of Sodom; doesn't the king's objection sound eerily similar to the question Abraham himself asked of the Lord, "Will you indeed sweep away the righteous with the wicked?" (18:23)? Subtle as it may

---

15. Ancient Egyptian ethics severely frowned upon lying (Kenneth A. Kitchen, "Egyptian Ethics," *Baker's Dictionary of Christian Ethics*, ed. Carl F. Henry [Grand Rapids: Baker, 1973], 202).

16. Arnold, *Genesis*, 188. Sarna speculates that Abraham relocated in order to trade, purchase supplies, or take advantage of "the rich pasturelands in the vicinity," (*Genesis*, 141).

17. Rather than a personal name, Abimelech ("my father is king") seems to have been a royal title similar to Egypt's Pharaoh.

18. This detail at the end of the story is not frivolous; otherwise, one might be tempted to think that Isaac was conceived illegitimately.

be, there is a strong condemnation of the patriarch in Abimelech's words—"just as God choreographed Abimelech's repentance, does the king speak unwittingly the words of divine correction to Abraham?"[19] The patriarch should have known better than to do this. He had just witnessed the salvation of his nephew Lot from Sodom's destruction. Such a recent occasion of God's faithfulness would hardly excuse Abraham's faith for giving way to fear.

And like Pharaoh, Abimelech was justifiably outraged with Abraham's blatant deception and thus interrogated him. This time, Abraham explained the reasons for his actions, confessing that Sarah was his half-sister[20] and that fear for his survival had motivated him to lie about his marriage. To make reparations, Abimelech gave the patriarch livestock, servants, and a thousand silver shekels[21] (the bride price in Deut 22:29 is fifty shekels). He also allowed Abraham to live and travel throughout the land without harassment, something Pharaoh had not conceded (12:20). Note, however, the very sarcastic way Abimelech says to Sarah, "I have given your brother..." not "I have given your husband..." It seems the king "still resented Abraham's behavior."[22]

In both stories, it's what Abraham planned to do should someone ever claim Sarah as a wife. If he lied about his marriage, then Sarah being taken as someone else's wife was inevitable. He placed his wife at risk for adultery, and in the ANE,

---

19. Kenneth A. Mathews, *Genesis 11:27–50:26* (Nashville: Broadman, 2005), 256.

20. Hamilton wonders if even this "half-truth" isn't "a total fabrication on Abraham's part," (*The Book of Genesis: Chapters 18–50* [Grand Rapids: Eerdmans, 1995], 68), and he has a point. We more or less assume that Abraham's claiming Sarah as a half-sister is the real truth, but nothing is said in 11:27–32 of her being his half-sister, though it does mention that Nahor married his niece (11:29).

21. "In Ugaritic literature this is the amount of silver paid as the bride price among the gods. In weight it equals about twenty-five pounds of silver, but in value it is more than a common worker could expect to make in a lifetime," (Walton, *Genesis*, 496). Waltke estimates an ancient Babylonian, "usually paid a half shekel per month, would have had to work 167 years to earn such a sum," (*Genesis*, 287).

22. Gordon J. Wenham, *Genesis 16–50* (Dallas: Word, 1994), 74.

adultery was known as "the great sin"[23] (cf. 20:9) and often legislated against.[24] What, then, did Abraham hope to accomplish, other than the preservation of his own life? We just don't know.

What is clear, however, is that Abraham refused to completely trust in God's promises. The Lord had affirmed that he would provide Abraham with protection when necessary (15:3), and would curse anyone who dared mistreat the patriarch (12:3). What need did Abraham have to lie in order to save himself? Whether his plan was a well-thought-out scheme—or a poorly devised, last-minute ploy—Abraham refused to trust, and that decision blew up in his face.

These are not the only recorded examples of Abraham's fear and faithlessness. There was also his lack of faith in God's promise to provide a son, which will be explored later. However, Abraham eventually experienced a remarkable transformation into the father of the faithful. This gradual metamorphosis on his part gives hope to his children who live today. Our walk of faith sometimes seems to be one step forward, two steps back. But in spite of our frailty, Christians live with the assurance "that he who began a good work in you will bring it to completion at the day of Jesus Christ" (Phil 1:6).

These stories, along with their parallel in Isaac's life (26:6–11), are problematic because the narrator never censures the patriarch. Did God approve of the deception? Such is hardly likely, for God hates falsehood (Prov 6:17). We are not in a position to judge Abraham, but we should take these episodes as examples of Walter Scott's admonition, "Oh what a tangled web we weave when first we practice to deceive." The patriarch simultaneously put in jeopardy his wife and God's promises, and it was only the Lord's intervention that gave both stories a happy ending. We have no right to expect God to do the same for us, but we certainly have every confidence in his willingness to forgive us graciously. This is where our story merges with Abraham's, the wonder of a God who at times stands between sin and consequences, and mitigates or abolishes our penalty when we deserve his full wrath. There is no word in any language to adequately describe such grace.

"Amazing" will have to do.

---

23. Jacob J. Rabinowitz, "The 'Great Sin' in Ancient Egyptian Marriage Contracts," *JNES* 18 (1959): 73; W. L. Moran, "The Scandal of the 'Great Sin' at Ugarit," *JNES* 18 (1959): 280–81.

24. Walton, *Genesis*, 495.

TALKING POINTS

When Abram embarked from Haran, he became the first of many to enter the wild frontier of faith. To succeed in his new life with God, Abram had to leave his old life behind, for "faith demands a ruthless abandonment of the past."[25] He had no doubt grown comfortable in Ur and Haran, but all of that comfort had not given him the one thing he desired most: a child and a future. Indeed, "departure from securities is the only way out of barrenness."[26] Before they know it, Christians can become too comfortable to do what faith requires: too cozy in a relationship we have no right to be in, too cozy with a habit that is not consistent with godliness, too cozy with a career that is leading us away from the heart of God. Relationships are important, habits are hard to break, and paychecks put food on the table, but they can also hijack an incredible opportunity to trust in God with our whole heart and see what great things he might do to rescue us from our silent despondency (Prov 3:5–6). We are thus presented with the dilemma—the great paradox—of faith: the only way to abandon hopelessness is to abandon all else but God.

In Gen 12, Abram twice built an altar to God and worshiped in a place normally reserved for pagan worship. So precarious is the life of faith that, upon entering it for the first time, we must ruthlessly replace our old habits, redeeming them with new rituals that exalt God to the proper place in our hearts. But these altars hold greater significance in that, upon arriving in Canaan, Abram did not set out to build a tower (as did the citizens of Babel) or a city (Cain), but a simple altar that honored the Lord. Long after his tents were gone, Abram's altars remained. May the most permanent things we leave behind not be relics of our misguided self-promotion, but reminders of the greatness and goodness of God.

When we act faithlessly, we negatively impact those around us. We cannot be faithful carriers of God's blessing to the nations and also be faithless to his will. It is speculated that the Pharaoh of Gen 12 was Wahkare Achthoes III (c. 2120–2070). "Interestingly, this Egyptian king wrote wisdom literature including advice concerning the treachery of Asiatics."[27] Had Pharaoh's

---

25. Waltke, *Genesis*, 209.

26. Brueggemann, *Genesis*, 118.

27. Ross, "Genesis," 99.

experiences with Abram colored his perception? It's possible. The apostle Peter urged his readers "as sojourners and exiles to … keep your conduct among the Gentiles honorable, so that when they speak against you as evildoers, they may see your good deeds and glorify God on the day of visitation" (1 Pet 2:11–12). Abram did not walk with integrity during his sojourn in Egypt or Gerar. By God's help, may we be better examples throughout our own on earth.

A bram's plan to save his skin almost backfired; Pharaoh easily could have executed Abram for his crime since the ancient world considered adultery such a grave offense. Abram's failed ruse is a warning that the faithless often lose the very thing they try so desperately to preserve in their self-sufficiency. As Jesus so eloquently reminds us, "Whoever would save his life will lose it, but whoever loses his life for my sake will find it" (Matt 16:25). And for those whose trust is completely in the Father, the very thing they surrender is often returned to them in a manner beyond their wildest dreams (Matt 19:29).

M ore overwhelming than Abram's deceit is God's devotion. As the apostle Paul put it, "if we are faithless, he remains faithful—for he cannot deny himself" (2 Tim 2:13). Mysteriously, disturbingly, Abram's moral failures did not earn for him a "Go to jail, go directly to jail. Do not pass Go, do not collect $200." Indeed, we are bothered by the very absence of censure of the patriarch. Isn't lying a violation of one of the commandments (Exod 20:16)? Isn't it something the Lord despises (Prov 6:16–19)? To be sure, there is nothing to be emulated in these stories, but the greatest take away might be that God is more patient with us than we sometimes imagine. "He knows what we are made of, remembering that we are dust" (Ps 103:14 HCSB; cf. 1 John 3:20). We must never confuse this as being God's tolerance of sin, but rather an acknowledgment from the Lord that nothing worthwhile happens overnight. Spiritual growth takes time! Sanctification can't be microwaved. We must content ourselves with the reality "that he who began a good work in you will bring it to completion at the day of Jesus Christ" (Phil 1:6). And not a moment sooner.

6

FOG OF WAR

C ivil wars are always the bloodiest and family feuds the bitterest. My dad once said that we tend to hurt the ones we love the most. So I am thankful that, from fraternal conflict between Cain and Abel, to congregational strife in first-century Corinth, the Bible is no stranger to our human proclivity towards squabbles and spats. Scripture never even attempts to gloss over our tendency to battle and bicker with one another. Rather, it portrays such as the frustrating and heartbreaking consequence of living in a fallen world, a reality that will never go away.

The Bible not only tells of conflict, however. It also uses stories to illustrate for us how to deal with our own disagreements—large or small—in a way that honors God. One such story is about Abram, Lot, and their decision to separate so as to prevent a minor frustration from escalating into a major family feud. The narrative that follows in the next chapter makes clear that Abram harbored no lasting resentment towards his nephew—Abram drew his sword in order to rescue Lot and the other prisoners from Sodom, encountering in the aftermath a mysterious priest named Melchizedek.

But despite what you may have learned in Sunday School, the narrative of Gen 13 is not *primarily* about how and why to be a peacemaker. Like the rest of the OT, these chapters were written for our instruction and correction (Rom 15:4; 1 Cor 10:11; 2 Tim 3:16), but they are first God's story, an account of how he faithfully fulfills his promises to his people.

As a unit, Gen 13–14 demonstrates how God began eliminating all obstacles in order for Abram (or rather, his descendants) to inherit the Promised Land. Particularly in Gen 13, "at stake is nothing less than Lot's elimination as heir to the covenant promise."[1] Lot was introduced to us in 11:27 as Abram's nephew, and we were told in 12:4 that he joined his uncle when the patriarch obeyed the call of God to leave his father's house. Mentioned again in 13:1, it seems like the text would have us see Lot as the patriarch's protégé and presumed heir.

But God had other plans. We have much to learn from Abram's peacemaking example, but even more from God's fidelity. He had promised the land of Canaan to Abram, land that would be given to his "offspring" (12:7), and Lot wasn't Abram's offspring. He thus needed to be dismissed from the stage. Terrible as they are, the Lord is not above using conflict and war to further his purposes in the world (cf. Amos 3:3–6).

GENESIS 13

After Abram and his entourage had been escorted to the Egyptian border by Pharaoh's guard, they traveled another 200 miles back to the Negeb. Abram's material wealth is mentioned (13:2) to set the stage for what happens next. Specifically noted is his possession of silver and gold, which means the patriarch held liquid assets that endowed him with financial stability in harsh economic times.

Upon arriving in Canaan, Abram moved "from place to place" (13:3 NIV), not unlike Israel's movement through the wilderness in stages (Exod 17:1). He most likely moved wherever pasture and water were available, ultimately returning to his previous residence near Bethel. His worship to God (13:4) could be interpreted as repentance on Abram's part following his sinful deception in Egypt. At the least, this gesture was a pledge to be more faithful to God's promises in the future. At an altar he had built previously, he declared that he wanted his faith to be as before,[2] and that intention was about to be tested.

For the first time, specific details are given about Lot other than his being Abram's nephew. Lot was also rich in livestock (13:5), but silver and gold are not mentioned as they were in his uncle's case. Lot's wealth was most likely due to his kinship with Abram, but the land surrounding their encampment simply could not support both of their herds. Mention of the Canaanites and Perizzites[3]

---

1. Larry R. Helyer, "The Separation of Abram and Lot: Its Significance in the Patriarchal Narratives," *JSOT* 26 (1983): 85.

2. "Abram has resumed the devout practices he observed on his first excursion in the promised land, indicating perhaps that he has returned home in ways other than physical," (Arnold, *Genesis*, 140).

3. Identifying the Perizzites has proven impossible. They are never mentioned in extra-

(13:7) meant that others already occupied the land, so that is why Abram and Lot were so hard-pressed for adequate pasture.

Abram is to be commended for addressing the quarrel in its early stages while it was still between the herdsmen (Prov 17:14). In addition, he took the high road by offering his nephew first choice when they decided to part ways; there is never an excuse to be selfish with God's blessings. As so today, ancient custom would have dictated that Lot defer to his uncle as the senior party. But Abram was selfless because he trusted God to care for him, regardless of the quality of land in which he resided (Phil 4:11–13).[4] He valued his relationships over his real estate. This is a very different Abram than the one in the previous episode; he is now magnanimous, rather than manipulative.

On this occasion, Abram and Lot perhaps stood at Burj-Beitin, "an elevation that affords a magnificent view of the Jordan Valley," about a mile SE of Bethel.[5] Facing the east, Abram encouraged his nephew to look north ("the left hand") and south ("the right hand") and choose a land to call his own in order to resolve the present conflict. Notice Abram's words carefully; it seems that he intended for he and Lot to partition the land of Canaan between them.[6] But Lot looked *east* (straight ahead, not to "the left hand" or to "the right hand"), and his gaze fell on the Jordan Valley. He surely knew that it was the choice land since it was not dependent upon seasonal rainfall for nourishment. This valley was so ideal that the narrator went out of his way to compare it to Eden. But whatever illusions of paradise we might thus conjure up are immediately dashed with a reminder that the infamous Sodom and her sister cities were located on this plain (13:10).

Nonetheless, Lot chose the fertile valley as his new home, parted ways with his uncle, and settled near Sodom. The move meant that Lot was now leaving Canaan, the land of blessing and promise. His move in the direction of the east again invites the observant student of Genesis to consider Lot as moving away from God (cf. 3:24; 4:16; 11:2). Abram's nephew was clearly choosing common sense over faith.

---

biblical sources.

4.   "A soul truly living in the contemplation of the future, and filled with God's promises, will never be eager to insist on its rights, or to stand on its dignity, and will take too accurate a measure of the worth of things temporal to get into a heat about them," (Maclaren, *Genesis*, 88).

5.   Sarna, *Genesis*, 98.

6.   Helyer, "Separation of Abram," 79.

Lot had to have known that the citizens of Sodom weren't exactly your run-of-the-mill boys and girls next-door. Just as many today are prone to do, Lot was attracted by the material prosperity of the Jordan Valley and failed to account for the spiritual impact it would have on his family. Moses' note concerning Sodom's wickedness is not exactly a glowing endorsement of Lot's character either. As Calvin put it, "Lot, when he fancied that he was dwelling in paradise, was nearly plunged into the depths of hell."[7]

After Lot made his ill-fated decision, God rewarded Abram's peaceable spirit by expanding upon his prior promises. Whereas the promise of land had previously been a general "the land that I will show you" (12:1), it was now specified. The vantage point that allowed Abram to see the whole of Canaan might have been Ramath-Hazor, a spot five miles NE of Bethel and the highest summit in central Israel.[8] From here, Abram was invited to look in all directions, and what he saw would one day be given to him and his offspring. Likewise, the promise of posterity had previously been a general "I will make of you a great nation" (12:2). Now it became a promise to make his descendants impossible to number.

A portion of God's call to Abram in 13:14 is often left untranslated in many versions. The Hebrew na' is a particle "used in entreaties or exhortations"[9] and at times is translated as "please" (19:2, 24:12; 32:29, 33:10; 34:8). But while this particle appears a total of 180 times in the OT (sixty times in Genesis), "it is found only four times in the entire Bible when God addresses a human being,"[10] (13:14; 15:5; 22:2; Exod 11:2). In each of these instances, God asked Abram or Israel "to do something that transcends human comprehension."[11] It certainly took extraordinary faith on Abram's part to believe on this occasion that the whole of Canaan would one day be given to his descendants. But such is the nature of biblical faith; it believes in the "unbelievable"—in a God for whom nothing is impossible.

---

7. Calvin, *Genesis*, 1:373. Sarna agrees: "Dazzled by the surface appearance of prosperity, he pays no heed to the moral depravity of his future neighbors," (*Genesis*, 99). On the other hand, the apostle Peter later called Lot a "righteous" man (2 Pet 2:7), one "troubled because of the filthy lives of evil people" (NCV). Taken together, Lot stands as evidence that good men can make poor decisions with disastrous consequences.

8. Sarna, *Genesis*, 100.

9. NIDOTTE 4:1033

10. Yehuda T. Radday, "The Spoils of Egypt," *ASTI* 12 (1983): 137.

11. Ibid.

The command to traverse the land (13:17) is reminiscent of ANE customs pertaining to the legal acquisition of property. Upon his coronation, a new regent would often tour his kingdom as a way of establishing his sovereignty.[12] A related custom, called *hazakah* by the rabbis,[13] may be reflected later in the OT: God assured Joshua, "Every place that the sole of your foot will tread upon I have given to you, just as I promised to Moses" (Josh 1:3; cf. Deut 11:24), and in Ruth 4:7, Boaz sealed a real estate transaction with the exchange of sandals, again reflecting the idea of acquisition by traversing the land.[14] In other words, the command to "Go, walk through the length and breadth of the land" (13:17 NIV) was God's assurance to Abram that the land would one day be his descendants' legal property.

After this, Abram relocated to Hebron,[15] a large settlement located halfway between Jerusalem and Beersheba. The area was very fertile (Num 13:23), undoubtedly the reason for the famous grove of oaks located there. In Josephus's day an oak tree in Mamre was said to have existed there from the day of creation (*Wars* 4.9.7, *Antiquities* 1.10.4). These oaks of Mamre would become Abram's chief home for the next several chapters; he later purchased the nearby cave of Machpelah as a family tomb. Arriving at Mamre for the first time, Abram responded to the reaffirmed promises by worshiping God (13:18).

GENESIS 14

On the surface, this narrative seems out-of-sorts with the scope of Scripture's main interest in Abram. We are accustomed to imagining the patriarch as a peaceful pastoralist—a tent-dwelling hybrid of Santa Claus and Mister Rogers. But this chapter violently presents us with Abram the Hebrew warrior (action figure sold separately). What's more, it is here that we stumble upon Scripture's first mention of the cruel reality of war.

The narrative as a whole seems to be a rude interruption in Abram's story. One could argue persuasively that this chapter's absence would detract little from the broader storyline! But this story illustrates yet again how God made good on

---

12. Waltke, *Genesis*, 222–23.

13. Sarna, *Genesis*, 100.

14. Ernest R. Lacheman, "Note on Ruth 4:7–8," *JBL* 56 (1937): 53–56.

15. The city of Hebron would not exist until c. 1700 B.C. (Num 13:22), a few hundred years after Abram had died. Mamre lay two miles north of the city.

his promise to bless, provide for, and protect the patriarch. In the narrative, we also glimpse growth in Abram's character; he values kinship and disdains illicit rewards. He is maturing as a man of faith before our very eyes.

The chapter is a tale of four kings going to war against five kings. But even though the kings are all mentioned by name, confidently identifying them with historical figures has proven impossible. The background of the episode is explained very quickly. Twelve years prior, the five cities of the Plain had been subjugated by an alliance led by the ruler of Elam, Chedorlaomer (such an alliance was a political norm for that time and place).[16] After being vassals for a dozen years, the five kings rebelled. In response, Chedorlaomer marshaled his allied forces and embarked on a military campaign, traveling as far south as the Gulf of Aqaba (El-paran) on the King's Highway running east of the Jordan (Num 20:17; 21:22). Pillaging as they went, Chedorlaomer's forces finally met their opponents, the armies of Sodom and her sister cities, in the Valley of Siddim.

This valley "was full of tar pits" (14:10 NIV; cf. "bitumen pits" ESV, "asphalt pits" NKJV); when Chedorlaomer routed the army of the five kings, they fled into the hills, and some of the soldiers fell into these tar pits by accident and perished. In the aftermath, Chedorlaomer and his allies made off with prisoners and loot from the five cities. Since he was now "dwelling in Sodom," rather than simply living in the general vicinity (13:12), Lot was among the POWs. Already, his move to the east was proving problematic.

A messenger brought to Abram news of the battle and the fate of his nephew, and the patriarch saddled a posse of "318 trained men who had been born into his household" (14:14 NLT). The Hebrew term translated "trained" is used elsewhere of dedicating a building (Deut 20:5) or training a child (Prov 22:6). The word was borrowed from the Egyptians, where it meant "armed retainers."[17] It seems Abram was wealthy enough to employ a group of men whose sole purpose was militant in nature,[18] i.e. a private security force. That these men had been born in his household meant they were more loyal than those only recently employed.

---

16. K. A. Kitchen, *Ancient Orient and Old Testament* (Downers Grove, IL: InterVarsity Press, 1966), 45.

17. Thomas O. Lambdin, "Egyptian Loan Words in the Old Testament," *JAOS* 73 (1953): 150.

18. "They are not shepherds who grabbed a spear or a sling and headed north for some 125 miles. They are individuals capable of making a successful attack against imposing odds," (Hamilton, *The Book of Genesis: Chapters 1–17*, 406).

In a scene reminiscent of Gideon (Judg 7:8–25), Abram's posse pursued the allied armies "as far as Dan," or Laish as it was then known according to 18th century B.C. Egyptian texts[19] (cf. Judg 18:27–29). It was a place often considered to be the northernmost point in Canaan (Judg 20:1; 1 Sam 3:20). Abram's posse attacked at night and completely routed Chedorlaomer's army, recovering prisoners and loot alike.

Returning home from battle, Abram was greeted by both the king of Sodom and Melchizedek (meaning "king of righteousness," Heb 7:2), the "king of Salem," in a place called "the King's Valley" (cf. 2 Sam 18:18), an area two and a half miles south of Jerusalem.[20] The king of Sodom brought nothing with him to Abram; on the other hand, Melchizedek produced bread and wine to duly honor Abram as a royal guest (cf. 1 Sam 16:20) and conquering hero.

That Melchizedek "was priest of God Most High" emphasizes that he and Abram had a mutual faith in the God of heaven. In his blessing, Melchizedek affirmed that it had been God who had won the victory for Abram. Specifically, he calls God the "Creator of heaven and earth" (14:19 NIV), a phrase that occurs regularly in the OT hymnal (e.g. Pss 121:2; 124:8; 146:6), praising God not only for his past work of creation, but also his present intervention in world events. There is little doubt that, in his blessing, Melchizedek attributed Abram's victory to the sovereignty of God, "the ultimate arbiter of human destiny."[21] Abram's subsequent tithe was thus an expression of gratitude to God for victory, and to Melchizedek for his blessing.

In very stark contrast to Melchizedek's grand generosity, the king of Sodom demanded Abram return the people and keep the plunder for himself. Melchizedek's first words in the narrative are "Blessed be Abram," while the king of Sodom's are "Give me!" But the patriarch had no desire to keep anything that did not belong to him—not even "a thread or a sandal strap," a phrase remarkably similar to those used in ANE legal texts renouncing property rights.[22] The phrase "is clearly a figure of speech signifying completeness" meaning "something like

---

19. Biran, "Dan (Place)," ABD 2:12.

20. Salem is the same as Jerusalem (cf. Ps 76:2).

21. Sarna, *Genesis*, 109.

22. E. A. Speiser, "A Figurative Equivalent for Totality in Akkadian and West-Semitic," *JAOS* 54 (1934): 200–203.

'down to the last shred.'"[23] Abram had once before allowed himself to be enriched at another's expense (12:16), and it had not ended well. Here, Abram would claim no right to Sodom's plunder except the provisions his men had already consumed.

The entire episode reminds us of one of God's earlier promises: "Him who dishonors you I will curse" (12:3). I don't think it a coincidence that Chedorlaomer experienced defeat only when he came up against the patriarch in battle, for opposing God's elect invites God's curse. "No foreign king can exercise power against the blessing of God."[24] Not Pharaoh, nor Chedorlaomer. And when the king of Sodom exhibited such a brusque, ungrateful attitude towards the patriarch, the dark storm clouds of God's judgment grew more ominous over the five cities of the Plain. In this story, the cowardly, scheming Abram we saw in Egypt has given way to a daring warrior who trusts that the battle belongs to the Lord.

But a more significant lesson is also put on display here. It is significant that the patriarch is called "Abram the Hebrew" in the narrative (14:13), but never again in the Bible. The term is often used in the OT to depict God's people as foreigners (39:14; Exod 2:11; 1 Sam 4:6; Jonah 1:9); used here, it called attention to the fact that Abram was a stranger in a strange land. But Abram vanquished Chedorlaomer and expelled him from Canaan, giving Abram a legitimate claim to the land. God had already made clear to him that he would inherit its length and breadth (13:17). Why not seize it all now? Why not strike while the iron was hot? If Abram had returned home eager to rule all of Canaan with his obviously superior fighting force, we could hardly blame him.

That's the thing about biblical faith—it sometimes requires us to surrender the bird in our hand for God's two in the bush. Abram reciprocated Melchizedek's overtures of peace with a tithe of battle spoils, and he refused to enrich himself at the expense of the king of Sodom, lest he exchange a righteous alliance for a wholly unholy one. The patriarch thereby declared that the land and its spoil were not his to take on his own. God would give it to him (or rather, to his descendants) in due time. It requires great faith to live in the uncertainty—the "fog"—of conflict and war. But on these occasions, Abram set a powerful example.

If Abram's magnanimity is our example, then Chedorlaomer's greed is our

---

23. Ibid., 200.

24. Eugene F. Roop, *Genesis* (Scottdale, PA: Herald, 1987), 107.

cautionary tale. Had he been content with the plunder of Sodom, he would have survived this expedition and returned home in glory. But by taking human prisoners, among them Lot, he overreached, and this proved to be his undoing. God's people struggle as well with overreaching in regards to God's promised blessings. Our instant-gratification world has conditioned us so. But if we are truly intent on allowing God to author the story of our lives, we must allow the plot to unfold his way.

TALKING POINTS

When we pursue peace in the midst of conflict, our efforts help fulfill God's plan for the world. He is a God of peace (1 Cor 14:33; 2 Cor 13:11), and his children are peacemakers when necessary (Matt 5:9). The reality of peace is one of the loftiest prayers of the church (1 Tim 2:2) and should be among our chief pursuits (2 Tim 2:22; Heb 12:14). Whether or not he realized it, by opting for a peaceful solution, Abram made it easier for God's will to become reality. This same principle is echoed in Paul's letter to Rome. After rehearsing God's grand scheme of redemption to bring the Gentiles into the church (Rom 9–11), Paul implores his readers to live transformed lives (12:2) characterized by humility (12:3–8), love (12:9–13), and peace in the face of conflict (12:14–21). Paul infers that seeking revenge interferes with (but does not thwart) God's will. Vengeance is God's; let him extract it. We may think that, by opting for peace, we are doing "nothing." But as Lincoln famously said, "The best way to destroy an enemy is to make him a friend." When we prove ourselves peacemakers, we do more than vengeance ever could. Though it seems a paradox, laying down the sword and extending the olive branch of peace could be the most courageous thing we ever do.

Settling for the short end of a stick in any disagreement isn't easy, especially if you're a hypercompetitive person as I am. It had to have annoyed Abram just a little when his graciousness was abused by Lot's greed. Christians are supposed to be magnanimous, but it doesn't always work out that way. The church at Corinth suffered from an epidemic of lawsuits, a problem of which Paul was quite critical (1 Cor 6:1–8). Opting to suffer instead of sue, however, depends on how much faith we have in God vs. fear of the unknown. When "Abram said to Lot, 'Let there be no strife between you and me'" (13:8), the word used for "strife" was *meribah*, the name Moses gave to the place where Israel quarreled in the wilderness (Exod 17:1–7). The linguistic link between these two stories reminds us that we have two options when things don't go our way: fear or faith. Fear causes us to complain out of our disappointment. Faith causes us to confess our dependence. Fear is the conviction that, if I was taken advantage of, then God didn't come through for me. Faith is the conviction that, if I was taken advantage of, then God must have something greater prepared for me in the future. Fear behooves us to reach out and take control. Faith motivates us to "let go and let God," confident that he is as benevolent as he is sovereign.[25]

M elchizedek is one of Scripture's most mysterious characters; he appears on the biblical page out of nowhere, and disappears just as rapidly. In one of the psalms, a hymn of coronation, Israel's new king was said to be "a priest forever after the order of Melchizedek" (Ps 110:4). In the NT, Jesus demonstrated this psalm's messianic overtone (Matt 22:41–45), and the author of Hebrews seized upon the same imagery when he claimed that Jesus' priesthood is superior to that of Aaron. If Aaron, a Levite, paid tribute to Melchizedek while still in Abram's loins, then Aaron's priesthood was clearly inferior to Melchizedek's, and also to Christ's (Heb 7:1–10). In this way, the Hebrews writer appropriates Melchizedek to affirm the obsolescence of the Aaronic priesthood and award credibility to the persecuted church of Christ.[26]

---

25. "Christians are to relinquish their rights in order to enrich others, trusting God's promises to provide. Abraham, secure in God, can give up his land. When we are secure in Christ, we do not have to grasp greedily for possessions," (Waltke, *Genesis*, 224).

26. Hamilton, *The Book of Genesis: Chapters 1–17*, 416.

7

IN BETWEEN

As this book was going to press, violence erupted in the powder keg that is the Middle East. In response to provocation, Israel launched missile strikes against Hamas on November 14, 2012, and Hamas quickly retaliated by firing on Tel Aviv and Jerusalem. Escalation to full war seemed likely until a tenuous cease-fire agreement was brokered a week later. By the time you read this, the situation will have developed in one direction or the other, and we pray now that events trend towards peace. But in spite of our hopes and prayers to the contrary, it is a fact that this is just the latest incident in a long string of violence between the children of Abraham. The three major religious groups in the world—Judaism, Christianity, and Islam—all claim a heritage with the patriarch, but the relationships between them have been characterized by conflict and war for untold generations. How did such hostility and antagonism begin?

It's in these chapters that we see Abram caught up in the tension between daring faith and doubt-riddled fear. One moment, he was staring up at the night sky's constellations in dumbfounded awe, trusting that God could make his descendants as numerous as those twinkle, twinkle little stars. The next moment, he was passively acquiescing to his wife's attempts to circumvent God's miraculous and benevolent provision. Abram was experiencing the gap—what I call the "land of in between"—that often exists between promise and reality. Our success in the land of in between depends on what we place in that gap.

Faith? Fear? Abram vacillated between both.

Most anyone who has studied the Middle East eventually concedes that it is a proverbial mess with no clear resolution, at least none that will pacify all parties for very long. And when Abram fathered a son by Hagar, he created this very mess. But God remained faithful to him, even when the patriarch was faithless. The Lord got involved and promised to bring redemption to the situation. It is in these three chapters that Israel's inheritance of Canaan is affirmed, Ishmael's destiny is secured, and the covenant mark of circumcision is ordained.

Whenever we feel deluged with the consequences of our own sin, these three things—inheritance, future, and covenant seal—are our rescuers, our guardian angels. They are the signposts and travel guides in the land of in between. Our heavenly Father isn't intimidated when doubts arise and fears dismay. Through many dangers, toils, and snares, he is patient with us. Even today, he still has his ways of reaffirming his covenant with us, of making grand gestures that assert his grace and grandeur, which together can engulf our guilt and shame if we surrender them to God.

Inheritance? Our hope of heaven outweighs any earthly suffering (2 Cor 4:17).

Future? Yahweh's mercies are renewed every morning (Lam 3:23).

Covenant seal? "All of you who were baptized into Christ have clothed yourselves with Christ" (Gal 3:27 NIV; cf. Col 2:11–12), and dressed in those robes, we stand immune to Satan's every attack (Rev 12:11).

GENESIS 15

This chapter is one of the most important in the Abra(ha)m story. The promises of property and posterity, soil and seed, merge here as never before. In fact, the Promised Land motif, which has dominated the previous chapters, will climax here and then recede into the background; meanwhile, the promise of offspring is reintroduced and subsequently assumes center stage.

Not long after vanquishing Chedorlaomer, God spoke to the patriarch in a vision, affirming Melchizedek's blessing. A militaristic theme runs through God's word to Abram; besides the obvious "shield," "reward" refers to the loot a soldier would carry from the battlefield (Ezek 29:19). In the previous story, Abram had voluntarily forfeited his share of the victor's "reward" to Sodom's surly king, and considering Sodom's extravagant wealth, such plunder would have been quite valuable. Yet God affirmed that Abram had walked away with something more precious than gold.

But as Abram heard those words, the scab of an old wound apparently fell away to reveal raw frustration. What good was God's reward when Abram had no one to whom he could pass on the blessing? Indeed, "No material reward can equal the blessing of having children,"[1] (cf. Ps 127:3). Twice in the opening verses, Abram gives voice to this painful frustration. "What will you give me, for I continue childless, and the heir of my house is Eliezer of Damascus?" (15:2). From a literary standpoint, that would have been enough to remind readers of Abram's plight.

Yet the patriarch seemingly begs God to really, truly, actually consider his dilemma. "Look, you have given me no son, so a slave born in my house will inherit everything I have" (15:3 NCV). One would have to forgive the patriarch for feeling vexed; God wanted Abram to trust in his goodness, but in the world of Genesis, God's favor was manifest in multiple descendants (cf. 1:28; 9:1; 26:24; 35:11), and the OT elsewhere considers childlessness to be God's curse (Lev 20:20–21; Jer 22:30). You and I have felt this tension of faith—it is the struggle to believe in God's favor in the face of his apparent failure (or worse, his displeasure).

It was not uncommon in the ANE for a childless man to adopt a son as his heir in exchange for the adoptee agreeing to discharge certain responsibilities expected of a son (e.g. care in old age, funeral preparations). Abram likely had planned to adopt his nephew Lot. But Lot had pitched his tents toward, and cast his lot with, Sodom (take your time on that one), so Abram apparently believed he would have to resort to making his chief slave the heir to his estate. And as common as it might have been for a man to adopt an heir in childless situations, to adopt one's own *slave* for this purpose was significantly less common[2] (cf. Prov 17:2).

In response to Abram's complaint, God made a grand declaration to Abram that clarified his earlier promise to make Abram into a great nation (12:2). He assured the patriarch that, literally, a son would be granted to Abram from his loins, "your own flesh and blood" (15:4 NIV). At that point, God countered Abram's challenge to "Look" (15:3) with his own: "Look toward heaven, and number the stars, if you are able to number them ... So shall your offspring be" (15:5; cf. 22:17).

The next verse—"Abram believed the LORD, and he credited it to him as righteousness" (15:6 NIV)—is among the most important statements in the OT, at least in view of its use in the NT. To believe God, as it says Abram did, means "to rely on someone, to give credence to a message or to consider it to be true, to

---

1.   Sarna, *Genesis*, 113.

2.   Waltke, *Genesis*, 241.

trust in someone."[3] More significantly, God credited righteousness to Abram as a bank teller credits an account following a deposit. After some of his past (and future!) failures, Abram had no hope of laying claim to moral righteousness on account of his actions. But God did for Abram what the patriarch could not do for himself; he declared Abram "righteous" by virtue of his faith.

On the heels of God's promise of a child came reaffirmation of the promise of land. Abram's request for a sign (15:8) should not be interpreted as a lack of faith (cf. Isa 7:10–14). Quite the contrary! That the promise might be firm in Abram's mind, God commanded him to bring five animals. The three heads of livestock were to be three years of age each, "perhaps indicating the optimum age of value."[4]

At the heart of what happens next is an ancient ceremony whereby two parties entered into an agreement. The details vary in ancient literature, but the basic scene that emerges is one of two people walking between the carcasses of slaughtered animals, striking an agreement, and wishing on themselves the same fate as these dead animals if their end of the pact is not fulfilled. There is an Assyrian text from the 8th century B.C. in which Mati'ilu of Arpad enters into a treaty with Assyria's Ashurnirari V. Mati'ilu gazes on a lamb's severed head and wishes on himself and his sons the same fate if he is not faithful to the treaty.

> If Mati'ilu sins against this treaty, so may, just as the shoulder of this spring lamb is torn out, and [...], the shoulder of Mati'ilu, of his sons, his officials, and the people of his land be torn out.[5]

Imagine if you purchased your next car in this manner.

The same ceremony seems to be the background of Jer 34:18. Yahweh was enraged that the nobles of Jerusalem had made a covenant (Hebrew *karath berith*) to free their Hebrew servants (cf. Exod 21:2), only to later renege on their word. Yahweh thus swore to bring on them the same fate as the calves that had been slaughtered as part of the covenant-making ceremony, and that the bodies of the faithless would be devoured by the birds of the air (cf. 15:11).

Such ceremonies were apparently so prevalent that they affected the lingo;

---

3. TDOT 1:308.

4. Mathews, *Genesis 11:27–50:26*, 170.

5. ANET 532–33.

when it says that Yahweh "made a covenant with Abram" (15:18), it literally reads that he "cut a covenant" (*karath berith*) with the patriarch. From elsewhere in the ANE comes similar phrases such as "to kill a donkey foal" and "cut the neck of a sheep" that mean the same thing.[6] One ANE text dating to the early 2nd millennium B.C. reads, "Abba-AN swore an oath of the gods to Yarimlim and he cut the neck of one lamb (saying): (May I be cursed) if I take what I have given to you."[7]

And if all of this seems hopelessly antiquated, or an extreme way of sealing a deal, bear in mind that self-imprecatory oaths are not as foreign as they seem—witnesses in court are still required to take an oath to tell the truth, the whole truth, and nothing but the truth, "so help me God" (i.e. "If I lie, may God punish me").[8] I personally have heard more than a few people use the phrase, "If I'm lyin', I'm dyin.'" Again, what God and Abram did here is not that antiquated.

In what follows, the narrator intends for us to imagine a rather ominous scene, one pregnant with expectation of what God would do. It is a dramatic crossroads where fear and faith collide. As they are prone to do, "birds of prey" gathered on the slaughtered animals, and Abram had to drive them away. This detail seems an odd one to mention unless we consider it an omen of Israel's enemies lurking like buzzards to devour them.[9] The notion isn't far-fetched: Egypt's Pharaoh identified himself with the god Horus who was depicted as a falcon.[10] And as we soon will learn, dark days lay ahead in Pharaoh's land for Abram's offspring.

Elsewhere in the OT, when we read the words "deep sleep" or "dreadful darkness" (15:12 NIV), it often suggests "awe-inspiring divine activity." It was into a deep sleep that God placed Adam when he created Eve (2:21; cf. 1 Sam 26:12; Jonah 1:5; Acts 20:9), and Abram likewise slumbered as God acted mightily to allay the patriarch's fears.

Israel's future enslavement in Egypt must have caused Abram great distress.

---

6.   Sarna, *Genesis*, 114.

7.   Richard S. Hess, "The Slaughter of Animals in Genesis 15," in *He Swore an Oath: Biblical Themes from Genesis 12–50*, eds. Richard S. Hess, Gordon J. Wenham, and Philip E. Satterthwaite, 2nd ed. (Grand Rapids: Baker, 1994), 57.

8.   Hamilton, *The Book of Genesis: Chapters 1–17*, 430, n. 15.

9.   G. J. Wenham, "The Symbolism of the Animal Rite in Genesis 15: A Response to G. F. Hasel," *JSOT* 22 (1982): 135.

10.   Waltke, *Genesis*, 243, n. 96.

Is there any consolation in one's seed becoming a great nation if they also become the neighborhood whipping boy? There is such consolation if God promises a mighty deliverance. "I will punish the nation that enslaves them, and in the end they will come away with great wealth" (15:14 NLT). Israel's sojourn in slavery was to last four "generations" (Hebrew *dor*), a rather elastic term that means a "lap in a race, cycle of time," or simply a "lifetime."[11]

But why was there a need for Israel to spend 400 years in Egypt? Why not cede Canaan to Abram's descendants immediately? It was because, from God's perspective, "the wickedness of the Amorites will not have reached its full measure until then" (15:16 NAB). And with those words, we are given an intriguing glimpse into the nature of Abram's God. It is easy to assume that the God of the OT was concerned exclusively with Abram and his posterity. But as the OT consistently bears out, Yahweh's sovereignty and concern knew no political boundaries. "God is the King of all the earth … God reigns over the nations" (Ps 47:7–8 NIV). The same God who grieved over Nineveh's sin in Jonah's day also mourned the wickedness of the Amorites. Whether in the OT (Deut 18:9–12; 2 Kgs 21:11) or the secular Baal cycle of Ugarit, the Amorites' abhorrent depravity is well attested.

This, then, is yet another testament to God's matchless mercy. Rather than execute immediate judgment, his delay betrayed his hope for Amorite repentance (2 Pet 3:9). When some read Joshua's account of Canaan's conquest, they impose upon the text a caricature of a capricious, vindictive deity ordering the genocide of a peaceful, indigenous people. But that is completely inconsistent with the biblical record. What kind of God gives a nation four centuries to get their moral act together? One who is as loving as he is sovereign, and as gracious as he is holy.

But it was not Abram's place to concern himself with the destiny of his people. He was assured that his future held for him peace and long life, a promise that God kept (25:8).

To affirm all of this, the presence of God in the form of "a smoking fire pot and a flaming torch" (cf. Exod 19:18; Isa 31:9) moved between the halved animal carcasses. Consistent with the cultural practice, God presumably assumed upon himself the sentence of death should he not keep his promise to the patriarch. And no, God can't die. But God can't break his promises either (Heb 6:18), and

---

11. W. F. Albright, "Abram the Hebrew: A New Archaeological Interpretation," *BASOR* 163 (1961): 50–51.

that is precisely the point. Israel's future possession of Canaan (its boundaries and present inhabitants listed in 15:18–20, nullifying any ambiguity) was as sure a thing as God's eternality.

C enturies later, the author of Genesis stood on the brink of the Promised Land and surveyed the children of Israel. "The LORD your God has increased your numbers so that today you are as numerous as the stars in the sky" (Deut 1:10 NIV). God had kept his promise.

A few years after that, and under Moses' lieutenant, Israel reached another milestone. "Joshua took control of the entire land, just as the LORD had instructed Moses. He gave it to the people of Israel as their special possession, dividing the land among the tribes" (Josh 11:23 NLT). God had kept his promise.

A few centuries after that, an anonymous historian in Israel would make this seemingly trivial comment. "Solomon ruled over all the kingdoms from the Euphrates to the land of the Philistines and to the border of Egypt" (1 Kgs 4:21). Hard to believe, but until that time, Israel's borders had never been so broad or encompassed so much territory. Through many dangers, toils, and snares, God had kept his promise.

And God will keep another promise made to us, the children of Abraham living 4,000 years later. Through faith in Jesus, God has sworn to credit righteousness to us (Rom 4:24), though we are so undeserving. In God's ledger, we are all in the red. We are all deficient. But in response to our deposit of trust in him, he ascribes to us Christ's riches. He moves us into the "balanced" column, reconciled by his grace.

One day, faith will give way to sight. One day, hope will give way to reality. One day, this world of "in between" will give way to one in which every one of God's promises will be fulfilled beyond our wildest imaginations. One day, "The Lord Himself will descend from heaven with a shout, with the archangel's voice, and with the trumpet of God" (1 Thess 4:16 HCSB).

What a day, glorious day, that will be.

GENESIS 16

In the previous chapter, Abram had been the one to express frustration at his childlessness; here, it is Sarai's agitation that drives the narrative. Barrenness was nothing short of devastating for women of antiquity; "to have a great brood of children was the mark of success as a wife; to have none was ignominious failure."[12] Like her husband, Sarai was caught between faith and either God's apparent failure, or his devastating displeasure. Her grief was compounded by the knowledge that God had ordained her condition (16:2; cf. Ps 113:9). So she responded as any other woman in her time and circumstance would: she suggested Abram take Sarai's servant, Hagar, and conceive a child for Sarai through her.

To accuse Sarai and Abram of sexual immorality is a bit problematic. For one thing, Abram did marry Hagar (16:3). But it was also ANE norm for a barren wife to provide her husband with a surrogate wife or concubine to produce children. So common was this reality that several legal codes sought to regulate it and its inevitable fallout.[13] Other options included divorcing the first wife and marrying a more fertile woman, but this was not economically ideal because a divorced woman took the bride price and her dowry with her (Code of Hammurabi §138). It was thus considered preferable for a barren wife to provide a surrogate for her husband. If what Sarai had in mind was consistent with the custom of the day, Sarai would have had a legal prerogative to consider any child born to Hagar as her own—"perhaps I can build a family through her" (16:2 NIV; cf. 30:6, 20).

And if this were a secular story, this plan would be all well and good. But Abram's (and Sarai's) story is a spiritual one about how wide life's pendulum can swing between faith and fear. "Faith is not easy. It calls for a persistence that is against common sense. It calls for believing in a gift from God which none of the present data can substantiate."[14]

Throughout the narrative, Abram's passivity stands in stark contrast to the valiant warrior who attacked Chedorlaomer's forces with tenacity and daring. He now seems resigned to the whims of his wife and reluctant to get involved with the subsequent fallout. Abram's lack of leadership in his own home is disconcerting. Here, as before Pharaoh, the patriarch is hardly the father of the faithful. No better is Sarai, who clearly knew her barrenness was the Lord's doing, but inexplicably opted not to turn to prayer and petition for a reversal of her condition. That she did what culture expected is no excuse. Hers cannot be

---

12. Wenham, *Genesis 16–50*, 7.

13. Hamilton, *The Book of Genesis: Chapters 1–17*, 444. If a man's wife proved barren after ten years of marriage, the rabbis accepted this as grounds for divorce (Gen Rab 45:3).

14. Brueggemann, *Genesis*, 152.

a model for us to follow. This is another immutable principle of the life of faith: what culture tolerates and God demands are often worlds apart.

Vivid language describes the dynamic between Sarai and Hagar. The text says that her maidservant treated her master "with contempt" (*qalal*), the same Hebrew word used in 12:3 when God promised to curse those who dishonored (*qalal*) Abram. The Law of Moses demanded the death penalty for children who cursed (*qalal*) their parents (Exod 21:17; Lev 20:9). Yet here we have Hagar, Abram's new wife, dishonoring his first wife!

Legal codes of the ANE were not unfamiliar to situations like this. The Code of Hammurabi (§146) would have prevented Sarai from selling Hagar, but at the same time allowed her to subject Hagar to slavery. The Law of Ur-Nammu (c. 2100 B.C.) went so far as to prescribe the following: "If a man's slave-woman, comparing herself to her mistress, speaks insolently to her, her mouth shall be scoured with 1 quart of salt."[15] Whether with salt or soap, I imagine that experience to be quite terrible.

Sarai was livid at Hagar's disrespect; she accused her husband of being culpable for the "wrong" (*hamas*) done to her, a word used elsewhere in Genesis to describe the violence of the pre-Flood world (6:11, 13) and of Simeon and Levi at Shechem (49:5). Elsewhere, the term "often occurs in passages pertaining to malicious liars and betrayal (e.g., Ps 27:12; Mic 6:12; Zeph 1:9; 1 Chr 12:17)."[16] Sarai was being overly dramatic, but when Abram refused to get involved, she started treating her servant "harshly" (Hebrew *'anah*), a word used to describe Israel's oppression in Egypt (15:13; Exod 1:12). They say hell hath no fury like a woman scorned.

We can scarcely blame Hagar, then, for fleeing from such a terrible situation (cf. Deut 23:15) in the direction of her homeland. Given her location, it is estimated that she traveled at least seventy miles over the course of a week.[17] Notwithstanding the fact that she had brought some of it on herself by treating Sarai as she did, the picture of an expectant mother alone in the desert arouses tremendous sympathy in the reader. Hagar is vulnerable and no doubt feels betrayed and abandoned.

Despondent in the desert, Hagar encountered divine intervention. "The

15. ANET 525.

16. Mathews, *Genesis 11:27–50:26*, 186.

17. Walton, *Genesis*, 448.

angel of the LORD" is mentioned 58 times in the OT ("the angel of God" occurs an additional eleven), but what is the exact identity of this being? It's hard to say. Early Christian writers believed it to be the pre-incarnate Christ[18] (cf. Mal 3:1). Modern scholars are dubious about this, but concede that the being is more than an angel, "more a representation of God than a representative of God."[19]

I believe it was Yahweh himself that Hagar encountered in the desert. She responded as if she had spoken to God himself (16:13). At the burning bush, "the angel of the LORD" appeared to Moses (Exod 3:2), but it was God who called out to him (3:4; cf. Judg 6:11–23). In other passages where "the angel of the LORD" appears, he accepts worship (Num 22:31; Judg 13:20; cf. Rev 22:8–9). That the being refers to Yahweh in the third person (16:11) isn't as problematic as it seems; Jesus did this all the time (e.g. Matt 26:45; Luke 18:8).

But again, we can become so entangled with trying to figure out the exact identity of "the angel of the LORD" that we miss the tenderness and care God exhibited towards Hagar. Realize that God is the first in the narrative to call Hagar by her own name. To Abram and Sarai, she had only been "my/your servant." But to the Lord, she was more; by calling her name, God expressed the great value he had placed on her.

The Lord knew more about Hagar than her identity. He knew she had suffered (Hebrew 'anah) under Sarai's authority, but he commanded her to return and submit ('anah) to it.[20] As vulnerable and alone as she might have felt, Hagar had captured God's concern. Remarkably, he ushered her under the umbrella of the promise made to Abram—"I will so greatly multiply your offspring that they cannot be counted for multitude" (16:10).

And it was at this point that Hagar realized she wasn't alone after all. God was not powerless; he was in control of everything. He was aware of her suffering, of her despair, of her impending pregnancy. He had already named her child and ordained a future for him. Hagar's story was not ending; it was only beginning. "A realization that God is in control of a given situation is the

18. *A Dictionary of Early Christian Beliefs*, ed. David W. Bercot (Peabody, MA: Hendrickson, 1998), 20–21; cf. G. B. Funderburk, "Angel," *The Zondervan Pictorial Encyclopedia of the Bible* (Grand Rapids: Zondervan, 1976), 1:162–63.

19. Hamilton, *The Book of Genesis: Chapters 1–17*, 451.

20. "The Lord delights to show mercy and give relief to the oppressed, but he also confronts them with their responsibilities," (Joyce G. Baldwin, *The Message of Genesis 12–50* [Downers Grove, IL: Inter-Varsity Press, 1986], 59).

antidote to despair."[21] Hagar therefore called her mysterious messenger "a God who sees" (16:13 NASU), and "in Scripture when God sees, he cares (cf. 29:32; Exod 3:7)."[22] Her son Ishmael ("God hears") would remind her always of the Lord's attentiveness to her despondency.[23] In the wilderness of vulnerability and despair, Hagar discovered what all the poor in spirit discover—the sun still shines on cloudy days, and despite what circumstances may indicate, ours is a God who hears, sees, and cares.

Hagar's faith in God's concern and care somehow motivated her to obey the command to return (16:9). She had no idea what to expect upon returning. The divine message had commanded her to submit to Sarai, but had given no indication whether the mistreatment would abate. Hagar had to trust that God would be with her. It is not always God's will to relieve our suffering, but rather for us to submit to it in faith, believing that his promises are greater than our pain.

Hagar gave birth, and eleven years after leaving Haran, Abram finally had a son. But it had come through human scheming, not the Lord's will. God predicted that Ishmael would be "a wild ass of a man" (16:12 NRSV), which isn't exactly the hope a mother has for her son. The phrase is deceptive, however. The narrator intends us to read this description as derogatory, but not in the way you might think; the ass didn't represent stupidity in ancient Israel as it does today, but rather despair and loneliness.[24] The prophecy (16:12) itself was one "of independent defiance and strength,"[25] meaning that Ishmael and his descendants would be an isolated, lonely group dwelling in abandoned wilderness regions on the fringe of civilization (cf. Job 39:5–8) where they would not only survive, but thrive. In the OT, the Ishmaelites indeed led a Bedouin existence.

The end of the chapter leaves us with a startling dichotomy. It is Hagar, not

---

21. McKeown, *Genesis*, 98.

22. Wenham, *Genesis 16–50*, 11.

23. Ishmael is only the first of several in Scripture whose birth was divinely announced. As would also be the case with Isaac (18:10), Samson (Judg 13:3), John (Luke 1:13), and Jesus (Luke 1:31), birth announcements signaled the revival of God's mighty redemptive acts on the behalf of his people.

24. Francis I. Andersen and David Noel Freedman, *Hosea* (Garden City, NY: Doubleday, 1980), 505.

25. Arnold, *Genesis*, 165. "Even today the Arab descendants of Ishmael ... manifest a rugged independence which makes co-operation with anyone uncertain and precarious," (Baldwin, *The Message of Genesis 12–50*, 59).

Abram and Sarai, who responded with faithful surrender to the Lord's will. If Abram and Sarai had reacted to their own despair with something approaching Hagar's faith, the present crisis would have been averted, and this story would have turned out very differently. As it stands, the last 4,000 years are stained with the blood of Isaac's and Ishmael's descendants. "The world has had to bear the consequences of this mistake ever since because of the tribal conflicts in the Middle East between the different sons of Abraham."[26] If there is to ever be lasting peace in the Middle East, it can only come through the children of Abraham affirming a common Savior in the Lord Jesus Christ—"he himself is our peace, who has made the two groups one and has destroyed the barrier, the dividing wall of hostility" (Eph 2:14 NIV).

That too would be a glorious day indeed.

GENESIS 17:1–14

Some thirteen years after Ishmael's birth, God again appeared to Abram. This was the fourth time this had happened (at least that we know of), but for the first time, God revealed himself as El Shaddai or "God Almighty." It was a name by which the patriarchs knew him (28:3; 35:11; 43:14; 48:3), and a name very appropriate for the subject God was about to broach. Promising an aged, barren couple to make their descendants into a nation was a tall order to fill, but God would deliver on that promise in a remarkable display of power.

By the authority of that name, God called Abram into a righteous relationship with him via the words "walk before me, and be blameless" (17:1; cf. 6:9). As previously noted, "walk before" is slightly different from "walk with." It has to do with submissive obedience to a superior; Sarna calls the phrase "a [possible] technical term for absolute loyalty to a king."[27] A similar phrase, "stand before" (1 Kgs 1:2; 10:8), represents the same idea.

It is confusing to read in 17:2 that God would only now "make" or "establish" (NASU) his covenant with the patriarch. Had not the covenant been established two chapters prior in some crazy slice-an-animal-in-half ceremony? Had not a covenant been struck even earlier when God had called Abram out of his father's house (12:1)? Note that, in Gen 12, God merely extended certain promises to the patriarch in exchange for his moving to Canaan. In Gen 15, God struck a

26. Ross, "Genesis," 115.
27. Sarna, *Genesis*, 123.

covenant agreement (and a one-sided one at that) to give the land of Canaan to Abram's descendants. But realize that on neither of these two occasions were moral expectations placed upon the patriarch's behavior.

Only now is he called, in light of a covenant, to characterize his relationship with God with submission and moral integrity, i.e. blamelessness. This covenant is different than the one in Gen 15 in that it contains obligations for both parties.[28] Just as he swore to give Canaan to Abram's descendants, God swore to give Abram said descendants, i.e. to multiply him greatly (17:2). For Abram, the covenant brings with it both behavioral expectations and a name-change.

Just as was noted in the first chapter, bestowing a name implied ownership and sovereignty in ancient times. But at the same time, a name-change said something about the destiny of the individual. Here, the Lord reaffirmed his previous promise to make the patriarch into a large nation (12:2; 13:16). And so sure was that promise that God altered Abram's name to *Abraham*; the former meant "exalted father," while the new name meant "father of many." To the previous promise of becoming a nation came the added vow "kings shall come from you" (17:6), and God promised to perpetuate the covenant to successive generations.

But for *how many* generations? How long would this covenant last? The text plainly says three times this was "an everlasting covenant" (17:7, 13, 19). Yet God also swore to Abraham, "I will give to you and to your offspring after you the land of your sojournings, all the land of Canaan, for an everlasting possession" (17:8), and history plainly bears out that the nation of Israel has not always been in possession of Canaan. As it did to the author of Ps 89, there appears to us a vexing gap between promise and fulfillment in this matter. So what is really meant when God swore this covenant, both of posterity and property, was an "everlasting" one?

The Hebrew term translated "everlasting" in this passage is *olam*. In certain OT passages, it very much represents the concept of eternity as we think of it, but this seems to be the exception rather than the rule for this word.[29] Consider how the term is used elsewhere. Just a few verses from now, God deemed the covenant of circumcision as an "everlasting" (olam) one, but we know this did

---

28. "Although in chapter 15 Abraham was a passive partner to whom God unconditionally committed himself, this supplement [Gen 17] calls Abraham into active partnership," (Waltke, *Genesis*, 263).

29. NIDOTTE 3:346.

not mean forever (cf. 1 Cor 7:19; Gal 5:6). Under the Law, the pierced ear of a slave meant he had committed himself to be his master's slave "forever" (Exod 21:6; cf. Deut 15:17; 1 Sam 27:12), though we understand that to mean "for the rest of his life"—he obviously will not serve his master in the afterlife! In Proverbs, the word can mean "ancient" (cf. 22:28; 23:10), but not "eternal." Jeremiah used *olam* to depict Babylon as an "ancient nation" (Jer 5:15), but it is obviously not an eternal one—it was conquered by another empire in 539 B.C. In Ps 78:69 and Eccl 1:4, it is said that the earth has been established "forever," but if we infer that to mean "eternally," Jesus stands ready to correct us (Mark 13:31).

My point is we may not have an English word that captures all the nuances of the Hebrew *olam*. It certainly *can* mean everlasting or eternal, but it doesn't *always* mean that. One final example very akin to the subject at hand is God's covenant with the Aaronic priesthood. Because Aaron's son Phinehas "was jealous for his God and made atonement for the people of Israel," he was given what is called "a perpetual [*olam*] priesthood" (Num 25:13). The Aaronic priesthood obviously did not last forever: the Temple was eventually destroyed, sacrifices ceased, and Christ (descended from Judah) is now our great high priest (Heb 7:11–14). We are thus left with the impression that olam can mean "open-ended perpetuity" or "'the most distant time,' a relative concept according to a text's horizon."[30]

And that means that God's promise of land to Abraham was for *olam*, but not necessarily "forever."

But the text also includes a condition on this promise, one that, if you noticed, I did not include when quoting 17:8 previously: "I will give to you and to your offspring after you the land of your sojournings, all the land of Canaan, for an everlasting possession, *and I will be their God*" (17:8). God's gift of land to Abraham's posterity (Israel) was conditional on Yahweh remaining their God. If Israel rebelled against him, all bets were off.[31] Both Lev 26 and Deut 28

---

30. Waltke, *Genesis*, 261.

31. "The land is not a possession that may be enjoyed without reference to God. Possessing this land is contingent on Israel's ongoing faithfulness to God and obedience to his law. The land therefore is a byproduct of the covenant, a gift of the covenant. It is not a possession that can be held independently," (Gary M. Burge, *Jesus and the Land* [Grand Rapids: Baker, 2010], 3–4). Later, and in response to the Christian Zionist movement, one that seeks to protect Israel's 1948 return to Palestine, Burge rightly points out that "these Christians fail to point out the indisputable biblical motif that land promise is strictly tied to covenant fidelity," (Ibid., 123).

enumerate certain covenant curses to be brought on Israel if she did not keep the Law, and a very prominent one is expulsion from the land.

> But if you will not listen to me and carry out all these commands, and if you reject my decrees and abhor my laws and fail to carry out all my commands and so violate my covenant, then I will do this to you: ... I myself will lay waste the land, so that your enemies who live there will be appalled. I will scatter you among the nations and will draw out my sword and pursue you. Your land will be laid waste, and your cities will lie in ruins.
>
> Lev 26:14–16, 32–33 NIV

> If you do not carefully follow all the words of this law, which are written in this book, and do not revere this glorious and awesome name—the LORD your God ... Then the LORD will scatter you among all nations, from one end of the earth to the other.
>
> Deut 28:58, 64 NIV

Also mentioned in these curses was that the womb of Israel would be cursed and her children would be in jeopardy (Lev 26:22, 29; Deut 28:18, 53–57). But while Israel continued to perpetuate her race in spite of her disobedience (and only due to God's grace!), she was expelled from her land on multiple occasions. Seventy years in Babylon was the penalty for her faithlessness in OT times, and though she returned to the land of promise by Cyrus' God-inspired edict (2 Chr 36:22–23), Israel was never her own independent nation again, save for the Maccabean period. In the NT, the four Jewish sects (Pharisees, Sadducees, Essenes, and Zealots) were borne of four different ideologies of how to cope with the dilemma of being an occupied nation when God had promised the land to father Abraham "forever." About forty years after Jesus' illegal crucifixion, Rome destroyed Jerusalem and effectively dispersed the Jews throughout the world. This happened because they rejected Jesus as their Messiah (Luke 19:43–44; 21:24).

I thus consider it a testament to the grace of God that his promise of land to Israel was not broken, but rather transformed and redeemed. Jesus eschewed an earthly kingdom (John 18:36) for he knew his Father would give him a better, heavenly one. Jesus also suggested in his teachings that there was something greater than living in the Promised Land—knowing the Promised One. In

Matt 21:33–46, Jesus spoke of a vineyard (Palestine) with a master (God) and tenants (Israel), and as anyone who has ever signed a rental agreement will tell you, being a tenant is a very conditional thing. In this case, rejecting the Master's Son brought with it something much worse than eviction. In other words, Jesus essentially called the four branches of Judaism to stop dealing with the tension of an occupied Promised Land, and instead deal with him![32]

Because of Israel's unwillingness to keep the covenant, not to mention their rejection of Jesus as the Christ, God had no obligation whatsoever to remain true to his promise of a special land. But today, the people of God—the church, the new Israel, the heirs of Abraham by faith—anticipate with the patriarch a better country than any earthly one: "a heavenly one" (Heb 11:16). "Based on His promise, we wait for the new heavens and a new earth, where righteousness will dwell" (2 Pet 3:13 HCSB). In that fair and happy land, we have the promise of dwelling with Jesus evermore.

T he sign of this Abrahamic covenant would be circumcision, a well-attested practice in the ANE (cf. Jer 9:25–26, so it would not have been a new idea to Abraham—of all the nations appearing in the OT, only the Philistines are known as the "uncircumcised" (Judg 15:18; 1 Sam 17:26, 36). Egyptian literature from the 22nd century speaks of circumcision,[33] and a scene from inside a tomb depicting a circumcision ritual may be older than that.[34] But while circumcision was practiced for a wide variety of reasons in ancient times, it was most often a rite of passage into purity, puberty, adulthood, or marriage. So what meaning did it have for ancient Israel in light of God's covenant with their father Abraham?

Notice that, going forward, every male born to Abraham's covenant lineage was to be circumcised, as well as every male bought as a slave (17:12). It was to

---

32. "*Ownership of the land* [i.e. Palestine] *is not a Christian question.* The New Testament instead asks if we know the landowner himself ... Amidst calls to reclaim holy land, to reconquer territory in the name of God, to assume religious privileges for one tribe and not another, the New Testament says: No. Jesus called for a faithfulness that abandoned such things, that envisioned a different era, a different kingdom, where old territorial claims backed by religious privilege were no more," (Ibid., 127, 131; emphasis his).

33. ANET 326.

34. Harold O. Forshey, "Circumcision: An Initiatory Rite in Ancient Israel?" *ResQ* 16 (1973): 152.

be a "sign" of the covenant, and while we are never told for whom it was a sign (God? Man?), the fact that the sign is never explained favors the interpretation that it was a sign to God. In other words, "God will see the circumcised penis of the Israelite before and during sexual congress, and will then 'remember' his promise to Abraham and to all his descendants to make them very fertile."[35]

But if the sign was a reminder to God, why was *man* punished (probably by premature death)[36] if he failed to be circumcised (17:14)? The ambiguity leaves us with the realization that this is not an either/or scenario, but one in which God and man are both reminded via circumcision of their obligations and promises under the Abrahamic covenant. God sees circumcision and is reminded of his oath to multiply the patriarch greatly. Man sees circumcision and is reminded of his obligation to trust in the promises and providence of God.[37] For national Israel, this would be critically important since they would dwell in a Canaan's land plagued by pagan fertility cults. It was not Baal whom they should trust to bless them with children, but in the God of their fathers (cf. Deut 7:12–16).

GENESIS 17:15-27

For the first time, Abraham's wife Sarai is made an explicit party to the covenant between God and the patriarch. The son of Abraham and Hagar is not the child of promise, for God's covenant is not with Abraham and Hagar, but with Abraham and *Sarah*—a new name that carried with it a renewed hope! Unlike Abraham's name, *Sarai* and *Sarah* are essentially the same because, as my wife likes to remind me, they both mean "princess"! But while the meaning of her name may not have changed, Sarah now has the assurance that her God is aware of her barrenness, and that his covenant with Abraham also holds just as much hope for her.

It's easy to forget that for the past thirteen years, "Abraham has not been anxiously awaiting the arrival of another son. He would not have seen a need

---

35. Hamilton, *The Book of Genesis: Chapters 1–17*, 470.

36. Cf. the use of "cut off" in 1 Sam 28:9; 1 Kgs 11:16; Ps 101:8. An example of the serious consequences of not circumcising each male child is found in Exod 4:24–26. "The threat of being 'cut off' by the hand of God, in His own time, hovers over the offender constantly and inescapably; he is not unlike the patient who is told by his doctors that his disease is incurable and that he might die any day," (Haim H. Cohn, "The Penology of the Talmud," *ILR* 5 [1970]: 72).

37. "Abraham's circumcision is as much an amen to Yahweh as was his affirmation in 15:6," (Hamilton, *The Book of Genesis: Chapters 1–17*, 472).

for another, nor has God informed him otherwise."[38] So it must have been odd for the patriarch to hear God again promise a son, and no less through Sarah. Abraham had been willing to adopt Eliezer as his heir in Gen 15, and he was here confused as to why Ishmael was not reckoned as the promised son. Abraham begged, "Oh that Ishmael might live before you!" (17:18), meaning "Why not let Ishmael inherit what you have promised me?" (CEV). To believe that he and Sarah would conceive a son was too much.

Evidently, God's people are at times willing to settle for less than what God has in mind. Instead of living by faith and receiving what is awesome, we are content to live by sight and settle for the ordinary. What would our families and churches, marriages and businesses look like if we were to seek God's true will, rather than asking him to acquiesce to our own? How might things be different if we fully embraced Paul's Ephesian prayer? "Now to him who is able to do immeasurably more than all we ask or imagine, according to his power that is at work within us, to him be glory in the church and in Christ Jesus throughout all generations, for ever and ever! Amen" (Eph 3:20–21 NIV). What if we, as the patriarch eventually did, learned to submit "impossible" to the sovereignty of God Almighty?

"No, Abraham," God says. No, Ishmael would not be the child of promise, for this is not what God had planned. Yahweh had a specific will in this matter, and no plan or purpose of his can be thwarted (Job 42:2; cf. Prov 19:21). Ishmael would receive God's blessing (17:20), and God kept every promise made here concerning Ishmael. But the oldest son of Abraham would not inherit the covenant. That privilege was reserved for Isaac ("he laughs"), one whose very birth and existence was met with skepticism, incredulity, and laughter. This was a sovereign decision on God's part. Note that this choice had nothing to do with Ishmael's or Isaac's salvation. The Lord was not predestinating one for eternal bliss or suffering. Rather, this choice had to do with membership in the covenant community of Israel and placement in the lineage that would culminate in the Incarnation of God's special Son, one that would be likened to Isaac (cf. John 3:16; Heb 11:17).

And as if to signal that this topic was no longer open to additional debate, God abruptly left (17:22). The patriarch's response is as commendable as was Noah's (6:22; 7:5).[39] Abraham saw to it that he, his son Ishmael, and all the

---

38. Walton, *Genesis*, 451.

39. "By repeating the phrase 'that very day,' the narrator stresses that the day Abraham circumcised his family was one of the turning points in world history, comparable to Noah's entry into the ark or the exodus from Egypt (cf. 7:13; Exod 12:17, 41, 51)," (Wenham, *Genesis 16–50*, 27).

males in his house were circumcised. The narrator takes up five verses to assert redundantly that this was done "as God had said." But redundant notice of the patriarch's obedience is not a literary burden as much as a call to us, his children, to emulate him concerning the commandments and promises of God.

When God speaks definitively, nothing else remains for his people but to trust and obey.

> *But we never can prove*
> *The delights of His love*
> *Until all on the altar we lay;*
> *For the favor He shows,*
> *And the joy He bestows,*
> *Are for those who will trust and obey.*

TALKING POINTS

We must not forget that Abram's time was one in which many believed that doing the will of God (or the gods) brought favor. On the other hand, misfortune had to mean one had angered deity; this was certainly the assumption of Job's three friends (Job 4:7–8). But God was clear to Abram that dark times lay ahead for his posterity, and Abram could do nothing about it except to trust that God would see his people through. The NT is unequivocal when it comes to the Christian and suffering (2 Tim 3:12), which is ironic considering our natural aversion to it. But our hope should be the same as the patriarch's; we trust that God will see us through every storm. And just as Israel was made to wait four centuries for God to act, we too are asked to wait for the consummation of all things (2 Pet 3:8–10). Our wait is not in vain. "Because God wanted to make the unchanging nature of his purpose very clear to the heirs of what was promised, he confirmed it with an oath. God did this so that, by two unchangeable things in which it is impossible for God to lie, we who have fled to take hold of the hope set before us may be greatly encouraged" (Heb 6:17–18 NIV).

Whenever we are made to suffer, or whenever God seems lax in keeping his promises (or both), we often ask, "Why?" Why doesn't God rain down justice? Why doesn't God honor his word? Why doesn't he show us kindness? According to 15:16, it might be because God has not seen fit in his wisdom and mercy to remove his blessing from another. Abram's offspring could not inherit Canaan just yet because God had not yet removed his blessing of land from the Amorites. Do you find yourself in a situation from which you have prayed for God's deliverance? Do you consider your present circumstances "suffering," and the other side to be "blessing"? It may be a zero-sum situation, one in which your gain is another's loss. God may not yet be willing to remove that blessing from another person. Perhaps their salvation hangs in the balance. Your willingness to patiently wait on the Lord could mean the salvation of a precious soul (2 Pet 3:9). And isn't that the greatest blessing of all?

Floundering in the undercurrent of Sarai's mistreatment of Hagar is a biblical principle concerning how we (mis)treat the disenfranchised of society. In the Law, God was clear that his people were to show kindness to, and maintain justice for, the down-and-out—the orphan, the widow, and the immigrant (Deut 16:11; 24:17; 26:12; 27:19). Israel's obligation in this matter was derived from God's identity as "a father to the fatherless, a defender of widows" (Ps 68:5 NIV). When Yahweh indignantly enumerated through the prophets the covenant failures of his people, social injustice always held a prominent place (Jer 22:3; Ezek 22:7; Zech 7:10; Mal 3:5). "Wash and make yourselves clean. Take your evil deeds out of my sight; stop doing wrong. Learn to do right; seek justice. Defend the oppressed. Take up the cause of the fatherless; plead the case of the widow" (Isa 1:16–17 NIV). This ethic is preserved in the NT, where we are commanded to "visit" (Jas 1:27) or "look after" (NIV) orphans and widows. If our concern for these individuals wanes, we lose out on seeing Jesus at work in our world, and our hearts grow calloused towards those who have much to teach us about daily reliance on the Father.

How should we reconcile God's sovereignty over all things with the tension between Ishmael's and Isaac's descendants? Wouldn't it have been easier for God to stand in the way of Ishmael's birth, rather than allowing it and thereby giving the world a 4,000-year-old headache? I have no answer for this question, for I do not pretend to know the mind of God. But this is a perfect opportunity to point to Paul's discussion of these things in Rom 9–11. An exegesis of that passage is beyond the scope of this chapter, but I am intrigued by the apostle's conclusion there and its application to the Isaac/Ishmael rivalry. It is all too common to question God's wisdom when certain events occur. I myself have asked God, "Why?" only to receive deafening silence as my answer. I am convicted that God cares deeply about suffering in the world, no less the ravaged portions of the Middle East where children of Ishmael and Isaac war against one another. But there comes a point where our questions are as futile as they are near-sighted. Like Job, we may be inquiring of things too wonderful for us to know (Job 42:3). The apostle Paul would have us rest secure in the fact that God is working out a plan to bring glory to his name (Rom 11:36). There is no headline, no natural disaster, no suicide bombing, and no war that he cannot use to his praise. The next time you hear of yet another act of senseless violence, even in the powder keg of the Middle East, remember that it will inconceivably find its end in these words: "Holy, holy, holy, is the Lord God Almighty, who was and is and is to come!" (Rev 4:8).

On the fourth finger of my left hand, the hand closest to my heart, I wear a gold wedding ring. It is a reminder that I once vowed before God and witnesses that I would love and be faithful to my wife Sara until death parted us. The ring has even greater significance to me because it was my dad's wedding ring, so it also reminds me of his love for and faithfulness to mom. Wedding rings are a symbol of the marriage covenant made between a man and woman. Likewise, circumcision was a symbol of the covenant God made with Abraham, and the Lord ordained that it be practiced in the future so that his people would carry a reminder that Yahweh was their God, a God of promises and provision. Circumcision was an affirmative affirmation of faith in this God. Trouble is, Israel eventually put too much stock in circumcision and too little in their faith. It became an empty ritual. In the NT, the apostle Paul drew parallels between Jewish circumcision and "the circumcision of Christ" (Col 2:11–13). The sign of the covenant for Christians is no longer something done in the flesh, but an event from 2,000 years ago: the crucifixion and resurrection of Jesus that is reenacted in baptism. We are buried with him in water and raised as a new creature (2 Cor 5:17) by God's matchless power. Like a wedding ring, our baptism is a reminder of God's oath to declare us "not guilty" before his judgment seat on the final day (Rom 8:1). We have that hope because Jesus died, was buried, resurrected, ascended to the Father, and has sworn to return again. To see him in the clouds…

What a day, glorious day, that will be.

8

JUDGMENT CALL

The cities of Sodom and Gomorrah have become bywords in Christian circles for homosexuality, and justifiably so. In our own time, the homosexual community has made alarming strides in gaining recognition from various sectors of our culture. It should be deeply disturbing to any godly man or woman to see homosexuals being granted the right to marry, adopt children, etc. Yet it should concern us even more that antiquity seemed to tolerate homosexuality more than our own society presently does—what does the future hold?

But this book is not about the sin of homosexuality; it is about how our struggle with faith and God's record of faithfulness collide in the pages of Genesis. In these chapters, the righteous judgment and destruction of Sodom by a holy God underscore broader principles that we shall explore. For just one example, an interesting contrast in these chapters is the hospitality shown by Abraham and Lot vs. the lack of such on the part of the citizens of Sodom.

These chapters begin with God visiting Abraham in the flesh and promising him a son within a year's time. He also engages Abraham in dialogue about Sodom's impending doom. Was the patriarch willing to lobby for the salvation of the righteous? Was his heart characterized by compassion? Would he defer to the Lord's justice and acquiesce to Sodom's sentence? Abraham's morals and values would likely pass on to his children, and they to their children; what kind of nation would they become? And what does that conversation tell us about God?

Even as he related these events several centuries later, I think Moses still wondered what kind of nation Israel would become. As he put pen to papyrus, did he breathe a prayer that this story would foster in Israel both a commitment to justice and a love of mercy (cf. Mic 6:8)?

As you can see, divine judgment of homosexuality is simply one of many themes in these chapters. Elsewhere in Scripture, we learn that showing hospitality is of great priority to the Lord, and a lack of it was among the reasons he destroyed these cities of the Plain. Hospitality flows from a heart that is saturated with compassion, even for those who do not love God or live lives that honor him. Sodom's sins had to have been upsetting to Abraham, but he was also grieved by their destruction.

There is a lesson there, I think, for the children of Abraham: we must love all those created in God's image, even homosexuals, and wish for them nothing less than a relationship with the One who wants to be their Savior before he becomes their Judge.

GENESIS 18:1–15

While Abraham was still residing in Hebron (13:18; 14:13), God visited him, accompanied by two companions. These individuals are referred to as "men" in this chapter, but elsewhere are called "angels" (19:1, 15; Heb 13:2). One of these men was perceived by Abraham to be the leader; the patriarch addressed him alone (18:3) before turning his attention to all three (18:4–5). It seems this leader was really God, who later lingered with Abraham while sending his angels on to Sodom. What is more, the reader is tipped off to the true identity of these visitors while Abraham remains clueless—his "O Lord" in 18:3 being more akin to "Dear Sir" than a recognition of the Almighty (cf. Heb 13:2).

The visit took place in the middle of the day (18:1), and this is more than a time-stamp. Per the custom of the day, the patriarch was likely preparing for an afternoon nap. But when he saw that he had company, Abraham dispensed with his personal agenda and welcomed these three travelers. There also may be unique significance in Abraham's running and bowing (18:2); elsewhere in Genesis, people only run to greet long-lost relatives (29:13; 33:4), and only bow in the presence of the powerful (37:9; 42:6).[1]

Abraham certainly displayed impressive hospitality by summoning bread (something resembling pita bread), curds of yogurt, goat's milk (highly valued in the ANE), and a choice roasted calf from his herd. The latter was "a rare delicacy and a sign of princely hospitality."[2] A lamb or young goat would have been

---

1. Wenham, *Genesis 16–50*, 46.

2. Sarna, *Genesis*, 129.

considered adequate (cf. Judg 13:15; Luke 15:27–30), but for the patriarch, it was not enough to honor his special guests (remember that he was still unaware of their divine identity). The patriarch's generosity is heightened by the terms "went quickly" and "ran" (18:6–7). He went to great and urgent lengths to care for the needs of his guests.

During the meal, God asked, "Where is Sarah your wife?" a question the answer to which God already knew. But as we have already seen in Genesis (e.g. 3:9; 4:9), God's questions are rhetorical devices to bring attention to something that should not be, not a means to learn new information. This also should have been a major hint to Abraham that his guests were supernatural.

It is here that OT scholar John H. Walton makes an interesting observation. He admits that his suggestion is "tenuous," but it is worth considering nonetheless. Walton wonders why the three guests would inquire as to Sarah's whereabouts. If these visitors were mere men, the question would have been rude; if they were supernatural and omniscient beings (and they were), the question was unnecessary unless the Lord was calling attention to something that was out-of-sorts (and he was).

Walton contends it was not the practice of that time for women to eat separately from men,[3] so Sarah might have confined herself to the tent because she had begun menstruating (cf. 31:34–35). At some point during the meal, Sarah became understandably alarmed when she began menstruating, something that should not have happened given her age (18:11). Walton thus asserts that the arrival of these three visitors triggered "the resumption of her fertility."[4]

Walton's suggestion is as plausible as it is outlandish, but we must not get so consumed with why Sarah was in the tent that we miss the subsequent scene. God specifically promised Abraham and Sarah that they would have a son within the year. The absurd thought of Sarah conceiving is expressed with the phrase, "The way of women had ceased to be with Sarah" (18:11), a reference to female menstruation. Most modern translations delicately gloss over the phrase with something like "Sarah was past the age of childbearing" (NIV), but I prefer the literal translation. The entire scene rudely calls attention to the fact that Sarah's pregnancy would not be confused as being ordinary or natural.

What is more, Sarah's retort that she and Abraham were old, and her rhetorical question, "Shall I have pleasure?" may indicate they had stopped

---

3. Wenham disagrees (*Genesis 16–50*, 47).

4. Walton, *Genesis*, 452–53.

having intercourse. Moses certainly went overboard in highlighting Abraham's and Sarah's ages; he says they "were old, advanced in years" (18:11), and quotes Sarah as saying that she is "worn out" and her husband is "old" (18:12). How was she to conceive when the complications of aging presented too much of a hurdle? The answer is that nothing is too hard for God (18:14)! As had been the case with Hagar, God was very aware of this couple's plight.

He saw. He knew. He cared.

There is a significant word in the text to which I want to call your attention. God promised this aged couple, "I will return to you at the appointed time next year, and Sarah will have a son" (18:14 NIV). This same word is used throughout the OT for something that is fixed, such as the time and place of a meeting (1 Sam 20:35), the migratory habits of birds (Jer 8:7), and even Israel's religious festivals (Lev 23:2). We are dealing with a word that means "predetermined," and with a nuance closer to "concrete" rather than "tentative."

Not only does God see and know our suffering; not only does he care. He has also determined a time for it to end, and if not in this life, most certainly in the one to come. In the midst of their unjust persecution, Paul promised the Thessalonians:

> [God] will give trouble to those who trouble you. And he will give rest to you who are troubled and to us also when the Lord Jesus appears with burning fire from heaven with his powerful angels. Then he will punish those who do not know God and who do not obey the Good News about our Lord Jesus Christ. Those people will be punished with a destruction that continues forever. They will be kept away from the Lord and from his great power.
>
> 2 Thess 1:6–9 NCV

Isn't it grand to know our suffering is finite, that our collective terrible-horrible-no good-very bad days won't go on forever? The God of Abraham has fixed an appointed time, unknown to all but him, when all suffering will come to a fantastic end! It will be the moment when the Son comes to be glorified in his church and render awestruck all who have put their faith in him (2 Thess 1:10). Knowing that our heartache will eventually give way to hallelujahs can help us bear the pain a little while longer. God sees. God knows. God cares. He has appointed a time when he will visit his people in their distress and bring with him the redemption of the ages!

GENESIS 18:16–33

As hospitality of the time dictated, when the three travelers arose to leave, Abraham journeyed with them to "see them off," and they came to a place where Sodom and Gomorrah could be seen. Traditionally, this place has been identified as the village of Beni Na'im, a location just three miles east of Hebron where the Dead Sea area can be seen on a clear day.[5] There and then, Yahweh decided to inform Abraham of the possible fate of these cities. But why? Why would a mere man be invited into God's counsel?

There is arguably nowhere else in Genesis that the gospel message shines through as plainly as it does here. When God had first called Abraham, it had been promised that "in you all the families of the earth shall be blessed" (12:3), a promise that found its ultimate fulfillment in Christ's atoning sacrifice at Golgotha—but not entirely. For whatever reason, God has invited his people to participate in his plan to bless the nations, and being proper channels of that blessing requires that we properly understand and practice the righteousness and justice of God.

We naturally understand what is meant by the phrase "the justice of God." We know that God is holy (Lev 19:2) and must therefore always do what is right. But what is meant by "righteousness" in this chapter? Is it the same as God's justice? In the OT, God's "righteousness" can refer to different things. In Ps 99:4, it is synonymous with "equity." In Ps 7:11, David praises God as "a righteous judge" for rewarding the good and punishing the bad. But God's "righteousness" can also mean his covenant faithfulness, i.e. his commitment to remain true to his promises. "In you, LORD, I have taken refuge; let me never be put to shame; deliver me in your righteousness" (Ps 31:1 NIV; cf. 71:1–2). And connected with this concept is God's salvation, which also appears synonymously with his righteousness. "The LORD has made his salvation known and revealed his righteousness to the nations" (Ps 98:2 NIV; cf. Isa 46:13; 56:1).

Abraham must have had an appreciation for the justice and judgment of God. He no doubt knew of the Flood that had destroyed the world in the days of his forefather Noah. And while we cannot know just how much of God's nature had been disclosed to Abraham, he had to have known that God must punish wickedness, or else he cannot be God. In fact, listening to Abraham's speech in 18:23–25, the patriarch seems to think God is "too just," a bit too eager to pour out his justice on everyone, regardless of the collateral damage. "If the righteous

---

5. Hamilton, *The Book of Genesis: Chapters 18–50*, 17.

are swept away with the wicked, so be it," (cf. 18:23).

And there is no denying that the wickedness of Sodom and her sister cities deserved punishment. We will discuss their crimes a bit later in this chapter, but here the text makes clear that an "outcry against Sodom and Gomorrah" had come up to God (18:20); that outcry is a scream of terror from those suffering grave injustice.[6] We are assured, "When the righteous cry for help, the LORD hears and delivers them out of all their troubles" (Ps 34:17). God could not ignore these cries because he is just.

But one of the great truths of this passage is that God's sense of justice is infinitely above our own. He does not enter into judgment and punishment rashly; he isn't a bloodthirsty, trigger-happy cowboy looking to damn first and ask questions later. For those who, like me, grew up believing in the omniscience of God, it is confusing why God would want to so thoroughly investigate Sodom's sins. Did he not already have all the information he needed? Had not all their sins been committed under his watchful eye? "The eyes of the LORD are everywhere, observing the wicked and the good" (Prov 15:3 HCSB). Was there any need to pull the cosmic security tapes and screen them so as to ascertain the validity of the accusation? The answer to these questions is obvious; God could have remained in heaven and said, "I've seen enough." But his commitment to justice is unassailable (1 Sam 2:3); he goes above and beyond. By actually sending his angels to investigate, God proved the unsurpassed integrity of his justice.

The history of 18:22 is intriguing. Most every translation reads, "Abraham remained standing before the LORD" (HCSB), but it is unlikely this is what Moses originally penned. Apparently, the scribes considered the original phrase, "the LORD remained standing before Abraham," to be blasphemous and changed it, leaving notice of their alteration.[7] But if the scribes' note is correct, and what we have is *Yahweh* standing before *Abraham*, then the Lord was doing so in a posture of exposure, an invitation to come and examine. By standing before Abraham, the Judge of all the earth was inviting the patriarch to discover a startling piece of God's nature of which the patriarch was ignorant.

And this is the truth that Abraham discovered on that occasion, that God's commitment to justice is greater than our own. As I said before, he goes above and beyond. But his commitment to *mercy* is equally greater than our own. Those two commitments, to justice and mercy, can conflict violently in the heart

6. Von Rad, *Genesis*, 211.

7. Hamilton, *The Book of Genesis: Chapters 18–50*, 23–24.

of our Lord. How else do we explain his reluctance to punish sin, even when he has been scorned and betrayed by those he loves the most? "How can I give you up, O Ephraim? How can I hand you over, O Israel? How can I make you like Admah? How can I treat you like Zeboiim?"—note that those are the two cities destroyed along with Sodom and Gomorrah—"My heart recoils within me; my compassion grows warm and tender" (Hos 11:8). The Lord wanted Abraham to feel the same burden, the same anguish for the wicked that God himself feels.

So in this narrative, we are presented with an odd, seemingly incomprehensible, scene in which the patriarch presumed to test the boundaries of the Lord. Abraham could not conceive how a righteous God, which he perceived Yahweh to be, could throw a moral baby out with the immoral bathwater. "Far be it from you to do such a thing—to kill the righteous with the wicked, treating the righteous and the wicked alike. Far be it from you! Will not the Judge of all the earth do right?" (18:25 NIV). So Abraham haggled with God. What the patriarch learned has the ability to change the world.

Nathan MacDonald provides us with an excellent summation of the haggling process so common in Middle Eastern culture:

> The technical rules of haggling are essentially universal. The buyer approaches the vendor, who gives the initial price; bids then alternate between the two and converge. If complete convergence is reached, the sale is consummated. In the haggle, backward moves are forbidden and accepted bids must be honored.[8]

MacDonald goes on to point out that, given this description, Abraham clearly entered into the discussion thinking it to be a haggling situation. He would ask for fifty souls and expected God to counter with a higher number—say, 100?—at which point Abraham would counter the counter-offer until the two parties met somewhere in the middle. In other words, I think Abraham believed it was his responsibility to soften the stance of a trigger-happy, overly-vengeful God, to invite "the Judge of all the earth" to be more reasonable.

What he discovered, instead, is that God has a greater capacity for mercy than we can imagine. Yes, his justice is above our own, but so is his mercy. At no

---

8. Nathan MacDonald, "Listening to Abraham—Listening to Yhwh: Divine Justice and Mercy in Genesis 18:16–33," *CBQ* 66 (2004): 31.

point in the conversation did God ever counter-offer Abraham, so the patriarch kept on going, eventually stopping with a deal in which Sodom would be spared if ten righteous souls were found. Why ten? MacDonald suggests Abraham may have stopped at ten, not because God somehow signaled that the limit was being reached, but because Abraham was confused or embarrassed at being able to go so far below his original "asking price"[9]—something that would have never happened while haggling in the marketplace. If you offer to buy a piece of fruit for $1, you can abandon any hope of getting it for less—unless the person you're dealing with is infinitely benevolent.

Abraham entered into the negotiation believing that he would have to talk Yahweh into being more merciful, yet it was Yahweh who taught the patriarch that the mercy of God is greater than we can comprehend.[10] The patriarch was willing to see Sodom destroyed in spite of nine righteous souls. God, it seems, might have been willing *to go lower*. Couple that with God's unnecessary plan to go and investigate for himself the wickedness of the city, and we are given a glimpse at just how reluctant God was to destroy a city that became a by-word for utter wickedness.

Remember when I said that God's dual commitment to justice and mercy can violently conflict in his heart? If you doubt that, just look at the Cross. God's justice demanded that a blood sacrifice be offered to atone for our sins. God's mercy demanded that a substitutionary sacrifice be offered to atone for our sins. Jesus was the solution. "God made him who had no sin to be sin for us, so that in him we might become the righteousness of God" (2 Cor 5:21 NIV).

And that isn't the only way in which Paul's message in 2 Cor 5 intersects with this narrative in Gen 18. God's plan did not end with Jesus' sacrifice. He has commissioned his people, Paul says, with "the ministry of reconciliation; that is, in Christ God was reconciling the world to himself, not counting their trespasses against them" (2 Cor 5:18–19). As Christians, you and I are to be conduits or vessels of God's good-news message to the world, a message that proclaims the glad tidings that no one has to stand condemned for even the worst offenses (Rom 8:1). We are to be "ambassadors for Christ" (2 Cor 5:20). In other words, we are to be mediators of God's blessing to the nations—just like Abraham.

I must confess that I have wrestled with this particular passage in Genesis as much as any other. The implications are staggering. The people of God are to

---

9. Ibid., 34.

10. Arnold, *Genesis*, 183.

value justice. We are to foster in both ourselves and our children a holy reverence for a holy God who must punish sin. But coupled with the call to do justly is also one to "love mercy" (Mic 6:8). Such means that while we must hate sin and warn of the coming Judgment (2 Cor 5:11), our hearts must always remain tender towards those ensnared in the schemes of Satan. If I were Abraham, I would have been content to see Sodom burn like a thousand Fourth of July's. Their king had been a jerk and their influence had corrupted his nephew's family. But remarkably, Abraham seemed to consider each citizen of Sodom a precious life fashioned in the image of God.

Like many of you, I often find myself less inclined to pray for and seek the good of the wicked. I'm more inclined to pray for Jesus to come quickly and sweep the lot of them into the eternal flames of a devil's hell. It's passages like this one that prick my conscience, that leave me grateful that God is slow in pouring out his wrath, for I too deserve a devil's hell, and you also. Too many of us express indignation and resentment towards those guilty of Sodom's sin. What we need is a greater appreciation of the grace and forbearance of God. What we need are a few more Abrahams: ambassadors for Christ, mediators of blessing, who will gaze down on cities of unspeakable immorality and petition the Lord's mercy, rather than his wrath.[11] To inherit the blessings of Abraham, we must emulate his character. And I, for one, could do a better job of that. How about you?

God is just. God is holy. God punishes sin. These were traits with which Abraham was apparently very familiar. But God is also merciful. Merciful enough that he was willing to subject his nature to Abraham's interrogation. Merciful enough to spare a den of iniquity for the sake of ten righteous. Merciful enough to spare the lives of Abraham's relatives when not even ten could be found. Merciful enough to offer up his sinless Son for the salvation of the wicked. And merciful enough to invite us, children of Abraham by faith, to partner with him as ambassadors for Christ, mediators of blessing, imploring a lost world to be reconciled to God before his wrath comes in its terrible fullness.

For the wicked—those who spurn the mercy of God—what a dreadful day that will be.

---

11. "How much more surely will real communion with Jesus lead us to look on all men, and especially on the vicious and outcast, with His eyes who saw the multitudes as sheep without a shepherd, torn, panting, scattered, and lying exhausted and defenceless! Indifference to the miseries and impending dangers of Christless men is impossible for any whom He calls 'not servants, but friends,'" (Maclaren, *Genesis*, 132; emphasis his).

GENESIS 19:1-29

Determining with certainty the location of Sodom has proven a bit problematic. "No archaeological remains exist or can be identified to provide material for scientific investigation. The ruined cities have vanished without leaving a trace,"[12] no doubt a powerful testament to how thorough God's judgment can be. Two options exist for locating Sodom and her sister cities. The first places them at the northern end of the Dead Sea, but there is little support for this location. The second option has these cities at the southern terminus of the Dead Sea. This area is well watered by several streams (13:10), and bitumen is present (14:10).

If you look at a map of the Dead Sea, you will notice a peninsula jutting out from its SE bank; the Sea north of the peninsula is 1,300 feet deep in some places, but only 20 feet in depth south of this peninsula. It's possible that at one time this peninsula was the Dead Sea's southern shore, and that the shallow end of the Dead Sea now was previously the Valley of Siddim (14:3), the location of Sodom and her sister cities.

It has been noted in several places that the city gates (19:1) in ancient times functioned as courthouses/town halls/community centers (cf. Deut 21:19; Josh 20:4; Ruth 4:1; 1 Kgs 22:10). The city gate uncovered at Tell Dan had a fifteen-foot-long stone bench around one of its towers.[13] Lot's presence at Sodom's city gates means he was considered a prominent member of the community, though his immigrant status was later thrown in his face (19:9). Lot had risen in Sodom's society, and while it would spell his downfall, it doesn't seem to have ruined his good manners or hospitable spirit.

The two angels who had journeyed to Sodom were greeted by Lot upon arrival, and he extended to them courtesy similar to what Abraham had done: he offered to wash their feet (18:4) and "made them a feast" including bread (18:6–7). Because it was already evening, social standards of hospitality dictated that he offer lodging, not just a simple meal. The angels initially refused Lot's offer, but he twisted their arm until they consented. Whether or not Lot knew their supernatural identity, he certainly knew about the immoral sexual desires of his neighbors, and he did not want his guests to be subjected to the violence of Sodom's men.

No sooner had Lot led his guests home but a mob formed outside his door.

---

12. Sarna, *Genesis*, 138.

13. Ibid., 134.

This wasn't limited to a few men. It was "all the people to the last man" (19:4) or "the whole population" (HCSB)—a phrase that creates serious doubt in the reader's mind that Abraham's ten righteous souls could actually be found in Sodom (18:32).

What did the mob want? Up until recently, it was universally acknowledged that their desires were not only immoral, but also unnatural. They wanted to have homosexual intercourse with Lot's guests. In more modern times, however, spectacularly vigorous attempts have been made to reinterpret the mob's (and by extension, Sodom's) sin. This movement began in some sense with the release of *Homosexuality and the Western Christian Tradition* by Derrick Bailey, an Anglican minister in Great Britain. In that book, Bailey presents arguments in an (overconfident) attempt to reinterpret the Gen 19 narrative, but his conclusions are as incorrect as they are brazen: "The story does not in the least demand the assumption that the sin of Sodom was sexual, let alone homosexual—indeed, there is no evidence to show that vice of the latter kind was prevalent there."[14] As we will see, that is a startling conclusion to draw in the face of so much contrary evidence.

In more recent times, Scott Morschauser employed these arguments in an article[15] in which he sets forth an alternative interpretation of the events of Gen 19: Lot was at the city gates partly on the lookout for spies since Sodom had recently been raided by Chedorlaomer (Gen 14). That he invited the strangers into the town (and into his house, no less) was unacceptable to the citizens of Sodom. These outsiders could be a security risk, and they must be detained and interrogated. The mob of men who arrived at Lot's door, as "the official members of the community—the ruling elite,"[16] intended to do just that. In short, Morschauser asserts, "It is completely unnecessary to take the Sodomites' oration as a demand for 'sexual intercourse.'"[17]

Instead, the mob was insisting they be allowed to interrogate these two men as potential spies, and Lot was reluctant because he knew how violent a

---

14. Derrick Sherwin Bailey, *Homosexuality and the Western Christian Tradition* (Hamden, CT: Shoe String, 1975), 5. He later contends, "It is significant that none of the Biblical condemnations of homosexual practices makes any mention of the Sodom story," (Ibid., 11). But the only way that can be true is if one penknifes Jude 7 right out of the NT.

15. Scott Morschauser, "'Hospitality', Hostiles and Hostages: On the Legal Background to Genesis 19.1–9," *JSOT* 27 (2003): 461–85.

16. Ibid., 469.

17. Ibid., 472.

process that could be (cf. 1 Kgs 22:24–27; Jer 20:1–3). So he offered up his daughters as a form of prisoner exchange (not unlike Reuben's offer of his sons as collateral should Benjamin not return from Egypt, 42:37). The mob refused Lot's offer, and the city was judged and destroyed—not because of perversity, deviancy, or immorality—but because Sodom did not respect the rule of law. They thus "become the prototype for a faithless and chaotic society."[18]

Much of Morschauser's case is built on reinterpreting the verb "to know" (Hebrew *yada'*), which appears regularly as a euphemism for sexual intercourse, both in Genesis (4:1, 17, 25; 24:16; 38:26), as well as the rest of the OT (Num 31:17–18, 35; Judg 11:39; 1 Sam 1:19; 1 Kgs 1:4), and even in the Code of Hammurabi (§130).[19] Morschauser claims the verb only elsewhere denotes homosexual intercourse/rape in Judg 19:22, and is thus evidence of a circular argument.[20] But the Hebrew term clearly can be a euphemism for sex; context, not the definition of this word, determines whether the intercourse is homo- or heterosexual.[21] The fact that the OT only narrates two occasions of homosexual gang rape means nothing.

Consider the scene in Gen 19 once again. If the mob of Sodom wanted to "know" (*yada'*) Lot's visitors, and if Lot offered his daughters to the mob as an alternative—daughters "who have not known [*yada'*] any man"—then are we seriously expected to conclude that the mob's original demand wasn't sexual? Arnold surmises:

> The use of "know" with an undeniably sexual denotation in the same context (19:8) makes it difficult to deny homosexual intent on the part of the men of Sodom, whether it is taken as the most serious offense of the text or not. Attempts to deny this are driven more by today's sensibilities rather by the text before us.[22]

---

18. Ibid., 485.

19. The code read, "If a seignior bound the (betrothed) wife of a(nother) seignior, who had had no intercourse with [literally "had not known"] a male ..." (ANET 171).

20. Morschauser, "Hospitality," 471, n. 35.

21. "The meaning of a word in a given passage is not determined solely on the basis of the number of times it is translated that way in the Bible. The context determines how it is to be translated," (P. Michael Ukleja, "Homosexuality and the Old Testament," *BibSac* 140 [1983]: 261).

22. Arnold, *Genesis*, 184.

What is more unconscionable than the mob's request is Lot's offer to satisfy their lust with his virgin daughters. So much for Lot's good manners, to say nothing of the daddy issues these girls must have had (the narrative of 19:30–38 seems par for the course in light of this). Walton suggests alternatively that Lot may have been sarcastic with this offer, akin to "saying to your mortgage company, 'Why don't you just take the clothes off my children's backs and the food off their plates?'"[23] But Lot's demeanor here seems panicked and placating instead of vexed and sarcastic; his offer was ghastly, cowardly, and indefensible. If he had been an Israelite, his proposal to the mob would have earned him the death penalty (Deut 22:23–24).

The mob began to wantonly beat the door down, seemingly intent on raping Lot instead of the angels—"now we will treat you worse than them" (19:9 NASU). That's when the divine agents of Yahweh struck the mob with "blindness." The only other place in the OT this word (Hebrew *sanwerim*) occurs is in 2 Kgs 6:18, where Elisha prays that the Aramean troops surrounding his home in Dothan be struck blind. The term, which is distinct from the OT's regular ones for "blind" and "blindness," is also rare in ANE literature and only occurs "in medical texts apparently referring to a corneal disease,"[24] possibly day- or night-blindness depending on the context.[25] What is unmistakable in this passage is that the angels' act was supernaturally debilitating and disorienting. Yet so determined was this mob in its degenerate lust that they did not disperse; "they wore themselves out groping for the door" (19:11).

Meanwhile, the urgency of the angels kicked in. They ordered Lot to gather up his family post-haste and get out of the city as quickly as possible. Lot implored his sons-in-law (since his daughters were still virgins, they were likely his sons-in-law to-be) to join him in leaving the city. But for whatever reason, Lot had zero influence on them. We are told that they thought he was "jesting" (19:14). "Perhaps their disregard for Lot's warning as a joke speaks also to the narrative's general picture of Lot as a confused, inept person who falls to his own short-sighted ambition and finally to the deceit of treacherous daughters."[26]

But what I find worse is the way in which Lot drug his feet and delayed in

---

23. Walton, *Genesis*, 477. For his part, Walton does cite the parallel story of Judg 19:24–25 as opposing his suggestion.

24. ZIBBCOT 1:93.

25. Marten Stol, "Blindness and Night-Blindness in Akkadian," *JNES* 45 (1986): 296–97.

26. Mathews, *Genesis 11:27–50:26*, 238.

getting out of Dodge. The text says Lot "lingered" or "hesitated" (19:16 HCSB), so much so that it seems God mercifully delayed the destruction until the angels had seized Lot and his family and almost drug them out of the city. And if that isn't enough, Lot whined that the distance he was expected to travel was too far (19:20). "Can I instead flee to this small, insignificant town of Zoar?" In the face of the terrible, awesome judgment of God, only a fool dares delay his own salvation, and only a gracious God stalls his wrath until we have gotten out of our own way (cf. 2 Pet 3:9).

I have always pictured Lot's wife looking back (19:26) in the sense of glancing wistfully over her shoulder at the city (i.e. the life) she was leaving behind, and then *poof!* she became a pillar of salt. But there may have been more to it than that. Jesus may have suggested she went so far as to return to the city:

> It was the same in the days of Lot. People were eating and drinking, buying and selling, planting and building. But the day Lot left Sodom, fire and sulfur rained down from heaven and destroyed them all. It will be just like this on the day the Son of Man is revealed. On that day no one who is on the housetop, with possessions inside, should go down to get them. Likewise, no one in the field should go back for anything. Remember Lot's wife!
>
> Luke 17:28–32 NIV

This suggests more than a knee-jerk glance over the shoulder; it evokes Lot's wife losing faith in her husband (and in God), saying in effect, "You're a fool, Lot, and I refuse to go one step further! I'm going home. I'll see you in a day or two or whenever you come to your senses!"[27] But this decision on her part proved fatal. In the face of God's judgment, it is foolishness to continue to identify with the objects of our past affections.

It is said that, even today, there are grotesque, human-like rock formations in the salt cliffs surrounding the Dead Sea. The apocryphal book Wisdom of Solomon speaks of how "Evidence of [Sodom's] wickedness still remains ... a pillar of salt standing as a monument to an unbelieving soul" (10:7 NRSV); Josephus also mentioned the pillar of salt and claimed to have seen it for himself (*Antiquities* 1.11.4).

---

27. Walton, *Genesis*, 480.

How exactly was Sodom destroyed? The text says sulfur and fire rained down from heaven, a statement Jesus later corroborated (Luke 17:29). Scientifically, it is suggested that an earthquake "overthrew" (19:25) natural gas and petroleum pocketed in the ground (cf. 14:10) and sent them skyward, only to be ignited by lightning and fall back to earth, giving the appearance of raining sulfur and fire from heaven. The whole Jordan Valley sits on the Syrian-African Rift,[28] so an earthquake isn't out of the question. But trying to understand what physically happened can undermine our appreciation for what spiritually happened.[29] From the Bible's perspective, God had had enough of Sodom's evil.

1.   The destruction was Yahweh's work; the divine name appears no fewer than three times in the destruction account (19:23–26).

2.   The destruction was warranted, for "the Judge of all the earth" always does what is right (18:25).

3.   The destruction was also total, for not even plant life survived the destruction (19:25).

In the final scene of the devastation, we are again reminded of Abraham. He returned to where he had previously bartered with the Lord for Sodom's survival and was met with confirmation that not even ten righteous souls had been found. I'm old enough to remember the Persian Gulf War images of Kuwaiti oil fields set ablaze by Saddam Hussein's retreating Republican Guard. I have to imagine that such thick, black, billowing smoke also greeted Abraham that morning (19:28; cf. Rev 9:2). Only one question remained on his mind:

Had Lot been spared?[30]

---

28. Sarna, *Genesis*, 138.

29. "Hebrew narrative is not interested in secondary causes, so that whatever natural phenomena might have been perceived as contributing to the disaster is irrelevant. It only matters that the rain of fire was 'from the Lord out of heaven,'" (Arnold, *Genesis*, 185).

30. "Presenting it through Abraham's eyes, the narrator makes us more conscious of the human aspect of the destruction. Abraham had relatives there. What had happened to them? The reader has been told, but Abraham was still unaware of Lot's escape. He had gone back to the place 'where he had stood before the LORD' and interceded for the city. What had been the point?" (Wenham, *Genesis 16–50*, 59).

The cities of Sodom and Gomorrah, as previously mentioned, have in the Christian community become bywords for homosexuality (why the other two cities, Admah and Zeboiim, have not been so branded is a mystery), and for good reason. It's hard to reinterpret the demands and desires of the mob at Lot's door: "Where are the men who came to spend the night with you? Bring them out to us so we can have sex with them!" (19:5 NLT). Coupled with this and other passages (Lev 18:22; 20:13; Judg 19:22–30), the OT is unique in ANE literature in condemning homosexual practices. "Most of the ancient Near East adopted an attitude to homosexuality very similar to that of classical Greece and Rome which simply accepted it as long as it was done among consenting adults."[31]

But contrary to popular belief, and not to detract from my strenuous arguments above, I maintain that homosexuality was not the *sole* reason for these cities' destruction. Indeed, their extermination is often attributed to something much broader. Consider the evidence: "Sodom" is not mentioned in Genesis again after this chapter, but when it is broached in the rest of the OT, it is almost always as a metaphor for utter destruction (Deut 29:23; Isa 1:9; 13:19; Jer 49:18; 50:40; Lam 4:6; Amos 4:11; Zeph 2:9). In Isa 3:9, the Lord laments that his people blatantly flaunt their guilt "like Sodom; they do not hide it." A very thorough illustration of Sodom's legacy is in Ezek 16. "This was the sin of your sister Sodom: She and her daughters were proud and had plenty of food and lived in great comfort, but she did not help the poor and needy" (Ezek 16:49 NCV).

"Wait, what?"

That was my response the first time I read that passage. I had long been conditioned to think that Sodom's sole sin, and a major one, was homosexuality. And it cannot be gainsaid in the least that the NT lays this charge at Sodom's feet (Jude 7). But Sodom's sin was not *limited* to this. Pride and a systematic disregard for the less fortunate were also on that checklist. And the extent to which Sodom and her sister cities were guilty of this is arresting.

The cities of this area evidently enjoyed great wealth gained from very little work (cf. the allegation in Ezek 16:49 of "idleness" NKJV, or "careless ease" NASU). The region was rich in a wide variety of natural resources. Sodom likely forced slaves to mine those minerals, then sat back as the lucrative profits rolled in. And if you're ridiculously wealthy, you're likely less inclined to share what you have with those in need. In his *Legends of the Jews*, Louis Ginzberg drew on varied

---

31. G. J. Wenham, "The Old Testament Attitude to Homosexuality," *ExpTim* 102 (1991): 360.

rabbinical sources, including the Talmud, to illustrate Sodom's efforts to keep her wealth and spurn the needs of the less fortunate. Consider these examples:

- The citizens of Sodom regularly practiced theft and extortion on those to whom they had offered hospitality. When lawsuits were brought against the offenders, the courts always found in favor of the Sodomites.

- At the suggestion of their own judges, the cities of Gomorrah, Admah, and Zeboiim placed beds in their city squares; when travelers arrived, they would seize them, strap them to the bed, and gang rape them while chanting, "Thus will be done to any man that comes into our land." I'm guessing these towns didn't have a Visitors Bureau.

- When travelers stopped and asked for food, they would be given gold and silver instead. Once the person starved to death, the citizens would steal back the gold and silver, as well as the traveler's clothes, and bury him naked.

- One traveler passed through Admah and requested bread and water from the daughter of a rich man, which she offered gladly. The town heard of her "crime" and brought her before the judge, whereby she was sentenced to death in this way: she was covered in honey and was allowed to be stung to death by bees.

- Sodom's laws stipulated that you had to pay a toll to use the ferry. If you opted to wade the water to save money, they would charge you double the toll.

- When a beggar once appeared in Sodom, the city prohibited anyone from feeding him, hoping he would die of starvation. One woman had pity on him and would sneak him bread in the bottom of her water pitcher as she went to the city well each day. When the city leaders couldn't understand how the beggar kept on living, they stationed three men on a stakeout. They caught the woman red-handed and burned her alive.[32]

I concede these stories may have been somewhat embellished over the

---

32. Louis Ginzberg, *Legends of the Jews*, 2nd ed., trans. Henrietta Szold and Paul Radin (Philadelphia: Jewish Publication Society, 2003), 207–9.

years, but they nonetheless paint a picture of Sodom that is wholly consistent with the Scriptures. The reality is that the Sodomites weren't just considered sinners, but "wicked, great sinners against the LORD" (13:13). Yahweh brought judgment upon them, and our inability to even find their ruins today foreshadows the eternal fate of all the wicked.

But lest we think that such a fate only awaits homosexuals, or those who practice other forms of sexual immorality, the OT leaves us with a cautionary tale that this fearful retribution also awaits those void of compassion for the less fortunate. In the judgment scene of Matt 25, Jesus says those who failed to show generosity to the needy will hear these fatal words as they enter into eternal punishment: "Away from me, you that are under God's curse!" (Matt 25:41 GNT). There is more to the life of faith than avoiding carnal lust or supporting a biblical definition of marriage. We must learn to regard all others as precious souls made in God's image, the *imago Dei*. This was a pursuit at which Sodom failed miserably.

GENESIS 19:30–38

For whatever reason, Lot and his daughters were "afraid to stay in Zoar" (19:30 NASU), and they left the village to live in a cave, even though they had rejected that option the night before (19:17–19). Because the devastation was so widespread, they may have assumed the entire world had been destroyed.[33] This explains why Lot's daughters desperately intoxicated their father and conceived by him.

Regardless, there is no denying that their desires were reprehensible, even by ancient standards.[34] The phrase "lie with" is not as innocent as it sounds; it is used elsewhere in Genesis for other illicit sexual relationships (cf. 26:10; 34:2; 35:22; 39:7). And in spite of what some have suggested, there is absolutely no salvageable nobility in the daughters trying to secure an heir. That they had to get their own father drunk to accomplish their goal proves they knew their actions to be morally abhorrent. On the other hand, no blame for what transpired is assigned to Lot; the narrator stresses he was completely unaware of what happened.

The two sons born to Lot's daughters were named *Moab*, meaning "from my father," and *Ben-ammi*, meaning "son of my family." Both became nations with

---

33. Walton, *Genesis*, 480–81.

34. The Code of Hammurabi dictated that a man who had intercourse with his daughter be expelled from the city (§154).

whom Israel had occasional (often violent) contact, and while God prohibited their extermination (Deut 2:9, 19), they nonetheless lived under his rejection (Deut 23:3–6), though not forever (Jer 48:47; 49:6).

A s we have already asked of the narrator, and will ask again before we are done, "Why record this story?" The narrative does explain the origins of the Moabites and Ammonites, something Genesis is always interested in doing. But I believe Moses' greater motive was to prompt the reader to contrast the fates of Lot and Abraham. Lot is never mentioned again in Genesis, as the spotlight will now return to Abraham.

We are thus left with the stark realization of what it means to live by faith vs. by natural instinct. Lot chose the best land, established himself in a city, and had only war and destruction to show for it, living out the rest of his existence in a nameless cave. On the other hand, Abraham chose the land God had promised, continued to live in temporary dwellings, and despite his hiccups of faith, eventually "died at a ripe old age, old and contented" (25:8 HCSB). The patriarch thus stands as an example of one who eschewed this world and its pleasures in exchange for the glories of endless fellowship with God (1 John 2:17). "Better is one day in your courts than a thousand elsewhere" (Ps 84:10 NIV).

Indeed.

TALKING POINTS

Throughout Scripture, the omnipotence and omniscience of God are often celebrated, but never more so than in 18:1–15. No sooner had he revealed his knowledge of Sarah's laughter than God asked, "Is anything too hard for the LORD?" At our lowest and most vulnerable, when we believe all hope is gone, we need reminding that God sees and knows our plight, and that he cares. We also need reminding that he is powerful enough to do something about our circumstances. As he often does with us, perhaps God intentionally delayed the fulfillment of his promise these many years until Abraham and Sarah were completely broken. He did so in order to teach them that the power and grace of God are never more matchless than when we believe things have passed the point of no return. Well did Jesus say that the poor in spirit, those so despondent in their soul, were qualified for citizenship in heaven's kingdom (Matt 5:3). Only when we abandon our own agenda can we see God's at work.

It demands remarkable faith to believe that God has appointed an end to our suffering *while we are suffering*! But how thrilling it is that we are invited to believe the impossible! This truth confronted Jeremiah near the end of the Jerusalem siege. Within a year, Nebuchadnezzar would prevail, destroy the city, and deport most of the inhabitants 500 miles across the desert. Yet the Lord commanded Jeremiah to buy a field from his cousin (Jer 32:7). What good was there in buying property when it was about to become the spoil of war (cf. Jer 32:25)? An aged couple hoping for a son might have wondered the same. At the heart of the narrative, Jeremiah heard God declare something similar to what Abraham and Sarah had been told: "I am Yahweh, God of all humanity. Is anything impossible to me?" (32:27 NJB). In the midst of our disappointment and despair, God's sovereignty is the only appropriate basis for our hope. When our hearts become convinced that God can do all things—that he is patiently working out his plan in the world—we will find no command of his too arduous, and no promise too ridiculous.

In 18:19, it is obvious that God considered it Abraham's obligation to teach his posterity about the righteousness and justice of God, and this obligation belongs to every family patriarch. The problem is that the once exalted position of father has been drug through the mud in recent times. In TV sitcoms, they are often portrayed as incompetent, bumbling idiots (e.g. Al Bundy, Homer

Simpson, Peter Griffin, Ray Barone)—we've come a long way from the examples of Ward Cleaver, Mike Brady, and Cliff Huxtable. Ignoring for a moment the mounting stack of studies heralding the necessity of strong, benevolent fathers, the biblical call is clear and decisive. A father is responsible for teaching his children the will of God and reaffirming the faithfulness of God (Exod 12:26–27; Deut 6:6–7; Isa 38:19). A father is responsible for loving and disciplining his children so that they might become men and women of God (Ps 103:13; Prov 3:12). It is admittedly a difficult balance to strike, the balance between love and fairness, mercy and fairness. But by praying to their heavenly Father and asking for his wisdom (cf. Jas 1:5), today's fathers can, like Abraham, teach their children properly about the righteousness and justice of God.

Among the Millennial generation, there is a declining commitment to a biblical definition of sexuality and marriage. That trend should give us pause because it is the duty of every professed Christian to preserve and proclaim God's values to the world (Matt 5:13–16). But on the other side of the equation are Christians whose stance against homosexuality is, well, militant. Listen to their vitriol long enough, and you are left with the impression that every homosexual is an Antichrist in the making, that homosexuality is the worst sin imaginable. Is it? Jesus said that those who rejected both his messengers (Matt 10:15) and his message (11:24) would be in worse shape at the Judgment than the citizens of Sodom. Consider that claim. As utterly immoral as homosexuality is, Jesus considered it a graver sin to witness his works yet reject his Lordship. For the church, those for whom Christ has done marvelous things, Jesus' words mandate that we make him Lord of our whole lives. Explaining away his difficult teachings (e.g. discipleship, service, sacrificial love, radical obedience, divorce and remarriage) in order to soothe our guilty consciences is a practice the church should renounce with bitter tears. Otherwise, Sodom will fare better on the final day than we will. That fact alone should truly give us pause.

Lot is indeed a tragic character in Scripture. Once a very wealthy man, all that he owns in life can now fit inside a small cave. "His ruin can hardly be more complete."[35] For all we know, this is his existence until death. "We are just left to pity Lot in his last and most painful loss of honor at the hands of those who should

---

35. Wenham, *Genesis 16–50*, 60.

have loved him most."[36] But this should not come as a surprise to us. For too long, Lot had lived by his own self-sufficiency instead of an abiding faith in God. Earlier in the chapter, he had been willing to offer up his daughters to be gang-raped by the lustful mob in order to secure his own safety. He was revered as a spiritual leader by absolutely no one. It should be expected, then, that his daughters would lose all respect for him and resort to tricks, not trust, to meet their needs. It is a truth of Scripture that the sins of the parents fester and spread to successive generations. David was righteous, "except in the matter of Uriah the Hittite" (1 Kgs 15:5). His son Solomon "was loved by his God, and God made him king over all Israel, but even he was led into sin by foreign women" (Neh 13:26 NIV). And by the time we come to Solomon's son, Rehoboam, we are not surprised to find that his biblical epitaph reads: "He did evil because he had not set his heart on seeking the LORD" (2 Chr 12:14 NIV). In the case of Lot, his (grand)sons spawned nations that were never known (not surprisingly) for their morality or righteousness. "Heavenly Father, give us more parents who set for their children a powerful example of what it means to trust and obey you in all things."

Genesis is often interested in explaining the origins of various nations (e.g. Gen 10), and it does so here for the Moabites and Ammonites. But "the narrator's main point is not that the Moabites and Ammonites owe their existence to incestuous acts but that they owe their existence to Abraham."[37] In other words, these nations existed due to God's faithfulness to his promises, which also happens to be the reason *Israel* existed. Moab and Ammon had as much a right to exist as Israel, which is why God prohibited their extermination and expulsion (Deut 2:9, 19). Unpopular as it may be to say this, the fact is that patriotism can become as much a vice as a virtue, especially if it dehumanizes citizens of other nations. Is an Afghani, Iranian, or Palestinian any less precious to God than an American? Isn't it true that our nation's establishment and subsequent success are due to God's unmerited blessing? And does not the Lord therefore have the right to bless any nation he wishes?

---

36. Ibid., 62.

37. Walton, *Genesis*, 485.

9

A FAITH ODYSSEY

For a quarter century, Abraham struggled to trust consistently in God's promises, proving that the life of faith is an odyssey with unexpected twists and turns. Though he was able to enjoy the blessings of Canaan, the Lord had made clear to him that his descendants would not inherit the land until after four centuries of oppression. The blessings of prosperity and protection were tenable, but the promise of a covenant child remained unfulfilled.

However, a year after God visited Abraham, he visited Sarah in a different way, and the promise was actualized. The significance of Isaac's birth does not go unnoticed elsewhere in Scripture. One NT writer referred to Isaac as Abraham's "only begotten son" (Heb 11:17 NKJV), a phrase used elsewhere only of Jesus (cf. John 1:14; 3:16). Though Isaac was not the only begotten of Abraham (he had Ishmael by Hagar and six other sons by Keturah), Isaac was Abraham's unique son (cf. Heb 11:17 HCSB), the child of promise, and a token of God's faithfulness.

Imagine, then, the agony in Abraham's heart as he faced the prospect of sacrificing his son to God, just as he had been instructed to do. The test of Abraham's faith on Mt. Moriah was no less significant than Isaac's birth, and it proved to be the pivotal moment of the patriarch's life. The story illustrates the purest and most mature expression of faith and obedience possible. Not only does the odyssey of faith have its twists and turns, but also its own agonizing moments on the mountaintop and the valley below. Through it all, our trust and confidence in God is being strengthened, as was father Abraham's.

The designation of "only begotten son" is not the only parallel between Isaac and Jesus in the NT. In many ways, Isaac embodied all the promises God had made to Abraham, and Christ certainly embodies the same for us—in him is our hope for forgiveness (Eph 4:32) and a verdict of "not guilty" (Rom 8:1). He is our hope for an abundant life here on earth (John 10:10) and an eternal one in heaven (Rom 6:23). Indeed, the most mature expression of our reliance on God would be to trust in the promise of Phil 4:19—"My God will supply every need of yours according to his riches in glory in Christ Jesus."

The section does not end before narrating the circumstances following Sarah's death. His beloved wife now passed, Abraham yet again demonstrated remarkable faith in his God by securing for her (as well as for himself and his posterity) a permanent resting place in Canaan. Abraham's purchase carries a profound message that speaks to our own traditions related to death and burial.

But we're getting ahead of ourselves. Before we can speak of death, let us speak of a very special birth...

GENESIS 21:1–21

God is faithful. As he has done on countless occasions throughout history, he remembered the despair of one in a hopeless situation. The text reads beautifully, "The LORD visited Sarah as he had said." The term "visit" in Scripture signals God's intervention in the lives of his people, both for judgment (Exod 20:5; 32:34) and redemption (Exod 4:31; Ruth 1:6; Jer 29:10). Before his death, Joseph promised his people that God would "visit" them and restore them to the Promised Land (50:24). Later, just as he did for Sarah, God would "visit" a barren Hannah and bless her with Samuel (1 Sam 2:21).

Sarah gave birth to a son, and he was given a name precisely as God had promised (17:19). This birth took place "at the appointed time" (21:2 NASU); God had appointed an end to this couple's suffering, and the Lord had been faithful! Moses artfully underscores the event's absurdity by noting both Abraham's and Sarah's shock over having a child at such an advanced age (21:5–7). There is much ado made over their elderly state—not out of rudeness, but in an effort to celebrate the unparalleled power of God. Their heartbreak had been transformed into a "Hallelujah!" and those around them surely chorused: "The LORD has done great things for them" (Ps 126:2). Nothing is said of Abraham's elation, but that probably goes without saying. Yet his excitement did not make him lax in meeting his covenant obligation. He did "as God had commanded him" by circumcising his son on the eighth day (21:4; cf. 17:12).

The joy over Isaac's birth was shattered a few years later by another family feud. During a celebration commemorating Isaac's weaning,[1] Ishmael was caught doing something (21:9), and we presume that it was directed at Isaac (so says the LXX).

So what was Ishmael doing? The Hebrew *sahaq* is admittedly ambiguous. Whenever this verb appears in the OT in the same form as it does here (19:14; Exod 32:6; Judg 16:25), it occurs "with nasty overtones, usually of someone being mocked."[2] It is variously translated here as "laughing" (ESV), "mocking" (NIV), "scoffing" (NKJV), and "playing" (NRSV), but this leaves us with a wide range of interpretations; it could mean something as innocent as Ishmael picking on his little brother (cf. Judg 16:25), or as serious as Ishmael molesting Isaac[3] (cf. 39:14, 17). The rabbis variously accused Ishmael of fornication, idolatry, and attempted murder (Gen Rab 53:11), while Paul in the NT simply says that Ishmael "persecuted" Isaac (Gal 4:29).

A much more innocent (yet arguably more dangerous) option is that Sarah saw Ishmael playing with Isaac in a loving, big-brotherly way and was concerned Isaac would grow up revering Ishmael. Perhaps Isaac, through Ishmael's influence, would adopt too many Egyptian practices or forsake the religious values of his parents. Abraham and Sarah were, after all, advanced in years; after their death, would Ishmael become a more significant role model?[4]

In the end, however, I am inclined to interpret this event in light of Paul's comments in Gal 4, that Ishmael was somehow mistreating Isaac (though I find far-fetched the suggestion of sexual abuse). Whatever the crime, it was enough to infuriate Sarah—she never even mentions Ishmael or Hagar by name, and she demanded that Abraham banish them from the family. Though the text does not specifically say, it seems Sarah wished Abraham to divorce Hagar. The word

---

1. According to the Egyptian text *The Instruction of Ani*, this milestone normally came at three years of age (ANET 420; cf. 1 Sam 1:22–25; 2 Maccabees 7:27). "In a society where infant mortality was high, to reach the age of two or three would be regarded as a significant achievement, so this in part explains the magnitude of the celebrations," (Wenham, *Genesis 16–50*, 81).

2. Wenham, *Genesis 16–50*, 82.

3. This is Hamilton's conclusion (*The Book of Genesis: Chapters 18–50*, 78), and it is not out of the question. The term *sahaq* is also used in 26:8 where Abimelech notices "Isaac laughing with Rebekah" and concludes they are husband and wife. Given the circumstances, it is suggested that Isaac was sexually fondling Rebekah on that occasion (David J. Zucker, "What Sarah Saw: Envisioning Genesis 21:9–10," *JBQ* 36 [2008]: 57).

4. Zucker, "What Sarah Saw," 58.

translated "cast out" (21:10) can also be rendered "divorce" (cf. Lev 21:7; 22:13; Num 30:9; Ezek 44:22); the same can be said for the phrase "sent ... away" (21:14; cf. Deut 22:19; 24:1; Mal 2:16).[5] Abraham, for understandable reasons, was not so easily inclined to throw his oldest son under the bus to satisfy the wrath of his first wife. The text says Sarah's demand was "displeasing" (21:11) to or "upset" (NLT) Abraham. But God gave assurances of his providence for Hagar and Ishmael.

Sarah's demand that Hagar and Ishmael be divorced may have been more than simple pettiness on her part. God had been clear in the past that Isaac was the child of promise (17:19), and Sarah may have only been playing the part of a protective mother. The Lipit-Ishtar legal code (c. 19th century B.C.) stated that "children born to slave-wives could inherit with the children of the primary wife,"[6] but such rights were forfeited if the slave and her child were freed as Hagar and Ishmael were here—"the children of the slave shall not divide the estate with the children of their (former) master,"[7] (cf. Judg 11:1–3). The reality is that Sarah's demand, harsh as it may seem to us, was consistent with God's plan. This does not legitimize any pettiness on her part, but rather affirms the truth that God sometimes uses human sinfulness to further unfold his plan in the world—a truth that saturates the pages of Genesis. Like Lot in Gen 13 and Eliezer in Gen 15, Ishmael was yet another potential heir of Abraham removed so as to clear the way for Isaac, the child of promise (cf. Ps 83:5–6).

As God had commanded, Abraham outfitted Hagar and Ishmael for their departure, but their provisions were rather sparse for a multi-day journey into the desert; the skin of water given to Hagar (21:14) held no more than three gallons. Such an oversight on Abraham's part was probably not due to his lack of concern as much as his "numbness at sending his son away."[8] If losing Ishmael caused Abraham this much distress, imagine the pain he would feel over the prospect of losing Isaac (22:2).

---

5. Hamilton notes a subtle distinction between these two Hebrew terms, arguing that "the former [*garas*, "cast out"] is invariably a hostile act," while "the latter [*shalah*, 'sent ... away'] often refers to a friendly release," (*The Book of Genesis: Chapters 18–50*, 82–83).

6. Wenham, *Genesis 16–50*, 83.

7. ANET 160. The Code of Hammurabi had a similar mandate (§171).

8. Wenham, *Genesis 16–50*, 84. Calvin believed that Abraham gave Hagar sparse provisions to make sure she could not travel too far, preferring that they live nearby so that he could continue to provide for their needs (*Genesis*, 1:548).

With the obvious inherent risks in desert travel, water is a precious resource that gets used up very quickly. The skin of water Abraham had given them would have only lasted them a few days. When it was gone, Hagar and Ishmael despondently resigned themselves to death. But God graciously heard their prayer, their cry for help. The Lord had promised Abraham that Ishmael would become a nation. The promise was reiterated here to Hagar (21:18), and we know that when God ordains a future, he also meets the needs of the present. Hagar's eyes were opened to a well that would quench their thirst.

Before moving on to the next passage, take just a moment to read and ponder the startling statement, "God was with the boy" (21:20). The passage is clear that Ishmael was not a part of the plan, the one that commenced with Abraham and would culminate with the Incarnation—for such an honor was reserved for Isaac. But that doesn't mean Ishmael was cast from the divine presence and made to live outside of God's favor. Rather, it may be that the Lord established Ishmael as the patriarch of his own nation in order to make up for the inheritance Ishmael lost when he was cast from Abraham's house and effectively written out of the will.[9]

Genesis is not finished with Ishmael. He would later reappear at his father's funeral, and there the "rest of the story" concerning his lineage is told. But here we learn that he became an expert archer[10] in the NW barrens of the Sinai desert, the wilderness of Paran. Hagar showed as much concern for her son's nuptials as Abraham would for Isaac's. She secured for Ishmael a wife of her own people, and the race of Ishmaelites was born.

GENESIS 21:22–34

Not too long after Hagar and Ishmael departed, Abraham was visited by Abimelech and Phicol, respectively the king and military commander of Gerar. They made this journey of about 25 miles to secure a treaty with Abraham because they discerned, "God is with you in all that you do" (21:22). The treaty they sought would not only be with the patriarch, but also with his God, whom Abimelech considered "at least equal to him and his army commander."[11] The

---

9. F. Charles Fensham, "The Son of a Handmaid in Northwest Semitic," *VT* 19 (1969): 318.

10. The descendants of Kedar, one of Ishmael's sons (25:13), were renowned in the prophet Isaiah's day for their archery skills (Isa 21:17).

11. Waltke, *Genesis*, 299.

reason he wanted the patriarch to "swear" is precisely because Abraham had been deceptive previously during their prior engagement in Gen 20. Simply put, Abimelech did not trust Abraham (cf. Matt 5:33–37).

But if the patriarch was going to consent to this pact of non-aggression, then he also wanted to raise concerns when his rights were violated. Moses says "Abraham *reproved* Abimelech about a well of water that Abimelech's servants had seized," and "the Hebrew verb suggests that Abraham had to make his complaint several times."[12] It is a verb that can mean "to make right" or vindicate, and in 20:16, vindication is exactly what Abimelech had wanted. Now it is Abraham's turn to seek the same.

In an arid region such as the one Abraham inhabited on this occasion, one that may have averaged only a foot of rain per annum, wells were quite valuable. What Abimelech's servants were doing was essentially stealing (cf. Hebrew *gazal* in Lev 6:4; 19:13; Judg 9:25; Ps 69:4; Prov 22:22; Isa 10:2; Ezek 18:18). The patriarch loved peace, but he now showed a bolder side to his character than the one we saw in Gen 12 when he stood before Pharaoh, and Gen 20 when he stood before this same Abimelech. On those occasions, when challenged to defend what was his (his wife, no less!), he had wilted. Here, he made a stand and was confident God would protect him.

In response to Abraham's complaint, Abimelech claimed he had no knowledge of the act, which was exactly his defense in 20:4–5. Abraham took sheep and oxen with which the two men "cut a covenant," likely in a way similar to that of Gen 15. But the patriarch also took seven ewe lambs as an additional witness that the well was his. The well was given the name "Beersheba," a word that can mean both "well of seven" and "well of oaths." This location, particularly the settlement that grew up around the well, would later become noteworthy as the southern terminus of Israel (cf. Judg 20:1; 1 Sam 3:20; 1 Kgs 4:25).

After Abimelech and Phicol had departed, we are told Abraham planted a tree and called upon "the name of the LORD" (21:33). He invoked a special name on that occasion: El Olam, "Everlasting God." As mentioned in chapter 7, *olam* is an elastic term that, at its most basic, means "a very long time." In this case, God is not only everlasting, but also eternal—he has no beginning and no end. There has not been a time when God has not existed, nor will there ever be. But when Abraham invoked the Lord as El Olam, he was praising the enduring nature of God and his faithfulness. In times past, Abraham had dealt

---

12. Kidner, *Genesis*, 141.

falsely (21:23) with others, and a lesser man on this occasion might have been tempted to parlay the perception of "God is with you in all that you do" into an unfair economic advantage. But if God had been faithful to the patriarch in regards to Isaac, he would surely be faithful to him in regards to Canaan.

Abraham sought a human solution to correct the injustice of a stolen well. Such required no violation of conscience on his part, and as a man of peace, he favored a treaty of peace. But as his actions at the end of the chapter bear out, Abraham's trust was not in his treaty with Abimelech, but in the provision only God can provide. The patriarch planted a tree to symbolize his trust in a God who indeed blesses and makes his people prosper. His faith was in El Olam, the Enduring God. "This awesome view of God would now inform all of Abraham's dealings."[13]

But that view, that faith, was about to be put to the supreme test...

An additional note: the Philistines of Gen 21, 26 are different from the Philistines who appear in the stories of Judges and 1–2 Samuel. Note the differences:

1. In Genesis, a king rules the Philistines. Later in the OT, theirs is a government of five established city-states—Ashdod, Ashkelon, Ekron, Gath, and Gaza.

2. The Philistines whom the patriarchs knew were a relatively peaceful people, while those that appear in Judges–Samuel were incredibly antagonistic.

With that said, however, the suggestion that "Philistines" is an anachronism in the text is not necessarily true. That two different groups of people at two different times could be known as "Philistines" seems confusing. But "Philistines" is actually derived from the Egyptian term *plst*, the name for the *territory* that the Philistines inhabited. This 50-mile-long by 15-mile-wide coastal plain in SW Canaan was settled by Egyptian colonists that bore the name "plst" (cf. 10:14). These people of the land of "Philistia" were the ones known to Abraham and Isaac. But sometime during the Judges period, Egypt lost its control of the region, and inhabitants of the island of Crete came and displaced the people of

---

13. Hughes, *Genesis*, 296.

Philistia[14] (cf. Deut 2:23; Jer 47:4; Amos 9:7). These new inhabitants became the Philistines we read about later in the OT.

If all this sounds rather confusing, then consider this analogy. My dad was born in California, but was raised in Texas and Oklahoma, finished high school in Tennessee, and lived most of his adult life in Mississippi. Would you say he was a Californian? A Texan? A Mississippian? Though his family has been in America for many, many years, the family name is an Irish one. So was my father Irish? American? My point is we tend to identify people based on both past and current residences. This seems to be the case with the Philistines of Abraham's day, a people who had given their group name to the land they occupied in Canaan. Centuries later, a new ethnic group displaced them, but also became known as "Philistines" because they now resided in Philistia, i.e. the land of the Philistines.

GENESIS 22

To this point, Abraham has run the gamut of spiritual maturity in the past four decades or so. He has endured many highs and lows. He was willing to displace his family from their homeland, but unwilling to be honest about his marriage. He was willing to attack superior enemy forces, but cowered before kings and subjected himself to his wife's occasional whims. Always at stake on these occasions was the question: "Does Abraham trust God to provide?"

Trusting in God's provision instead of relying on our own is what the life of faith is all about. From birth to death, life is filled with moments, large and small, where our trust in God's provision is tested. Will we allow him to work his plan, to reveal his will, to meet our needs? Or will we fall for Satan's lie? Remember that Adam and Eve had been surrounded by a multitude of trees in Eden, each one of them ripe with the fruit of God's provision. But the serpent convinced them that, in order to move forward—to be in better shape tomorrow than they were that day—they had to reach out and grab hold of what God was denying them.

Since then, undermining faith in God's provision has been the bread and butter of Satan's playbook:

It's the young lady who knows she's in a relationship that doesn't please her heavenly Father, but her beau might be the last train coming through the station.

It's the business professional whose income—not to mention his self-

---

14. K. A. Kitchen, *On the Reliability of the Old Testament* (Grand Rapids: Eerdmans, 2003), 137–38.

esteem—relies on that next big deal. He knows even a white lie doesn't please his heavenly Father, but "this is how the business world works."

It's the wife or mother who knows her quick temper doesn't please her heavenly Father, but throwing a fit is her only real way of getting what she wants from her family. "Sometimes you have to do what you have to do."

It's the father who knows his drinking doesn't please his heavenly Father, but it's what he needs to get him through the day. "I can stop when I want to."

Doubt in God's provision is the root of our rebellion. It's why the alcoholic needs his drink and the junkie his fix. It's why successful people quit on God— why trust when you can make it happen for yourself? It's why suffering people quit on God—why trust when he isn't coming through for you? It's why families fracture and churches decline. Somehow, someway, they lost their confidence in God's provision.

I am convinced that, at some critical juncture in life, we are put to the supreme test by being called to surrender to God that which is most dear to us. A relationship. A deal. A habit. A possession. Only when God is most dear to us can we fully experience the greatness of life with him. In Gen 22, Abraham found himself facing this very test.

Before you read any further, I'd like to ask you to do something I believe will be very helpful. Open to Gen 22 in your Bible and before reading it, pray this prayer: "Heavenly Father, please bring clearly to my attention those things that I have not yet fully surrendered to you." As you read the text, consider the value and affection Abraham felt for his beloved son Isaac. Imagine his pain as he placed this son on the altar of sacrifice. Reflect on how willing Abraham was to surrender the one thing dearest to him if it meant greater obedience to God. Too often, we read Scripture in order to see how it applies to everyone else except ourselves. But this is a painfully personal narrative, one that summons us to reflect inwardly, examine our true spiritual selves (2 Cor 13:5), and judge whether we have sincerely surrendered all to the lordship of Christ.

The Hebrew phrase *lek leka* acts as a pair of bookends to Abraham's story. It occurs in 12:1 when God commanded him to "Go from…" It appears again in 22:2 when God commanded him to "Go to…" but it occurs nowhere else in the OT, "strongly suggesting that the narrator intends his audience to see the frame."[15]

---

15. Waltke, *Genesis*, 301.

The narrative opens by telling us that God intended to test Abraham, something he would later do for Israel (Deut 8:2; Judg 3:4). The translation of the KJV, that God tempted Abraham, is not correct, "for God ... tempts no one" (Jas 1:13). Learning as we do that God was testing the patriarch should shift our focus away from our concern for Isaac's life to concern for Abraham's faith. Too often, a newcomer reads the text, wondering, "Oh no! Does Isaac survive?" when it should be asked, "Oh no! Will Abraham obey?"[16] Even in the worst-case scenario, sincere faith is more valuable than long life in God's economy (Matt 16:25).

It is a maxim of the life of faith: "God *tests* every person who would receive eternal life."[17] As he did with Abraham, God also did with Moses and Israel, with David and Elijah, with Jeremiah and Daniel, with Peter and Paul, and even Jesus. He tests us in order to help us fear him and keep us from sin (Exod 20:20), to reveal what is in our heart (Deut 8:2; 2 Chr 32:31), and to build our faith to the point that we will respond with "praise and glory and honor" when Jesus comes again (1 Pet 1:7). When he tests us, God is not hidden away, observing us behind one-way mirrors like a research scientist conducting experiments. Rather, he equips us to withstand the test and brings us safely through the storm (1 Cor 10:13).[18]

The Lord made an inconceivable request of Abraham. "Take your son, your only son, whom you love—Isaac—and go to the region of Moriah. Sacrifice him there as a burnt offering on a mountain I will show you" (22:2 NIV). The enormity of what God was asking of Abraham is underscored by the triple designation of his son: "your son, your only son, whom you love—Isaac." "With astonishing and unmistakable clarity, God makes it impossible to misunderstand or redirect the imperative."[19]

Isaac's designation as Abraham's "only son" should arrest our attention and

---

16. "The focal point of this story is not the danger to Isaac but the danger to Abraham in his relationship to God," (Ibid., 304).

17. James Burton Coffman, *Commentary on Genesis* (Abilene, TX: ACU Press, 1985), 291–92; emphasis his.

18. "God's proving does not mean that He stands by, watching how His child will behave. He helps us to sustain the trial to which He subjects us," (Maclaren, *Genesis*, 153).

19. Arnold, *Genesis*, 203. The rabbis fabricated an exchange between God and Abraham that fostered this triple designation of Isaac. God said, "Take your son." Abraham replied, "Which son?" "Your only son." Abraham responded, "This one is the only son of his mother, and that one is the only son of his mother." "Whom you love," God answered. "I love them both." "Isaac," God finally says (Gen Rab 55:7).

give us pause. The OT prophets used the phrase "mourning as for an only son" (Jer 6:26; Amos 8:10; Zech 12:10) as a euphemism for the deepest expression of grief. The death of an only son wasn't just the death of a beloved child, but "the end of the family line," and was thus considered "a terrible catastrophe."[20] Abraham had loved Ishmael and been quite reluctant to dismiss him. How much more so would Isaac's certain doom be the capstone on his life of grief? Surely this was too much for God to ask of the patriarch. But Abraham realized that only when we have surrendered what is most valuable to us, making God the sole Author of our story, can we fully experience the glory of life with the Lord.

Abraham was ordered to journey to "the land of Moriah," and Mt. Moriah is later said to be the future site of the Temple (2 Chr 3:1; Josephus, *Antiquities* 1.226); Jerusalem is indeed about a two- or three-day journey (about fifty miles) from Beersheba. In addition, Moriah is known after this story as "the mountain of the LORD" (22:14 NIV), a designation that elsewhere in Scripture only applies to Sinai (Num 10:33) and Jerusalem (Ps 24:3; Isa 2:3; Zech 8:3). But considering the fact that Jerusalem has already been called "Salem" in Gen 14, one wonders why it should be considered the same as "the land of Moriah" in this chapter.[21]

As narrator, Moses makes clear that Abraham did not delay in obeying the divine command. But he is silent as to Abraham's emotional state. Surely the patriarch had to be upset, but why are his feelings not specifically expressed? Walton points out, "There is sufficient emotional drama in the scenario alone—the narrator does not have to build it up literarily,"[22] and I believe he's right. Imagine receiving such a special child of promise, only to face the prospect of losing him forever. Imagine the many years of anticipation for something so precious, only to lose it almost as soon as you had received it. "Isaac is the child of the promise. In him every saving thing that God has promised to do is invested and guaranteed. The point here is not a natural gift, not even the highest, but

---

20. NIDOTTE 2:435. "In ancient Hebrew mentality, Abraham is being called to sacrifice more than just his son; he is really being called to sacrifice himself, his very future. ... For some inexplicable reason, God is recalling the heart of the promise," (Rick R. Marrs, "Sacrificing Our Future (Genesis 22)," *ResQ* 29 [1987]: 48).

21. In spite of this final concern, I agree with T. C. Mitchell's conclusion: "There is no need to doubt therefore that Abraham's sacrifice took place on the site of later Jerusalem, if not on the Temple hill," ("Moriah," NBD 783).

22. Walton, *Genesis*, 511.

rather the disappearance from Abraham's life of the whole promise."[23]

As the fateful party neared Moriah, the narrator intentionally slows the pace of the storytelling. He does this that we might reflect on how grave an act Abraham is about to commit, and one borne of his faith in God. An affectionate father is about to sacrifice the life of his so-very-special son.

Questions arise in our minds as we read this story. How old were Abraham and Isaac on this occasion? Was Sarah ever told of God's command? Why did Abraham tell his servants that both he and Isaac would return (22:5)? Was it out of faith that God would not actually make him go through with the act? Or did he simply not want to arouse any suspicions? And what did Isaac think of all this?[24] His question in 22:7 is a valid and innocent one; Abraham's reply had to have left him wondering. "God will provide for himself the lamb for a burnt offering."

Once on the mountain, Abraham and his son went about preparing the sacrifice. We would have to conclude that Isaac was quite dense if we assume he was unaware of his role in this drama. He seems to have willingly allowed himself to be bound and placed upon the altar. And here we have a startling picture of Abraham prepared not simply to stab his son and then walk away to be alone in his grief. No, he is prepared to "slaughter" (22:10) his son as one would a sacrificial animal (e.g. Lev 1:5; 3:2; 4:4; 7:2)—to disembowel Isaac as if he were an ox from Abraham's herd. Such is the depth of the patriarch's commitment to obey his God.

But then Abraham heard a voice, and a most blessed one. It was the same voice that had commanded him to make this journey. It now ordered him to stand down. And just as that voice spoke, a sacrificial ram caught Abraham's eye. There would be a sacrifice offered this day, but it would be a substitutionary one. So overwhelmed was he with this turn of events that Abraham marked this mountain with the Hebrew words *yhwh yireh*—"Yahweh will provide." The patriarch had named a well in the chapter previous. He now renamed a mountain, and in so doing spawned a proverb that became famous in ancient Israel. "To this day it is said, 'On the mountain of the LORD it will be provided'" (22:14 NIV).

I wonder if, on this occasion, God revealed to Abraham his great plan to redeem the world, specifically the suffering of Christ on that same location many, many years later. In John 8:56, Jesus said quite cryptically, "Your father Abraham rejoiced at the thought of seeing my day; he saw it and was glad." "This 'day' may

---

23. Von Rad, *Genesis*, 244.

24. Tradition holds that, upon their return home, Isaac gave his father a brochure about the local assisted-living facility called "Beth Zaqen."

have been a reference to the coming of the Messiah to make the perfect sacrifice. It may be that at that moment at Moriah God allowed Abraham to see more of the divine plan [i.e. the scheme of redemption] than the text has put into words."[25]

If this Mt. Moriah was indeed the future site of Solomon's Temple, then the ram as a substitute sacrifice foreshadowed the substitutionary atonement of animal sacrifices that dominated the OT beginning with Leviticus. The only other places where "burnt offering," "ram," and "to see/provide" all occur in the same passage are Lev 8–9 (the ordination of priests) and Lev 16 (the Day of Atonement). For centuries, faithful men of Israel brought animals to the Tabernacle and Temple to be offered in their place. When the animal was slaughtered and burned upon the altar, the Israelites were reminded that their sins came at the cost of life. They also called out to God to "see" the sacrifice and make provision for atonement. And the proper response to this reconciliation was faith—a faith that caused one to "revere [God] as sovereign, trust him implicitly, and obey him without question or protest."[26]

The ram (and by extension, Isaac) also foreshadowed a dark day two millennia later when God offered up his own special and unique Son upon an altar of sacrifice. As Isaac had been compelled to do, God also laid wood on the back of his Son and made him carry it to the place of sacrifice (John 19:17).[27] And as was the case in Gen 22, this sacrifice had to do with God's provision—a necessary and substitutionary atonement for our sins (John 1:29). A ram took Isaac's place. Jesus took ours.

The NT considers faith to be a proper response to what God did for us in Christ. Faith is not a cerebral acknowledgement of God's existence; that is not biblical faith. One does not "believe in God" as if he were Santa Claus or the Tooth Fairy. Rather, biblical faith considers uninterrupted fellowship with God as the most valuable thing one can possess. Biblical faith manifests itself by submission to God's sovereignty, confidence in his provision, and obedience to his authority.

Relationships? They are subjected to God's authority, fully convinced that love lost can be found again by God's grace.

---

25. Ross, "Genesis," 143.

26. Ibid., 142.

27. Concerning Isaac carrying the wood up the mountain (22:6), the rabbis commented, "It is like one who carries his own cross on his shoulder" (Gen Rab 56:3), an absolutely remarkable statement for a group of people who rejected Jesus as their Messiah and once-for-all substitutionary atonement.

Success? It is subjected to God's authority, fully convinced that God's definition of success has less to do with achieving material gain and more with discovering endless fellowship with him.

Bad habits? They too are subjected to God's authority. Resorting to our own devices and efforts in order to meet our needs is never a good idea. Instead, we trust that any need God has given to us, he will also meet, for he has sworn to supply our needs in Christ (Phil 4:19). It's why the Christian doesn't have to pitch a fit to get attention or have a drink in order to relax. It's because God provides. Always and forever, he provides.

This one truth is what I believe Abraham was clinging to as he journeyed to Moriah and told his servants he and Isaac would return. It's what he trusted in as he ascended the mountain and prepared to slaughter his son. Biblical faith, the faith of Abraham, believes God will remember his promises, even when God's promises and God's will seem hopelessly at odds with one another.[28] Biblical faith believes that God gives, God takes away, and that God can restore again.[29] Biblical faith believes that God alone provides.

Somehow, someway, always and forever—God provides.

And if we ever doubt that great reality, we need only look back to Golgotha and the heartbreaking slaughter of a special, promised Son—one who, more so than Isaac, was obedient to the point of death (Phil 2:8; cf. Heb 5:8). Just as Satan deceived Adam and Eve, the prince of this world wishes to convince us that God is holding out on us. That God is cruel or mean. That God is not interested in providing for our needs. That he is keeping us from true happiness. That we must seize the reins in order to discover the satisfaction for which our hearts long. But the apostle Paul exposed these lies: "He who did not spare his own Son, but gave him up for us all—how will he not also, along with him, graciously give us all things?" (Rom 8:32 NIV).

Let me ask again: How will he not graciously give us all things?

And how can we but respond in kind?

---

28. "Though he [Abraham] knew not how, still he held by the hope that somehow God would not forget His promise. ... So he goes straight on the road marked for him, quite sure that it will not end in a blind alley, from which there is no exit. That is the very climax of faith—to trust God so absolutely, even when His ways seem contradictory, as to be more willing to believe apparent impossibilities than to doubt Him, and to be therefore ready for the hardest trial of obedience," (Maclaren, *Genesis*, 156–57).

29. Hamilton, *The Book of Genesis: Chapters 18–50*, 108.

Take a moment to step back from Abraham's life and appreciate how far he has come. In the beginning, he showed great promise by following God to Canaan. But in so many other ways, he struggled to trust in the promises of God. Until Gen 22, the patriarch's life had been characterized by as many failures as successes. Which, now that I mention it, makes me wonder about the legitimacy of Paul's statement concerning Abraham, "He did not waver through unbelief regarding the promise of God" (Rom 4:20 NIV). In the next verse, Paul adds that Abraham was "fully convinced that God was able to do what he had promised" (4:21). I'm not in the habit of disagreeing with inspired writers, but Paul seems to be fuzzy on the facts. Have we not seen clear examples of Abraham's numerous failings in faith? Have we not seen indisputable evidence that he did waver, that he did doubt that God had power to do what he promised? How do we reconcile Abraham's life with Paul's words?

Perhaps an old woodsmen's proverb can resolve this tension. As he was authoring his famous biography on the life of Abraham Lincoln, Carl Sandburg searched in vain for an appropriate title for the chapter detailing with the immediate aftermath of Lincoln's assassination. What one phrase could adequately express the aftermath of that dark moment in our nation's history? Sandburg was at a loss until he discovered this old woodsmen's proverb: "A tree is best measured when it's down."[30]

The Bible encourages the people of God to live every moment as if it will be our last. Death could come at any moment. *Jesus* could come at any moment. Both Paul and Peter described the Lord's return as a thief in the night (1 Thess 5:2; 2 Pet 3:10); in light of this, Peter then asked, "What kind of people ought you to be? You ought to live holy and godly lives" (2 Pet 3:11 NIV). If my relationship with God is not what it should be, Scripture implores me to make it right immediately. "The 'right time' is now," Paul exhorted, "the 'day of salvation' is now" (2 Cor 6:2 NCV).

On the other hand, God looks at our lives with a wide-angle lens, not a telephoto zoom. The final verdict will not be rendered on our life until the end of our life. Our tree will not be measured until it's lying down. God did not strike Abraham dead when he first lied about his relationship with Sarah, nor did he send fire from heaven when Ishmael was conceived. Rather, God sought to create in Abraham, to borrow a phrase from Friedrich Nietzsche, "a long obedience in the same direction." The life of faith is a marathon, not a sprint.

---

30. Carl Sandburg, *Abraham Lincoln: The War Years* (New York: Scribner's, 1950), 6:357.

Have you stumbled? Pause and regain your balance.

Have you fallen? Get up. The race is not over.

This is why Paul could write concerning Abraham, "He did not waver through unbelief regarding the promise of God," and that the patriarch was "fully convinced that God was able to do what he had promised." Paul could write those words because this was the divine verdict when Abraham's tree was measured lying down. After Abraham left Moriah, the place where he had almost sacrificed his son to God, we do not read of the patriarch ever having another failure in his faith. Though it took him more than a hundred years to get there, Abraham finally learned that God provides, that he will do what he has promised. The patriarch learned that it is God who supplies all of our needs (Phil 4:19). He discovered that, while "some trust in chariots and some in horses," the people of God "trust in the name of the LORD our God" (Ps 20:7).

T he final few verses of the chapter concern the growth of Abraham's extended family. They have not been mentioned since Abraham left them behind in Haran at the beginning of Gen 12. But here he receives word that his brother Nahor had been blessed with a dozen sons. Among them was Bethuel, who had fathered a daughter, Rebekah. The stage is thus set for a transition from Abraham's life to Isaac's.

But first, a requiem...

GENESIS 23

The death of the Hebrew matriarch was a sad, yet significant event. It reminds us that not even the covenant family was immune from the curse of death. Sarah is the only woman in Scripture whose life span is given at her death: 127 years. When she passed away at Kiriath-arba, apparently an older name for the site later known as Hebron (Josh 14:15), the text says Abraham mourned and wept for her. Biblical customs concerning grief entailed various combinations of fasting, tearing of garments, disheveling or shaving one's hair or beard, throwing dirt on the head, and sitting in ashes (cf. 2 Sam 1:11–12; 13:31; Ezra 9:3; Job 1:20; 2:12; Ezek 27:30). Abraham no doubt engaged in at least some, if not all, of these practices in order to mark his beloved's passing.

It was then that he approached the local Hittites to secure a burial place.

Custom of the day required that a person be buried in the ancestral homeland[31] (cf. 49:29; 50:25). But by burying Sarah in Canaan, Abraham was boldly declaring this new land to be his home just as God had promised. Abraham was not negotiating for a place to dig a hole in the ground; caves were used as resting places for the remains of family members. "Bodies would be laid out on rock shelves until nothing remained but the bones, at which point the bones would either be cleared to the back of the tomb or relocated into a container of some sort to make room for another body."[32]

The Hittites' offer to allow Abraham to bury his dead in any of their tombs (23:6) seems gracious, but it could be a cover for something else. One interpretative option is to say that they wanted to haggle the purchase price.[33] But it is also true that people of the ANE were often reluctant to sell their land to outsiders. Naboth's oath to Ahab was the prevailing sentiment: "The LORD forbid that I should give you the inheritance of my ancestors" (1 Kgs 21:3 NIV). Ephron's offer of the land as a free gift may have been "to prevent Abraham from acquiring ownership of land. This proposition is not too startling: Abraham is a 'stranger and sojourner', and many societies show reluctance to allow a foreigner to acquire land, short of actually forbidding it outright."[34] He isn't a native, so he shouldn't own land. Either way, it is highly unlikely the Hittites, or Ephron, intended to give anything to Abraham for free.

But the patriarch proved persistent and seemingly didn't blink when Ephron named his price. It's impossible for us to know for sure the exact value of Abraham's 400 shekels of silver, but the price seems exorbitant. By means of comparison, the standard annual wage of a laborer at this time was a mere ten

31. Ross, "Genesis," 145.

32. ZIBBCOT 1:99.

33. "Those who have made purchases from a Near Eastern market will recognize that the initial offer, 'I will give it to you,' is not a serious suggestion but a way of opening the haggling," (McKeown, Genesis, 120). Arnold specifically notes several parallels between this passage and ancient/modern methods of haggling (Genesis, 211–12).

34. Raymond Westbrook, Property and the Family in Biblical Law (Sheffield: Sheffield Academic, 1991), 28–29. Some ancient societies may have indeed forbidden this practice outright; from correspondence between Niqmepa king of Ugarit and Hattusili III king of Ura (a city of the Hittites), it seems merchants from Ura were forbidden from purchasing real estate in Ugarit (Cyrus H. Gordon, "Abraham and the Merchants of Ura," JNES 17 [1958]: 28).

shekels.[35] David purchased the threshing floor of Araunah and oxen to sacrifice there for a total of fifty silver shekels (2 Sam 24:24); Jeremiah purchased a field from his cousin for 17 shekels (Jer 32:9). If he had wanted to save the money, Abraham would have had the option to lease the land, but he instead wanted to pay the full price so as to secure the land for himself and his descendants in perpetuity.[36] The sale was thereby indubitable.

This passage reads much like a typical real estate transaction record from antiquity. The Hebrew phrase translated "according to the weights current among the merchants" is almost identical to that used in other ANE contracts, as is the explicit stipulation that the trees be included in the sale.[37] Such tells us that this chapter has importance beyond being an account of the burial of the great Hebrew matriarch.

Realize that this cave will be the first and only plot of land owned by Abraham.[38] That's it—a cemetery! And that sole detail is the perfect capstone to Abraham's journey of faith. His call to leave Haran had begun with a promise of land, one reiterated when Lot separated (Gen 13), and reiterated yet again after defeating Chedorlaomer in battle. God had elaborately sworn that he would give this land to Abraham and his descendants, albeit after 400 years (Gen 15). And the patriarch had responded to that promise in faith.

So much faith, in fact, that he was willing to pay a ridiculous price for a field so that he could bury his wife in this promised land and thereby renounce his citizenship in the one he had left behind. In buying this cave, the patriarch was saying to God, "Lord, I believe you will indeed give this plot of ground, and much more, to my posterity." Abraham expressed his faith with a burial. God would fulfill his promise with a resurrection (Heb 11:39–40).

---

35. Walton, *Genesis*, 529.

36. On the phrase "full price" in 23:9, Waltke comments that it "is likely a legal term signifying full payment for an irrevocable sale. The term has been considered the equivalent of common Sumerian and Akkadian (and more rarely Ugaritic) legal terms, which indicated that a sale was for cash and final. These terms always accompanied clauses establishing the sale's irrevocability," (*Genesis*, 319).

37. Gene M. Tucker, "The Legal Background of Genesis 23," *JBL* 85 (1966): 77–84.

38. The well at Beersheba scarcely counts as a plot of land.

TALKING POINTS

I s it a violation of biblical principles to enter into contractual agreements with non-believers? Sandwiched between the gift of a son and the call to give up that son, we find that Abraham entered into a covenant with Abimelech. Was this a violation of his faith? The likely answer is no since he later praised God for being faithful (21:33). Likewise, it is not necessarily a violation of faith to enter into similar agreements today. But we should nonetheless always monitor ourselves lest our confidence be in the wrong things. A contract and the security it provides can tempt us to misplace that confidence, and Scripture warns us time and again: "Don't trust in man" (cf. Pss 33:16–18; 127:1; 146:3; Isa 2:22; Jer 17:5; John 15:5). I admit it is borderline ludicrous even to suggest contracts are sinful. But at the same time, Christians have an obligation to guard against anything that could undermine their faith in God. Paul gave us the principle, "Whatever does not proceed from faith is sin" (Rom 14:23). Therefore, if I were convicted that an activity would prompt me to trust man and not God, Scripture would have me steer clear, no matter how innocent others may think that activity to be (cf. Prov 3:5–6; Matt 4:3–4).

I n July 2012, President Barack Obama elicited a backlash from political opponents and conservative business owners when he said to an audience in Roanoke, Virginia: "If you've got a business—you didn't build that. Somebody else made that happen." The words "You didn't build that" quickly went viral on social media. Now, for the record, I don't believe that government deserves much credit for the success of hard-working people. But neither do I believe that *hard-working people* deserve much credit for the success of hard-working people. Biblical faith demands we acknowledge God as the source of all blessings (Jas 1:17). As Israel prepared to enter the Promised Land, Moses was concerned the nation would forget what it was like to depend on God's provision as they had done for forty years via daily manna. "Beware lest you say in your heart, 'My power and the might of my hand have gotten me this wealth.' You shall remember the LORD your God, for it is he who gives you power to get wealth" (Deut 8:17–18). Translation: "You didn't build that; God did." This principle is important because only when we acknowledge God as the source of our blessings (including those things most valuable to us) can we surrender those blessings to him. The text makes abundantly clear how ridiculous it would be to suggest Isaac's conception was a natural event. He was unequivocally God's blessing to Abraham and Sarah. And since God was the Author of Isaac's life, Abraham believed he could sacrifice Isaac at God's command, convinced "that God was able even to raise him from the dead" (Heb 11:19). If you are having difficulty surrendering to God what is most valuable to you, perhaps you have never acknowledged it as coming from him to begin with. But when you come to the place where your faith allows you to withhold nothing, your eyes are then opened to see the glorious things God can do with your life as he continues unfolding his epic.

E ver since I first considered it, I have planned to be cremated at death. It repulses me to see the lengths our culture goes to in order to make the body appear alive: nice clothes, makeup, perfumed funeral parlors. Cremation certainly offers a much more economical alternative. But after reading Gen 23, I wonder if cremation declares something wholly incompatible with the biblical doctrine of the afterlife. Scripture does not give definitive guidance as to how we are to dispose of the dead. Some in the Bible were cremated (e.g. Achan, Josh 7:25), but most of those individuals were under God's curse. Albert Mohler writes, "The early church rejected the pagan practice of cremation because of a belief that the body is to be respected. The early Christians observed the Roman pattern of cremation and agreed that it represented an intentional destruction of the human body — a belief that conflicted with the believers' understanding that death was to be understood as sleep, and that the dead are awaiting the resurrection to come."[39] Our word "cemetery" comes from the Greek *koimeterion* and the Latin *coemeteria*, both literally meaning "sleeping place." I have absolutely no intention to call into question the salvation of those who were cremated in the past. But this point is nonetheless worthy of further consideration. By burying his beloved Sarah in Canaan, rather than in their homeland, Abraham boldly asserted his faith in the promises of God. So we also, by being interred in the earth, declare our faith in the promises of God, including his oath that death is not the end (John 11:25), that there will one day be a resurrection (John 5:28–29), and that "we will be with the Lord forever" (1 Thess 4:17 NIV). What a day, glorious day, that will be.

---

39. R. Albert Mohler, Jr., "Cremation Gains Ground in Colorado — Why?" entry posted June 6, 2005, http://www.albertmohler.com/2005/06/06/cremation-gains-ground-in-colorado-why (accessed July 31, 2012).

10

TO BE CONTINUED...

As this book was nearing its final stages, my wife and I learned a bit of very-unexpected news: she was pregnant. Since then, we have been on the typical roller coaster all first-time expectant parents experience, and I don't expect the roller coaster to ever end. Questions such as "What should I eat while I'm pregnant?" and "What's the safest carrier, stroller, and crib?" turn into "What are the best schools" and "Should I make my kids join Boy Scouts/play sports/learn a musical instrument?" Good parents are always seeking a better future for their kids. It's why they push them to eat their vegetables, do their homework, and brush their teeth.

But Christian parents should also be concerned about their child's spiritual development, and according to statistics that have been released over the last few decades, it is becoming increasingly challenging to raise faithful kids in today's world. How can Christian parents successfully pass down their faith to their children? My dad left me a rich heritage of walking with the Lord—how can I ensure that such a legacy continues with my kids, that they enjoy more of God's blessings than I did? As my wife and I prepare to welcome our first child into the world, these are my questions, and I don't think I'm alone.

So far in Genesis, the focus has been primarily on the story of Abraham. But the life of the patriarch is winding down, and the covenant promises are about to pass to the next generation. As any parent can relate, the reader is confronted with several questions at this juncture. Will God be as faithful to Isaac as he had been to Abraham? Will Isaac enjoy as many covenant blessings as his father? And what of Isaac's relationship with God? Will he be as faithful as his father? What if he does not marry well? Will the immoral influence of the neighboring

Canaanites consume this unique heir of Abraham as it had Lot, the patriarch's nephew? This section of Genesis narrates how God's plan continued to unfold within the covenant family.

The narrative of Gen 24 is especially a Janus of sorts. It is a beautiful epilogue to the story of Abraham: whereas the patriarch had struggled to trust God in the past, he seems very much at ease surrendering the marriage of his son to divine providence. But this story also shifts the spotlight to the next generation of promise. As we will discover, yes, Isaac marries well. Yes, God's promises and providence continue with him. But so also do the failures of faith his father experienced, which simply underscores the fact that God is faithful in all things.

GENESIS 24

This chapter is the longest in Genesis, but it is also among the most touching. We are presented with a father committed to finding a godly wife for his son, a servant committed to honoring his master's wishes, a young woman committed to leaving her family behind if it means doing God's will, and a young man in need of comfort following his mother's death.

It is also in this chapter that we observe the mysterious dance between divine sovereignty and human responsibility. Is God directing the events? The text says so definitively. But what part does the obedient servant and the willing Rebekah play in the "success" of God's providence?

Abraham is, at this point, 140 years old; he will live for another 35 years, but he did not know that. The text makes clear in no uncertain terms that he is a blessed man. So how does a blessed man behave when there is one final concern before death? Scripture answers that question for us: he trusts unequivocally in the providence of God. Abraham's wealth is a prominent feature in this chapter (cf. 24:10, 22, 30, 35, 36, 47, 53), and he gave the command to use his wealth in whatever way necessary to secure for Isaac a good wife. The patriarch had no pretension of hanging on to his wealth indefinitely, or of taking it with him in death. Nor did he intend to spend it on himself (the RV bumper sticker "I'm spending my kid's inheritance" comes to mind). Rather, Abraham became the father of all those determined to spend their wealth to further the purposes of God.

For a special mission, the patriarch called to his side "his servant, the oldest of his household" (24:2), and this has been commonly assumed to be Eliezer, the servant mentioned in 15:2. However, we cannot be sure since the servant remains anonymous throughout the narrative.

Abraham did not want Isaac to marry a Canaanite woman because of their immoral values. Esau would later displease Isaac by doing this (26:35). Not only was this Abraham's desire, but he also believed it was God's will. "The patriarchal fear of such contact with foreigners was not xenophobia but a justified bulwark against corrupting religious influences," (Judg 3:5–7).[1] So the patriarch was convinced an angel would go with his servant and direct events to a favorable end. "Abraham is so confident that Yahweh will direct the mission, he releases the servant from the oath altogether if either Yahweh's angel or the young woman should fail to cooperate."[2]

Abraham's request for his servant to swear to him with his hand on Abraham's thigh (cf. 47:29) seems odd to those of us accustomed to simply raising our right hand and placing the other on a Bible. In effect, the servant was expressing his understanding that the perpetuation of Abraham's family was dependent upon the success of the servant's mission. He was to be faithful to his master beyond death, for it was not an oath to Abraham alone, but to all his posterity. Obscene as it may sound, Abraham was asking his servant to place his hand just under the patriarch's genitals; the word translated "thigh" in this passage (Hebrew *yarek*) can mean "descendants" (46:26; Exod 1:5; Judg 8:30) in that they come from the "thigh." This method of swearing an oath is also attested outside the OT.[3]

Abraham's last recorded utterances in Scripture come in 24:6–8. Pause and ponder the faith exemplified in these words: concern for his son's spiritual welfare, commitment to the promises of God, conviction in the providence of God. Abraham has come a long way from his first words in Scripture, which were expressions of doubt (15:2, 8).

Thus the servant set out on his mission, and nothing is said about the actual journey, one that would have taken at least a month. The mention of camels, however, merits comment. The presence of camels in the patriarchal narratives of Genesis has led several scholars to question whether (at best) their presence is anachronistic, or (at worst) this story is inauthentic. Historical evidence indicates that camels were not widely used until the 12th century B.C., but they served as beasts of burden in very small, exclusive, and wealthy circles as early

---

1.   Mathews, *Genesis 11:27–50:26*, 600.

2.   Arnold, *Genesis*, 220.

3.   Meir Malul, "Touching the Sexual Organs As an Oath Ceremony in an Akkadian Letter," *VT* 37 (1987): 491–92.

as 3000 B.C. Babylonian texts (c. 2000–1700) corroborate their domestication in Abraham's day,[4] but their ownership would have been a mark of wealth and prestige at that point,[5] not unlike "status symbols" in our culture that lose their prestige once they gain widespread adoption.

Arriving at the well in the city of Nahor, the servant began to beseech the God of Abraham. His prayer expresses remarkable faith in God. "Nothing is more characteristic of biblical man than a profound and pervasive conviction about the role of divine Providence in everyday human affairs."[6] He essentially asks God to make his will known through a verifiable sign, and that is exactly what happens! In fact, so remarkable is God's faithfulness and providence that he began revealing his will "before [the servant] had finished speaking" (24:15; cf. Isa 65:24).

The sign the servant sought wasn't really a conspicuous miracle (cf. Judg 6:36–40), but a noted oddity (cf. 1 Sam 6:7–12)—something in the realm of possibility, but unlikely at the same time. One thirsty camel having gone several days without water can drink as much as 25 gallons of water, meaning Rebekah would have drawn her pitcher 80–100 times to satisfy all ten.[7] And since it would have taken each camel at least ten minutes to drink its allotted amount,[8] this chore would have taken almost two hours!

Rebekah is described as both attractive and a virgin—a perfect match for the chosen son of Abraham. The gold ring and bracelets the servant gave to her would have been worth tens of thousands of dollars (ten *silver* shekels was an average annual salary, and gold was more valuable), which may have represented the bride price due her family.

The genealogy of 22:20–24 already informed us that Abraham's brother Nahor had fathered a son named Bethuel, who in turn had fathered a daughter named Rebekah. When the servant realized God had providentially led him to Abraham's family as the source of Isaac's wife, he was overjoyed and offered up

---

4. Lawrence, "Zoology," DOTP 917.

5. "It is likely that the domesticated camel at first spread very slowly and long remained a rarity. A wealthy man might acquire a few as a prestige symbol for ornamental rather than utilitarian purposes. This would explain their presence in Abraham's entourage, their nonuse as beasts of burden, and their special mention in situations where wealth and honor need to be displayed, as, for instance, in Genesis 24," (Sarna, *Genesis*, 96).

6. Ibid., 164.

7. ZIBBCOT 1:101.

8. Sarna, *Genesis*, 164.

praise. It is notable that he gave thanks for Yahweh's "steadfast love" (24:27), the term used throughout the OT for God's covenant love for his people (Isa 54:10). In other words, the servant praised Yahweh for being faithful to his covenant with Abraham.

From here, the narrative moves quickly before slowing down again. Rebekah "ran" to tell her family what had happened, and her brother Laban "ran" to greet the man at the spring. The sight of such expensive jewelry on his sister told Laban that a very wealthy suitor was vying for her hand in marriage; as we will see later in his dealings with Jacob, Laban never outgrew his greed. In the ANE, it was not uncommon for the brother to negotiate the marriage of his sister (rather than the parents), and Laban certainly assumed that role in this narrative, while Rebekah's parents seem to be secondary participants at best (cf. 24:50, 55).

It may be that we are intended to see a comparison between the hospitality shown Abraham's servant and the hospitality Abraham/Lot gave their divine visitors in Gen 18–19. The family of Rebekah rolled out the red carpet for their guests. But Abraham's servant was still overwhelmed at this point with the sovereign providence of God, and he refuses to eat his food until he was allowed to recount the story so far.

Much of the chapter's length is due partly to the sixteen verses in which Abraham's servant rehearses the story (24:34–49), though he tactfully leaves out Abraham's prohibiting Isaac from making the trip. Why raise questions in Laban's mind that could lead to an uncomfortable conversation? This section is not simply repeated for redundancy's sake; repetition in Hebrew literature "elevates and intensifies the suspense of the narrative and anticipates a resolution."[9] God has providentially led the servant to Rebekah. Will her parents and brother consent to her marrying Isaac? Will they consign her to living so far away? Will they trust this stranger who has come laden with expensive gifts?

Rebekah's family responded favorably to the servant's words. Though they were not monotheistic (Josh 24:2), I don't agree with Walton's contention "that Abraham's relatives are no more monotheistic than the Canaanites. They are not worshipers of Yahweh."[10] This is a bold assertion since Laban and Bethuel interpreted these events as being directed by Yahweh (24:50–51; cf. Acts 5:38–39). They may have been worshipers of the moon god, but they were also reverent of Abraham's God. In his later dealings with Jacob, Laban still exhibited a healthy fear of the Lord.

---

9. Arnold, *Genesis*, 223.

10. Walton, *Genesis*, 529.

The servant and Rebekah departed the next morning; the nurse that accompanied her is later identified as Deborah (35:8). The servant knew that the God of his master Abraham had blessed his journey thus far, so he did not want to tarry any longer in returning to the patriarch lest he lose that blessing. Rebekah is also to be commended for her willingness to travel such a long distance to marry Isaac. In the ANE, for a woman to leave her family and travel so far to marry was to incur considerable risk. What if her husband was abusive or divorced her once she proved barren?[11] The latter, as it turns out, would be Rebekah's lot for twenty years.

At the end of the narrative, we learn that Isaac was dwelling in the Negeb at this point, and it was his habit in the evenings "to meditate in the field" (24:63). The Hebrew *suah* ("meditated") is difficult to translate since the word occurs only here, and there have been no less than 63 options proposed. It was not until the Latin Vulgate that Isaac was said to have been meditating, and this understanding is now prominent in English translations, though Isaac could have simply been "walking" (cf. HCSB, NJB, NRSV). The rabbis believed him to be praying (Gen Rab 60:14). But in comparing the word to similar ones used elsewhere (Job 7:11; Pss 55:17; 77:4, 6), it may mean "to complain, lament."[12] Isaac was going out into the fields in the evenings to lament before God the death of his mother Sarah. The arrival of Rebekah, then, is portrayed as a significant provision of divine comfort. Her veiling herself as she met Isaac was her way of identifying herself as his bride-to-be.

A s I reflected on this chapter, it occurred to me how important it is that we go about our daily responsibilities as if they matter a great deal in the grand scheme of things. I don't mean in a compulsive, unhealthy way. But Jesus spoke of our being faithful in small things (Luke 16:10–12), and we become better instruments in the hands of Providence when we are faithful in the seemingly mundane events of life. The tone we take with friends, the courtesy we show our waiter, the choices we make as to how to spend our time or money—these can prove vitally important in our efforts to enlarge the boundaries of God's kingdom. If that seems far-fetched, consider the seeming insignificance of a

---

11. ZIBBCOT 1:102.

12. For this understanding of *suah*, see Gregory Vall, "What Was Isaac Doing in the Field (Genesis XXIV 63)?" *VT* 44 (1994): 513.

young woman who offered to draw water for a stranger and his ten thirsty camels. By her faithfulness in a small act of hospitality, Rebekah fulfilled the will of God and became a matriarch in the lineage of Christ. Divine sovereignty and human responsibility are like two pedals on a bike, and if we believe in the sovereignty and providence of God, we will act faithfully in as many ways possible in order to give him opportunities to bring glory to his own name.

GENESIS 25:1–11

Sometime after the death of Sarah, Abraham married a woman named Keturah (known in 25:6 and 1 Chr 1:32 as his concubine), and by her the patriarch fathered six sons. A handful of scholars believe this happened before Isaac was born;[13] their reasoning seems to be their difficulty in believing the patriarch could sire six sons past his 140th birthday, making these sons "even more supernatural than Isaac, which is theologically unlikely."[14] Point taken. But it would seem odd for the narrator to have not noted this in Gen 16–18. Additionally, what made Isaac theologically significant is that he was the elect son chosen by God to perpetuate the seed of woman and the covenant promises.

Of these sons and their descendants, most are unknown to history, and attempts by a few scholars to identity them often prove problematic. Many of these clans settled in northern Arabia on the fringes of the Negeb, but that's as much as we know for certain. But of the sixteen sons and grandsons that came from Keturah, here is how a few of them fit into latter developments in the OT. Nothing is known about Jokshan, but it's a different story concerning his son. Sheba became a nation in SW Arabia, and its queen visited Jerusalem during the reign of Solomon (1 Kgs 10:1–13). Sheba's brother, Dedan, also settled in Arabia. The place known as Dedan was "an important commercial settlement located at one of the major oases in NW Arabia."[15] It is assumed that the descendants of Dedan's three sons populated the place Dedan, but beyond that, very, very little is known about Asshurim, Letushim, and Leummim.

However, of Abraham's fourth son by Keturah, we know a good bit. The tribe of Midian is somewhat of an enigma in Scripture. They are portrayed as neutral traders later in the Joseph narrative (37:28), and Moses married into

---

13. Arnold, *Genesis*, 226; Sarna, *Genesis*, 172; Waltke, *Genesis*, 335.

14. Waltke, *Genesis*, 335.

15. Graf, "Dedan (Place)" ABD 2:121.

the family of Jethro, the priest of Midian (Exod 3:1). But in Numbers, the Midianites and Moabites conspired against Israel (22:4–7; 25:1–9; 31:1–54), and in the Judges period, they are the antagonists in the story of Gideon (Judg 6–8). Midian's first son, Ephah, may have gained notoriety as a camel breeder (cf. Isa 60:6), and Assyrian records from the time of Tiglath-pileser III and Sargon II mention Ephah as a tribe in NW Arabia.[16] Of Midian's other five sons, virtually nothing else is certain.

The sixth son of Abraham and Keturah was Shuah. One of Job's three friends is Bildad the Shuhite (Job 2:11). The land of Shuah may be the same as Suhu, "a country (and Assyrian province) on the middle Euphrates" and a summer pasture for Arabian tribes during the reign of the Assyrian king Sargon II (722–705 B.C.).[17]

Before he died, Abraham bequeathed all he had to Isaac. He had already sent Ishmael away at Sarah's behest. Now he sent his other six sons away "to the east country," i.e. "those desert areas on the eastern fringes of the land of Israel."[18] We can assume that he sent them away as regretfully as he had Ishmael; Abraham seems to have been a man with a lot of love for his family. He gave gifts to Keturah's six sons, which was extraordinarily generous since he technically owed them nothing. But the larger point is that he sent them away so that Isaac could receive everything and also dwell alone in the Promised Land. Even to his death, Abraham was committed to living out his faith in the promises of God.[19]

As was made clear in Gen 5, death is a fate from which none of us can escape, not even Abraham. But if we have to die, what better condition can we ask for than the one Abraham experienced? "It is one thing to live a long life. It is another thing to live a long life that is also a happy life."[20] The narrator says that the patriarch passed "at a ripe old age, old and contented, and he was gathered to his people" (25:8 HCSB). He had experienced many blessings and had become, by the power of God, "a father of many nations" (17:5 NIV). But Abraham died not having received all of God's blessings or realizing all of his promises. Even

---

16. Knauf, "Ephah (Person)," ABD 2:534.

17. Knauf, "Shuah," ABD 5:1226.

18. Wenham, Genesis 16–50, 160.

19. "Nothing disparaging is said about Keturah, the concubines, or their offspring, but there is a clear demarcation between them and Isaac," (McKeown, Genesis, 124).

20. Hamilton, The Book of Genesis: Chapters 18–50, 167.

now, those promises await a fulfillment at the end of time when you and I will be made perfect with Abraham (Heb 11:39–40).

Yet another of Genesis' "Hallmark moments" is narrated here. Though separated when they were just boys, Ishmael and Isaac had apparently stayed in contact. They now came together in peace to bury their beloved father beside the body of Sarah in the family cemetery, the cave of Machpelah. After the funeral, the narrator is careful to say that God began to bless Isaac as he had his father. In the previous chapter, we had been told that Isaac had dwelt for some time at Beer-lahai-roi before returning to the Negeb (24:62). Now he returned to Beer-lahai-roi, the place where God had previously heard and answered Hagar's prayer (16:14). As a man of prayer (24:63; 25:21), Isaac wanted to be in a place where he could commune with God and have his petitions heard.[21]

A s children, many of us learned the tune "Father Abraham and His Many Sons," a fun song sort of like a spiritualized Hokey-Pokey. One phrase of that song, however, always confused me until recently. Concerning Abraham's many sons, the song claims: "I am one of them, and so are you." I remember being six or seven and thinking, "How can I be a son of Abraham? My dad's name is Daniel!?" Only in my young adult years did I discover the truth. The apostle Paul claims that all those who abandon themselves to God, putting their faith solely in him, are children of Abraham and rightful heirs to all his promises (Rom 4:16).

The promise of property? On the other side of Jordan, God has prepared for you a land fairer than day. To Canaan's land, we're on our way! It is only by faith that we can see it afar, but it is real nonetheless. Jesus assured us that there was ample space in his Father's house to accommodate us all, and that he was returning to God's right hand to make final preparations (John 14:2–3). It is thus with eager anticipation that we await the coming of our Lord who will carry us beyond the Jordan where our faith will become sight.

The promise of prosperity? Abraham may have given small gifts to his other children before bequeathing everything to Isaac. But every child of God stands to inherit unspeakable riches in Christ Jesus (Phil 4:19), in whom is found every spiritual blessing (Eph 1:3). The Christian life will not necessarily bring health and wealth in this life; Jesus taught that his message was one at odds with the values of this world (cf. John 16:33; 1 John 3:13). But what the child of God

---

21. Ross, "Genesis," 153.

may lack in material things is more than compensated by "the surpassing worth of knowing Christ Jesus" (Phil 3:8). Only in Christ can a man be a pauper, yet inherit a kingdom.

The promise of protection?

> Who will bring any charge against those whom God has chosen? ... Who then is the one who condemns? ... Who shall separate us from the love of Christ? Shall trouble or hardship or persecution or famine or nakedness or danger or sword? ... No, in all these things we are more than conquerors through him who loved us.
>
> Rom 8:33–39 NIV

As children of Abraham, we are all heirs of these promises. As God rewarded the patriarch, so he will reward those whose faith is solely and securely in him.

> *Father Abraham had many sons,*
> *And many sons had Father Abraham.*
> *I am one of them, and so are you,*
> *So let's all praise the Lord!*

GENESIS 25:12–18

As the narrator has done before, he does so here: he dispenses with the non-elect lineage (Cain, Japheth, Ham) before continuing the story. Like his nephew Jacob, Ishmael was blessed with twelve sons who became "princes" of their respective tribes, or better translated "chiefs" (NJB; cf. Num 1:16). God had promised Hagar that her son would become "a great nation" (21:18), and this genealogy is proof that God's promise was fulfilled. "If God did not overlook his promises to Ishmael, how much more certainly will he fulfill those guaranteed by oath to Abraham about Isaac and his descendants."[22]

As with the sons of Keturah, we do not know a whole lot about Ishmael's sons. The tribes settled in the Sinai and Arabian peninsulas (25:18); some make appearances in the preaching of Isaiah, Jeremiah, and Ezekiel. Many of these names are also mentioned in the Assyrian records of Tiglath-pileser III and Ashurbanipal, and the Babylonian records of Nebuchadnezzar and Nabonidus.

---

22. Wenham, *Genesis 16–50*, 166.

Kedar became the most powerful of the Ishmaelite tribes. Nebuchadnezzar led a campaign against Arabian tribes in 599 B.C., and Kedar seems to have been among his conquests (Jer 49:28–33). In Ezek 27:21, Kedar is said to be a trading partner with Tyre.

Before his birth, it had been prophesied that Ishmael would "dwell over against all his kinsmen" (16:12). That promise is also fulfilled. "His descendants settled in the area from Havilah to Shur, near the eastern border of Egypt, as you go toward Ashur. And they lived in hostility toward all the tribes related to them" (25:18 NIV).

GENESIS 25:19–34

With the phrase "These are the generations of," Moses marks what is essentially a new chapter in the story of the patriarchs. Abraham has been gathered to his people, and the covenant promises now passed fully to Isaac. Would he continue the rich legacy of faith?

Well, we shall soon see since that faith was tested in the form of barrenness (it ran in the family). There is tension embedded in this fact. Was Rebekah really the one Isaac should have married? Since she is barren, how can she perpetuate the covenant lineage? Had Abraham's servant misread the "signs" from Yahweh? Had there been a mistake?[23]

Isaac responded to his wife's barrenness in a greater way than did his father (or his son Jacob, for that matter, who will have sons by Leah's and Rachel's servants). The text simply, yet beautifully, reads: "Isaac prayed to the LORD" (25:21). More exactly, he "pleaded with the LORD" (NKJV); the same verb translated "prayed" is used in Exodus when Pharaoh asked Moses to petition God to remove the plagues from Egypt (8:8–9, 28–30; 9:28; 10:17–18). "The man who prays persistently for twenty years is a man of strong faith."[24]

Arnold notes that "prayed" and "granted his prayer" in 25:21 are from the same Hebrew root, and thus proposes that "this turn-of-phrase denotes that Yahweh was emotively stirred into action, not against his will, but precisely to accomplish his will through the urging of his servant."[25] In this is a powerful example for our own prayers. It is not necessarily wrong to ask God for the desires

---

23. Hamilton, *The Book of Genesis: Chapters 18–50*, 175.

24. Waltke, *Genesis*, 356.

25. Arnold, *Genesis*, 231.

of our heart, for he loves giving "good things to those who ask him!" (Matt 7:11). But we should not pout when those prayers are not answered favorably. And if we are constantly entreating the Lord for things that are, well, trivial and petty, we shouldn't be surprised when our prayers never seem transcendent.

Following Isaac's example, we are better served investing our prayers in those things consistent with the will of God (e.g. salvation of the lost, glorification of his name, strength to face temptation). It was in the will of God that Abraham's seed become a great nation, and Isaac knew this. How could a barren Rebekah perpetuate the seed of woman? "This is the confidence that we have toward him, that if we ask anything according to his will he hears us" (1 John 5:14). It seems redundant to say God will answer prayers that are according to his will; if it's already in his will, won't it happen anyway? What's the point in praying?

Therein lies the lesson we should take away from Isaac's two decades of prayer. Prayer is for our benefit, not God's. Praying for something that is in the will of God shapes us spiritually in ways few other things can. God's desires become our own, and we start to see things as he does. It wasn't that Isaac wanted children to satisfy an emotional need or to avoid the social stigma that barrenness brought. Isaac wanted children so that God could continue being faithful to his covenant promises. Isaac begged the Lord to answer his prayer so that Yahweh could bring about the blessing to the nations through Abraham's seed and thereby glorify his own great name. Isaac wanted his prayer answered as much for the Lord's sake as his own.

And Yahweh indeed answered his prayer. "Rebekah his wife conceived." But this was a troubled pregnancy, for it says that her "children *struggled* together within her." The Hebrew *rasas* means "to crush" or "smash up." We read of Abimelech's skull being crushed by a millstone (Judg 9:53), and of a bowl and wheel being broken (Eccl 12:6). Used here, we're supposed to see Rebekah's discomfort as something more painful than "the baby kicking."

When she couldn't take it anymore, she went to inquire of Yahweh. It is frequent in Scripture that, in times of great distress, God's people come to inquire of him (cf. 1 Sam 9:9; 1 Kgs 14:1–5; 2 Kgs 8:8; 22:18). This is preferred to other means in the ANE of obtaining information from the gods, i.e. divination, which could be pretty gross. "A widely practiced technique involved the observation of the entrails of slaughtered sheep or goats, particularly the liver ... The findings of such methods were collected in manuals or handbooks in which a typical entry might use the following casuistic formulation: 'If the liver has the shape of *X*, then the outcome of the situation will be Y."[26] Put a liver in front of me, and the outcome of the situation will be my losing my lunch.

The question Rebekah asked of the Lord is actually an incomplete sentence in Hebrew, which explains why translations vary—"why is this happening to me?" (ESV) or "why do I live?" (NRSV). In response to her inquiry, God informed Rebekah that the struggle in her womb between her twin boys portended struggle between two nations, and that in a reversal of the norm, "the older shall serve the younger" (25:23). As had been the case with Isaac and Ishmael, and would be the case with Judah (not Reuben!), Perez (not Zerah!), David (not Eliab!), and Solomon (not Adonijah!), the whole lineage of Christ showed a preference for the younger over the older. In a national sense, Israel could lay claim to God's birthright (Exod 4:22), despite being the "smallest of all nations!" (Deut 7:7 NLT). "All of these bear witness to God's gratuitous choice in which the factor in the choice is not age but God's sovereign will."[27] Which is another way of saying that the election of God is based on his grace, not our merit (Rom 11:6).

At birth, Esau "came out red," meaning he had a ruddy complexion; the same term is used to describe David (1 Sam 16:12; 17:42). Esau was also born very hairy, which will become a significant detail later in the narrative. His twin brother came out grasping his heel, and the twin was named "Jacob." The name was probably derived from *ya'qub-alel*, "may God protect," which was "a typical Amorite name of the early second millennium."[28] But the narrator here reinterprets the name as derived from the Hebrew *'aqab*, meaning "heel" (Hos 12:3). Figuratively, the word could also mean "deceive" (cf. 27:36; Jer 9:4). No parent would name their kid "Liar" from birth, but the narrator's twist foreshadows events to come.

As adults, Jacob and Esau were characterized as polar opposites. Esau was an outdoorsman and kind of redneck-ish, while Jacob was said to be a "quiet man," a translation of a Hebrew adjective that means "blameless" or "perfect" (cf. Job 1:1; Prov 29:10). Jacob was anything but perfect, so the word here probably means "well-cultured" or "civilized."[29] But their unique personalities made them

---

26. Hamilton, *The Book of Genesis: Chapters 18–50*, 176.

27. Ibid., 177. McKeown comments further that this narrative about the birth of Jacob and Esau "highlights Yahweh's independence; his plans are not constrained by human traditions or what is the expected norm. Yahweh does the unexpected and makes no apology for ignoring the traditional rights of the firstborn in favor of his younger brother," (*Genesis*, 127–28).

28. Wenham, *Genesis 16–50*, 176.

29. Waltke, *Genesis*, 362.

the favorite of different parents. This unhealthy favoritism would also plague Jacob's family as it did Isaac's.

The scene shifts to what at first seems like a perfect anecdote for the twins' polar personalities: Jacob cooking and Esau hunting. In actuality, Esau came in "exhausted" from a hunt, a word Gideon used to describe his men who were giving chase to fleeing Midianites (Judg 8:4–5). Esau noticed his brother preparing a delicious soup and demanded some. Jacob seized the opportunity to lay claim to his brother's birthright; he would give food to his starving brother in exchange for it (this in contrast to the grand hospitality his grandfather Abraham had exhibited). Esau didn't blink at the offer, but Jacob demanded he swear to it. The rest of the narrative is rushed away hurriedly: Esau "ate and drank and rose and went his way" (25:34).

But the narrator cannot turn away from the narrative before offering a final criticism: "Thus Esau despised his birthright." Considering the things that Moses never explicitly censures in the Genesis text (drunkenness, lying, incest), this is a serious statement. Indeed, "explicit moral commentary is rare in the Bible."[30] But here it is before our very eyes. And this was not an insignificant slight; Esau despised his birthright as others despised God's word (Num 15:31; 2 Sam 12:9), God's name (Mal 1:6), and God's servants (1 Sam 17:42; Neh 2:19).

The birthright due the firstborn son was a precious thing. For a son, it meant the right to inherit the largest piece of his father's estate; for a prince, it meant to inherit his father's crown (2 Chr 21:3). According to Deut 21:17, the firstborn was entitled to two portions of the estate. For example, if there were six sons in the family, the inheritance was divided seven ways, and the oldest received two portions; if there were three sons, the oldest received half the estate (i.e. two-fourths).[31] But it wasn't unheard of for this tradition to be ignored and for the oldest to receive the entire inheritance as Isaac had from Abraham (25:5).

In this particular case, Esau could expect to receive a minimum two-thirds of the inheritance. And when Esau so carelessly gave his birthright away, the original audience would have recoiled in horror at his being so careless with something so precious. Even in the secular literature and legal codes of the ANE, this was completely unheard of. As we will discover in the "Talking Points" section of this chapter, the NT considers Esau an example of one who sacrifices

---

30. Wenham, *Genesis 16–50*, 178.

31. TDOT 2:126; cf. I. Mendelsohn, "On the Preferential Status of the Eldest Son," *BASOR* 156 (1959): 38–40.

a future sacred blessing in order to gratify here-and-now desires (Heb 12:16).

GENESIS 26

When Isaac's father first arrived in Canaan, there had been a famine in the land forcing him to go to Egypt (12:10). As was discussed in chapter 5, famine in Canaan remains a frequent occurrence. This narrative is introduced with notice of another famine, and the narrator explicitly says it was not the same one Abraham had faced. Whether Abraham on that occasion had sought refuge in Egypt against God's will, we cannot be sure. But we know for a fact that God precluded Isaac from doing the same. In the process, the Lord reaffirmed to Isaac the promises he had made to his father Abraham (cf. 12:1–3; 13:14–16; 22:17–18).

If you gain a sense of déjà vu as you read the story, then it's not just you. In this entire chapter, we are given glimpses of Isaac's life that illustrates how he experienced similar blessings and frustrations to those of his father. This narrative "portrays Isaac as very much walking in his father's footsteps. He receives similar promises, faces similar tests, fails similarly, but eventually triumphs in like fashion."[32]

Presumably at the Lord's direction (26:2), "Isaac settled in Gerar" (26:6) as his father once had (20:1). Just like his daddy had done, Isaac lied about his relationship with Rebekah out of fear for his own life. "The force of *a long time* is that Isaac's fears have proved groundless; yet he persists in them."[33] And like his father, Isaac was busted, though not in the same way. Notice there is a key difference in this story from the narratives of Gen 12 and Gen 20; Abimelech, nor any other man in Gerar, ever touched Rebekah. Nonetheless, the king noticed Isaac sexually fondling his wife, instantly deduced their true relationship, and he became furious. The phrase "laughing with" is the translation of the Hebrew *sahaq*, which described what Ishmael had done to Isaac (21:9). Though the ESV reads in 26:8 that Isaac was "laughing with Rebekah," the translators admit in a note that the "Hebrew may suggest an intimate relationship," a fact reflected in other translations' use of "caressing" (e.g. HCSB, NASU, NIV).

As had been the case in Gen 20, Abimelech was justifiably angry. He acknowledged that if someone had taken Rebekah as a wife, Isaac's deception "would have brought guilt upon us" (26:10). And with that, Abimelech banned anyone from touching Isaac (violently) or Rebekah (sexually) under penalty of death.

---

32. Wenham, *Genesis 16–50*, 196.

33. Kidner, *Genesis*, 153.

It is certain that Isaac was to blame for the situation; his excuse was as flimsy as Abraham's had been. In Gen 12, God had just promised Abraham that he would curse those who dishonored Abraham. Why did Abraham feel the need to lie to the Egyptians? In 15:1, Abraham received the assurance that God would shield him. In Gen 19, God spared Lot from the destruction of Sodom for Abraham's sake. Why did Abraham feel the need to lie to the Philistines in Gen 20? In 26:3–4, God affirmed the Abrahamic covenant to Isaac. Why did Isaac feel the need to lie to the Philistines?

There is no good reason for Abraham and Isaac to have acted as they did, yet their behavior is a reminder that we all—myself as much as anyone—are weak at times in living out the promises of God. Our failures do not mean God is less trustworthy, but that we need to do a better job of living as if his promises are real and reliable, because they are on both counts. Isaac was discovering that it is one thing to stand in awe as God reaffirms to you the blessing of the ages; it is quite another thing altogether to live in light of that blessing in the cruel, hard world of reality. God's people have always been called to "walk by faith, not by sight" (2 Cor 5:7).

Despite Isaac's faithlessness, God was faithful (2 Tim 2:13) to Isaac as he had been to his father. This is shown in the fact that, while in the area of Gerar, Isaac's harvest was 100x what he had planted. To get an idea of how ridiculously high this was, consider that the highest crop return recorded in ANE documents is 75x, and "in medieval Britain a yield of two or three times was normal."[34] That Isaac's yield was this high is nothing short of remarkable, especially considering that it came in the middle of a famine![35] Such happens to those who enjoy Yahweh's blessing (cf. Matt 13:8).

The Lord kept blessing Isaac until he became wealthy just like his father. But as Abraham had discovered in Gen 13, those blessings can sometimes cause problems; "whenever an outsider moves in and becomes very prosperous in someone else's backyard, the natives feel resentment."[36] In Isaac's case, his blessings created significant envy among the Philistines, and he was expelled from the area. They also spitefully filled in the wells Isaac held rightful claim to since it had been

---

34. McKeown, Genesis, 130.

35. Eliezer Oren reports, "Frequently, low yields or crop failures are the result" of planting in this region of Palestine ("Ziglag—A biblical city on the edge of the Negev," BA 45 [1982]: 157). Isaac's yield, no matter how one considers it, was miraculous.

36. Hamilton, The Book of Genesis: Chapters 18–50, 200.

his father's servants who had first dug them (presumably while Abraham had sojourned there in Gen 20–21). Wells in antiquity were very valuable; once metal tools were developed, they could range in depth from 70 to 150 feet.[37]

Isaac chose to leave peacefully instead of fight back, but he knew he was surrendering a valuable resource. He redug more of his father's wells and "gave them the names that his father had given them" (26:18), which was a way of theoretically establishing clear ownership of a place—as we saw in the days of Creation, the prerogative to name something meant authority and ownership. One of the wells was actually a freshwater spring, a very valuable find since a spring meant a continuous supply and would not dry up like a well could. But the Philistines ran Isaac off from that well, and then again from another; he named those wells "Esek" and "Sitnah," meaning "quarrel" and "accusation" respectively. Isaac finally found peace when he dug the third well, so he named it "Rehoboth," meaning "wide open spaces." But eventually, Isaac relocated to Beersheba. God appeared to him again and reaffirmed his promises and blessings. Isaac responded in the way his father often had: he built an altar (cf. 12:8; 13:18).

It was also at Beersheba that Isaac was visited by Abimelech, who had in tow his counselor Ahuzzath and military commander Phicol. It's unlikely that these are the same Abimelech and Phicol of Gen 20–21 since a minimum of 40–60 years had elapsed since the events of those chapters. Abimelech wanted to secure a treaty with Isaac. He acknowledged that Yahweh was the source of Isaac's wealth, though he seems oblivious to the mistreatment Isaac had suffered at the hands of his countrymen (26:29; cf. 21:26). When they first arrived, Isaac appeared indignant. But he evidently settled down and confirmed the treaty by inviting them to a feast. "In the ancient world, treaty-making often was accompanied by a ceremonial meal, the purpose of which was to create an auspicious atmosphere of harmony and fellowship for the pact to go into effect"[38] (cf. 31:54; Exod 24:11). The scene ends with Isaac's servants informing him that they had successfully dug another well; God's blessings were indeed great in the life of Abraham's son.

F or as long as I can remember, my grandparents haven't used public water on their property in Choctaw County, Mississippi. Their home is outfitted with

37. Oleson, "Water Works," ABD 6:886.

38. Sarna, Genesis, 188.

indoor plumbing, but for the first several years of my life, Pop would tote water from the pond in a large barrel, and a water pump allowed it to be used in the house. But dirty pond water isn't ideal to shower or wash your dishes in. So Pop had a well dug on the property in the late '90s, and their water has been relatively cleaner since then. I was visiting them on Spring Break when the men came to install the well, and I remember what a complicated process it was. Isaac's wells weren't dug with late-20th century technology like Pop's was, and east-central Mississippi isn't as arid as southern Canaan, a region that can easily see less than a foot of rainfall annually.[39] But nonetheless, that experience as a kid provided me with a very minute window into the frustration Isaac felt.

A wise man once told me, "People want you to succeed, but not too much." God's people today at times experience conflict with those envious of their success and blessing. We would do well to follow Isaac's example and "move on" from such people. Allow them to wallow in their envy and insecurity. It may not help you to confront it—if a person covets your blessing, then you're likely the last one they want giving them a spiritual wake-up call. By moving on from springs of conflict and wells of accusation, you show yourself to be a peacemaker. Who knows? Maybe others will envy your agreeable spirit! "When the LORD takes pleasure in anyone's way, he causes their enemies to make peace with them" (Prov 16:7 NIV).

I know the difficulty in opting for peaceful, not punitive, measures. But as with everything else in life, our faith is at stake when confronted with this issue. It takes faith to abandon blessings, confident that God can restore what we have lost. But if we truly believe that God is greater than any adversary we might ever face, this is the course we will choose. Remember, our God is peace, and he calls us to pursue the same (2 Cor 13:11; 2 Tim 2:22).

A t the end of the narrative, we learn that Esau married two Canaanite women named Judith and Basemath, thereby departing from the wishes of his grandfather Abraham and the example of his father. Esau thereby proved himself to be an unfit heir of his father's estate because he

---

39. Thomas L. Thompson, "The Background of the Patriarchs: A Reply to William Dever and Malcolm Clark," *JSOT* 9 (1978): 25. Wells are still crucial in that part of the world due to a lack of rainfall; while the U.S. military was in Iraq, they set about building wells for the populace. "It makes people think good things are on the way," said one Iraqi (James Glanz, "Rebuilding Iraq, a Well at a Time," *New York Times*, July 20, 2004).

1.   Did not allow his parents to arrange his marriage.

2.   Married outside the extended family.

3.   Married a Canaanite.[40]

Esau's choice of wives greatly embittered Isaac and Rebekah (cf. 1 Sam 1:10; Job 7:11; 10:1), so why he remained his father's favorite is anyone's guess. But the stage is thus set for the next narrative in Genesis.

---

40. Sarna, *Genesis*, 189. "Esau's indifference to the law's demands, which Abraham held so dear, suggests that perhaps he does not deserve to inherit Abraham's blessing," (Wenham, *Genesis 16–50*, 205).

TALKING POINTS

Abraham's refusal to allow Isaac to marry a Canaanite woman bears a principle worth emulating. The Law of Moses warned Israel of the danger in intermarrying with her neighbors (Deut 7:3–4), and when Solomon disobeyed this command, it was widely considered the beginning of the end for the glorious kingdom of Israel (cf. 1 Kgs 11:4; Neh 13:26). In the NT, Paul forbids a widow from marrying outside of the Lord (1 Cor 7:39), and in general warns of being "yoked with unbelievers" (2 Cor 6:14). I am in no way saying it is a sin to marry a non-Christian. But just because something is not a sin does not also mean it is wise (1 Cor 6:12). We can look around a church auditorium and single out a handful of those who were brought to obedient faith in Christ through the influence of a godly spouse. But we must also acknowledge the dozens more who were led away from their faith by an ungodly spouse. We tend to forget about the ones who are no longer among us. As a consequence of the Fall, marriage is complicated as it is. Why unnecessarily make it more so?

There is a great deal parents can learn from Abraham's example in Gen 24. I'm not sure I want to return to the days when parents arranged marriages for their children, but neither does our culture, where shows like *The Bachelor* and *The Bachelorette* are a hit with television audiences, have much wisdom to offer in this regard. Parents would perform a great service to their children (and to the church) by lifting them up in prayer. Why not, from their birth, pray for the future mates of your children? Pray for God's guidance as you raise someone's future spouse, and that God would likewise guide the parents of your future son- or daughter-in-law. Pray that your daughter is as passionate about being Mrs. Right as she is about finding Mr. Right. Above all, affirm to your heavenly Father his sovereignty over all things—for your sake, not his. "Trust in the LORD with all your heart, and do not lean on your own understanding. In all your ways acknowledge him, and he will make straight your paths" (Prov 3:5–6).

The love story of Isaac and Rebekah had a beautiful beginning. It was, in some ways, a match made in heaven. Rebekah brought great comfort to Isaac in light of Sarah's death. But just because a marriage has a great beginning does not mean it will end well. By the time their sons are grown, their "marriage has become dysfunctional. Each speaks and acts secretly against each other in their machinations to secure the divine blessing on the favored son."[41] A successful marriage that will last a lifetime as God intends requires hard work and constant investment. Couples should never make the mistake of allowing their child(ren) to come between them. Children are only a temporary assignment from the Lord. Marriage, on the other hand, is a lifelong commitment.

I t is admittedly obscure in the ESV, but Esau requested of Jacob "a *swallow* of that red stuff there" (25:30 NASU), which is a unique word appearing nowhere else in the OT. It portrays an awkward Esau wanting just a little bit of stew in order to gratify a base instinct, no matter the cost. It seems he was exaggerating when he exclaimed, "I am about to die." The NT uses Esau as a cautionary tale for the sexually immoral person. "See to it … that no one is sexually immoral or unholy like Esau, who sold his birthright for a single meal" (Heb 12:15–16). The rabbis alleged that Esau was promiscuous with married women (Gen Rab 65:1), and in light of this passage from Hebrews, there may be some truth to that. Either way, Esau embodies the person who cannot resist temptation in exchange for some future reward, but would rather take a little here-and-now, even if it means surrendering something greater in the hereafter. Sexual temptation specifically appeals to the hunger of the flesh, persuading us to forget about the glory and honor of an undefiled marriage bed (Heb 13:4). But as was the case for Esau, the tradeoff is never worth it, and only leads to many years (if not a lifetime) of heartache.

---

41. Waltke, *Genesis*, 334.

11

HE'S THE CHEATIN' KIND

I don't know anyone who doesn't wish they had the perfect family. And while we would each define that in different ways (e.g. certain profession, standard of living, number of children, kids' achievements), for all our strenuous efforts, the perfect family is an impossible ideal to achieve. All families are flawed in one way or another, and it almost seems as if the more "perfect" a family appears in public, the more dysfunctional they become behind closed doors.

From the moment we met them in the latter verses of Gen 11, Abraham's family—the covenant family God chose to bless!—has been quite dysfunctional. His wife was barren and attempted to solve it by fixing her servant up with her husband. We've already seen how great an idea that turned out to be. Isaac and Rebekah seemed to have a happy marriage until they had twins and quickly chose sides.

When the covenant promises passed to the third generation, Jacob established a completely new standard for family dysfunction. It began with a command from his mother and was severely provoked by her brother Laban, but Jacob wasn't exactly a Boy Scout himself. In fact, though he was the clear victim in a few instances, this section is about his proclivity to cheat and deceive whenever he had the opportunity to advance. Jacob was a profoundly, disturbingly self-sufficient man, and none of his relationships were immune from this inclination.

Can God possibly work his plan through such dysfunctional families and moral scoundrels as the ones we encounter in Genesis? He can, and he does. That gives me hope for my family, and it should give you hope for yours. Whether it is overbearing parents, rebellious children, or an unfaithful spouse, God has the ability to transform our brokenness and use it to further his purposes. He also has a habit of using our dysfunction to deepen our devotion to him.

But, and this is a crucial point, we cannot realize God's power to redeem dysfunction if we trust in the wrong things. In this section, we will see Jacob trust in his deception, Laban in his trickery and superior bargaining power, and Rachel in her mandrakes and household idols. Their examples warn us not to misplace our trust in this life (cf. 1 Cor 10:11).

To whom do you turn for help with your personal and family problems? The secular advice a talk-show host might dispense? Self-help books and magazine advice-columns? Internet message-boards (God help us all)? The people of God must learn not only to trust him to provide, but also to trust his Word to guide us in all things (Ps 119:105). The law of the Lord is perfect and makes us wiser than both the aged and the educated (Pss 19:7; 119:99–100). All of us have baggage and dysfunction, but God's counsel can help us avoid a lot of heartache if we will heed it. For example…

GENESIS 27:1–28:9

With the exception of a brief and famous story explaining how Jacob manipulated Esau out of his birthright, the two brothers have not been the stars of the show so far. That changes as the narrative spotlight shifts from Isaac to Jacob.

In ancient times, it was customary for the family patriarch to give a blessing to his children before death. This was always considered to be an important event carrying significant ramifications for the future.[1] By this point, Isaac was about 137 years old. While he wasn't on his deathbed (chronologically, he didn't die until a year before Joseph's ascendency in Egypt), he still wanted to put his affairs in order "just in case." He was also going blind,[2] so he summoned Esau and asked him to prepare a special meal, at which point he planned to give Esau the blessing due the firstborn. When a father blessed his oldest son, clan leadership passed from father to son, and the blessing could not be rescinded once given.[3]

---

1.   "The deathbed blessing, or testamental blessing, is of vital importance in Israelite culture. Such blessings, pronounced when death was imminent, were more than simple wishes or prayers but were legally binding wills," (Arnold, *Genesis*, 374).

2.   Notice of Isaac's blindness "may also have a figurative significance: Isaac's perception of reality about Esau's worthiness to receive the blessing appears to have been clouded," (Sarna, *Genesis*, 190).

3.   McKeown (*Genesis*, 134) correctly points out that the gravity of the patriarchal blessing is underscored by 1.) Rebekah's acknowledgment that her deception could invite a

But it is odd that Isaac wanted to keep private this very public act (cf. 49:1), one that required witnesses. Why did he not want Rebekah and Jacob to know what he was doing? Was not Jacob also eligible for a blessing? And what right did Isaac have to bless Esau when he had to have known of the prophecy that Jacob would be greater than his brother (25:23)? Was Isaac willfully opposing the will of God? It could be that Isaac was intentionally ignoring the tension of Esau being the firstborn and his father's favorite vs. Esau not deserving the blessing in light of his choice in women. I press this point because we often consider Isaac to be a victim in this story, but some of his intentions and actions are indefensible.

Rebekah overheard Isaac's command to Esau. Because of her favoritism of Jacob, she initiated a plan to deceive her blind husband, something the Law would have denounced (Lev 19:14; Deut 27:18). There is absolutely nothing favorable we can say about the actions of Rebekah and Jacob except that they were used by God to further his divine purposes. There is no denying that, as Calvin put it, Jacob's "seeking the blessing by fraud, and insinuating himself into the possession of it by falsehood, was contrary to faith."[4] And he was clearly less concerned with the morality of his actions than he was what would happen to him if he were caught—"I'll bring down a curse on myself instead of a blessing" (27:12 Msg).

But Rebekah seems worthy of greater blame since she played the greater role. This ruse was no mere suggestion on her part, but rather a "command" to Jacob (27:8).[5] By preparing the food Isaac liked, dressing Jacob up in Esau's clothes, and placing animal skins on Jacob to make him feel as hairy as his brother, Rebekah sought for Jacob the position of leadership in the clan. She may have been acting consistently with the oracle she had received at birth, but she should have realized that God does not need the immoral aid of his children to accomplish his deeds.[6]

When Jacob went in to receive his father's blessing, something he said may be very telling of Jacob's spiritual status at this season of his life. Not only did he

---

curse (27:13), 2.) Jacob's awareness that his act would mean Esau's wrath and Isaac's displeasure (27:12), 3.) Isaac's violent trembling when he learned what had happened (27:33), and 4.) Esau's bitter weeping (27:38) and his threat to kill his brother (27:41).

4.   Calvin, *Genesis*, 2:88.

5.   Wenham (*Genesis 16–50*, 207) draws attention to the anomaly of "command" having a feminine subject (cf. Esth 4:5).

6.   "Here Rebekah sins again, because she burns with such hasty zeal that she does not consider how highly God disapproves of her evil course. ... Yet no one will deny that this zeal, although preposterous, proceeds from special reverence for the word of God," (Calvin, *Genesis*, 2:87).

invoke the divine covenant name of Yahweh in a deceitful way, but he also called him "the LORD *your* God" (27:20). This is a phrase he will use often (31:5, 42; 32:9). In fact, not until after his midnight encounter with the divine warrior (32:22–32) did Jacob speak of Yahweh as his God (33:20; cf. 28:21).

The sudden return of "Esau" did not seem right to Isaac—"he is old and blind, not stupid."[7] The voice had to be Jacob, but his other senses (the feel of Esau's hairy arms, the strong odor of his scent)[8] led Isaac to conclude that Esau indeed stood before him, so he commenced.

Isaac's blessing was one of fertility and dominion; he desired for Esau (Jacob) rich crops, large herds, and many children. The mention of "the dew of heaven" (27:28) is significant since most of the rain received by the Promised Land falls in a four-month period. For the remaining eight months of the year, dew is very necessary for plants to grow and is thus considered a great blessing. According to the rabbis, when the high priest would emerge from the Most Holy Place on the Day of Atonement, he would pray for Israel's welfare and ask for, among other things, "an abundance of dew."[9] Isaac finished his blessing with a line from God's promises to Abraham: "Cursed be everyone who curses you, and blessed be everyone who blesses you!" (27:29; cf. 12:3).

Note the timing of the next scene: "As soon as ..." (27:30). It would be easy to assume that timing throughout the patriarchal narratives (e.g. 24:15; 37:25) is merely coincidental. But Genesis adamantly maintains that God directs the events as they unfold.[10]

No sooner had Jacob exited than Esau entered with precisely the meal his father had requested. Isaac was horrified when he realized what had happened. It may confuse us as to why he couldn't simply annul the blessing; deception had to be legitimate grounds for doing so. But in the ANE, the spoken word was not simply recalled by honorable individuals; they knew it was like putting toothpaste back into the tube. How much more so a blessing which, once spoken, had a life and power all its own and could not be undone (cf. Num 30:2; Judg 11:30–35)?

---

7. McKeown, *Genesis*, 135. For all of his own secrecy, it is clear that Isaac's senses are failing him. "He is as much to be pitied as to be blamed," (Wenham, *Genesis 16–50*, 208).

8. "The clothes of the shepherd reek of the flock and the herd, whereas the hunter's emit the odor of the fields, which Isaac relished more," (Sarna, *Genesis*, 192).

9. Ibid., 193.

10. "Our times are in God's hand; not only events themselves, but the times of them," (Henry, *Commentary on the Whole Bible*, 1:147).

Meanwhile, Esau was livid. His outburst, "Is he not rightly named Jacob? For he has cheated me these two times" (27:36), is a deliberate pun since the words "Jacob" (*yaqob*) and "cheated" (*'aqab*) are from the same Hebrew root. What is most alarming is that Esau fully intended to kill his brother, making him almost as bad as Cain (but he was not so impulsive).

It is painful when a valuable object, once the recipient of our carelessness or scorn, is taken away from us. But while he had scorned his *birthright*, we are never told whether Esau had scorned his *blessing*; these were two different things. Nonetheless, Isaac had no other blessing to give than one that resigned Esau to an inferior future. Isaac's prophecy regarding Esau serving, then breaking his brother's yoke, was fulfilled centuries later. David subjugated the Edomites (2 Sam 8:14), but "during Jehoram's reign, Edom rebelled against Judah's control and appointed their own king. ... So Edom is still in rebellion against Judah's control today" (2 Kgs 8:20–22 HCSB).

It also alarmed Rebekah, who somehow discovered Esau's intention. She did not want to lose one son to murder and the other to exile or retribution all in the same day. To avoid losing both sons, Rebekah sent Jacob to live with her brother until Esau simmered down. Her conversation with Isaac at the end of the chapter is Rebekah's final appearance on Genesis' stage. Not even her death is narrated; some believe this was the narrator's way of censuring her for deceiving her husband. It's also possible her own words, "My son, let the curse fall on me" (27:13 NIV), came true. "As it turned out she did bear a considerable curse, for she would never see her dear son Jacob again."[11] What we can say for sure is that "the career of the woman whose bright start promised to make her the female equivalent of Abraham eventually ends in shadow."[12]

Instead of coming and expressing her fear that Esau would murder Jacob, Rebekah shrewdly couched her request to Isaac in terms of her disgust for Esau's wives, a feeling she knew her husband shared. Sure enough, Jacob was summoned to his father's side and given a strict command not to marry a local woman, but to head to the home of Laban and marry one of his daughters. Isaac called on El Shaddai to bless Jacob and expressed the hope that his son would inherit the covenant promises of Abraham (28:3–4). I suspect Isaac was still upset on this occasion, but that he had resigned himself to the fact that the end result of the deception was God's will anyway—Jacob, not Esau, was the rightful heir to the covenant (cf. Rom 9:10–12).

---

11. Baldwin, *The Message of Genesis 12–50*, 115.

12. Wenham, *Genesis 16–50*, 212.

Finally, we are left with a parting image of a very vacuous Esau. Throughout these narratives, he "is portrayed as someone who tries hard but who does not really understand the main issues."[13] Even now, Esau recognized his parents were upset with his marrying Canaanite women, but he attempted to rectify it in a terrible way. The final verses of this section leave us with an image of "Esau as a marginalized family member who deeply wanted to belong."[14] In a last ditch effort to please his parents, he married Ishmael's daughter Mahalath. But a third wife does not make a right. Incidentally, this may have been the beginning of the alliance between the Edomites and Ishmaelites (Ps 83:6).

GENESIS 28:10–22

Jacob was now on the run from his brother's fierce fury; we can easily assume he had the "fish out of water" feeling everyone experiences when having to embrace a new normal. "The home-loving favorite of an overprotective mother is now an exile, utterly alone and friendless, embarking on a long perilous journey."[15] This perilous journey would be over 500 miles, and it would have taken at least two or three days to cover the almost sixty miles between Beersheba and Bethel. But a few days into his journey of escape, God appeared to Jacob in a mighty way in order to ease his anxiety. It was a noteworthy occasion since this was the first time God spoke directly to Jacob, the third generation of the Abrahamic covenant.

Consistent with the mythology of the ANE, it was often thought that if one slept in a sacred place (e.g. a temple precinct), the gods would reveal a revelation. But Moses completely disassociates that pagan concept from this event in Jacob's life. The overnight stop was unplanned and circumstantial, the place (until the end of the story) was unknown, and it was God who took the initiative in speaking to Jacob. We cannot choose the times that God powerfully makes himself known in our lives; if we could, such moments wouldn't be acts of grace. This nighttime encounter with the divine would not be an isolated incident in Jacob's life; he would also experience another on his return to Canaan twenty years later.

While sleeping, Jacob envisioned "a stairway" (28:12 NIV; cf. ESV note) rising to heaven with angels going up and down. From the top of the stairway, God spoke to him. This concept may seem strange, but the basic idea was not

13. McKeown, *Genesis*, 139.

14. Roop, *Genesis*, 187.

15. Sarna, *Genesis*, 197.

as foreign to Jacob. A structure rising to heaven as a means of communication between God (or the gods) and man was at the heart of the ziggurats so common in the ANE (cf. 11:1–9). We are intended to see the angels as ascending and descending, not as if on parade, but going out and returning from missions on behalf of Yahweh. From his position atop the stairway, God presided over the process. The Lord was thus revealing that these "ministering spirits" would be working as his agents on Jacob's behalf (Heb 1:14; cf. Ps 91:11; Zech 1:10).

In the dream, God affirmed to him that the covenant promises made to Abraham and Isaac would also perpetuate to Jacob. Specifically, he would inherit the Promised Land, his posterity would be very numerous, and he would be an agency of blessing to the nations (28:13–14). But more relevant to Jacob's immediate dilemma was the next promise: "I am with you and will watch over you wherever you go, and I will bring you back to this land. I will not leave you until I have done what I have promised you" (28:15 NIV). Jacob may have been able to swindle Esau and deceive Isaac, but Yahweh held sovereign sway over Jacob's future. "The Deceiver" didn't have to deceive to gain a bright future for himself.

I'm sure the covenant promises of land, children, and blessing mattered to Jacob, but I think the thought of never seeing his home and parents again mattered to him a great deal more on this occasion. So God spoke to those anxious worries. Jacob was assured that God's presence—his sovereign guidance and protection—would not climax until Jacob returned home.[16] And it didn't matter where Jacob journeyed; God's efficacy was not limited to Canaan.[17] For a book that focuses so much attention on the special relationship between Yahweh and Israel, the OT is emphatic that he is Lord over all the earth (e.g. Josh 3:11; Ps 47:2; Isa 54:5; Mic 4:13; Zech 4:14).

As had been the case with Abraham and Isaac, God's promises meant God's provision, and this is a key realization; Jacob struggled mightily to trust in God's provision in a greater way than his fathers ever did. It proved profoundly difficult for Jacob to eschew the lifestyle his name embodied. He was a deceiver by nature, one who sought to get ahead at others' expense. This directly contradicted the life of faith God was proposing to him. Jacob could choose to trick or trust, but real blessings come only through faith (Ps 40:4; Prov 16:20).

---

16. "'Until I have done for you what I have promised' does not mean that God's protection of Jacob will end some day, but that it will outlast all his journeyings," (Wenham, *Genesis 16–50*, 223).

17. "Unlike the pagan deities of the ancient Near East, God is not limited to a particular land," (Waltke, *Genesis*, 392).

Jacob's fear and amazement the following morning is understandable; how could God exhibit so much favor toward one so undeserving? At this stage in the narrative, Jacob has been no saint. He has certainly done nothing to merit the blessings and promises God had extended to him. But neither have I, nor you, done anything to merit God's favor. He extends to us the greatest blessing of all: salvation through his Son, that we might enjoy every spiritual blessing (Eph 1:3). Such an offer is made on the basis of his grace, not our goodness, and we accept it through whole-hearted faith and obedience (Eph 2:8–10; Rom 6:17).

Consistent with the idea that name-change marked important events, Jacob gave a new name to the place where he had spent the previous night. No longer would it be known as Luz, but Bethel, meaning "God's house." Jacob made a vow to God: if he was indeed given divine protection and provision, Jacob would return to Bethel and give to God a tenth of his possessions—i.e. he would sacrifice a tenth of his flocks as burnt offerings. Most notably, however, is the oath, "the LORD shall be my God" (28:21).

Hamilton claims, "Jacob is throwing himself on God's mercy, not calculating whether to accept God."[18] But Brueggemann argues that Jacob "sounds like a bargain-hunter,"[19] and I am inclined to agree if only because this side of Jacob is consistent with the one that emerges henceforth. In the OT, vows were often made under duress (Num 21:2; Judg 11:30–31; 1 Sam 1:11; 2 Sam 15:8; Jonah 1:16), and Israel was thus warned of the gravity of forgetting or not keeping these vows (Num 30:2; Deut 23:21; Eccl 5:4–5). I contend that making a vow to God is not a Christian practice, and "the church should abstain" from it.[20] Making a vow to God smacks of bargaining our way out of a tight spot as if God were a genie in a lamp. Is it not better to respond in faith when our backs are against the wall? Our example should not be Jacob, but the three Hebrews who boldly believed God was able to deliver them from Nebuchadnezzar's fury, and even resolved to stand firm should Yahweh choose not to do so (Dan 3:17–18). Our examples should be Job, who resolved to trust even if it killed him (Job 13:15), and Paul, who turned to prayer in the face of trial and so learned to rely on God all the more (2 Cor 1:8–11).

Incidentally, Jesus echoed this narrative when he said to his disciples,

---

18. Hamilton, *The Book of Genesis: Chapters 18–50*, 248.

19. Brueggemann, *Genesis*, 248; cf. Baldwin, *The Message of Genesis 12–50*, 119; Walton, *Genesis*, 573–74.

20. Waltke, *Genesis*, 397.

"Truly, truly, I say to you, you will see heaven opened, and the angels of God ascending and descending on the Son of Man" (John 1:51). By virtue of the Crucifixion and Resurrection, Christ is the mediator between God and man (1 Tim 2:5). He himself is God's greatest blessing and promise.

GENESIS 29:1–30

As we have already discussed, wells were of great importance in the ANE and remain so today. At this point in time, they would not have had the iconic protective wall. They would have only been covered with a large rock in order to camouflage the existence of the well, to prevent contamination, and to keep animals from falling in. Single-handedly moving the stone from the well's opening would have required near-superhuman strength. Some have suggested that this well is the same as the one in 24:11, but we can't know for sure.

In spite of their similarities,[21] one cannot help but notice a stark difference between Jacob's arrival in Haran and the arrival of Abraham's servant in Gen 24. Both stories involved a well, but Abraham's caravan had been loaded with riches; Jacob came empty-handed. Abraham's servant committed his mission to prayer, but if Jacob prayed, we don't know about it. He seems to have stumbled onto the scene resolved to survive on his self-sufficiency. His ability to remove the stone by himself does not spark awareness of God's presence (cf. Judg 16:20–21, 28). And when he discovered he had arrived at his intended destination, he did not thank God profusely as Abraham's servant had done.[22]

Rather, he became instantly infatuated with Rachel, his uncle Laban's younger daughter. One might say he experienced love at first sight with Rachel. The comment that Leah's eyes were "weak" means that they were tender or soft (cf. Deut 28:54; 2 Sam 3:39; Prov 15:1; Isa 47:1). Leah was pretty, but the text presents Rachel as stunningly beautiful. Notice that, as soon as Jacob saw Rachel for the first time, he flexed his muscles for her, after which he "kissed Rachel and wept aloud" (29:11). Incidentally, I tried this exact same tactic for meeting women several times in college. Five restraining orders later, I gave up. I think it was the loud weeping.[23]

---

21. Hamilton, *The Book of Genesis: Chapters 18–50*, 254–55.

22. Waltke, *Genesis*, 399.

23. In all seriousness, kissing was a form of greeting and farewell in biblical times (cf. 33:4; Exod 4:27; Ruth 1:14; 1 Kgs 19:20; Luke 7:45; Acts 20:37; Rom 16:16; 1 Pet 5:14).

After he had stayed a month, Jacob was offered wages for his labor to Laban. This may seem to us like a generous offer by Laban. Why should Jacob work for free? But Waltke points out:

> Laban is degrading the blood relationship between himself and Jacob (29:14a) into an economic arrangement. What Laban should have done as a loving relative is to help Jacob get a start on building his own home, as Jacob asks of Laban in 30:25–34 (esp. vv. 26, 30, 33). Instead, Laban keeps Jacob as nothing more than a laborer under contract, as Jacob bitterly complains in 31:38–42.[24]

Since he was so smitten with Rachel, Jacob asked for her hand in marriage in exchange for work. He agreed to work seven years in order to pay the bride price, and this was not an unusual arrangement in the ANE.[25] This payment was a sort of insurance payment in the event of divorce, desertion, or death. An average bride price would have been thirty or forty shekels.[26] Since the average annual wage of a laborer was ten shekels, Jacob was being forced to pay almost double the customary amount for Rachel. "Perhaps Laban can take advantage of Jacob because Jacob, being penniless and moonstruck, is in a poor bargaining position."[27] But Jacob arguably thought it was a bargain since the years flew by for him (29:20).

When the time came for the wedding, Laban threw the customary celebration. The text does not say so explicitly, hence we cannot know for sure, but it is suspected that Jacob was quite intoxicated due to the party (Josephus, *Antiquities* 1.301). The Hebrew *mishteh* ("feast") involved drunkenness (cf. 1 Sam 25:36; Esth 1:3, 7–8; Isa 25:6; Jer 51:39), so that may be why Jacob did not recognize which sister he spent the night with. The narrator invites us to be as shocked as Jacob was. "Morning came: There was Leah in the marriage bed!"

---

24. Waltke, *Genesis*, 404; cf. Sarna, *Genesis*, 203.

25. Hans Jochen Boecker, *Law and the Administration of Justice in the Old Testament and the Ancient East*, trans. Jeremy Moiser (Minneapolis: Augsburg, 1980), 109.

26. Katarzyna Grosz, "Dowry and Brideprice in Nuzi," in *Studies on the Civilization and Culture of Nuzi and the Hurrians*, eds. M. A. Morrison and D. I. Owen (Winona Lake, IN: Eisenbrauns, 1981), 176–77.

27. ZIBBCOT 1:109.

(29:25 Msg). The Deceiver had been deceived (cf. Gal 6:7)![28]

Laban's excuse was that it was not their custom to allow a younger sister to marry out-of-turn, but why hadn't he explained this seven years prior? Evidently, "That's the way we've always done things" can be a self-righteous cop-out for cowards. Furthermore, what Laban did would have been illegal under the Code of Hammurabi, and the fine would have been double the bride price Jacob had paid—fourteen years of wages![29]

Jacob was clearly not happy, and though he was permitted to marry Rachel also[30] (he first had to finish the marriage week[31] with Leah), he would have to work another seven years to pay his debt. And where was God in all this? Hadn't God sworn to look out for Jacob? Would Jacob trust, or would he have to resort to self-sufficiency in order to provide for himself and his growing family? At stake was Jacob's confidence in the God of his fathers in light of this terrible turn of events.

Finally, what is so unfortunate in this story is how Leah, through no fault of her own, was caught in the crossfire of a contentious relationship between Jacob and Laban. As we are about to see, the names of her children bore witness to her very troubled marriage.

GENESIS 29:31–30:24

A regular theme of Genesis appears yet again: the barrenness of Israel's matriarchs. God is the sovereign giver of life, and it is his prerogative to open or close a womb (cf. 20:17–21:2). In this case, he gave Leah the blessing of children because of the heartache she felt in her marriage; Rachel, on the other hand, remained barren for quite a while.

We are also told that Jacob "hated" Leah, and while the Hebrew can mean that (e.g. 37:4; Lev 19:17; Josh 20:5; 2 Sam 13:22), a better understanding here

---

28. Wenham believes in Laban's response (29:26) may be an undertone of "poetic justice ... a barbed underhanded dig" concerning Jacob's prior deception of his father and brother (*Genesis 16–50*, 237).

29. "If a seignior had the betrothal-gift brought to the house of the (prospective) father-in-law (and) paid the marriage-price, and the father of the daughter has then said, 'I will not give my daughter to you,' he shall pay back double the full amount that was brought to him," (§160).

30. The Law of Moses would have never allowed this (Lev 18:18).

31. The marriage week was apparently a long-standing custom in biblical times (cf. Judg 14:12; Tobit 11:18).

is "loved less" or "unloved"[32] (cf. Deut 21:15; Mal 1:3; Matt 6:24). Leah believed her bearing children would give Jacob an additional reason to love her more, but she proved sadly mistaken. These two sisters are at tragic odds with one another in this narrative since both have what the other does not.

Names in Genesis are quite meaningful, and the names given in this passage reflect the thoughts or attitudes of the mothers at birth. The names Leah gave to her sons expressed her hope for kindled romance with Jacob, as well as her gratitude to God for the blessing of sons—Reuben: "The LORD has looked upon my affliction…" Simeon: "The LORD has heard that I am hated…" Levi: "Now this time my husband will be attached to me…" Judah: "This time I will praise the LORD" (29:32–35). It is clear Leah named her children out of faith in God.

But Leah's fertility, which is attributed directly to God's blessing, became an object of jealousy between Leah and Rachel. Are you noticing this theme running through Genesis of God's blessing creating envy in others? In response to her own barrenness, Rachel blamed God as Sarah had done (16:2), and Rachel was correct. Her outburst to Jacob, "Give me children, or I shall die!" (30:1), seems a bit too dramatic, but the reality was that a wife without children was a social disgrace in ancient times. The horrible irony is that she later died in childbirth (35:16–19). Unlike his father (25:21), Jacob did not intercede on his wife's behalf. He clearly knew that God was sovereign over life (30:2; cf. Ps 113:9), but he did not seek to affect God's will on this matter. The Lord wanted both Jacob and Rachel to realize that the only way out of hopelessness is through faith in him,[33] but neither one got the message.

Instead, Rachel suggested Jacob take her servant as a surrogate wife; children born to that relationship would legally be Rachel's. Her literal statement to Jacob, "Go in to her [Bilhah] that she may bear *on my knees*" (30:3 NASU), means Rachel intended to adopt her servant's children (cf. 48:12; 50:23). If God refused to give her a child, she would take the matter into her own hands.

Sure enough, two more kids were born to Jacob through Bilhah. But their names did not reflect faith in God as Leah's son's had. Rachel named her first surrogate son Dan, meaning "judged," for Rachel felt vindicated in that she finally had a son (cf. Ps 43:1). Her second son via Bilhah carried a name that symbolized her struggle with her sister: Naphtali. In spite of her four sons, Leah

32. Sarna calls it "a relative degree of preference," (*Genesis*, 206).

33. "Faith is bringing our fears and weaknesses to God and believing that somehow God will transform our pain into a moment of grace," (Waltke, *Genesis*, 416).

became intensely jealous of Rachel's maidservant, and she gave her own to Jacob. Zilpah bore Gad and Asher.

And just when you thought this family feud couldn't get any worse, Leah's oldest son brought her a prize from the fields "in the days of wheat harvest" (i.e. about May).[34] The aroma of mandrake roots,[35] sometimes called "love apples," was considered an aphrodisiac in ancient times (cf. Song 7:13) and a cure for sterility.[36] In an ancient Egyptian love song, a man fantasized about his lover: "If only I were her Nubian maid, her attendant in secret! [She would let me bring her love apples; when it was in her hand, she would smell it, and she would show me] the hue of her whole body."[37] In addition, Aphrodite, the Greek goddess of love and sex, was known as "Lady of the Mandrake."

Rachel likely thought that, with these mandrakes, she would not only become fertile, but also irresistible to her husband. He would then stop sleeping with Leah altogether, and Leah would become increasingly irrelevant. Leah may have been taunting Rachel (cf. 16:4; 1 Sam 1:6), so Rachel in effect said, "Fine, sleep with Jacob tonight. It will be the last time you do so if I can help it." But in divine irony, Leah conceived Issachar on that very night, his name acting as a memorial of the night Leah had "hired" Jacob to sleep with her. And God wasn't through blessing Leah—she gave birth to a sixth(!) son, Zebulun, and a daughter, Dinah.[38] "Leah, who gives up the mandrakes, bears three children; Rachel, who possesses them, remains barren for apparently three more years."[39] God really has a sense of humor at times.

Finally, "God remembered Rachel" just as he had remembered Noah during the flood (8:1). In other words, the Lord turned his attention to delivering Rachel from her suffering and opened her womb. Joseph's name has double-significance

---

34. Wenham, *Genesis 16–50*, 246.

35. The mandrake plant itself "has dark green, wrinkled leaves, from which rise a violet, bell-shaped flower. Its fruit is a yellowish berry approximately the size of a small tomato, which can be consumed," (Walton, *Genesis*, 588).

36. Marvin H. Pope, *Song of Songs* (New York: Doubleday, 1977), 648.

37. Othmar Keel, *The Song of Songs* (Minneapolis: Fortress, 1994), 257.

38. If anyone was *not* at fault in this episode, it was Leah. She was obviously troubled that Jacob no longer had any sexual interest in her (grounds for divorce under the Law of Moses, Exod 21:10–11), and Rachel seemed to be controlling which wife got to sleep with Jacob on any given night.

39. Sarna, *Genesis*, 209.

in that it embodied etymologically his mother's hope for another son, as well as (via wordplay) her gratitude to the Lord for removing the social stigma of barrenness (cf. ESV note). God had succeeded where Rachel's manipulation and mandrakes had failed.

He alone is the Creator and Sustainer of life.

GENESIS 30:25–43

All the while, the relationship between Laban and Jacob deteriorated rapidly. Laban had mistreated him in more ways than tricking him into marrying his two daughters (31:38–42). Weary of the injustice, Jacob had wanted to return home, but what had kept him around was the barrenness of his favorite wife.[40] So it was not until Rachel had given birth to Joseph that Jacob expressed his desire to be released from service (cf. 1 Kgs 11:21). Laban, however, convinced him to stay under certain conditions. He said he had "learned by divination"[41] that he had been blessed by God because of Jacob (30:27; cf. 12:2–3; 39:2–6). Why should Laban lose an employee he knew to be so valuable?

In ancient times, divination was an attempt "to gain supernatural knowledge, usually either to understand why something has occurred or to predict the future."[42] It isn't stated what methods of divination Laban used, but some of the more common ones were observation of animal entrails, flight patterns of birds, movement of oil in water, or casting lots.[43] Divination was a forbidden practice in ancient Israel (Lev 19:26; Deut 18:10) because it was not consistent with trust in the sovereignty and benevolence of God, but he did at times make his will known through the Urim and Thummim (Lev 8:8; Num 27:21; 1 Sam 28:6; cf. Prov 16:33).

For the first time since arriving at Laban's house, Jacob was in a superior bargaining position. He devised a scheme purposed to increase his flocks. He would be allowed to keep every newborn sheep or goat that was speckled,

---

40. Walton, *Genesis*, 589.

41. It is not absolutely certain that this is a correct rendering of the Hebrew (Hamilton, *The Book of Genesis: Chapters 18–50*, 282). But I find the arguments typically given for alternatives to be mostly unpersuasive, particularly since Laban owned "household gods" (31:19), which were possibly used for divining purposes.

42. O'Mathúna, "Divination, Magic," DOTP 193.

43. Ibid., 194–95.

spotted, or dark-colored.[44] Such animals usually made up only a small part of the herd, less than 20% (most sheep were white, and goats were dark), and the average commission for a shepherd would have been more than this. Laban thought he was getting the better deal,[45] but in his greed, he went so far as to remove all of the current speckled, spotted, or dark-colored animals from his herds (30:35–36) to keep Jacob from gaining a "starter herd" of such animals.[46] Jacob had the last laugh, however. Not only did this not deter his ability to grow a large herd, but the three-day distance gave him a head-start when he escaped from Laban six years later. "Whoever digs a hole and scoops it out falls into the pit they have made. The trouble they cause recoils on them; their violence comes down on their own heads" (Ps 7:15–16 NIV; cf. Job 5:13).

Jacob took branches and peeled part of the bark away so that the branches looked to be striped, i.e. alternating bark/no bark. He seemed to have believed, quite superstitiously, that if the animals looked at these alternating colors while mating, their offspring would be multi-colored, and would thus belong to Jacob and not Laban. He also made sure the stronger animals mated with one another in order to produce a superior flock for himself, a process that makes sense to modern readers since we understand the principles of genetics and heredity. But the belief that animals looking at stripes while mating would produce striped or spotted offspring was a completely unfounded superstition.[47]

There are some elements in this section that are admittedly confusing, but the text makes two things very clear. Jacob became a very wealthy man as is evident from the flocks, servants, and other animals he acquired (camels, if you remember, were a major status-symbol at that time). But the text is also unequivocal that God was the real source of Jacob's prosperity. Whether Jacob

---

44. The Hebrew *hum* occurs only in Gen 30 and is variously rendered "black" (ESV), "brown" (NKJV), and "dark-colored" (NIV); either of these last two is the most appropriate translation (Athalya Brenner, *Colour Terms in the Old Testament* [Sheffield: JSOT, 1982], 121–23).

45. Walton, *Genesis*, 589.

46. "Jacob has only the monochrome members of the flock to tend, and they will produce few, if any, irregulars," (Hamilton, *The Book of Genesis: Chapters 18–50*, 283). "Thus he [Laban] believes he is ensuring a minimal return on Jacob's investment," (Arnold, *Genesis*, 272).

47. If Jacob's superstitions sound nutty, similar ones abound on the Internet. If a couple wants a boy, moms-to-be should eat red meat and salty snacks before conception, and dads-to-be must drink lots of soda. It also helps, so the Internet says, to make love when there is a quarter moon and on odd days of the month. For girls, it is recommended that a couple maintain a diet of fish and vegetables, as well as place a wooden spoon and a pair of scissors under the bed.

actually believed in the superstitions, or simply employed them to fool Laban, the take-away here is that God is the sole arbiter of life and blessing, a point on which Genesis is definitive.

GENESIS 31

After twenty years of working for Laban, Jacob had had enough. The catalyst of his departure was learning about Laban's sons' disparaging remarks. But the true straw that broke the camel's back was the Lord speaking to him directly: "Go back to the land of your fathers and to your relatives, and I will be with you" (31:3 NIV). With that, Jacob called a family meeting.

In his speech to his wives, we learn the depths of Laban's mistreatment of his nephew/son-in-law, but also of his own daughters (31:14–15). The bride price for each of them had been seven years of labor, and Laban should have stored away for his daughters seven years of wages for each of them (or at least a portion thereof). He had apparently burned through the money already, money that technically should have been reserved for Leah and Rachel as insurance policies in case of death, divorce, or desertion.[48] So they were just fine with leaving their selfish father behind.

But notice also that Jacob acknowledged God as the source of his prosperity while being mistreated by Laban (31:5–13). Over the past two decades, I think Jacob had learned through many trials that deception and abuse beget deception and abuse, that "God cannot be mocked. A man reaps what he sows" (Gal 6:7 NIV). His mistreatment had impressed upon the patriarch that Yahweh is the sole arbiter of prosperity, and that an abusive employer can no more thwart divine blessing than a hummingbird can obstruct a hurricane. "Jacob's speech begins, continues, and ends with God's victories over Laban: Laban is against him, but God is with him (31:5); Laban cheated him, but God did not allow harm (31:6–7); Laban changed wages, but God changed flocks (31:8–9)."[49]

Jacob and his family escaped while Laban was out shearing sheep, which would have been in the spring. Laban pursued and quickly caught up with them. He was understandably angry, but God had warned him about retribution

---

48. Hennie J. Marsman, *Women in Ugarit and Israel* (Boston: Brill, 2003), 103.

49. Waltke, *Genesis*, 424.

(31:24),[50] thereby corking "the bottle of his aggressiveness."[51] Over Jacob's life had hovered the sovereign hand of God. He had sworn to Jacob that he would be with him and would protect him (28:15), just as he had sworn the same to Abraham and Isaac (12:3; 26:3). Even today, no harm can befall the people of God that God does not allow (cf. Job 1:12; 2:6), and he will never license more than we can handle (1 Cor 10:13), nor will he sign-off on that which cannot bring him glory (Rom 11:36). Here, it was his sovereign decision to protect the grandson of Abraham, and he made good on that promise.

A lot of commentators like to incredulously point out the impossibility of a large family with servants, herds of animals, and small children traveling so great a distance in so little a time.[52] The distance between Nahor and Mizpah is well over 400 miles—does the text really expect us to believe Jacob's family covered this much ground in ten days before Laban caught up to them? We forget that this is as close as we will get to an ANE version of a high-speed chase. Jacob "is fleeing for his future,"[53] so he and his family would have been moving faster than a normal caravan, and Laban would have been able to cover even more ground since he was traveling lighter. Laban also may have taken his time before giving chase, believing that Jacob could not have been traveling too quickly.[54]

When he finally caught up to Jacob, Laban falsely accused him of forcibly taking Laban's daughters with him. If Laban was sincere in everything he said to Jacob in 31:26–30 (and I'm fairly confident he was), it is profoundly evident that

---

50. In his *Homilies on Genesis* (57.19–20), Chrysostom asked why God simply warned Laban instead of directing him to return home. His answer: "For the good man [Jacob] to learn in fact and by experience the degree of care he was accorded by God. You see, had Laban turned back, how would the good man or his wives have known this? Hence God allowed Laban to come and from his own lips to confess the words spoken to him by God. He did so that the good man might also gain greater enthusiasm for his journey and embrace it in confidence and that his wives might come to know how much care Jacob was accorded by the God of all and so reject their father's deception and imitate the good man. They thus gained from the incident considerable instruction in knowing God. ... This in fact is a sign of God's creative wisdom, when he turns the enemies of truth into the very witnesses to truth, who then by their own mouth fight on its side."

51. J. P. Fokkelman, *Narrative Art in Genesis* (Amsterdam: Van Gorcum, 1976), 166.

52. Hamilton says that the "seven days" should be interpreted "nonliterally" (*The Book of Genesis: Chapters 18–50*, 299), and Wenham claims it is a rough approximation (*Genesis 16–50*, 274).

53. Waltke, *Genesis*, 428.

54. Coffman, *Genesis*, 388.

Laban's self-deception ran deep within his soul. Consider that he:

1. Believed his daughters would have never left him willingly.

2. Fancied himself willing and capable of sending Jacob off with a grand celebration.

3. Thought he had the "power" to do Jacob harm.

How much self-awareness does a man have to lack not to notice his daughters' bitterness towards him, bitterness over being treated as property—and by ANE standards no less! How difficult is it to believe Laban would have actually thrown a great celebration over Jacob's departure? And notice that Laban thought he had the "power" to harm Jacob, but he knew deep down that the sovereign hand of Jacob's God would have never allowed such. It is clear that Laban felt threatened and wounded. He knew he no longer had the superior bargaining position. By virtue of Jacob's God, Jacob now had the upper hand.

When Jacob and his family had fled, Rachel had stolen her father's household gods (31:19), and Laban thought Jacob was the culprit. "Household gods" is a translation of the Hebrew *teraphim*, about which we do not know much. It is suggested that Rachel took them because she believed they gave her or her husband a greater claim to her inheritance,[55] or that the idols could solidify her superior status in Jacob's family.[56] The problem with the former interpretation is that both Jacob and Rachel were leaving Laban's house forever, and Jacob was not Laban's son—what inheritance would they potentially have received?

These teraphim do seem to have been treasured good-luck charms passed down from generation to generation within families, but they also may have been used as objects of divination (cf. Ezek 21:21; Zech 10:2). I am inclined to accept this understanding of the function and value of teraphim because 31:20 says Jacob thereby "stole the heart of" Laban (cf. ESV note). "To 'steal the heart' can mean 'to deceive,' but elsewhere it involves taking away a person's ability to discern and act appropriately," (cf. 2 Sam 15:6; 1 Kgs 12:27).[57]

Whatever Rachel's reason for taking them, her father clearly cherished these

---

55. Kidner, *Genesis*, 165.

56. Ktziah Spanier, "Rachel's Theft of the Teraphim: Her Struggle for Family Primacy," *VT* 42 (1992): 404–12.

57. Waltke, *Genesis*, 427.

teraphim. Laban accused Jacob of stealing them, and when Jacob adamantly denied doing so,[58] Laban humiliated his nephew by searching through the tents in an effort to prove him wrong. No one but Rachel knew where the idols really were, and when Laban attempted to search her tent, she used menstruation as an excuse for "not getting up" (there is no way for us to know whether such was really the case). Whether she herself meant to insinuate such, the narrator certainly intends for us to see this as a contemptible rejection of these teraphim having any real power. For one thing, her sitting on them while menstruating would have rendered them ritually unclean (Lev 15:20).

When Laban returned from his search empty-handed, Jacob released an absolute torrent of verbal rage on his head. Using language very similar to that of a lawsuit, Jacob vented his frustration at the mistreatment he had suffered while working for Laban. It was humiliating enough that Laban had accused him of stealing personal property, but Jacob was also angry that Laban had been quite the unpleasant employer. He had changed Jacob's wages "ten times," a phrase that may be hyperbolically understood as "time and time again"[59] (cf. our non-literal use of round numbers, e.g. "I've said it a thousand times").

One thing Jacob mentioned specifically is that Laban had required restitution when a sheep or goat had been lost to a wild animal. In that day, it was standard practice for a shepherd to pay restitution to the owner if an animal became lost or stolen, but *not* if the animal were attacked by a wild animal (cf. Exod 22:11–12; Code of Hammurabi §263, 266). Additionally, Jacob further said that he had had to repay Laban "whether [an animal was] stolen by day or stolen by night" (31:39). In contrast, most shepherds were only liable if the animal were stolen during the day since "attacks on the fold at night by lions or wolves would have been almost impossible to defend against."[60] Laban's employment demands had been quite unreasonable, and Jacob was family!

But embedded within Jacob's tirade is the belief that God had mitigated his suffering (31:42). It had been God who had allowed him to prosper under such difficult circumstances. It had been God who had rebuked Laban, and it is this

---

58. There is no question that Jacob's oath, "Anyone with whom you find your gods shall not live" (31:32), was very rash. However, the Code of Hammurabi (§6) mandated the death penalty for anyone who stole temple property.

59. Wenham, *Genesis 16–50*, 271.

60. J. J. Finkelstein, "An Old Babylonian Herding Contract and Genesis 31:38f.," *JAOS* 88 (1968): 36.

same God who still rebukes leaders and masters on the behalf of his people—
"Touch not my anointed ones" (Ps 105:14–15). This is only consistent with
the promise God had made to Abraham, the promise to curse those who dared
dishonor the patriarch (12:3). And while the NT forbids us to seek revenge
against those who mistreat us, especially those in power, we are also promised
that God sees the abuse we experience (2 Thess 1:6–9). Those who dare to touch
the anointed of God will find themselves under his curse forever, "punished with
everlasting destruction and shut out from the presence of the Lord and from the
glory of his might" (2 Thess 1:9 NIV).

Laban was clearly not happy with Jacob's rebuke, nor was he willing to
apologize and make things right. He was still under the impression that all Jacob
possessed rightfully belonged to Laban (31:43), but he also realized he could
not compel Jacob to do as he wished. God had spoken. So Laban made a pathetic
attempt at generosity; he offered a treaty. They had a large pile of stones heaped
up as a witness to their cease-fire—each of them gave it a name, but it was the
same name in two different languages (Laban's in Aramaic, Jacob's in Hebrew).
In addition to Galeed (i.e. Gilead), the monument would also carry the name
Mizpah, meaning "watchtower," "for he said, 'The LORD watch between you
and me, when we are out of one another's sight'" (31:49).[61] What Jacob and
Laban did on this occasion to ceremoniously ratify their covenant was culturally
consistent with the times, including their sharing a meal and calling their
respective God/gods to be witnesses to their treaty.[62]

The formation of a pile of stones, the bestowment of two names in two
languages, and the invoking of two deities together carry significance that can
be easily overlooked. Before our eyes is the establishment of the house of Laban
and the house of Jacob as two separate entities. The pile of stones had the force
of a political boundary that must not be crossed. In lieu of the separation at
Babel, the two languages (Aramaic and Hebrew) represented two heritages. But
most notably, Laban invoked "the God of Nahor" in a way that makes clear he

---

61. Walton notes the terrible irony of this verse being quoted in benedictions and at
wedding ceremonies. He points out that Jacob and Laban made this statement with a very
suspicious tone. Since neither would be around to keep an eye on the other, they essentially
resigned the other to the all-seeing eye of God. "It is hardly the sentiment that one would want
on a wedding ring, and although a minister may feel that way about a congregation, it is not in
good taste to express it so unequivocally," (*Genesis*, 592).

62. Sarna, *Genesis*, 221–22.

considered such a deity to be different from the one patronized by Abraham's family. Henceforth, Jacob and Laban would be two "distinct peoples."[63] Laban would remain polytheistic, but Jacob would go on to a deeper relationship with his God, known here as the "Fear of his father Isaac" (31:53).

I n many ways, Moses' audience experienced for themselves what Jacob endured at Laban's hands. Pharaoh had manipulated and cheated Israel for a long time; it would have been easy to think that the God of Israel, the Fear of Isaac, was no match for Pharaoh's craftiness. But as these stories from Jacob's life bear out, the suffering of God's people is not evidence of God's impotence. The purposes of God cannot be deterred by sin, especially by cheating, deception, and manipulation. He either uses such attempts for his own ends, or he thwarts their power altogether.

When it seems as if God's will and Kingdom are being put at a disadvantage, it takes great faith to believe otherwise. It requires great faith in things not seen. Satan would have us believe that personal sin or family dysfunction is an insurmountable setback. Satan would have us believe that being wronged or suffering injustice is a setback. Satan would especially have the church believe that losing an election, a vote, a court decision, or the totality of our cultural relevance is a setback. But "setback" is not a part of God's vocabulary, for God always moves forward.

Forward for our good.

Forward for his glory.

Forward with his story.

---

63. Waltke, *Genesis*, 433.

TALKING POINTS

Hamilton astutely notes, "Jacob's life is laced with fear."[64] He was fearful of his dream at Bethel (28:17), fearful of Laban (31:31), and fearful of Esau (32:7). This is the unavoidable end of the self-sufficient man: fear. Anxiety and worry are the fruit of not trusting in God. Over and over, the Bible calls the people of God to exchange their fear for faith. And over and over, we see the victories faith can deliver when fear would have collapsed into inglorious destruction. "When I am afraid, I put my trust in you. In God, whose word I praise—in God I trust and am not afraid. What can mere mortals do to me?" (Ps 56:3–4 NIV). The reason self-sufficiency breeds fear is because our own strength will eventually fail us (Isa 40:30). It is inevitable that our best won't be good enough. And the failures of the past cause us to fear the challenges and unknowns of the future. The most dangerous form of fear comes when we have proven failures at achieving righteousness by our own efforts. But God, with his great and faithful provision, casts out our fear. The NT labels such provision God's "perfect love" (1 John 4:18). When we behold that perfect love, why in the world would we continue to strive for what God has already so graciously provided us in Christ? Why would we not exchange our fear for faith and trust in the One who has sworn to give us all things (Rom 8:32)?

For much of his life, Jacob was a pathological liar and deceiver. But Laban gave him a dose of his own medicine by giving him Leah in marriage when Jacob believed he was getting Rachel. In such situations, we are tempted to exclaim, "What goes around, comes around." The Bible expresses the same reality in a different way; the apostle Paul warned, "Do not be deceived: God cannot be mocked. A man reaps what he sows" (Gal 6:7 NIV). None of us are perfect. We have all mistreated others and consequently reap what we had sown. But Christians are always to be interested in redemption, so we must transform those painful moments into appreciation for the suffering we have caused with our own sin.

Reading the narratives of Gen 29–31, it is quite evident there was an atrocious tendency toward dehumanization in Laban's family. Laban believed he had a higher obligation to tradition than to his nephew, one whom he had acknowledged as being "my bone and my flesh" (29:14). So he deceived Jacob by giving him Leah,

---

64. Hamilton, *The Book of Genesis: Chapters 18–50*, 244.

not Rachel. Over and over, Laban was intent on milking Jacob for every economic advantage he could, and he evidently was so greedy that he stole from his daughters a portion of money rightfully theirs. No less guilty is Rachel; in the mandrake scene, the horror of what actually transpires should not be lost on us—she pimps out her husband to his first wife! Broken relationships of any kind are most always the product of one person dehumanizing another, of a failure to regard others as precious souls made in God's image and in need of God's love. No wonder, then, that Jesus considered there to be two great commands of equal significance, not just one: love God and love others (Matt 22:36–39). Indeed, all of God's rules for human relationships spring from this simple command: "Love" (cf. Rom 13:8–10).

I n modern western cultures, work-place abuse is nowhere near as epidemic as it once was, especially when compared with the poor working conditions that plague third-world countries. Nonetheless, it is still possible to serve an employer that can be quite unreasonable. If we are honest, some of the mistreatment we endure at work are petty qualms, but some of it can be quite real. And when the economy is poor and jobs are scarce, some employers are sadly not above acting in a heavy-handed way since they know they can more easily get away with it. What is a biblical response to mistreatment by those in power over us? In a culture where many can join a union, strike against the status quo, or turn to social media to blow the whistle on their boss, a Christian has a lot to think about. Jacob certainly suffered under Laban's unfair employment demands, but he learned to deal with such mistreatment from a position of faith, not fear. Faith demands that we serve our bosses/masters as we would Christ—"not by the way of eye-service, as people-pleasers, but as bondservants of Christ, doing the will of God from the heart" (Eph 6:5–6). After he said almost identical things to the Colossians, the apostle Paul added that any employer who dares mistreat us will be punished severely by a God who does not show partiality or favoritism (Col 3:25; cf. Eph 6:9). Too often, Christians mitigate "Turn the other cheek" with "Don't become a doormat," but that can easily become an excuse not to do the very thing faith demands we do: submit. In the end, Christians suffering mistreatment from an unreasonable master must remember that those things most precious to us cannot be affected by anyone in anyway (Matt 10:28), and that we "will receive an inheritance from the Lord as a reward" (Col 3:24 NIV). "Whenever we bear people's wrongdoing meekly and mildly, we enjoy help from on high in a richer and more abundant measure."[65]

---

65. Chrysostom, *Homilies on Genesis* 57.13.

One of the hallmarks of Genesis, and of the rest of Scripture, is the power of God to use human sin for his own purposes. In this narrative, and through the deceitfulness of his uncle/father-in-law, Jacob married the wrong woman. But God used Laban's sin to bring Judah into the world; through Judah, God gave us the strength of David, the wisdom of Solomon, and the atonement of Christ. Later, in the Joseph narrative, God would use the sin of Joseph's brothers to deliver the known world from a devastating famine (50:20). To paraphrase Alexander Maclaren, the wicked deeds of evil men cannot sidetrack the stream of divine purpose anymore than a child can divert the Mississippi River with a mud dam.[66] The greatest example of this magnificent truth is Judas' betrayal of our Lord. Such an evil deed was necessary for the salvation of our souls (cf. 1 Cor 2:8). "God's purposes are not thwarted by human sin, but rather advanced by it through his good graces."[67] This did not exempt Judas from eternal condemnation (Matt 26:24), but Christians should, with the apostle Paul, stand in awestruck wonder at God's ability to take something so terrible and remake it into something so wonderful. "Oh, the depth of the riches both of the wisdom and the knowledge of God! How unsearchable His judgments and untraceable His ways!" (Rom 11:33 HCSB).

---

66. Maclaren, *Genesis*, 263.

67. Arnold, *Genesis*, 361.

12

FAMILY MATTERS

Very early in my junior year of college, I was watching a baseball game comfortably on my dorm-room couch one Sunday night when I began to feel an increasingly severe pain. Over the phone, my dad advised me to visit the ER, and there I learned that I had kidney stones. In the past eight years, these minions of Satan have plagued me on five different occasions. Dad struggled with them as well, and he claimed to have it on good authority from several mothers that kidney-stone pain is worse than labor pains. So even though I will never experience childbirth, I can still relate to Paul's statement in Gal 4:19—"My children, I am again suffering labor pains for you until Christ is formed in you" (HCSB). Every Christian minister and parent has felt the anxiety and pain Paul speaks of here; it is the agony of anticipating life-change in those for whom you are spiritually responsible.

This section of Genesis marks a new era in Jacob's life. He had made a covenant of peace with Laban and continued his return to Canaan. However, his homecoming remained marred by nightmares of his petty dealings with Esau. It had been twenty years, but had Esau's rage softened? Had it festered and intensified like a nasty sore? Jacob had no way of knowing as he and his family journeyed towards the Promised Land. And we readers have our own questions. Is Jacob a changed man after his midnight struggle? Will he continue to be duplicitous? Will he be more trusting? And what of Jacob's children—will they be people of faith? Fear? Will they be trusting or self-serving?

After his reconciliation with Esau, the focus slowly shifts to the lives of Jacob's children, but not before recounting his return to Bethel in order to fulfill a vow he had made to God. The birth of Benjamin, the deaths of Deborah,

Rachel, and Isaac, and the descendants of Esau are all discussed in this section of Genesis. As you can tell, there is a lot that goes on! Yet these events can be challenging and difficult to digest. What are we to make of the massacre of Shechem by Simeon and Levi? And what of Reuben committing adultery with his father's concubine? In all of these events, both good and bad, God continued to work out his plan to redeem the world and transform the hearts of his people. In my experience, God uses both the routine and the unique events of life—both good days and bad—to make us more like Jesus.

Moses presents these stories in such rapid-fire sequence that the significance of each event can become eclipsed by what happens next. So as you read these stories, pause occasionally and see if you can feel the tension and anxiety that comes from the anticipation of life-change. At the beginning of this section, Jacob had much to address regarding his relationship with God and with Esau. In addition, his children proved to be just as frustrating. But God didn't give up on Jacob's children, nor did he give up on Jacob. Rather, God is willing to endure pain worse than childbirth until Christ is formed in us.

And why? So that we can be a part of his story.

GENESIS 32:1–21

After his encounter with Laban, Jacob continued home accompanied by angels. The appearance of these heavenly beings had marked his departure years before (28:10–12), and they now signaled his return. Jacob named the camp Mahanaim ("two camps"), possibly an acknowledgment that both he and God had been encamped there. The Hebrew phrase translated "God's camp" elsewhere signifies a large army (1 Chr 12:22). To a casual observer, Jacob had been fending for himself since fleeing from his brother so many years earlier, but he had in actuality been under God's sovereign watch the entire time despite his repeated failures. The details given at the beginning of the chapter, therefore, are an "indication that God is directing the events of Jacob's return."[1]

Encouraged by God's presence, Jacob sent messengers to Esau to give advance notice of his arrival, rather than risk the appearance of sneaking around his brother's back. Jacob knew it was time to face the music. Throughout the ordeal, Jacob used "lord" or "master" (NIV) to refer to Esau, and "servant" for himself, attempting to soften his brother's potential rage. Under normal

---

1. Walton, *Genesis*, 603.

circumstances, such courtesy would have been unusual between twin brothers in the ANE,[2] but these were anything but normal circumstances. Jacob intimated he was completely willing to buy Esau off if necessary.

There is a very crucial wordplay in Hebrew often missed in English. God sent his angels (Hebrew *malak*) to meet Jacob (32:1), and Jacob sent his messengers (*malak*) to meet Esau (32:3). These angels were a reminder that God would protect his people (cf. 2 Kgs 6:16–17), but they were also notice that Jacob needed to tend to unfinished business before meeting his brother. Jacob was attempting to reconcile with Esau, but he first needed to reconcile with his God, to wrestle and come to grips with him. For too long, he had been shirking the Lord, holding him at arm's length. Until this chapter, there had been a distance between God and Jacob that had not existed between God and Jacob's fathers. Peace with God is the catalyst or springboard for peace with others (Eph 2:11–22), so attempting to reconcile earthly relationships before harmonizing the one with our Father in heaven is a rather pointless undertaking.

The messengers returned to Jacob with news that Esau was on his way with 400 men. This same number "seems to have been the standard size of a militia" (cf. 1 Sam 22:2; 25:13; 30:10) and "is therefore ominous."[3] It would certainly explain why Jacob was so terrified when he heard the news. If Abraham had defeated the standing army of four kings with 318 men, imagine the devastation a vindictive Esau could effect with just 400 on a defenseless family? And Jacob couldn't very well return the way he had come; life under Laban's thumb was no life at all. So Jacob put a plan into action intended to minimize his losses should Esau attack.

But notice that the patriarch also threw himself upon God's mercy and prayed for protection (32:9–12). "This prayer is the outpouring of a heart that is being torn apart by fear and doubts. Jacob, on the verge of the land he has been promised, is also on the brink of disaster."[4] Jacob's self-sufficiency was running out. If God's protection was not sought, he had no chance against Esau's wrath. Specifically in the prayer, Jacob mentioned three things:

1.   In his opening and closing words, Jacob reminded God of his promises. Yahweh had sworn to make Abraham into a nation, and he had ordered Jacob to return to Canaan. Neither of these

2. Wenham, *Genesis 16–50*, 290.

3. Sarna, *Genesis*, 224.

4. McKeown, *Genesis*, 153.

would be fulfilled if Jacob and his family were destroyed. But God obviously did not need to be reminded of his promises; the benefit of mentioning them in prayer belonged to Jacob. When we repeat in prayer what God has promised, our confidence that he will keep his word is renewed.

2. He affirmed that God was the source of all his blessings. For far too long, Jacob had been living by the ethos of his name: "Grabber" or "Deceiver." But even the most duplicitous individuals eventually learn their provision comes from God, not by trickery and deception. To acknowledge God's providence was a major step for Jacob.

3. He made a simple request and confessed his underlying fear. The salvation of God becomes sweeter when we fully realize exactly what we have been saved from. God knew Jacob's plight—he knew his fears before they were articulated (Matt 6:8). But only when we have made specific requests of God can we more clearly see his work on our behalf.

Jacob was learning to trust in the God of his fathers, but it is significant that nowhere in this prayer did Jacob refer to him as "my God" (cf. 28:21). Greater faithfulness remained for the patriarch.

Following his prayer, Jacob sent to Esau 550 animals (not counting the young), divided into their respective herds. He ordered his servants to present them to Esau in such a way that the escalating nature of the gifts would overwhelm his brother[5] (cf. Prov 18:16). Jacob's plan, which seems to have been very sincere, had the vibes of both a sacrifice to placate wrath and tribute paid to a king (cf. "appease," "present," 32:20–21). Walton claims Jacob's gift was actually "larger than towns were likely to pay in tribute to foreign kings," and in a footnote, he cites the 9th century town of Hindanu paying tribute to Tukulti-Ninurta II in the form of silver, bread, beer, 30 camels, 50 oxen, and 30 donkeys.[6] Writing in 1985, Coffman suggested, "It would take at least $100,000.00 today to put together such a drove as that which Jacob sent Esau."[7] Jacob knew this wasn't

5. Shubert Spero, "Jacob and Esau: The Relationship Reconsidered," *JBQ* 32 (2004): 245–50.

6. Walton, *Genesis*, 605.

7. Coffman, *Genesis*, 398.

the time to be stingy; he wanted to overwhelm his brother with generosity.

GENESIS 32:22–32

While Jacob's servants drove the herds toward Esau, Jacob transported his family to the north bank of the Jabbok River, a tributary emptying into the Jordan about twenty miles north of the Dead Sea. The Jabbok's course cuts a deep canyon before it joins the Jordan, so crossing this river in the middle of the night would have been a rather precarious undertaking. But Jacob did so because, at this point, he was anxious and desperate. His chickens were coming home to roost, and Esau was the red fox waiting in the henhouse. With nothing more than a river standing between his family and his brother, Jacob settled in for the night—until a visitor appeared.

The identity of this visitor is still a mystery. He is called a "man" throughout the story, "God" in 32:28, 30, and an "angel" in Hos 12:4. As had been the case with the angel of Yahweh that had appeared to Hagar, the possibility exists that this was a manifestation of the pre-incarnate Christ. It would certainly not be the first time he mysteriously appears in the OT as an "angel" or "man" (cf. Josh 5:13–15; Judg 13:3, 6). Ambiguity aside, it is clear from the details that Jacob encountered God in some form.

This night was a watershed moment for both Jacob and his descendants. All his life, Jacob had been practicing a profane self-sufficiency. Before his birth, great things had been forecasted for him (25:23), but Jacob had swindled Esau out of his birthright and deceived his father in order to receive the blessing. He who had been hoodwinked by his uncle (29:23) had turned the deception back onto Laban (30:25–43). Simply put, Jacob had been living out his own name (27:36). Even now, the parting request for a blessing and his assailant's name (32:29) was a last-ditch effort to regain some control in the struggle. Jacob was seeking to manipulate a situation in which he had no advantage into a blessing. That's how we are sometimes with God's blessings—Grab, grab, grab—as if it's a one-day-only fire sale at our favorite retail store. Such behavior makes blessings appear to be the product of our striving, rather than evidence of the great mercy and amazing grace of God.

That means neither you nor I can fully experience the warm embrace of grace until we have allowed God to break us of our self-sufficiency. "Dependence on self must be broken and lamed in order that, in the very moment of discovered impotence, we may grasp the hand that smites, and find immortal power flowing into our weakness from it."[8] The apostle Paul put it this way: "When I am weak, then I am strong" (2 Cor 12:10).

Not surprisingly, Jacob's request for his assailant's name was ignored. Instead, the midnight visitor asked for Jacob's name, not because he didn't know, but because he wanted Jacob to confess that he had been "the Deceiver" all his life. A new name was then conferred upon the patriarch, and the sun rose on a changed Jacob.[9] Not insignificantly, the mysterious visitor says Jacob had "prevailed" (32:28) in this struggle with God and man. In other words, he had finally come to grips with his "Grabber" ethos, with his penchant to trick and deceive in order to provide. His new name held the promise of a new future. And if the night needed to become even more remarkable, Jacob suddenly realized it had been God with whom he had wrestled. "So Jacob called the place Peniel, saying, 'It is because I saw God face to face, and yet my life was spared'" (32:30 NIV). "If he could meet God this way and walk away, he had nothing to fear from Esau."[10]

More so than his grandfather Abraham, Jacob's penchant for self-sufficiency was borderline pathological. He sought blessing and success through his own efforts. Such had blown up in his face, destroying his relationship with Esau and, later, with Laban. But there is a release when we invest our faith and confidence in the promises of God. There is a release in heeding God's call to get out of our own way. If necessary, he will be both relentless and ruthless in expelling self-sufficiency from our hearts. He will "cripple" us if doing so makes us lean harder on him. He will bring us to the very point of death if it helps us trust him more (2 Cor 1:9; 12:7–10).

When the sun rose the next morning, I think there were still a lot of uncertainties weighing on Jacob's mind. But he now had a limp to remind him of that eventful night on Jabbok's stormy banks. Going forward, every step Jacob

---

8. Maclaren, *Genesis*, 227. Calvin (*Genesis*, 2:196) wrote, "While he assails us with one hand, he defends us with the other; yea, inasmuch as he supplies us with more strength to resist than he employs in opposing us, we may truly and properly say, that he fights *against* us with his *left* hand, and *for* us with his *right* hand. For while he lightly opposes us, he supplies invincible strength whereby we overcome," (emphasis his).

9. The euphemism "will no longer say" (Jer 3:16; 7:32; 16:4; 23:7; 31:29; Ezek 12:23; 18:3) indicates "a spiritual metamorphosis of some kind" (Hamilton, *The Book of Genesis: Chapters 18–50*, 333). "By giving his name, Jacob was confessing his nature, his way of doing things. He was the heel-grabber, the deceiver, the crafty opponent. All that had to be radically changed before he would be blessed. He had to acknowledge who he was," (Ross, "Genesis," 191).

10. Ibid., 192.

took would be a silent declaration of just who was authoring his life's story.

The narrator makes one final note before shifting to the next scene. We are told that ancient Israel did not eat "the sinew of the thigh that is on the hip socket" (32:32), what scholars consider to be "the central nerve of the hip region."[11] However, this ban on eating that part of an animal is not mentioned again in the OT, though it does show up in certain rabbinical writings.

GENESIS 33

Having come to terms with the God of his fathers by very dramatic means, Jacob faced the next day with a little less anxiety than that which had plagued him during the previous night. As Esau and his entourage approached, Jacob grouped his wives and children in preparation for the reunion. And while the 400 men are again mentioned (33:1), Jacob does not seem as panicked as he had been the day before (32:7–8).

In keeping with his overtones of "lord" and "servant," Jacob bowed prone to Esau seven times out of respect,[12] an ironic reversal of Isaac's blessing (27:29). However, the pain of past injustices had faded from Esau's mind; he ran to hug his brother (cf. Luke 15:20) and both men wept as they embraced each other for the first time in many years. Jacob introduced his brother to his wives and twelve children. When Esau inquired about the herds that had been brought to him the previous day, Jacob explained they were intended as a gift meant "to find favor in your eyes" (33:8 NIV). Esau protested that such gifts were unnecessary,[13] but Jacob further insisted that Esau accept them, perhaps to recompense his brother for stealing his birthright.[14]

There is no doubt the events of the previous night were on Jacob's mind as he embraced his brother. He told Esau that seeing him was "like seeing the face of God" (33:10); when Jacob limped away from his midnight altercation on the banks of the Jabbok, he had named "the place Peniel, saying, 'It is because I saw God face to face, and yet my life was spared'" (32:30 NIV). In Esau's forgiveness,

---

11. HALOT 729.

12. The Amarna letters frequently mention the custom of bowing seven times before a king (ANET 483–90).

13. Sarna suggests that Esau's refusal and reluctant acceptance of Jacob's gift was merely in keeping with ANE etiquette (*Genesis*, 230), but Waltke finds it sincere (*Genesis*, 455).

14. "By word and gesture, prostrating himself and giving gifts, he [Jacob] is trying to undo his sins of many years earlier," (Wenham, *Genesis 16–50*, 299).

Jacob noticed a reflection of the mercy God had extended to him the previous night. The patriarch also knew it was only by the protection and providence of God that Esau had not attacked with vindictive fury.[15]

Esau offered to travel with Jacob to provide protection, but Jacob politely refused his brother's offer. His stated reason was that travel with women, children, and young livestock would be slow. When Esau offered to leave some of his men behind to assist, Jacob again refused and promised to continue towards Esau's home in Edom. Jacob, however, had little intention of going there since he settled elsewhere. It is difficult to see how Jacob was anything but outright deceptive about this,[16] proving that sincere life-change never occurs overnight—literally in this case. But at the same time, and this does not excuse his lie, it appears Jacob was at a loss as to how he can refuse his brother's gracious invitation.

Jacob's family made their home at Succoth, a location on the east bank of the Jordan near its confluence with the Jabbok. In this very fertile area, Jacob remained for a while, perhaps "to recoup what he gave away to Esau."[17] He then moved on to the outskirts of Shechem, a city 35 miles north of Jerusalem, where he purchased property. We don't know the precise amount paid since the Hebrew kesitah is an unknown unit of money, and it appears only two other times in the OT (Josh 24:32; Job 42:11). This property would become Joseph's final resting place (Josh 24:32), and Jacob built an altar here in worship to God, just as his grandfather Abraham had done decades before (12:6). This act was a significant one because unlike his prayer in 32:9–12, Jacob here makes his relationship with God a personal one, calling him "El-Elohe-Israel" ("God, the God of Israel").

It cannot be ignored, however, that Jacob is taking his precious time getting back to Bethel where he has a vow to fulfill (28:20–22). Kidner believes Jacob found Shechem an attractive home because it sat "at the crossroads of trade."[18]

---

15. "We must conclude that God had been working on Esau as well as upon Jacob during the intervening twenty years of their long separation," (Coffman, *Genesis*, 406).

16. Coffman speculates that Jacob, instead of being deceptive, simply promised to come and visit his brother, "a promise that he might very well have kept," (Ibid., 408). More plausible is Arnold's assertion that Esau knew he and Jacob were parting company (*Genesis*, 290). But the conclusion most consistent with a plain reading of the text is "that post-Peniel Jacob is not above making false promises and offering misleading expectations to Esau," (Hamilton, *The Book of Genesis: Chapters 18–50*, 347).

17. Sarna, *Genesis*, 231.

18. Kidner, *Genesis*, 172.

Without question, obeying God's will sometimes invites trouble (John 16:33). But delay in obeying God's will *always* invites trouble. Jacob's delay invited trouble...

GENESIS 34

Over the passing years since his reunion with Esau, Jacob's daughter Dinah grew into a young woman. While away visiting friends, the son of the area ruler raped her. There is a fair amount of literature debating whether she was "raped" (HCSB) or simply "humiliated" (ESV) since the Hebrew verb *'ana* is ambiguous here. It is a fact that "rape" is clearly meant when this word occurs elsewhere in similar contexts (Judg 19:24; 20:5; 2 Sam 13:12, 14, 22, 32; Lam 5:11). In addition, the narrator calls this "an outrageous thing in Israel" (34:7), and we later learn Dinah was being held apparently against her will (34:26). At the end of the story, her brothers alleged she had been treated "like a prostitute" (34:31). Thus I believe Dinah was raped.[19]

Regardless of what actually went on, the act itself was illicit. Yet in its aftermath, Shechem fell in love with and wanted to marry Dinah—"he tried to win her affection with tender words" (34:3 NLT)—so he asked his father to make the arrangements. Jacob and his sons were approached with the proposition, although they already knew of the rape. Shechem and his father offered no apology and pretended they did not have Dinah locked up in the city. Shechem offered to pay whatever bride price was demanded; in this particular case, the Law of Moses would have stipulated an amount of fifty shekels (five years salary for a laborer) and no possibility for divorce (Deut 22:28–29). Jacob's sons agreed to the marriage proposal on the condition that the area men become circumcised. The narrator carefully notes this condition was merely a ploy to mask their real plans (34:13).

The deal, however, had to be ratified by all the men of the area, and such was done at an impromptu meeting. Notice that, when speaking to his own citizens, Hamor was silent about his "promise" to Jacob that inter-marriage would mean property (30:10). Did he intend to honor such a vow? Regardless, the area men agreed to the mandated circumcision. While they were recovering from the

19. See Yael Shemesh, "Rape is Rape is Rape: The Story of Dinah and Shechem (Genesis 34)," *ZAW* 119 (2007): 2–21. For alternative interpretations of the Hebrew *'ana*, see Lyn M. Bechtel, "What If Dinah Is Not Raped? (Genesis 34)," *JSOT* 62 (1994): 19–36; Ellen Van Wolde, "Does 'INNÂ Denote Rape? A Semantic Analysis of a Controversial Word," *VT* 52 (2002): 528–44.

surgery, one that was painful and debilitating for several days, Simeon and Levi attacked the city. The other sons of Jacob plundered the town, but Simeon and Levi were focused solely on avenging their sister. Jacob angrily confronted them both when they returned,[20] claiming they had jeopardized their family's peaceful existence in the area; the patriarch later recalled the incident on his deathbed, cursing his sons' violent overreaction (49:5–7).

This story is admittedly difficult to interpret for several reasons. The original audience would have read the narrative in light of the OT's *lex talionis* ("eye for an eye") doctrine (Exod 21:23–25), but Christians must now study it through the lens of Jesus' teaching concerning revenge and forgiveness (Matt 5:38–42; 18:21–35). Jacob was furious that his sons had resorted to violence, though one wonders why he wasn't so grieved when he learned his daughter had been raped (cf. 2 Sam 13:21). In fact, I think Jacob was angrier at how Simeon and Levi had left the family vulnerable (34:30) than he was over their deception.

Meanwhile, Moses as narrator appears to place little (if any) blame on Jacob's sons. English translations read that Jacob's sons "deceitfully" (Hebrew *mirmah*) proposed their stipulation to Shechem and his father (34:13), while Moses may have only meant that they did so "with cunning" (Msg).[21] He certainly allowed Simeon and Levi to have the last word in the story, which effectively legitimized their actions.[22] It could be said that they only did what Israel was later mandated to do to all the Canaanites (cf. 34:25–29; Deut 20:13–14).

Ancient Jewish literature certainly sanctioned what Simeon and Levi did. The Apocryphal book of Judith credits the Lord with giving Simeon "a sword to take revenge on those strangers who had torn off a virgin's clothing to defile her" (9:2 NRSV), and Jubilees 30:5 claimed that "judgment was ordered in heaven against them that they might annihilate with a sword all of the men of Shechem because they caused a shame in Israel." Philo later characterized Simeon and Levi as "prepared to avenge themselves on such profane and impure dispositions,"

---

20. Von Rad calls Jacob's condemnation of Simeon and Levi "a peevish complaint" (*Genesis*, 334), but his fear of retaliation may have been justified (cf. 35:5).

21. Some scholars disagree that the Hebrew *mirmah* can be translated so innocently (cf. Mathews, *Genesis 11:27–50:26*, 601; Waltke, *Genesis*, 465).

22. Arnold notes that the chapter's abrupt ending reminds "one of another text ending in a rhetorical question, Jonah 4:11," (*Genesis*, 298, n. 484). So also Sarna, who concluded the story leaves us with the principle that "the women of Israel are not to be regarded as objects of abuse. They cannot be dishonored with impunity," (*Genesis*, 238).

(*Names* 36.200). On the one hand, we should be cautious in accepting these statements at face-value since later Jewish writers could be motivated "to purge the character of the patriarchs from negative traits," preferring instead "to portray Israel's ancestors as virtuous and pious persons who not only did not have blameworthy traits in their characters but were also zealous to guard the purity of Israel at all costs."[23]

But on the other hand, and to complicate matters further, the Lord mitigated Jacob's fear of retaliation by striking fear in the hearts of area inhabitants (35:5). This could be interpreted as grace in spite of sin, but it also could be no different than God promising Abraham he would shield the patriarch from retaliation at the hands of Chedorlaomer (15:1). Had Abraham's plan (attacking at night) been any less "cunning" than that of Simeon and Levi?

What, then, is to be gained from this story? On an individual level, we can absolutely and definitely say it is always wrong to seek revenge—that belongs to God alone. "Do not take revenge, my dear friends, but leave room for God's wrath, for it is written: 'It is mine to avenge; I will repay,' says the Lord" (Rom 12:19 NIV). It requires remarkable trust to forgive a sin similar to the one Shechem committed, but this is the only way for Christians to live. And while forgiveness may be difficult to extend in the immediate aftermath of a crime, it *must* be extended at some point, and sooner rather than later, lest we burn the bridge over which we too must cross (Matt 6:14–15). In all things, Christians are to consign themselves "to him who judges justly" (1 Pet 2:23).

However, on a societal level, evil must not be tolerated, but rather punished by neutral parties. Note that Paul's remarks on revenge in Rom 12 are immediately followed by an endorsement of civil government as God's agent to punish those who violate moral law (Rom 13:4). This principle was arguably Moses' motive for recording this story. The phrase in 34:7, "he [Shechem] had done an outrageous thing in Israel" (cf. Deut 22:21; Josh 7:15; Judg 20:6; Jer 29:23), makes no sense unless we remember this narrative was preserved for the entire nation of Israel. Levi's descendants would exhibit the same passion as their ancestor whenever they perceived the Lord being profaned (Exod 32:25–28; Num 25:7–8); their brutality (no less than Levi's) secured for them an eternal blessing on both occasions (Exod 32:29; Num 25:11–13). Are we then expected to condemn Levi and Simeon for doing the same?

---

23. Reinhard Pummer, "Genesis 34 in Jewish Writings of the Hellenistic and Roman Periods," *HTR* 75 (1982): 180–81.

I thus contend that Moses meant for Simeon's and Levi's closing words to be a warning to Israel's tribes: if there is sin in the camp, it cannot go unpunished, or the moral fabric of a godly society will quickly unravel. "When the sentence for a crime is not quickly carried out, people's hearts are filled with schemes to do wrong" (Eccl 8:11 NIV).

GENESIS 35

Warren Wiersbe writes, "Moving from Genesis 34 to Genesis 35 is like going from a desert to a garden or from an emergency room to a wedding reception. The atmosphere in Genesis 35 is one of faith and obedience, and the emphasis is on cleansing and renewal."[24] I couldn't agree more. God had been with Jacob through many dangers, toils, and snares. In this chapter, Jacob acknowledged the protection and provision he had received from the hand of God. Much can be (and has been) said of Jacob's negligence in fulfilling his vow sooner. But he did fulfill it, and that seems to be the focus of the narrator in this text.

At God's command, Jacob left the area of Shechem and journeyed to Bethel. This had been the place where he had previously vowed his allegiance to God if he were protected on his flight from Esau (28:18–22). God had indeed been with Jacob since that time, and now that he was about to return to this sacred place, Jacob ordered his family to cast out all the pagan objects in their possession and purify themselves.

It seems quite strange that Jacob's family was not yet monotheistic, but we must concede that Jacob was never the strongest spiritual leader. It is a sad thing when men prove to be ineffective leaders of their families (sometimes through no fault of their own). But just because a man has proven to be an ineffective leader does not make him a poor Christian. The latter portions of Genesis portray Jacob as having little control over his sons, but as this chapter proves, he nonetheless sought renewal in his walk with the God of his fathers. When Jacob demanded his family surrender their false gods, they complied. No man or woman can be called a failure who seeks first God's kingdom and his righteousness (Matt 6:33).

One very odd detail in the family's purification ritual is that they gave to Jacob, along with their idols, "the rings that were in their ears" which Jacob buried under an oak (35:4). Elsewhere in the OT, earrings are associated with idolatry

---

24. Warren W. Wiersbe, *Be Authentic* (Colorado Springs: Cook Communications, 1997), 66.

(Exod 32:2; Judg 8:24; Hos 2:13), and it's possible "that the earrings were in the ears of the idols. In other words, the earrings proscribed for eradication are not pieces of human jewelry but elements of divine regalia."[25]

It's clear in the text that God protected Jacob's family from retribution for the Shechem massacre; "a terror from God fell upon the cities that were around them" (35:5). Regardless of whether God approved of Simeon's and Levi's act, he had sworn to protect the patriarchs (12:3; 15:1; 28:15), and God is always faithful to his promises.

Jacob's rededication to the Lord was followed by three deaths. While the family was at Bethel, his mother's nurse died and was buried there (35:8). We can only speculate as to why notice of Deborah's death is given when we are never told of the deaths of Rebekah or Leah. One possibility is that Deborah represented Jacob's final connection with the pagan culture of Mesopotamia, the homeland of his grandfather Abraham, his mother Rebekah, and other relatives. With all ties now severed, the family of Israel was now free to become exclusively monotheistic.[26]

While at Bethel, God appeared to Jacob and reaffirmed several elements of the Abrahamic covenant, including Jacob's prior name change to Israel, the promise that Jacob's lineage would produce a nation with kings, and the promise of land. It is to the praise of his glory that we serve a God who is not content with making promises once and never mentioning them again, but instead regularly reaffirms his covenant with us. He does so, lest we forget that his faithfulness reaches to the skies (Ps 57:10).

As the family traveled from Bethel, Rachel gave birth to Jacob's twelfth son. But the woman who had cried to her husband, "Give me children, or I shall die!" (30:1), died tragically in childbirth. Difficult as it may be to believe, it has only been in recent times that death during childbirth (for mother or child) has become a rare occurrence, and only in developed nations.[27] In ancient Babylon, it was believed that the demon Lamashtu (known as Lilith in Jewish literature)

---

25. Victor Avigdor Hurowitz, "Who Lost an Earring? Genesis 35:4 Reconsidered," *CBQ* 62 (2000): 29–30. Alternatively, Wenham (*Genesis 16–50*, 324) says these earrings were considered plunder from the massacre at Shechem and had to be disposed in order for the family to be pure in God's eyes (cf. Num 31:50).

26. Sarna, *Genesis*, 241.

27. The World Health Organization cited for 2010 only 21 maternal deaths in the U.S. and 12 in the U.K. for every 100,000 live births, as opposed to over a thousand deaths per 100,000 live births in places like Chad and Somalia.

preyed upon women and infants, and maternal mortality was so common that spells were developed and amulets worn to protect expectant mothers.[28]

Rachel's last words bestowed on the child the name Ben-Oni, meaning "son of my sorrow." But Jacob renamed the child Benjamin. The meaning of Benjamin is debated, being variously interpreted as "son of my right hand" or "son of the south." But this is the same thing since, in ancient Hebrew thought, one faces the east (with the south at the right hand), whereas we today often orient ourselves to the north. The third option is to interpret Benjamin as "son of my old age." This may have been Jacob's understanding of the name's meaning (cf. 44:20), and it is the interpretation preserved in the *Testament of Benjamin* 1:6, a work of pseudepigrapha from the 2nd century A.D. Following the death of his beloved wife, Jacob buried Rachel in a tomb near Bethlehem, a landmark that remained famous centuries later (1 Sam 10:2).

After Rachel's death, Reuben slept with Bilhah, his father's concubine and Rachel's servant. The narrator does not tell us why he committed such an atrocity,[29] but the most reasonable explanation is that Reuben intended to usurp his father's position as leader of the family. When Abner slept with Saul's concubine, Ish-bosheth considered it an act of treason and betrayal (2 Sam 3:7–8). God allowed David to take Saul's concubines in order to exhibit the very same thing (2 Sam 12:7–8). When Absalom revolted against his father and seized the abandoned capital, he slept with his father's concubines on the palace roof as an exclamation point on his rebellion (2 Sam 16:21–22). Later, Solomon had his brother Adonijah executed for seeking permission to marry David's concubine (1 Kgs 2:13–25); again, Solomon evidently perceived this request as a treasonous attempt to usurp the throne. Reuben's act is referenced later as the reason why the firstborn's birthright was given to Joseph's sons instead (cf. 49:3–4; 1 Chr 5:1). So if Reuben did this to usurp his father's authority and establish himself as clan leader, he failed miserably.

The chapter ends by narrating Isaac's death, though chronologically, Isaac wouldn't die until Joseph had been in Egypt for a dozen years. The narrator is clearing the way for the Joseph narrative by effectively shuffling Isaac, then Esau, off the stage. Notice that, like his father Abraham, Isaac "died and was gathered to his

---

28. Handy, "Lilith," ABD 4:324–25.

29. The obscene nature of Reuben's act is reflected in the fact that the Mishnah legislated this story to be read, but not translated, for a synagogue audience (Megillah 4:10). Ironically, the story of Judah and Tamar (Gen 38) could be read *and* translated. Go figure.

people, old and full of days" (35:29, cf. 25:8). And as he and Ishmael had reunited to honor their father in burial, so also Jacob and Esau came together to honor theirs by interring him in the family cemetery, the cave of Machpelah (49:31).

Of the three patriarchs in Genesis, Isaac lived the longest, but less is narrated about him than Abraham or Jacob. His life was a special one. His birth had been a divine miracle. His father had ordered a special expedition to secure for Isaac a good wife. He had been blessed by God as much as his father had been—possibly more so. All of the covenant promises were reaffirmed to him, and Isaac seemed to have enjoyed an intimate relationship with God seen in his devotion to prayer. But Isaac was not without his faults, as we have seen, including his preferring Esau over Jacob when it was clear the former did not merit such favor. Isaac, then, stands as an example of a godly man with earthly flaws. Yet he nevertheless lived "by faith" (Heb 11:20), and that is how we also can overcome this life and inherit the one to come.

GENESIS 36

This chapter is a perfect example of Moses' penchant for weaving admonitions into the genealogical lists of Genesis. While still in the womb, God had promised that Esau's lineage would become a nation (25:23). Later, Isaac further expounded on Esau's violent nature and inferiority to Jacob (27:39–40), but Yahweh had vowed to make Esau into a nation, and this chapter details how that promise materialized.

Two of Esau's three wives were Canaanites, and this was a constant source of aggravation for his parents (26:34–35; 27:46; 28:6–8). By marrying foreigners, Esau exhibited contempt for his father's (28:1) and grandfather's (24:3) wishes. The Law prohibited an Israelite from intermarrying with the Canaanites (Exod 34:16; Deut 7:3), so when Moses noted this detail, he likely intended it "to be an indictment of [Esau's] character."[30]

There is some confusion with the record of Esau's wives given here vs. their mention elsewhere. The record of 26:34 has him marrying two Hittite women: "Judith, the daughter of Beeri, and Basemath, the daughter of Elon" (NLT), but 28:9 says he married Ishmael's daughter Mahalath. In Gen 36, Basemath is supposedly Ishmael's daughter and the two Hittite women are named Anah and Oholibamah. Scholars reconcile this discrepancy in various ways; the simplest

---

30. Arnold, *Genesis*, 309.

238 THE EPIC OF GOD

is that these women had more than one name, as did Esau (Edom) and Jacob (Israel). But another theory, one that is rather elaborate but also possible, is that Esau changed the names of his wives to pacify his parents' rancor.[31]

Esau and his family settled in the cliffs and plateaus of Seir, an area SW of the Dead Sea, and this region would become the Edomites' ancestral lands. Moses goes out of his way to note that Esau didn't move away from Jacob because of lingering resentment, but of a true lack of real estate (36:6–7). If you see in this an echo of Lot leaving Canaan because there wasn't enough room (13:5–12), you're correct. We are learning that, as far as Genesis is concerned, there is only room enough in the Promised Land for heirs of the Abrahamic covenant (cf. 37:1). But God was also looking out for Edom: the nation of Israel was later commanded to treat Edom as family, and to not confiscate their land, because God had reserved it for Esau's posterity (Deut 2:5; Josh 24:4), just as Canaan had been reserved for Abraham, Isaac, and Jacob.

Though Jacob and Esau made peace with one another, their posterity became perpetual enemies. As a nation, Edom is referenced in Egyptian texts as early as the 15th century B.C., and Israel was commanded to accept them as citizens on the third generation (Deut 23:7–8). But there was also the prophecy that Edom would be subservient to Israel (25:23; 27:40), and that was fulfilled during the days of Israel's monarchy. Saul warred against Edom (1 Sam 14:47), but it was David who reduced the nation to a vassal state and installed governors over the sons of Esau (2 Sam 8:13–14; 1 Kgs 11:14–17). Edom freed herself from Israelite domination in the days of Jehoram (2 Kgs 8:20–22), only to be subdued again by Amaziah (2 Chr 25:11–14). The book of Obadiah is a condemnation of Edom because she celebrated the destruction of Jerusalem by the Babylonians in 586 B.C. (cf. Ps 137:7), and both Scripture (Mal 1:2–4) and archaeological evidence testify to Edom's ruination not many years later.[32] But the nation would linger, becoming known as Idumeans in the NT and spawning the Herods.

Included in the list of Esau's family tree are a few persons of interest. Born to Esau's son Eliphaz by way of a concubine was Amalek (36:12). His descendants are well known in the OT as some of Israel's bitterest enemies (cf. Exod 17:8–16; Num 14:45; 1 Sam 15:1–9). The Simeonites later wiped them out during Hezekiah's reign (1 Chr 4:41–43). Also of interest in Esau's lineage is his grandson Teman (36:11); one of Job's three friends was "Eliphaz the Temanite" (Job 2:11).

31. Jed H. Abraham, "Esau's Wives," *JBQ* 25 (1997): 251–59.

32. MacDonald, "Edom," ISBE 2:20.

And then there is mention of Anah, a Horite[33] "who discovered the hot springs in the desert while he was grazing the donkeys of his father Zibeon" (36:24 NIV), a reference to a legend that is now unknown. The translation "hot springs" is based on the Latin Vulgate; Jewish tradition translated the Hebrew phrase as "mules," making "Anah a culture hero, the first to crossbreed the horse with the donkey to produce the hybrid mule." But this doesn't seem to be based on anything more than the similarity between the Hebrew *ha yemim* and the Greek *hemionos* (mules).[34] Others suggest that Anah thought he saw "lakes" in the desert when it was just a mirage, and that "later and more unimaginative generations have failed to see the joke."[35] Again, Genesis sometimes alludes to traditions known to the original audience, but that have since been lost to us.

The statement that Edom had kings before Israel (36:31; cf. Num 20:14) is significant. Though not a child of the Abrahamic covenant, Esau's posterity was greatly blessed by Yahweh; like Israel, they too became innumerable as the sand and stars. Genesis has repeatedly illustrated that God is responsible for the rise and fall of nations, Edom included.

What are we to make of Esau? He scorned his parents' wishes by marrying women who brought them much misery, but he also attempted to rectify (albeit wrongly) that mistake. He is portrayed in early narratives as a brute and a slave to his desires. Later in life, he was magnanimously eager to make peace with his brother—as far as we know, that peace lasted for the rest of their lives. But in the NT, he is remembered as "unholy" (Heb 12:16), and stands as an example of what will happen to those who cannot master their passions through the power of God. Like many other personalities in Scripture, Esau is an enigmatic figure, from whom we must dissect the good and strive not to emulate their mistakes.

33. The Horites were the peoples displaced in Seir by Esau's clan (Deut 2:12). The inclusion of their genealogy in this list reflects the fact that they were later assimilated into Edom.

34. Sarna, *Genesis*, 251.

35. A. F. L. Beeston, "What Did Anah See?" *VT* 24 (1974): 110.

TALKING POINTS

The entire narrative of Gen 32 is a powerful lesson of what it means to trust in God's providence and protection. Many centuries later, David would flee to Mahanaim when his son Absalom revolted against him and seized the throne (2 Sam 17:27). The king had to have known the significance of this place-name; he certainly trusted on that occasion that God would provide and protect. In a psalm he authored during this season of his life, he proclaimed, "I lay down and slept; I woke again, for the LORD sustained me. I will not be afraid of many thousands of people who have set themselves against me all around. Arise, O LORD! Save me, O my God!" (Ps 3:5–7). When Jacob petitioned the Lord's blessing (32:9–12), his display of faith may have been mitigated in part by his decision to split his camp in two. Some may consider that simply to be a shrewd move, but "guilty fears will do this to prayer, for somewhere in the back of the mind is the idea that the answer to the prayer is not deserved and that justice will be meted out instead."[36] I certainly believe that we should "put legs on our prayers" as my dad used to say, but never to the point that we consider our prayers to be little more than insurance in case something goes horribly wrong. The life of faith requires action, but always with the conviction that God is directing the events of life, and that it is ultimately up to him whether we live or die (Dan 3:17–18). As Jacob discovered in Gen 32, angels "are arrayed around God's children to keep them from all evil while He wills that they should live, and their chariots of fire and horses of fire are sent to bear them to heaven when He wills that they should die,"[37] (cf. Ps 91:9–13; Heb 1:14).

Quite a troubling development in these chapters is Jacob's loss of control over his family. Beginning in Gen 34, he failed to respond appropriately to Dinah's rape and was equally unable to restrain his sons from retribution. In Gen 35, his oldest son threatened his leadership of the clan by sleeping with Bilhah. In coming chapters, Jacob would watch helplessly as his family fractured even further; his sons' hatred towards Joseph spilled over into the latter being sold into slavery. This is not the first time we have seen the breakdown of male leadership in Genesis. Adam, Abraham, Lot, Isaac, and Laban have all been culpable to varying degrees. The importance of strong spiritual leadership is

36. Ross, "Genesis," 189.

37. Maclaren, Genesis, 222.

apparent when it is absent. One of the greatest benefits of strong and sound leadership is that it can prevent tendencies toward excess; i.e. it has a mellowing effect on human sinfulness. This fact holds tremendous bearing both on how Christians choose their leaders, and on how Christian leadership is exercised. We are to prefer, as well as strive to be, leaders who exercise moderation (cf. the qualifications for elders in 1 Tim 3:2–7). If we fail in this endeavor, balance will be swallowed up by extremes, and we can expect a lot of unnecessary heartache and trouble (Prov 25:16).

With that said, the opening verses of Gen 35 represent Jacob's efforts to make Yahweh, the God of his fathers, the Lord of his life. Even after his struggle with God and reconciliation with Esau, Jacob took his time returning to Bethel to fulfill the vow he had made (28:20–22). By purchasing land at Shechem, it seems Jacob intended to settle there for quite a while and was only forced to move by the call of God in 35:1. Only then did he fulfill his vow and expel idolatry from his household. Many years later, and on the site of Shechem, an aged Joshua would challenge Israel to do the same. Many Christian homes feature decorations with the text of Josh 24:15, "Choose this day whom you will serve … But as for me and my house, we will serve the LORD." This is a sentiment all parents should take to heart. God has tasked a father and mother with being the primary agents of spiritual instruction in a child's life. Spiritual training of the young is not the *primary* responsibility of the preacher, youth minister, elder, Bible class teacher, or any other person. Such belongs to parents, and as all parents know, children learn more by example than verbal instruction. Therefore, it is imperative that parents be vigilant concerning the examples they set. In the modern family, nothing competes for our affections and attention more than academics and athletics—how many of us have been guilty of forgoing the pursuit of the spiritual in order to attend ball games or complete homework? It is natural and healthy for parents to want their children to succeed in every area. But what shall it profit a child if he becomes a Rhodes scholar or wins the Heisman trophy, yet loses his own soul? Godly parents must emulate for their children, in word and deed, the truth of Matt 6:33—"Seek first the kingdom of God and his righteousness, and all these things will be added to you." That command/promise ranks among the most precious ever given to the people of God.

Separation from the world is difficult to live out. You may be familiar with various religious groups who have tried to separate themselves from the world to significant degrees. One thinks of Amish or Mennonite communities in various places in the U.S. Driving through their communities, one is overwhelmed with sweet nostalgic feelings—that is until you notice some of their barns have electricity and sophisticated hay-balers. We also occasionally read in the newspaper tales of sexual abuse and other crimes committed in Amish and Mennonite communities. We are thus reminded that not even *they* are able to avoid sin and family dysfunction through quaint living. The harsh reality is that "the whole world lies in the power of the evil one" (1 John 5:19). In the wake of the Shechem massacre, perhaps Jacob hoped that, by asking his family to surrender their false gods, such would lead to their leading a holier lifestyle. But such hopes were dashed when Reuben committed his sin. Spiritual renewal and separation from the world is a process that takes place in the inner man. I must be careful about the people with whom I associate, the media I consume, and the places I visit. But the NT increasingly speaks of putting away via baptism the sinful desires of the inner self and replacing them with the power of God's Word (cf. Eph 4:22–25; Col 3:7–8; Tit 3:5; Jas 1:21; 1 Pet 2:1–2). Indeed, only through Christ and his Word can we overcome the world (Rom 10:17; 1 John 5:4).

13

O BROTHER, WHERE ART THOU?

No star shines as brightly on the pages of Genesis as Joseph arguably does. The story of his life is a staple of Sunday school curriculum. However, its compelling nature is due to more than its kid-friendly factor. Joseph's story captivates us so because he rose above the worst circumstances to become second-in-command of a dominant world power while maintaining remarkable perspective. In a dramatic twist, he found himself with the surreal opportunity to extract revenge on those who had hurt him the most, but chose to forgive them instead.

In many ways, Joseph serves as the perfect climax for Genesis. Unlike those before him, he was willing at an early age to completely surrender his life to God's authorship. If anyone had the right to abandon faith and morality, it was Joseph. But even as a slave, he acted out his faith in the God of his fathers. And when promoted to a remarkable place of prominence, he continued to honor God with his decisions. The failures of faith that had plagued Abraham, Isaac, and Jacob are strangely absent from Joseph's story, and his circumstances were arguably the most difficult. So it is that, by this story, Moses began to illustrate for Israel what a faith-full life with God looked like.

But almost as soon as it begins, a bizarre and risqué narrative about Judah and Tamar briefly interrupts Joseph's story. On the surface, the story seems out of place, but as we will see, it highlights several themes prominent in Genesis. It also foreshadows the conclusion of Joseph's story several chapters later. In other words, the story of Judah and Tamar fits its context in more ways than may be readily apparent.

As has been the case throughout Genesis, however, these stories are primarily about God. He is both the play's director and lead-role. In both Joseph's story and Judah's, God proves no circumstance can thwart his plan or leave us hopelessly despondent. Joseph was an imprisoned slave in Egypt's dungeon—what future could he possibly have? Judah incestuously fathered two sons through his daughter-in-law whom he thought was a prostitute—what possible part could he play in God's glorious scheme of redemption? The reality is that no sin makes us useless, and no circumstance makes things hopeless, for it is God who graciously equips us and gives us a future.

Beginning here, the remainder of Genesis is very much about two brothers, in two very different places, so far apart in almost every conceivable way, both assuming the mantle of leadership among the tribes of Israel.

GENESIS 37

As the Joseph story commences, we're left with the impression that he was a bratty, bragging tattletale.[1] The text says he carried "a bad report" to Jacob about Dan, Naphtali, Gad, and Asher (cf. 30:5–13); everywhere else that the Hebrew *dibba* occurs in the OT, it represents a message that is at best derogatory, and at worst deceitfully slanderous (cf. Num 13:32; 14:36–37; Ps 31:13; Prov 10:18; 25:10; Jer 20:10; Ezek 36:3). Due to this and the special coat given to Joseph, his brothers "hated him and could not speak a kind word to him" (37:4 NIV). And this wasn't "hate" in the sense of our own colloquial, very flippant, expression (e.g. "I hate blue/broccoli/the BCS"). Westermann explains:

> When we use the word "hate," we usually mean something that is a personal position or attitude. However, in the Hebrew, the verb "to hate" has a different meaning: it is a deed or the inception of a deed. To practice this kind of hate is like pulling a bowstring taut — it has no purpose unless an arrow is then unleashed. By the same token, hate makes no sense unless one follows through with a corresponding deed. ... Thus, when our storyteller says that the brothers hated Joseph, we should expect that a hatefulfilling deed will follow.[2]

---

1. "God's future agent and mouthpiece in Egypt could hardly make a worse impression on his first appearance: spoiled brat, talebearer, braggart," (Meir Sternberg, *The Poetics of Biblical Narrative* [Bloomington, IN: Indiana Univ. Press, 1987], 98).

2. Claus Westermann, *Joseph: Eleven Bible Studies on Genesis*, trans. Omar Kaste

The favoritism that had plagued Isaac and Rebekah continued with Jacob. He had favored Rachel over Leah, and now favored Joseph over his other sons.[3] Though Joseph was the next-to-youngest, Jacob gave him a special coat. The translation "coat of many colours" (37:3 KJV) originated in the LXX and has become a church- and pop-cultural icon (e.g. children's Bible classes, Andrew Lloyd Weber's *Joseph and the Amazing Technicolor Dream Coat*). But this translation of the Hebrew "has been nearly universally abandoned in scholarly circles"[4] in favor of phrases like "ornate robe" (NIV) and "long robe with sleeves" (NRSV). Whatever its physical appearance, "we can assume the garment was a luxury item that only those who did not have to work could think of having."[5] Little wonder, then, that his brothers resented his authority, especially when he was so much younger than them.

And we can imagine that the dreams didn't help either. In one, sheaves of grain that had been bound by Joseph's brothers bow down to Joseph's sheaf of grain, indicative that Joseph would one day reign over his brothers. Twice it is said, both before and after the account of the dream, that his brothers "hated him even more" (37:5, 8). In the second dream, the sun, moon, and eleven stars bowed to him.[6] This particular dream invited further hatred, as well as Jacob's stern reprimand, but he also "kept the saying in mind" (37:11; cf. Luke 2:19, 51).

Joseph's dreams are powerful indicators that God was directing the events of Joseph's life just as he had for Joseph's ancestors. What others may consider to have been luck, karma, or coincidence is made clear in the Joseph story to be the providence of God. In these dreams, the Lord gave to Joseph a vision (yet unclear) of the course his life would take, and at every juncture in the narrative

---

(Minneapolis: Fortress, 1996), 7.

3. "How strange it is that Jacob, who himself had been brought up in a household of foolish parental preferences between their sons, and who thus had accurate knowledge of the foolishness of such parental preferences, should have, himself, foolishly indulged in the same wickedness," (Coffman, *Genesis*, 449). The favoritism exhibited by the patriarchs was a fault, but it was also evidence that Isaac, not Ishmael; Jacob, not Esau; Joseph, not his brothers, was the elect son. Even through human weakness, God works out his plan (Job 42:2; Isa 55:9).

4. Walton, *Genesis*, 662.

5. Arnold, *Genesis*, 318. The Hebrew phrase for this coat is used elsewhere in the OT only for Tamar's special robe that signified her as David's daughter (2 Sam 13:18).

6. Chronologically, it is not altogether impossible for "mother" (37:10) to refer to Rachel since she may not have died before Joseph had this dream.

is a reminder that the story is unfolding according to God's plan. Nothing was left to fate.

The next scene of the story happened sometime later. Joseph was sent by Jacob fifty miles north to Shechem to check on his brothers and the family flocks (when he bid Joseph farewell that day, he had no idea that he would not see his favorite son for more than twenty years). Jacob's anxiety no doubt had something to do with the massacre that had happened at Shechem only a few years before (Gen 34). But we have to wonder why Jacob sent Joseph out alone if he knew about the family fracture. And for Joseph, this wasn't a quick day-trip to the factory to check on the boys. This was an expedition that would take well over a week. When the brothers were not at Shechem as expected, Joseph, off of a tip, headed some fifteen miles farther north to Dothan on the Via Maris, an international trade route running all the way to Egypt.

Joseph's brothers saw him coming from quite a ways; they no doubt easily identified him from a long distance by his unique coat. They snidely called him "this dreamer" (37:19), or more literally in the Hebrew, a "master of dreams." There is no doubt in the text that the special coat Joseph wore was a source of consternation, but it seems the dreams had been the final straw. They hated their brother to the point that they wanted to be rid of him by any means necessary. What the brothers wanted to do to Joseph (Hebrew *harag*) is what Cain had done to Abel. They didn't intend to club Joseph "accidentally" over the head, but to brutally murder him in a gruesome, grizzly manner. As was the case with Cain, the fact that Joseph's brothers were willing to commit fratricide indicates to us the depths of their depravity.[7]

It is Reuben, however, that comes to Joseph's defense. He convinces his brothers to indeed throw Joseph into a cistern, but not to take his life. The narrator then lets us in on the fact that Reuben intended "to rescue him from their hands and return him to his father" (37:22 HCSB). Reuben could have wanted to save Joseph because he felt some affection for his little brother,[8] but he might have also been motivated by a desire to restore himself to his father's good graces after his earlier indiscretion (35:22).

---

7.   "All sinful thoughts and emotions are freighted with terrible and devastating potential, ever waiting for the right opportunity to reach the natural climax of evil," (Coffman, *Genesis*, 452).

8.   Calvin believed Reuben to have been sincere, and thereby "we are taught that the characters of men are not to be estimated by a single act, however atrocious, so as to cause us to despair of their salvation," (*Genesis*, 2:267).

As soon as Joseph arrived, he was stripped of the symbol of his father's favoritism and thrown into a cistern, pits dug to a depth of 6–24 feet in order to collect water during the rainy season in Israel (the rest of the year, they could be quite dry inside).[9] There may be more to the verb "threw" (37:24) than first appears; Hamilton explains that this verb, when a person is the direct object, "almost always refers to the placing of a dead body in a grave" (2 Sam 18:17; 2 Kgs 13:21; Jer 41:9), "or to the placing of a living body into what is assumed will be its grave" (21:15; Jer 38:6).[10] Joseph's brothers may have intended to leave Joseph in the pit indefinitely and allow him to die from thirst, starvation, exposure to the elements, a wild animal, or whatever else might happen by chance. It's quite certain that they were callously indifferent to Joseph's cries for help (cf. 42:21) as they sat down to their meal.

While they were eating, it "just so happened" that a caravan passed their way. The merchants are at first identified as Ishmaelites (37:25), then Midianites (37:28), Ishmaelites (37:28), Midianites (37:36), and then Ishmaelites (39:1) again. So which were they? Midian was descended from Abraham through Keturah, and Ishmael through Hagar. Scholars go back and forth on how to resolve this; one popular suggestion for quite a while was that the discrepancy proved that Moses had used two different sources to compile this story, and that those sources had disagreed as to the ethnicity of the traders. But in more recent times, commentators have suggested that "Ishmaelites" and "Midianites" simply became synonymous terms at some point, a fact reflected in Judg 8:24.

I say that this caravan "just so happened" to pass by because it seems coincidental or bad luck for Joseph, but it really wasn't. As previously mentioned, Dothan sat on a major trade route, the Via Maris, that ran all the way to Egypt. So "it is no surprise that a caravan should pass that way, but the timing is providential."[11] As narrator, Moses wants us to pick up on the fact that very few details in Joseph's story—the dreams, the anonymous tipster, the caravan—are coincidental. Every specific of Joseph's life (as is yours and mine) was unfolding under the sovereign watch of a loving God who was orchestrating his plan to preserve the world from a deadly famine.

When Judah saw the caravan on the horizon, he suggested the brothers

---

9. Sarna, *Genesis*, 259.

10. Hamilton, *The Book of Genesis: Chapters 18–50*, 417.

11. Walton, *Genesis*, 665.

would better profit from selling Joseph into slavery instead of murdering him. He hoped his reasoning, "after all, he is our brother, our own flesh and blood" (37:27 NIV), would make him appear humane and merciful. But while some may see the brothers' selling Joseph as a more humane alternative to murder, Moses' original audience may not have agreed. Investigation of ANE documents from the 13th and 12th centuries B.C. indicates people were commonly sold into slavery in Egypt as punishment for various crimes, including defaulting on debts. But the demand for slaves became so high that people began kidnapping others and profiting from their sale,[12] so legislation sprang up in ANE societies to squelch this morally horrific act (e.g. the Code of Hammurabi §14). Under the Law of Moses, kidnapping and selling someone into slavery was a capital offense (Exod 21:16; Deut 24:7). My point is that both the brothers' plans were equally damnable.

Nonetheless, hatred and greed make cozy bedfellows. The price of twenty shekels appears to have been the going rate at that time for a slave according to the Code of Hammurabi (§116, 214, 252) and the Law of Moses (Lev 27:5). Since ten shekels was an annual salary for a day laborer of that time, each brother stood to make several thousand dollars in today's money off the sale of their brother (and let's be honest, we have all fantasized at some point about selling our bratty little sibling into slavery).

When Reuben discovered Joseph was no longer in the pit, he became visibly and sincerely upset; the process of tearing one's garments in grief is known as *keri'ah* in Hebrew, and is still practiced by Jews to this day.[13] Meanwhile, the brothers devised a scheme to deceive Jacob concerning Joseph's fate, they would show him the precious coat—torn and blood-soaked—and allow him to draw his own conclusions. The depth of their heartless indifference is seen in their use of "your son" (cf. Luke 15:30) instead of "our brother."

It is difficult to empathize completely with Jacob because, in many ways, he was reaping what he had sown so many years before. The irony is rich in the story: Jacob had deceived his father with goats and his brother's coat (27:15–16). And though he has now presumably reformed, Jacob's past misdeeds continue to haunt him. "Sin always works out its tragic retributions upon the head of sinners. ... Only the merciful providence of God could have woven all of the shameful threads

---

12. Ignacio Márquez Rowe, "How Can Someone Sell His Own Fellow to the Egyptians?" *VT* 54 (2004): 335–43.

13. Sarna, *Genesis*, 261.

of this chapter into a pattern that would conform absolutely to the divine will."[14]

Jacob was understandably bereaved beyond comprehension. He "tore his clothes, put sackcloth around his waist, and mourned for his son many days" (37:34 HCSB). Jacob's grief was inconsolable; no one could comfort him, for he had resigned himself to spend the rest of his days mourning his son's presumed death.

Specifically, Jacob mentioned going "down to Sheol" (37:35), a place that is mentioned here for the first time in Scripture. Sarna writes that Sheol is

> The most frequently used term in biblical Hebrew for the abode of the spirits of the dead. The region was imagined to be situated deep beneath the earth and to be enclosed with gates. There is no concept of "heaven" and "hell" in the Hebrew Bible. The underworld received all men—good and bad, great and small—and all are equal there. It was a place of unrelieved darkness and gloom and of complete silence. None who entered it could return. The etymology of the word "Sheol" is uncertain, and the term is unknown in other ancient Semitic languages.[15]

Occurring 66 times in the OT, the NIV often translates the term as "the grave," and both the LXX and the NT use the Greek *hades*. But we simply have no idea about the origins of this word, and an exact universal meaning is elusive. Therefore, I like that the ESV, in all but one place (Song 8:6), simply renders it as "Sheol" and then allows us to draw our own conclusions. Sheol is a very flexible term in the OT. It can refer to death (Prov 5:5), the grave (1 Sam 2:6), the realm of the departed (Job 7:9), or the state of being in extreme danger (2 Sam 22:6).[16] It seems Sarna is right when he claims that both good and bad people enter Sheol (cf. 37:35; Num 16:30); "nowhere in the OT is Sheol described as a place of torment or punishment for the wicked. At most it is a place of confinement away from the land of the living."[17]

There is a tremendous amount of debate on the exact nature of Sheol, not to mention the broader topic of the OT's understanding of the afterlife. I think that it would be irresponsible at best, and arrogant at worst, to try and settle this

---

14. Coffman, *Genesis*, 455.

15. Sarna, *Genesis*, 262–63. See also Waltke, *Genesis*, 505.

16. Ross, "Genesis," 227.

17. Stuart, "Sheol," ISBE 4:472.

debate once and for all in a book like this. But in this specific instance of Jacob mourning what he believed to be his favorite son's death, it seems the patriarch was essentially saying, "I'll go to the grave mourning my son" (37:35 Msg). If we infer anymore from the text, we run the real risk of forcing it to say something it doesn't.

The final verse of Gen 37 informs us of what happened to Joseph while his father mourned his "death." He was sold as a slave to a man named Potiphar, whom the text calls "an officer of Pharaoh, the captain of the guard" (37:36). The phrase "captain of the guard" is used of Nebuzaradan (2 Kgs 25:8; Jer 39:9) and Arioch (Dan 2:14) who served Nebuchadnezzar. Whatever the scope of Potiphar's responsibilities, it is certain that he exercised oversight over the prison (40:3–4; 41:10, 12). With this note as to Joseph's fate, we would expect the narrative to now segue into his life and experiences in Egypt.

Boy, are we ever in for a surprise…

GENESIS 38

The chapter commences with brief details of Judah's marriage to a Canaanite woman,[18] an event that must have agitated his father as it had Isaac (26:35; 28:1) and frightened Abraham (24:3). Moses certainly seems to have not approved since he never mentioned the woman's name.

Judah's oldest son, Er, married a woman named Tamar, but the Lord put him to death because of some unexplained sin[19] (the first biblical occurrence of this phenomenon). As was expected in that culture, if the deceased had no children, an unmarried brother was required to provide an heir for his brother. But Onan, Judah's middle child, had no intention of doing so (cf. Deut 25:5–10).[20] As the oldest surviving son, he stood to inherit two-thirds of Judah's estate; if an heir for Er were fathered, Onan would have been left with only a fourth.[21] So to prevent this, Onan would ejaculate on the ground during coitus.

---

18. Simeon also married a Canaanite (46:10).

19. The 12th century Jewish exegete Bekhor Shor suggested Er did not want to consummate his relationship with Tamar, perhaps to avoid having children (Sarna, *Genesis*, 266).

20. Objections that the Law of Moses was not yet in effect miss the point. Levirate (from the Latin *levir*, "a husband's brother") marriage was an oriental custom that had been codified into law in several societies. Hittite Law #193 mandated, "If a man has a wife and then the man dies, his brother shall take his wife, then his father shall take her. If in turn also his father dies, one of his brother's sons shall take the wife whom he had," (ANET 196).

21. Paul Watson argues the "double portion" of Deut 21:17 is actually "two-thirds,"

This was not a one-time thing; the use of "whenever" (38:9) indicates Onan did this repeatedly,[22] and it angered God because it showed scorn for his deceased brother, was a violation of his levirate obligations, and was even tantamount to incest since he was evidently only in it for the sex.[23] As a result, God killed him.[24]

Judah's youngest son was not yet marrying age, so he sent Tamar back to her father with the promise that Shelah would one day be her husband when he was old enough. But Judah had no intention of keeping his promise. He may have believed the death of his sons was punishment from God for how he had (recently?) treated Joseph. That, or he simply believed Tamar was cursed; becoming a quick widow in two successive marriages would raise a few questions with anyone, but in the ANE, "women who seemed prone to become widows were in danger of being suspected of witchcraft."[25] Years later, it became evident that Judah had lied to Tamar, so she devised a plan to become pregnant and provide an heir for Er. Tamar's plan was wholly consistent with the custom of the day that called for a widow to marry her husband's father if her husband's brother died without providing an heir.

"After a long time" (38:12 HCSB), and perhaps as much as twenty years later (cf. 1 Sam 7:2), Judah journeyed to Timnah to shear sheep. This event was often accompanied by raucous celebration and inebriation (cf. 1 Sam 25:4, 36; 2 Sam 13:23, 28). Presumably under both the influence of alcohol and the impression

---

meaning the firstborn received two-thirds of the estate, and the final third was divided among the remaining inhabitants. If this is true, Onan stood to inherit even less (one-half of one third) if an heir was conceived for his older brother ("A Note on the 'Double Portion' of Deuteronomy 21:17 and II Kings 2:9," *ResQ* 8 [1965]: 70–75).

22. Eryl W. Davies, "Inheritance Rights and the Hebrew Levirate Marriage, Pt. 2," *VT* 31 (1981): 17, n. 1. Davies demonstrates persuasively in this article that levirate marriage served to protect the plight of a childless widow, but also required a surviving brother to act against his own interests.

23. Sarna, *Genesis*, 267.

24. Note that birth control or masturbation had nothing to do with Onan's demise. Rather, "The text is describing a man who took advantage of the levirate law ... for his own sexual pleasure. He would have sexual intercourse with the woman, but would not fulfill the intent of the law that allowed him to do that, i.e, to raise up a child for the deceased relative," (Ross, "Genesis," 213). Coffman points out that if this text legislates against birth control or masturbation, then it also mandates the execution of any man who refuses to marry his brother's widow (*Genesis*, 461–62).

25. Walton, *Genesis*, 668.

that Tamar was a random prostitute, Judah solicited her, promising her later payment. As a "pledge" or collateral, Tamar insisted that Judah temporarily forfeit his signet ("seal" NIV), cord, and staff (cf. Num 17:2)—"in modern terms, items akin to someone's driver's license."[26] Tamar now had undeniable evidence to later prove Judah's identity.

When Judah sent payment to the prostitute, she was nowhere to be found, so he assumed the incident was closed until he received word from his daughter-in-law three months later that she was pregnant. Believing that she had become so illegitimately (she had), he swore that he would execute her by having her burned alive, a sentence that was unusually cruel since stoning would have been more common (Deut 22:20–24). Tamar countered Judah's oath by producing his seal, cord, and staff, dramatically declaring that the owner had impregnated her. To his credit, Judah instantly recognized that he had forced Tamar into these circumstances by not honoring his word. His statement, "She is more righteous than I" (38:26) was an admission that Tamar's priorities—perpetuating the covenant family of Abraham—were greater than his own.

From my childhood, I have held a deep respect for the Bible as the inspired Word of God, but I'm not sure I could ever preach a sermon on this chapter[27]—mentioning masturbation and prostitution tends to make teenagers giggle and parents of young children squirm. This is arguably the most difficult chapter in Genesis to interpret, and for many good reasons. If the scandalous nature of its contents doesn't make it difficult, its placement sure does. One has to wonder why such a bizarre story about Judah is placed in the middle of the *Joseph* narrative. The end of Gen 37 left us all wondering what would become of Joseph in Egypt. Will he live or die in this foreign land? Will he prosper? Will he ever see his family again? His future is bleak, and no one could fault us for anticipating "the rest of the story." For a book that is 3,500 years old, Genesis is a real page-turner!

So why must Gen 38 come along and ruin the flow of the narrative? Some scholars claim that the story has no connection whatsoever to preceding or

---

26. Ibid., 669.

27. In his exposition of Genesis, H. C. Leupold gives what he calls "Homiletical Suggestions" at the end of each chapter. At the end of his commentary on Gen 38, he writes in full, "Entirely unsuited to homiletical use," (*Exposition of Genesis* [Grand Rapids: Baker, 1942], 2:990).

subsequent events.[28] In his *Antiquities of the Jews*, Josephus omitted the narrative entirely.

But nothing in Scripture is arranged by accident, and this salacious story actually has several connections with Gen 37. It also portends what is to come in the narrative. Anyone who has seen films directed by M. Night Shyamalan will understand this principle. In his films, (spoiler alert!), certain details and objects cryptically augur future developments (e.g. the half-empty water glasses in *Signs*, the red-hooded costume in *The Village*). In Gen 38, several details in Judah's life either hearken back to or foreshadow events in Joseph's:

- In the narratives of Gen 37–38, both stories have a goat at the center of the story (37:31; 38:17, 20), and both turn on a dramatic identification of Joseph/Judah using their respective personal items (cf. 37:32; 38:25), a twist that will occur again in the next chapter (39:13–18).

- In these three chapters are important literary links. The Hebrew verb meaning "to go down" is found three times (37:25; 38:1; 39:1). The verbs "to recognize" (37:32–33; 38:25–26) and "to comfort" (37:35; 38:12) are found twice each.

- God's preference for the younger over the older (Abel over Cain, Isaac over Ishmael, Jacob over Esau) is again put on display. Perez defied the odds and "broke out" before his older brother. Joseph would defy the odds and "break out" over his brothers, as would Judah over his oldest brother Reuben, and Ephraim over Manasseh.

- In Gen 38, Judah succumbed to sexual temptation. In the next chapter, Joseph resisted it.

- The most important principle of this chapter is one that will become the central theme of Joseph's story as well: "God turns

---

28. Brueggemann concludes, "This peculiar chapter [Gen 38] stands alone, without connection to its context. It is isolated in every way and is most enigmatic. It does not seem to belong with any of the identified sources of ancestral tradition. It is not evident that it provides any significant theological resource. It is difficult to know in what context it might be of value for theological exposition," (*Genesis*, 307–8). Similarly, von Rad writes, "Every attentive reader can see that the story of Judah and Tamar has no connection at all with the strictly organized Joseph story at whose beginning it is now inserted," (*Genesis*, 356).

good from evil in order to preserve life (45:5–8; 50:20)."[29] One might argue that this is among the most prominent themes in Scripture, for Christ descended from Judah through Perez (Matt 1:3), and it was the deeds of evil men that led providentially to the salvation of the world (Acts 4:27–28).

One thing that isn't clear is when the events of this chapter took place relative to the rest of the Joseph narrative. We assume they occurred while Joseph was in Egypt, but that is unlikely, as Walton points out. Joseph was in Egypt for 22 years before his family joined him there, yet it is ridiculous to assume that the following happened during that time:

1. Judah marries.

2. Judah has three sons.

3. Two (possibly all three) mature to marrying age.

4. Judah's wife dies and he, "after a long time," sleeps with Tamar.

5. Tamar's sons grow up and Perez had two sons of his own (46:12).[30]

All of this to say that this chapter introduces us to the fact that Judah is on a spiritual journey of his own. Tamar's revelation and Judah's subsequent humiliation most likely occurred after Joseph had been sold into slavery, so this story may be the reason why the Judah of Gen 43–44 seems kinder and gentler than the one in Gen 37. Rough and calloused, he had sold his little brother into slavery and was willing to see his daughter-in-law burned for her sexual immorality. But when challenged, he owned and confessed his sin (38:26). From this point forward, Judah was painfully conscious of his father's grief, and his transformation into a righteous family leader arguably began with his confession. Wenham concludes:

> Without this account of Tamar putting her father-in-law to shame, we should be hard pressed to explain the change in his [Judah's] character. And in its biographical sketches, character change

---

29. Arnold, *Genesis*, 329.

30. Walton, *Genesis*, 667.

is what Genesis is all about: Abram becomes Abraham; Jacob becomes Israel. Particularly in Jacob's family we see examples of character change: Reuben, violator of his father's concubine, later shows great concern for both Joseph and his father, while the upstart cocky Joseph becomes the wise statesman who forgives his brothers. Thus, this chapter has a most important role in clarifying the course of the subsequent narrative; without it we should find its development inexplicable.[31]

GENESIS 39

Meanwhile in Egypt, the narrative spotlight shifts back to Joseph. Purchased by Potiphar as a slave, he subsequently rose to power because "the LORD was with Joseph" (39:2), an important phrase that occurs three additional times in the chapter (39:3, 21, 23). Eventually, Joseph became overseer of his master's entire estate, and things went very well. The situation Joseph found himself in was not necessarily unique in that day; an Egyptian papyrus from the 18th century B.C. "lists the names of nearly eighty slaves in an Egyptian household, together with their occupations. Strangely, the Asian slaves clearly enjoyed superior status and performed the skilled jobs while the Egyptian slaves were given the more onerous and strenuous labors in the fields."[32] But while other slaves might have gained promotion through luck or hard work, Joseph gained his primarily through divine favor (Prov 10:22).

Then comes "the" statement, the type that seems as if it should be accompanied by ominous background music on the biblical soundtrack. Scripture hardly ever describes the physical appearance of someone unless it is crucial to the story, and it does so here: "Joseph was a strikingly handsome man" (39:6 Msg). His appearance did not escape the eye of Potiphar's wife, who began seducing Joseph and was rebuffed on every occasion. Joseph displayed an appreciation for moral absolutes and explained that accepting her proposition would be a gross abuse of trust, a violation of her marriage vows, and a sin against God (39:8–9).[33]

This scene is a stunning one since nowhere else in Scripture "does a woman

---

31. Wenham, *Genesis 16–50*, 364.

32. Sarna, *Genesis*, 271.

33. "[Joseph's] moral excellence can be appreciated all the more if one remembers that he is a slave and that sexual promiscuity was a perennial feature of all slave societies," (Ibid., 273).

brazenly proposition a man in this manner."[34] One tradition claims Potiphar's wife badgered Joseph for up to a year (Jubilees 39:8). Eventually, she tried to force herself on Joseph, but he fled from the house, leaving his coat in her hands. The phrase "to do his work" (39:11) effectively exonerates Joseph from any mischief or wrongdoing; it is clear he was simply going about his regular responsibilities when he was attacked and framed.

They say hell hath no fury like a woman scorned, and Potiphar's wife unleashed a torrent on Joseph for having rejected her. To the other servants in the house, she called Joseph a "Hebrew" in a pejorative tone, appealing to racial prejudices that existed in that day. She also accused her husband of having brought Joseph into his employ in order to "laugh" at her (39:14, 17). This is the same word used to describe Ishmael "playing" with Isaac; it's possible that all Potiphar's wife meant was that Joseph was brought in to taunt her, but she seems to mean Potiphar purchased Joseph that he might sexually harass her (cf. 26:8; Exod 32:6).

In response to these allegations, Potiphar "burned with anger" (39:19 NIV). But who was he angry with? The fact that Joseph was transferred to the king's prison—likely another part of Potiphar's house—instead of being executed immediately seems to indicate Potiphar had a hard time believing his wife's story. This may not have been the first time something like this had happened, and for all we know, Joseph might have been given the opportunity to plead his case to the point that Potiphar had enough doubt in his mind to preserve Joseph's life.[35] My point is that we tend to see Joseph's imprisonment as something nearing the worst possible scenario, and it certainly was not. God was quite obviously looking out for him.

Imprisonment was a form of punishment unique to Egypt in the ANE. It was here that Joseph's neck and feet were shackled (Ps 105:17–18). He surely must have felt as if he had hit rock bottom in life, but Moses surprisingly repeats his previous claim: "the LORD was with Joseph" (39:21). That Joseph somehow escaped a death sentence for attempted rape simply proved God was protecting him in this foreign land. It was in prison that Joseph befriended the prison warden, proved himself a capable manager,[36] and again rose to power in his circle

---

34. Ibid.

35. Coffman suggests the possibility of God revealing the truth to Potiphar in a dream (*Genesis*, 477).

36. A 19th century B.C. document known as the Brooklyn Papyrus lists various levels of prison staff in ancient Egypt, including the Director, and his subordinate, the "Keeper of the

of influence, just as he had in Potiphar's employ (cf. 39:6, 23).

GENESIS 40

When Joseph was 28, two important officers in Pharaoh's administration were imprisoned. It is not said what crime they committed, but given their position, it could be that they were implicated somehow in a plot to assassinate the king.[37] The chief cupbearer would have been responsible for tasting the king's food and drink to insure no one tried to poison Pharaoh. "These officials (often foreigners) became in many cases confidants and favourites of the king and wielded political influence,"[38] (cf. Neh 1:11). The chief baker was almost as important a station since they too were responsible for protecting the king.

While in prison, these two men both had dreams and were distraught that they had no one to explain the meaning. In Egyptian society, dreams were considered an important means used by the gods to communicate with man, especially to foretell future events. As a result, an entire system of dream interpretation sprang up in Egyptian culture. Professional dream interpreters were in Pharaoh's employ. This explains why the cupbearer and baker were so distraught and troubled—they had no access to these professionals and their dream-interpretation manuals,[39] and "a dream without an accompanying interpretation is like a diagnosis without a prognosis."[40] The word "troubled" (Hebrew *za'ap*) in 40:6 appears elsewhere in Dan 1:10 where it has the meaning of "looking sickly, emaciated."[41] Our own idiom, "looking like death warmed over," would be very similar.

How fortunate or lucky that Joseph "just so happened" to arrive (I need a towel to wipe up the sarcasm spilling all over my keyboard). We know better

---

Prison" (K. A. Kitchen, "A Recently Published Egyptian Papyrus and its Bearing on the Joseph Story," *TynBul* 2 [1956]: 1–2).

37. Several rabbis believed that the imprisonment was because "a fly was found in the cup prepared by the butler, and a stone in the cake of the baker," and another rabbi suggested that they both wanted to marry the daughter of Pharaoh (Gen Rab 88:2). A separate and rather obscure tradition maintains they were both beating Pharaoh in Egyptian Fantasy Football.

38. Kitchen, "Cupbearer," NBD 248.

39. James K. Hoffmeier, *Israel in Egypt* (New York: Oxford Univ. Press, 1997), 89.

40. Hamilton, *The Book of Genesis: Chapters 18–50*, 476.

41. TDOT 4:111.

than to consider this occasion a random twist of fate. While Joseph arguably had no idea that this occasion would catapult him from his miserable circumstances, his great faith informed him that the interpretation to these two dreams could only be discerned by God (40:8), not by consulting "dream books" as was done by Egyptians and Babylonians.[42] Joseph's statement was thus a polemic against ANE dreamology.

After hearing the dreams described, Joseph told the cupbearer that his dream portended his release and restoration in just three days time. When this came to pass, Joseph asked the cupbearer to remember the injustices done to Joseph and to mention his situation to Pharaoh. A professional dream interpreter would have expected payment for his services (cf. Num 22:17), and Joseph may have considered fulfillment of this small favor to be an even swap.

The interpretation of the baker's dream was exactly the opposite; in fact, Joseph links the two by saying to each "Pharaoh will lift up your head" (40:13, 19), but to the baker he adds the phrase "from you!" In other words, the baker would be beheaded in three days and his corpse impaled on a stake. Hanging was considered a dishonorable death in ancient times (Deut 21:22–23; Josh 8:29; 2 Sam 4:12). Considering the lengths Egypt went to in a quest to preserve the body after death (e.g. mummification), the phrase "the birds will pick your bones clean" (40:19 Msg) meant his death would be especially ignoble.[43] In the baker's dream, it was rather ominous that he was unable to drive the birds away (cf. 15:11), and that detail foreshadowed his fate.

Bizarrely, we are not told how the cupbearer or baker responded to their respective interpretations. But we do know that everything happened just as Joseph predicted—though arguably not as he planned. The cupbearer was restored, and the baker was destroyed. "Yet the chief cupbearer did not remember Joseph, but forgot him" (40:23).

Joseph would languish in prison for two more years.

---

42. Walton, Genesis, 672.

43. Sarna, Genesis, 280.

TALKING POINTS

Was it only coincidence that Joseph ran into the anonymous tipster[44] at Shechem who told of his brothers' new location? Imagine how the course of Joseph's life would have been different if he had returned home to Jacob and reported: "I couldn't find them." When tragedy strikes, we often play the what-if game. What if I had swerved in the other direction? What if I had not gone to this place? Did Jacob spend the subsequent decades wondering "What if I had not sent Joseph on that errand?" The reality is that free will often brings unintended consequences. But it is not healthy, nor does it deepen our faith, to play the what-if game. The story of Joseph is a testimony to the fact that God is greater than the dark powers; he can and will work all things for our good and his glory (Rom 8:28; 11:36). God was providentially behind Joseph's sale to Potiphar and the false accusation of rape, for it meant that Joseph would be placed in prison where he would meet Pharaoh's cupbearer. When we find ourselves in the throes of suffering and pain, we must refuse to play the what-if game. Ask instead, "What if God is greater than my current circumstances? If God is indeed working out a plan to bring himself greater glory, how should I react?" Then respond accordingly, confident that he can use our disappointment to deepen our faith and bring our lives into greater harmony with him.

In the bizarre story of Gen 38, Tamar is made out to be the heroine. This does not mean that all her actions are commendable or should be emulated, but she nonetheless emerges as an empathetic figure that deserved better than what she received. Not only did Onan not do right by her in refusing to father an heir, but Judah also scorned her when he deceived her concerning Shelah, and he was also quick to condemn her to death when he learned of her pregnancy. The Law of Moses would later call for compassionate treatment of widows, and in the NT, this concern is reflected in the early church's charitable distributions (Acts 6:1; 1 Tim 5:9). Admittedly, women without husbands have greater access to resources today than they did in the ANE. But this does not mean they are somehow less in need of emotional and (if necessary) financial support in the aftermath of so great a loss. There is a connection between the spiritual vibrancy of a church and the amount of concern it shows towards widows—not to mention orphans, immigrants, and the poor. Jesus warned that we will be judged on how we treat

---

44. The rabbis claimed this man was actually an angel (Gen Rab 84:14).

"the least of these" (Matt 25:31–46).

It is hard to imagine that Paul didn't have Joseph in mind when he exhorted the Corinthians to "flee from sexual immorality" (1 Cor 6:18). Once he knew of her desires, Joseph refused to be alone with Potiphar's wife. I find it intriguing and significant that *sexual* temptation is the only kind from which the NT admonishes us to flee (2 Tim 2:22); against all else, we are told to stand firm (1 Pet 5:9). It is the one temptation that appeals to the most primitive of our desires. Against all else, a will that is empowered by the Spirit of God equips us to stand our ground. But God created our sexual nature with a particular weakness, one that is beautiful in the context of marriage (1 Cor 7:5), but terrible outside of it. Christians, whether single or married, should exercise extreme caution and wisdom around members of the opposite sex. Quite simply, there are places we should never go and things we should never do. One meal, one conversation, or one text message may seem completely innocent, but it can certainly lead to your destruction. "Keep your way far from [a forbidden woman], and do not go near the door of her house" (Prov 5:8)—advice Solomon himself would have done well to heed.

We frail and pathetic humans have a bad habit of gauging God's presence based on our circumstances. When times are great, God seems very close and friendly; when the storm clouds gather, he feels distant and hostile—if we believe in him at all. But veterans of the life of faith know that circumstances are no better a barometer of whether God is with you than overcast skies are proof that the sun has vanished completely. That's what faith is all about—being convicted "of things not seen" (Heb 11:1; cf. 2 Cor 5:7). Joseph had no circumstantial reason to believe that Yahweh was with him in Egypt. Can someone really enjoy divine favor that has been sold into slavery by his brothers and then framed for rape and thrown into the dungeon? The answer in Genesis is that they can and do, for God had great things in store for Joseph. Even the cupbearer forgetting about Joseph for two years was, I believe, a part of God's plan (Acts 7:10). "If before Pharaoh's dreams the chief cupbearer had by his own intervention freed him from prison, perhaps his virtue would not have become known to many people. As it was, however, the wise and creative Lord, who like a fine craftsman knew how long the gold should be kept in the fire and when it ought be taken out, allowed forgetfulness to affect the chief cupbearer for a period of two years so that the moment of Pharaoh's dreams should arrive and that by force of circumstances the good man should become known to the whole of Pharaoh's kingdom."[45]

45. Chrysostom, *Homilies on Genesis* 63.11–12.

14

BRAVE NEW WORLD

One of the great disadvantages to reading history, and thus the challenge to every historian, is that readers can lose appreciation for the passage of time. When months, years, and even decades are summarized in a few sentences, it's difficult to feel the agony of prolonged suffering or the drama of a pivotal moment. Knowing the end of the story spoils us. As compelling as films like *Gettysburg* and *Titanic* may be, viewers already know the South loses and the ship sinks in the end.

When reading Joseph's story, it's hard to appreciate his suffering unless we transport ourselves into his context. He was ripped away from his family at seventeen. He was wrongly framed for rape and thrown into the dungeon. Just when he thought he had caught a break at the age of 28, Pharaoh's cupbearer forgets about this helpful Hebrew for two years. For those two years, questions must have whizzed through Joseph's mind in prison: "What happened to the cupbearer? Why did he not remember me? Did his pleas on my behalf fall on deaf ears? Will I be executed? Exonerated?"

Did Joseph have any idea what awaited him?

As I said before, Joseph's story is the perfect climax for Genesis. Moses used it to beckon the children of Israel into a brave new world of faith. And how different is the land of faith from the one we experience by our five senses. Ours is a world that blames God for disasters, but credits fate, karma, or luck for the blessings. Ours is a world in which, if you don't toot your own horn enough, you're quickly left behind. Ours is a world that considers forgiveness a sign of weakness. Ours is a world in which self-promotion and self-advancement are the driving ideals.

But Joseph opted to live in a different world, one of faith. Faith says that God is always with his people, that he will never forsake them, and that circumstances are a terrible way to measure the validity of these things; when Joseph found himself in trials, he believed just that. Faith dictates that we give God all the credit; when Joseph stood before Pharaoh, he did just that. Faith dictates that we forgive those who have hurt us the most, for God forgave us when we had hurt him the most (Rom 5:8); when his brothers stood before him, Joseph did just that. Faith dictates that we serve others rather than ourselves, confident that our heavenly Master sees and smiles upon the work of our hands. When the opportunity was the greatest for personal gain, Joseph did what was best for others.

In all things, Joseph's faith shone brighter than that of his predecessors or contemporaries. His example teaches us what it is to live in the brave new world of faith.

GENESIS 41

It was only by God's providence that Joseph didn't spend the rest of his life in prison. After two years, Pharaoh[1] had two dreams: the first about seven healthy and unhealthy cows, the second about seven healthy and unhealthy heads of grain, the latter being damaged by the "east wind" (cf. Ezek 17:10; 19:12; Hos 13:15; Jonah 4:8).[2] These dreams disturbed him because dreams were considered communication from the gods in ancient times, and unlike other dreams in Genesis, Pharaoh was not the central figure. "It is therefore clear to Pharaoh that his dream experience has a wider, national significance. The customary fawning and flattering expositions of the magicians are therefore unconvincing."[3] Pharaoh summoned his dream-interpretation specialists, but they were powerless (cf. Dan 2:1–11). It was only then that the cupbearer remembered Joseph and his ability to interpret dreams.

---

1. There is little agreement as to the exact date that Joseph rose to power in Egypt, so we are not sure which pharaoh sat on the throne at the time. Even if an exact date were known, Egyptologists are not in agreement on the exact dates of each pharaoh's reign. The most educated guesses include Amenemhet II, Senusret II, or Senusret III (ZIBBCOT 1:129).

2. John Skinner noted that the "east wind" of 41:6 was likely "the dreaded sirocco ... which blows from the SE from February to June, destroying vegetation, and even killing the seed-corn in the clods," (*A Critical and Exegetical Commentary on Genesis* [New York: Scribner, 1910], 466).

3. Sarna, *Genesis*, 282.

Joseph was quickly summoned to Pharaoh's court. He shaved his head and face (cf. Lev 14:9) and changed his clothes (cf. 2 Kgs 25:29). We may think these details mean nothing more than his "cleaning up" to be presentable at court, but "cleaning up" for a Hebrew did not entail shaving since they wore beards from puberty onwards. When Joseph shaved before appearing in Pharaoh's court, it might have been for the first time ever. So this detail is preserved for us as notice that Joseph was allowing himself to be "Egyptianized"[4] or transformed in a way that would render him unrecognizable to his brothers a few years later.

This scene is a dramatic polemic on Moses' part against the pagan practices of sorcery and divination. This same Moses, along with his brother Aaron, would expose Pharaoh's magicians (Exod 8:18–19) as frauds and warn Israel to steer clear of such practices since they were not consistent with faith in God (Lev 19:26; Deut 18:10). When Joseph appeared before him, Pharaoh expressed his belief that Joseph was one of these magicians capable of special powers. "I have heard it said of you that when you hear a dream you can interpret it" (41:15). Joseph's response was stunning and unwise in a context where conventional wisdom dictated the virtues of tooting your own horn. "It is not in *me*; *God* will give Pharaoh a favorable answer," (41:16). In ancient Egypt, pharaoh considered himself to be a god, so Joseph's response wasn't exactly a page out of Dale Carnegie's *How to Win Friends & Influence People*. But Joseph credited the true God of heaven with the revelation (cf. Dan 2:27–28, 30) because that was the truth, and people of faith speak what is true.

The seven healthy cows/heads of grain were seven years of abundant prosperity, while the seven unhealthy cows/heads of grain were seven years of severe famine.[5] That Pharaoh had two dreams of the same substance "shows that God has firmly decided that this will happen, and he will make it happen soon"

---

4. Joshua Berman, "Identity Politics and the Burial of Jacob (Genesis 50:1–14)," *CBQ* 68 (2006): 13–14. "In Egypt, white linen dress and clean-shaven face are customary in the tomb- and temple-scenes and are presupposed in Genesis 41:14, 42; while in Western Asia, the Semitic and other peoples appreciated fine beards and often multi-coloured garments," (Kitchen, *Ancient Orient and Old Testament*, 167).

5. Egypt's fertility was dependent upon the annual flooding of the Nile (see comments on Gen 12). That the Nile would not flood for seven years had to have been difficult for Pharaoh to believe, but it would not have been unprecedented (ANET 31–32; Sarna, *Genesis*, 290). It *was* unusual, however, for both Egypt and Canaan to experience famine at the same time (Waltke, *Genesis*, 536), a clue that God would use this famine to further his purposes for the covenant family and bless the whole world through Abraham's seed.

(41:32 NCV). Have you noticed that, for Joseph, dreams always come in pairs!?

Bizarrely, Joseph then proceeded to give his unsolicited advice as to what should be done in order to prepare Egypt for the severe famine:

1.   Appoint a "wise man" to be in charge. Otherwise, when the famine worsened, food would only go to the influential. Joseph knew all about misplaced favoritism and its cruel consequences. He also knew what it was like to be the disenfranchised of society.

2.   Establish regional overseers. This job was too much for one person (cf. Exod 18:13–26).

3.   Collect 20% of the crop yield for the next seven plenteous years and warehouse it for use during the famine. The grain would be sold back to the very people who had contributed it. This scheme would prove very advantageous to Pharaoh.

Pharaoh recognized Joseph's wisdom, but also that he had been endowed with "the Spirit of God" (cf. Dan 5:14).[6] He made Joseph the second-most powerful person in the country, bestowing him with special privileges and titles in order to fulfill his duties. Several of these titles are known to us from ancient Egypt records, titles such as "Overseer of the Domain of the Palace," "Chief of the Entire Land," "Royal Seal-Bearer,"[7] and "Overseer of the Granaries of Upper and Lower Egypt."[8] The signet ring given by Pharaoh allowed "Joseph to do business in Pharaoh's name since it was used to seal official documents,"[9] (cf. Esth 3:10).

The fine clothes and gold chain likewise designated Joseph as a VIP, and to top it all off, Joseph received a sweet ride to bring attention to his status—his very own chariot complete with runners who acted as an ancient version of the modern-day motorcade (cf. 2 Sam 15:1; 1 Kgs 1:5; Esth 6:9)! It's interesting that all four of the objects given to Joseph as symbols of his exalted position (ring, clothes, gold chain, a chariot) also appear in a 7th century B.C. document

6.   In the rest of the OT, this is a major clue that God is about to accomplish something great on behalf of his people (cf. Exod 31:3; 35:31; Judg 6:34; 13:25; 14:6; 15:14; 1 Sam 10:6; 16:13; Ezek 37:1).

7.   Sarna, *Genesis*, 286.

8.   Waltke, *Genesis*, 534.

9.   Walton, *Genesis*, 676.

detailing the installation of Pharaoh Neco by Assyria's Ashurbanipal.[10]

According to the Brooklyn Papyrus, the prison system in ancient Egypt "maintained, as would be expected, close links with the Department for Agriculture and the Labor bureau."[11] That statement intrigues me because I had never really wondered how Joseph seemingly knew so much about the inner workings of Egyptian agriculture in his day. We obviously must conclude that Joseph's knowledge was God's providence at work, and one option is that Joseph miraculously knew this information in the same way the apostles knew the languages they spoke at Pentecost. But it is just as possible that, during his many years in prison, the Lord providentially exposed Joseph to the inner bureaucratic workings of the Egyptian Department of Agriculture.

The chapter ends by portraying Joseph as enjoying God's lavish blessing and facing the future with great confidence in God. He married into a powerful priestly family in one of ancient Egypt's greatest cities (On, later known as Heliopolis, was located NE of Cairo and was the second most powerful religious center in Egypt). Joseph also received a new name, the meaning of which was derived from an Egyptian word that meant "the creator/sustainer of life."[12] The Lord blessed he and his wife with two boys, and their names confirmed Joseph's belief that God was with him (39:2, 21, 23). God had been faithful to Joseph in times of distress and success, and I find the latter to be the most noteworthy. It is possible for suffering to drive us away from God, but it can also lead us to God—the books of Job, Psalms, and Lamentations attest to this. It is much more difficult, however, to remain faithful to God in times of great success (cf. Deut 6:10–12; 8:17–18; Prov 30:7–9; Luke 12:16–20). Notice that Manasseh and Ephraim are Hebrew names; Joseph had experienced a startling rise to power, but he hadn't forgotten his home or heritage.

Joseph also knew that God was the true sovereign over all that was happening. He knew that God had given him the ability to interpret dreams and bestowed on him wisdom and discernment. In contrast, the sovereign(!) of Egypt appears in this story to be quite terrified of his dreams and their meaning (41:19). Pharaoh was certainly eager to trust Joseph with Egypt's salvation after knowing him a whopping ten minutes. He comes across as little more than a puppet in the hands

---

10. ANET 295.

11. Kitchen, "Egyptian Papyrus," 2.

12. Sarna, *Genesis*, 288.

of God (cf. Prov 21:1; Dan 5:23; John 19:11). And since Yahweh is indeed Lord of all, everything that had been revealed to Joseph came to pass, including the seven years of severe famine.

Ironically, Joseph interpreted God's sovereignty over the future famine as a "call to action." Several translations read that Joseph warned Pharaoh to adopt his plan so that Egypt "may not perish" (41:36; "ruined" NIV). But the Hebrew term is actually the same one translated "cut off" elsewhere in Genesis (e.g. 9:11; 17:14; cf. Exod 31:14; Lev 7:21), possibly suggesting that Egypt didn't face natural disaster so much as divine judgment if Pharaoh didn't heed Joseph's warning. "This moves Joseph's words to Pharaoh out of the category of option and into the category of mandate."[13] What we have in Gen 41 is a paradigmatic collision of divine sovereignty and human responsibility.[14]

The closing words, "the famine was severe over all the earth" (41:57), set the stage for what would happen next. Joseph may have been very content in his settled life, but more challenges awaited him—challenges that would be greater than any he had already faced.

GENESIS 42–45

As the close of Gen 41 had led us to believe, the famine indeed affected Canaan. Jacob's question to his sons is comical, "Why do you just keep looking at each other?" (42:1 NIV), but it also underscores the dysfunction of Jacob's family. Upon learning of Joseph's "death," it seems Benjamin had replaced his older brother as his father's favorite son. So when Jacob sent them down to Egypt, he retained Benjamin. Reading between the lines, there is cause to wonder if Jacob had not all this time secretly suspected his sons' culpability in Joseph's disappearance. If he didn't, he at least feared that harm would befall Benjamin.

It had been more than twenty years since his brothers had sold Joseph into slavery, so it is not unusual that they did not recognize him. Joseph also had a different name at this point (41:45), and in both speech and dress, he would have seemed every bit a native Egyptian. But the hearkening back to Joseph's dreams (42:9) is an indication to the reader that what is unfolding is from the

13. Hamilton, *The Book of Genesis: Chapters 18–50*, 500.

14. "What is theologically noteworthy is the way in which the strong predestination content of [Joseph's] speech is combined with a strong summons to action. The fact that God has determined the matter, that God hastens to bring it to pass, is precisely the reason for responsible leaders to take measures!" (von Rad, *Genesis*, 376).

hand of God. He had given the dreams to Joseph, and he was now fulfilling them as part of his divine plan to save Jacob's family, as well as the whole world.

Much has been speculated regarding Joseph's intentions in these four chapters. Was he punishing his brothers? Teaching them a lesson? Testing them? Did Joseph intend all along for his brothers to spend three days in prison? Did he release them, save Simeon, because he had a change of heart? The narrator never reveals his thoughts, so we are left with an enigmatic portrayal of Joseph. But if he is anything, Joseph is incredibly shrewd; it seems his plot was an attempt to deduce how Jacob and Benjamin had been treated in his absence. Had his brothers mistreated their father? Had they been as hateful to Benjamin as they had been to Joseph? Why was Benjamin not with the others on this first visit—had they disposed of him as they had Joseph? When Benjamin enjoyed favor at Joseph's banquet (43:34) and received lucrative gifts (45:22), would the brothers be jealous? When the silver cup was found in Benjamin's sack (44:12), would the brothers abandon him to a dungeon in Egypt as they had done Joseph? I think these are the questions to which Joseph sought answers. He wanted his brothers to be "tested" (42:15), and the same Hebrew term is used in Ps 66:10, "For you, O God, have tested us; you have tried us as silver is tried." The idea is a "test in the sense of determining or finding out the value of something."[15]

Joseph's accusation of espionage (42:9) wasn't trivial. Spies were common in ancient times, especially when one nation had an apparent advantage over her neighbors during international instability (e.g. a famine). In Egypt's case, their NE border (the one they shared with Canaan) was the least secure, so about a century before Joseph, Amenemhat I constructed a line of forts to protect the border and placed guards there to check each traveler thoroughly and prevent spies from entering the country.[16] Joseph accused his brothers of trying to locate "the nakedness of the land" or "the undefended parts" of Egypt (NASU), "a forceful way of saying 'to pry into all our private affairs.'"[17] If Egypt's storehouses could be located, they were at risk of being plundered.

In response to the accusation, the brothers' rightfully reasoned that no family would risk all of its sons in order to engage in espionage. After three days in prison, the brothers were allowed to leave, but Simeon was kept as collateral

---

15. Hamilton, *The Book of Genesis: Chapters 18–50*, 522.

16. Kitchen, *On the Reliability of the Old Testament*, 343.

17. Kidner, *Genesis*, 199.

until the brothers could produce Benjamin in a return visit. Via his outburst (42:22), Joseph deduced for the first time that Reuben (the oldest) was not culpable in selling him into slavery, so this may explain why he detained Simeon (the second oldest).

In Joseph's presence, and unaware that he could understand their conversation, the brothers conceded to one another that their misfortune in Egypt was retribution for how they had treated Joseph (42:21; cf. 42:28; 44:16), "a reckoning for his blood" (42:22; cf. 2 Sam 4:11). This will become a recurring theme in the Joseph narrative: the brothers' guilt haunted them, even after their father had passed away (50:15). When his brothers discussed their betrayal before him, Joseph often had to leave the room sobbing (42:24; 43:30; 45:2). They say that time heals all wounds, but even after twenty years, the injury of fraternal betrayal was still fresh.[18]

The nine brothers returned to Canaan with hearts as heavy as their grain sacks. The discovery of their money in the grain sacks was embarrassing; it would have caused their families back at home to assume that the money had either been stolen, or that they had sold Simeon into slavery as they had Joseph two decades before (truth is stranger than fiction). Their worst fears were confirmed when Jacob stubbornly refused to allow Benjamin to make the requisite return journey. And why should he? Twice his sons have returned home less one brother and richer in silver. Why risk Benjamin to such odds? Plus, Jacob's refusal to accept Reuben's offer isn't surprising; why should Jacob trust the son who had such little regard for his father's wife, and appears here to have even less regard for his own sons (42:37)?

At the end of Gen 42, we are left wondering about the fate, not only of an incarcerated Simeon, but also of Jacob's entire clan. Their food cannot last forever. Sure enough, it seems an empty stomach changed Jacob's mind, and so he sent his sons to purchase more grain, even including gifts and extra money (43:11–12). But convincing Jacob wasn't any easier this time around. He accused his sons of intentionally disclosing Benjamin's existence (43:6), and Judah had to offer himself as collateral (a more noble act than offering one's two sons) if Benjamin was harmed or didn't return. Jacob's contentiousness concerning Benjamin "betrays his self-absorption that he still saw the threat to Benjamin

---

18. Joseph's private weeping is also a clue to the reader that his public actions may not reflect his private feelings.

primarily in terms of himself."[19]

As was discussed in the last chapter, Judah is the son who emerges as a leader among his brothers throughout the Joseph narrative. They listened to him when Joseph was sold into slavery. Jacob listened to him here and relinquished Benjamin into his trust, and Judah would be the spokesman in Egypt before Joseph. It might even be said that Judah was developing into a better leader than his father; his statement in 43:10—"If we had not delayed, we would now have returned twice"—is a stinging indictment of Jacob's belligerence that had almost starved the clan.

When his brothers arrived in Egypt, Joseph threw a banquet in their honor, a fact that astonished the Egyptians as much as Joseph's seating his guests per birth-order astonished his brothers. Egyptians of antiquity possessed feelings of racial and religious superiority towards their neighbors. Plus, meats that were staples in the diets of Greeks (beef) and Hebrews (lamb) were sacred to the Egyptians and therefore offensive. The Greek historian Herodotus notes that no Egyptian would even go near the eating utensils of the Greeks (*Histories* 2.41). This might explain why the Egyptians would not eat with Israel's sons, an act they considered to be "an abomination" (43:32) just as certain sins are abhorrent to God (Lev 18:22, 26, 29).

Nonetheless, Joseph's fondness for Benjamin is very clear in the scene. When he met Benjamin, he had to leave the room sobbing (43:30). At dinner, Benjamin received five times what his brothers received (43:34). Indeed, Joseph shunned cultural norms and enjoyed a very lively party with all his brothers; the phrase "they drank and were merry with him" means they all got drunk (cf. 9:21; 1 Sam 1:14; 2 Sam 11:13).

After the meal, the brothers were again sent on their way, only to be chased down by Joseph's guards. The silver cup that Benjamin allegedly stole was one that Joseph claimed he used for purposes of divination (44:5). "From Mesopotamia we are familiar with a couple of techniques that use liquids. Lecanomancy functions by observing the shapes that oil makes when poured into water. Hydromancy gains information from the ripples or reflections in the water itself."[20] But while this was common in ANE, it is doubtful the practice existed in Egypt during

---

19. Kidner, *Genesis*, 215.

20. Walton, *Genesis*, 681.

Joseph's time,[21] and divination was later outlawed in Israel (Lev 19:26; Deut 18:10–11), so it is hard to imagine Joseph actually engaging in divination when God revealed future events to him through dreams. It's more likely that Joseph wanted his brothers to *think* he was capable of divination (cf. 44:15).

In response to the accusation that one of them had stolen Joseph's cup, the brothers protested that they could not be dishonest men if they had willingly returned the money from the previous visit (44:8). But their protests fell on deaf ears. Upon their return, the speech that Judah gave is a rather eloquent one. Much of it rehearses the story so far, an attempt on his part to give the brothers' side of things. Note especially that Judah's opening statement, "God has uncovered your servants' guilt" (44:16 NIV), may be a confession of how they had treated Joseph.

But the main thrust of Judah's speech is that if anything should happen to Benjamin, it would be the end of Jacob. Judah loved his father, and after seeing Jacob grieve Joseph's "death" the last two decades, Judah was willing to spend the rest of his life in an Egyptian prison if it meant salvaging his father's joy. This is a very different Judah than the one who had sold Joseph into slavery with little regard for how it would affect his father. "Twenty-two years earlier, he stood with his brothers and silently watched when the bloodied tunic they had brought to Jacob sent their father into a fit of anguish; now he is willing to do anything in order not to have to see his father suffer that way again."[22] Judah's speech is well summarized by his final words: "How can I go back to my father if the boy is not with me? Oh, don't make me go back and watch my father die in grief!" (44:34 Msg).

Upon hearing Judah's impassioned plea, Joseph yet again "could not control himself" (45:1) and began sobbing—so much so that "the king's palace heard about it" (45:2 NCV). Clearly, the brothers had a greater love for their father's second-favorite son than they had had for his first. Joseph emptied the room of everyone else except his brothers. This, right here, is the climax of Joseph's entire story. Joseph was in the very position that any emotionally-wounded person would love to be in—to have the opportunity to punish those who have hurt you the most, and with no repercussions whatsoever. No wonder that, when Joseph revealed himself to his brothers, "they were terrified at his presence" (45:3 NIV), a term the OT uses to describe that sickening gut-wrench or paralyzing fear an army has when they realize all hope is lost in battle (Exod 15:15; Judg 20:41; Ps

---

21. Kidner, *Genesis*, 205.

22. Robert Alter, *The Art of Biblical Narrative* (New York: Basic, 1981), 175.

48:5). Joseph's brothers sensed the Grim Reaper in their midst.

Joseph's speech to his brothers ranks among the most important passages in Scripture. His ability to forgive is as remarkable as was his perspective. He urged his brothers not to wallow in their guilt because God had used their sin to his glory. During his 22 years in Egypt, Joseph had at some point glimpsed the plan of God at work. He understood that his brothers had sinned, but that God had used their sin to deliver many from certain destruction. And because he could see God at work in his suffering, Joseph was able to forgive his brothers' evil act. Joseph concluded: "God sent me before you to preserve for you a remnant on earth, and to keep alive for you many survivors" (45:7).

Joseph went so far as to invite his family to move to Egypt so that he could care for them during the remaining years of famine, years in which the famine would reach a greater severity; all agricultural production would reach a devastating halt (45:6). Pharaoh, out of gratitude to Joseph for his shrewd management of the famine, generously reserved land in Goshen for Jacob and his family, an area located in the NE portion of the Nile delta that made for excellent pasture. He also commissioned carts (likely two-wheeled carts drawn by oxen)[23] for use in moving the family of Israel from Canaan. In a parting act, Joseph gave his brothers a change of clothes,[24] and to Benjamin five changes of clothes. Jacob had exhibited his favor of Joseph with a special coat. Here, Joseph did the same for his little brother.

Joseph's urging his brothers not to "quarrel" on their way home (45:24) would be better translated "do not fear" (cf. NKJV). The Hebrew *ragaz* has to do with fear or anxiety (cf. Exod 15:14; Mic 7:17; Hab 3:16); it is often used in the OT to describe a violent earthquake (1 Sam 14:15; 2 Sam 22:8; Ps 18:7; Amos 8:8). Joseph's brothers weren't prone to argue on their way home so much as fear for their lives. What if Joseph sent his posse after them to arrest them again or, worse, to execute them? "Our suspicions are the reflections of our own hearts."[25]

The section ends with an aged Jacob, one who thought his only hope was to see his beloved Joseph in Sheol (37:35), learning that Joseph was alive and well.

---

23. Cyril Aldred, "An Unusual Fragment of New Kingdom Relief," *JNES* 15 (1956): 150–52.

24. Tradition holds that among the clothes Joseph's brothers received were shirts that read, "My bratty little brother became vizier of Egypt and all I got was this lousy t-shirt."

25. Maclaren, *Genesis*, 263. Matthew Henry added, "Guilty consciences are apt to take good providences in a bad sense, and to put wrong constructions even upon those things that make for them. They flee when none pursues," (*Commentary on the Whole Bible*, 1:235).

His heart was at first "numb" or hardened to the fact that such could be true, but then his spirit "revived." God had transformed the patriarch's bitterest heartache into a heartfelt "Hallelujah!"

Joseph's perspective, one that was convinced of God's sovereignty over all things (Prov 19:21; 20:24), is a model for us to follow. Many of you reading these words have endured unspeakable hardship, as have I, and such often comes at the hands of evil people. If we were to collectively tell our stories, the world would not contain enough Kleenex to dry our eyes.

But no matter the severity of your suffering, recovery and healing are impossible until you come to grips with this truth: God is sovereign. When we enjoy great blessings, God is at work. When we endure great suffering, God is at work. In all things, God is at work. He does not cause evil people to make our lives miserable (Jas 1:13), but he is always mysteriously at work in their evil deeds to bring great glory to himself and great good to his people. You and I will never heal from our hurt until we have made our peace with that reality, until we can acknowledge to our Father in prayer, "The sword is theirs; the hand is Thine."[26]

Whenever God's people are made to suffer at the hands of evil people, we must find a way to surrender our grief to the Lord and ask that he use it to glorify himself. We must strain to see even the faintest glimmer of God at work in our heartache, for that is the only way the heart can heal.[27]

GENESIS 46–47

With his entire clan, Jacob moved to Egypt. No one and nothing was left behind because this was not a "Hold the fort down; we'll be back soon" kind of move. At Beersheba, the border of the Promised Land, God appeared to him.[28] Jacob was promised that this move was consistent with God's will—remember

---

26. Maclaren, *Genesis*, 265.

27. "There will be little disposition in us to visit offences against ourselves on the offenders, if we discern God's purpose working through our sorrows … If we would cultivate the habit of seeing God behind second causes, our hearts would be kept free from much wrath and bitterness," (Ibid., 269).

28. This divine revelation, beginning with "Jacob, Jacob," is significant, not only because it is the last that Jacob receives, but it is also the last until a voice called out to a lowly desert shepherd from a burning bush, "Moses, Moses."

that the Lord had previously prohibited Isaac from visiting Egypt during famine (26:2). Jacob may have been apprehensive about the move for this reason, which may also explain why he stopped at Beersheba (the border of Canaan proper) to worship "the God of his father Isaac" (46:1). Yahweh also affirmed to the patriarch that he would continue to work out his plan to make Abraham's seed a mighty nation, and that Jacob and Joseph would not be separated again before Israel passed, something Jacob had not envisioned since he had been made to believe that Joseph was dead. For all of Jacob's scheming in life, his story would enjoy a happy ending due entirely to the grace of God.

The roster of Jacob's family (46:8–27) is given primarily as an illustration of how truly small Jacob's family was when it entered Egypt vs. when it left four centuries later (Exod 1:5; Deut 10:22). "Jacob is, indeed, in the process of becoming the great nation promised to Abraham."[29] This list does not seem to be a comprehensive one (what of Jacob's daughters-in-law and granddaughters?). But since the number seventy represents completeness (cf. Gen 10), this roster seems indicative that all of Jacob's family made the move. No remnant was left behind at the old homestead to keep an eye on things until the rest could return.

And who is it that went ahead of the family to arrange the reunion of Jacob and Joseph? It was Judah, the one brother most responsible for separating father and son decades earlier. When Joseph went to meet the caravan, the reunion with his father (46:29) becomes one of the most touching scenes in Scripture, and is in need of no comment.

A confusing theme in this section is the attitude Egyptians held towards shepherds. Joseph's claim that they all were "detestable to the Egyptians" (46:34 NIV) has puzzled scholars because there exists nothing in Egyptian literature that expresses such disdain, and Pharaoh later entrusted his flocks to the care of Joseph's brothers (47:6).[30] What unpleasantness, then, could Joseph have been attempting to avoid when he "coached" his brothers for their audience with Pharaoh? Perhaps Joseph meant that Egyptians despised *foreign* shepherds. It is known that, during this period, strained relations existed between Egyptians and an ethnic group known as the Hyksos who were from the same region as

---

29. Arnold, *Genesis*, 369.

30. "Ramses III is said to have employed 3,264 men, mostly foreigners, to take care of his herds. The appointment of some of Joseph's brothers to supervise the king's cattle means that they are to be officers of the crown and thus will enjoy legal protection not usually accorded aliens," (Sarna, *Genesis*, 319).

Jacob's family. The Egyptians derogatorily referred to them as "shepherd kings."[31] Another possibility is that Joseph meant wealthy Egyptians found shepherding an "abomination," i.e. they thought it was beneath them.[32] By being honest about their occupation, Pharaoh would be assured that he wasn't welcoming a family who would mooch off the government in the middle of a famine. Rather, Joseph hoped his family would receive a favorable welcome in Egypt, be allowed to live separately on their own, and even enjoy a decent living as stewards of Pharaoh's flocks and herds.

When Jacob was introduced, he blessed Pharaoh, and rightfully so since the regent had done so much to bless the family of Israel. What is quite strange in this scene is that Jacob characterized his years on earth as "few and evil" (47:9), particularly to a complete stranger and leader of a world power. It is especially noteworthy that Jacob considered his life a sojourn (Heb 11:13–16).

As the family settled in Goshen (known to the narrator as "the land of Rameses," Exod 12:37), Joseph kept his promise and provided for all his family. The famine, however, worsened in Egypt. The remainder of Gen 47 provides further details of Joseph's actions to save Egypt and enrich Pharaoh. The people first exchanged their money, then their livestock, and finally their own land for food. This practice led to all of Egypt's land and wealth being centrally owned by the government, and it contributed to Egypt's rise to dominance in the ancient world.

The fifth of the harvest that the people paid as rent was a much lower percentage than exemplified elsewhere in the ANE (a third was more common).[33] Joseph's shrewd management skills brought blessings to Pharaoh and the entire nation of Egypt, a fulfillment of God's promise to Abraham: "all peoples on earth will be blessed through you" (12:3 NIV). It's also worth pointing out that Joseph did nothing to enrich himself during this period. He was unselfishly faithful to Pharaoh in all things, and the people considered him to be a kind, not cruel, administrator.

While the Egyptians suffered through the famine, Jacob's family prospered and "multiplied greatly." Within 400 years, they would go from a small group of 70 to numbering 603,550 fighting men on the occasion of the exodus (Num 1:45–46). As for Jacob, he knew his days were drawing to a close, so he made Joseph swear to him (cf. 24:2–3) that he would be buried in Canaan. Even in

---

31. Hamilton, *The Book of Genesis: Chapters 18–50*, 603.

32. Ibid., 608.

33. Waltke, *Genesis*, 591. In contrast, a sharecropper in the old American South kept at best one-third to one-half of his harvest; certainly nothing approaching 80%.

his death, the patriarch wanted to declare his great faith in the promises of God.

The final phrase of Gen 47 is rather ambiguous. The ESV reads, "Israel bowed himself upon the head of his bed," while the NIV renders it, "Israel worshiped as he leaned on the top of his staff."[34] Walton prefers the former translation— "bowing down at the bed acknowledges divine care and protection. We can conclude, then, that Jacob's bowing at the head of his bed is an acknowledgment of divine care that has allowed him to pass clan leadership successfully to his son Joseph,"[35] (cf. 1 Kgs 1:47).

As he had declared to Pharaoh, Jacob had lived a difficult life and his sojourn on earth was about to end. But God had been faithful to the patriarch, particularly through the providential guidance and care that had been exercised concerning Joseph, and thereby to Jacob's entire family. For all of his spiritually-troubled past, Jacob died full of faith.

But not before receiving from God a powerful glimpse into the future.

---

34. In a footnote, the NIV gives an alternative translation nearly identical to the ESV.

35. Walton, *Genesis*, 710; cf. Raymond de Hoop, "'Then Israel Bowed Himself...' (Genesis 47.31)," *JSOT* 28 (2004): 467–80.

TALKING POINTS

It is natural to hate pain and want desperately to avoid discomfort. When submerged in suffering, it is common to wonder if any possible good can come of it. But in exchange for confessing God as the sovereign Author of life, we gain with that confession the hope that he will orchestrate something truly beautiful from something so terrible. Our pain will give way to pleasure; temporary suffering will vanish into eternal serenity. For Joseph, all of his unjust mistreatment brought him closer to his exaltation as vizier of Egypt. "Not one thread in the tapestry could have been withdrawn without spoiling the pattern."[36] Had he not been betrayed by his brothers and framed for rape, what are the odds he would have ever met Pharaoh's cupbearer? If the cupbearer had secured Joseph's release instead of forgetting him for two years, would Joseph have returned home to Canaan?[37] Would he have proven an effective manager of Egypt's pantry without experience as head of Potiphar's household? So also must Christians hope in faith that "this light momentary affliction is preparing for us an eternal weight of glory beyond all comparison" (2 Cor 4:17).

How does one foster the perspective Joseph possessed, one in which evil and suffering are considered redemptive tools in the hand of God? At the risk of oversimplifying a process fraught with great emotional strain, let me suggest the following: 1.) Make every decision assuming that God cares about you. God seems most hidden when we suffer, and Satan would like nothing more than to deceive us so. We thus should actively affirm God's presence and concern for us. Joseph went so far as to bestow names to his sons that reminded him of God's providential presence (41:51–52). 2.) Ask God to reveal to you the reason for your suffering, and then learn to be content with whatever answer he gives, even if it's silence. I believe the Christian can withstand untold hardship if he is convinced it is for the greater good. By seeing God work circumstances for "the saving of many lives" (50:20 NIV), Joseph found it easier to forgive. 3.) Seek out ways for your pain to bring God praise. If victims are not careful, they can become victimized by their own self-absorption. Many of the psalms of lament (e.g. Pss 57, 142) begin with self-pity but end in worship. When we lose ourselves in praise of God's greatness, we are better able to see his plan at work

---

36. Maclaren, *Genesis*, 257.

37. Henry, *Commentary on the Whole Bible*, 1:228.

and remain steadfast in our suffering.

It seems that Jacob and his family went down to Egypt somewhat expecting to return home to Canaan after the famine had abated. But seventeen years later, even after their father had died, they remained. In fact, Jacob's family sojourned in Egypt for more than four centuries until God brought them out in a mighty way just as he had prophesied to Abraham (15:13–14). Funny, isn't it, how our plans for the future so rarely turn out as we expected or intended? Though still in my 20s, I know what it is like to expect to stay in one place for years, only for God to shorten it to a few months. Perhaps our focus should not be on the length of our stay in any one place, but rather on how we conduct ourselves while we are there. We have no control over the morrow, only our motives and actions. Let us allow God to handle the rest.

The text is unequivocal about the fact that Egypt survived this devastating famine because of Joseph (and, in truth, because of God). Pharaoh particularly prospered via God's blessing through the seed of Abraham. Years later, another Egyptian regent would mistreat Abraham's seed (Exod 1:8–22); he subsequently fell under God's curse (Exod 7:4). God was serious when he promised the patriarch, "Him who dishonors you I will curse" (12:3). As heirs of the Abrahamic promises, Christians can rest secure in the knowledge that those who mistreat us will receive greater retribution from the Judge of all the earth (Col 3:25; 1 Thess 4:6) It is his to remember and repay; ours is to forgive and forget (Rom 12:17–21). There is coming a day when the Son, the Word of God, will reappear in the skies. His spoken word will be his fearsome weapon, vengeance will be poured out on all enemies of the King (Rev 19:11–15), and all his saints will praise him (2 Thess 1:10). What a day, glorious day, that will be.

15

FOR YOUR FAMILY'S SAKE

My father passed away suddenly during my junior year of college, and as you can guess, it was a very traumatic experience for my family. In spite of his imperfections, sins, and personality quirks, dad had been a wonderful father to me, so in the aftermath of his death, I felt profoundly disoriented. Dad had been my best friend. Dad had been my mentor and counselor. Dad had been my role model as a preacher, minister, husband, and father. Dad had been my rock. When his life ended, I felt as if my future had gone up in smoke.

I thank God for godly fathers, particularly my godly father. But I have since realized that I had conferred on my dad a very unhealthy status, one that he would not have been thrilled with had he known about it. This was brought home to me about six months after his death; a beloved college professor, using a simple illustration of a pen and paper clips, demonstrated that I had been relying upon my dad for too much, and on God for too little.

In all of our relationships, especially the very important ones, you and I have a tendency to invest too much. Fill in the blank—"I couldn't live without _____." See my point? As much as we have invested in those we love, there is coming a day when those individuals won't be around anymore. Death comes to us all. Losing my dad caused me to feel as if I had lost my future also, but that is never the case when we put our trust in the Lord.

Genesis' final scenes focus on the death of Jacob. After seventeen years in Egypt, he knew the end of his life was imminent, and it was now time to impart a final blessing to his sons. The patriarchal blessing was a means of symbolically passing on the promises of God to the next generation. We have seen multiple occasions where a father's blessing to his son held significant sway over future events; Jacob's blessing of his sons is a sort of capstone to this idea in Genesis.

What follows is an unprecedented scene in Scripture. So far, no word of prophecy has come from mortal lips, and no recorded words have been uttered on one's deathbed. But Jacob was given remarkable vision into the future, particularly to the time when the Promised Land would be conquered and settled, and even beyond. As he blessed his sons, the events of the future unfolded before Jacob's dim eyes like movie scenes.

The author of Hebrews considers this event to be Jacob's greatest act of faith (Heb 11:21). In the face of death, it indeed requires tremendous faith in God to look forward into the future, but Jacob was confident that his death did not also mean death for the promises of God. Those would continue for the next generation. Like all the heroes of faith, Jacob recognized that his was a small part of a grander story, a temporary task in the context of a grander scheme (Heb 11:13–16). And his children needed to know that their father's death did not also spell the death of their future—far from it. For the people of God, death is always a new beginning.

GENESIS 48:1–49:28

Notified that his father was ill, Joseph brought his two sons (now aged about twenty years) to see their grandfather. Jacob's condition was quite grave since he had to summon his strength in order to sit up in bed. But even at such an advanced age, one at which many have forgotten so much that was once dear to them, Jacob still remembered and rehearsed the great promise that God had made to him at Bethel, notably the promise to make the patriarch "fruitful and multiply" him (48:4).

When Jacob asked, "Who are these?" referring to Joseph's sons, I don't think it was because he could not recognize them. We are told just a few verses later that his eyes "were dim with age, so that he could not see" (48:10), but that detail may be provided to explain why Joseph thought his father was mistaken in 48:17. By asking, "Who are these?" in 48:8, Jacob rhetorically called attention to Ephraim and Manasseh being Joseph's sons, and what follows is Jacob's formal adoption of these two boys as his own (48:5), "thereby elevating them to full membership in the Israelite tribal league."[1] In effect, these two boys split

---

1. Sarna, *Genesis*, 325. "Such adoptions within a family are well attested in the ancient Orient," (Wenham, *Genesis 16–50*, 463); cf. I. Mendelsohn, "A Ugaritic Parallel to the Adoption of Ephraim and Manasseh," *IEJ* 9 (1959): 180–83.

the double-portion of blessing and inheritance due the firstborn.[2] Jacob also considered these sons as replacements for the ones Rachel might have produced had she not died prematurely (48:7).

Joseph presented Manasseh (the oldest) at Jacob's right hand and Ephraim (the youngest) at his father's left so that Manasseh would receive the firstborn blessing. The right hand was considered "the position of strength, honor, power, and glory" (cf. Exod 15:6; Ps 89:13; Prov 3:16; Eccl 10:2; Matt 25:33; Acts 2:33).[3] But in a twist that should by now come as no real surprise, Jacob unequivocally expressed his preference for the younger and gave Ephraim the birthright.[4]

Such an unexpected move disturbed Joseph, for he knew that a blessing, once given, was irrevocable (cf. 27:35; Num 23:20; Rom 11:29). Several translations portray him as "displeased," but the Hebrew ra'a elsewhere in Genesis is translated "wicked" (19:7; 38:10) or "evil" (44:5; cf. Exod 5:22–23). At worst, Joseph thought his father was doing something immoral; at best, that he was so physically blind that he was mistaken. It's likely that only Joseph's profound respect and affection for his father prevented him from giving full expression to his anger. However, and in contrast to Isaac (27:1), "Jacob may be losing his sight, but he is not losing his insight."[5] The patriarch had selfishly once gained the preferred blessing over his brother by deception, but he now understood that God's ways, though mysterious at times, are to be followed with radical obedience.

To Joseph specifically, Jacob gave the property he had obtained at Shechem (33:19; cf. Josh 24:32; John 4:5). His reference to it as land "that I took from the hand of the Amorites with my sword and with my bow" (48:22) points to an event not preserved in Genesis. Some suggest he is referring to the massacre launched by Simeon and Levi, but considering his disapproval (34:30), I find this unlikely—Jacob clearly inferred he personally took this particular plot of land. It should also be noted that translators are divided over how to render the Hebrew shekem in 48:22—"mountain slope" (ESV, HCSB; cf. "ridge" NIV), "portion" (NASU, NRSV), or "Shechem" (NCV, NJB)? We simply aren't sure. The word is most often translated as "shoulder" when it appears elsewhere in Genesis

2. Walton translates the Hebrew literally as, "Like Reuben and Simeon they will be to me," (Genesis, 710).

3. Waltke, Genesis, 98.

4. "As surprising as this appears to be to Joseph, to the readers of Genesis it occasions only a wry grin (here we go again!)," (Walton, Genesis, 711).

5. Hamilton, The Book of Genesis: Chapter 18–50, 636.

(e.g. 9:23; 21:14; 24:15) and the OT (e.g. Josh 4:5; 1 Sam 9:2; Ps 81:6), so it's plausible that it means a shoulder (i.e. "ridge") of land.

Jacob's great faith on his deathbed is absolutely remarkable for several reasons. When Jacob spoke of Abraham's and Isaac's relationship with God (48:15), he used Hebrew verb forms that insinuated completed action (which makes sense as both were no longer living). But when he spoke of God's action, he used participles that translate to continuous or on-going action.[6] Abraham was dead; so was Isaac, and Jacob would soon join them. But the patriarch made clear to his family that God wasn't going anywhere. Jacob had no reason to fear, and neither did his tribe. He also promised that God would restore Israel, not to "Canaan," but "to the land of your fathers." "Canaan" was a geo-political term; by calling it "the land of your fathers," Jacob affirmed that it rightfully belonged to Abraham's descendants. God had sworn to it, and he would be faithful, for none of his promises can ever fail (Josh 21:45; Ps 119:140; 2 Cor 1:20; Tit 1:2).

Physically, Jacob was nearly blind, but on his deathbed, God gave the patriarch a very special, prophetic glimpse of what was in store for his children. I believe that, as he saw the faces of his sons around him, Jacob saw the future of their tribes stretching to the reign of David and beyond. "Gather yourselves together, that I may tell you what shall happen to you in days to come" (49:1). In this way, God reaffirmed to Jacob that the covenant promises would live on. He would continue to provide for Israel's posterity just as he had provided for the patriarch's. Full of faith, Jacob imparted a blessing to each of his sons, beginning with Joseph's.

EPHRAIM & MANASSEH

Jacob blessed his grandsons by invoking Yahweh as a covenant God committed to honoring the promises made to Abraham and Isaac, as a shepherding God who had guided and provided for Jacob "all my life long to this day" (48:15), and as a redemptive angel who had bailed him out of so many trials. Jacob called on this God to bless his grandsons with the covenant promises. Later, he asked that Ephraim and Manasseh become paradigms or "outstanding examples of divine blessing"[7] (48:20).

---

6. Ibid., 637.

7. Wenham, *Genesis 16–50*, 466.

In many ways, Joseph's two sons indeed took his place among the tribes of Israel. Here, Jacob predicted that Ephraim would become greater than his older brother. In the first census taken after the Exodus, the tribe of Ephraim numbered 40,500 to Manasseh's 32,200 (Num 1:33, 35). Strangely, this reality is reversed a generation later (Num 26:34, 37)—scholars point to an obscure story in 1 Chr 7:20–23 as the possible cause. But it is a very significant fact that, in the second census, the combined tribes of Ephraim and Manasseh outnumbered those of Reuben and Simeon. In his farewell address to Israel on the banks of the Jordan, Moses referred to the "thousands of Manasseh" and the "ten thousands of Ephraim" (Deut 33:17). When it came time to dole out land-allotments in Canaan, Joshua (himself a man of Ephraim, Num 13:8, 16) found it difficult to accommodate all of Joseph's many children (Josh 17:14–18); if you consult a map, you can see just how enormous the territories of Ephraim and Manasseh really were.

During the Judges period, Ephraim became quite powerful, even to the point of their developing a little hypersensitivity (Judg 8:1; 12:1). During the divided monarchy, the tribe became synonymous for the entire northern kingdom of Israel (e.g. Isa 7:9; Jer 31:9; Hos 5:3; 7:1).

REUBEN

Jacob acknowledged Reuben as the true firstborn, but then rebuked him for his character. Reuben lost the double inheritance due him (1 Chr 5:1) because he had committed adultery with his father's concubine (35:22). Consequently, Jacob called him "unstable as water" (49:4); the root of the Hebrew translated "unstable" is later used in the OT to describe a "reckless" mob (Judg 9:4). The phrase indicates that Reuben had acted "in an irresponsible, impetuous manner, casting off all moral restraint."[8]

Jacob's anger is palpable in this scene. He had had such high hopes for his firstborn, but he turned to the rest of his sons with repulsed horror at the end and exclaimed, "He went up to my couch!" (49:4). Jacob's switch to the third-person was damning and distancing from Reuben; it is "one of the fiercest denunciations in Genesis."[9] Solomon would later claim, "A man who takes part in adultery has no sense; he will destroy himself. He will be beaten up and disgraced, and his shame will never go away" (Prov 6:32–33 NCV). A single

---

8. Sarna, *Genesis*, 333. Kidner calls Reuben "a man of ungoverned impulse," (*Genesis*, 216).

9. Wenham, *Genesis 16–50*, 471.

moment of indiscretion, whether motivated by ambition or passion, had cost Reuben "an eternal blessing."[10]

The prophecy that Reuben's tribe would "not have preeminence" indeed came true. The composite biblical picture of the tribe is certainly not positive. In the wilderness, two of the leaders in Korah's rebellion against Moses—Dathan and Abiram—were Reubenites (cf. Num 16; 26:5–10); "it is likely that their actions involved an attempt to reassert the declining influence of Reuben among the tribes."[11]

The tribe settled in Canaan on the eastern bank of the Jordan along with Gad and half of Manasseh, but they never produced a prophet, judge, or king. They apparently ignored the call of Deborah and Barak to fight against the Canaanites (Judg 5:15–16). Some argue that the tribe maintained their distinct identity until Assyria deported the northern kingdom (cf. 1 Chr 5:26), but other evidence suggests that the tribe began to fade as early as Saul's reign. David's census (2 Sam 24:5–6), as well as the Moabite Stone (c. 9th century B.C.), both mention Gad, but not Reuben. It is suggested that some catastrophe (possibly a Moabite attack during Ehud's day) devastated the tribe, and that they subsequently "merged with the tribe of Gad."[12]

SIMEON & LEVI

Given Reuben's demotion, Simeon and Levi were next in line to receive the firstborn birthright. But they too were dismissed as a result of their "violence" at Shechem (34:25), the same word used in 6:13 to describe God's reasons for the Flood. Here, Jacob consequently distanced himself from Simeon and Levi as he had from Reuben.

The Hebrew *mekera*[13] is translated "swords" in this passage because of its similarity to the Greek *machaira*, but it's difficult to believe that a Greek word made its way into Hebrew this quickly. Further, the normal Hebrew term for "sword" (*hereb*) is used in 34:25–26, but not here. One writer, however, makes

---

10. Waltke, *Genesis*, 606.

11. Wright, "Reuben," DOTP 692.

12. Roland de Vaux, *The Early History of Israel*, trans. David Smith (Philadelphia: Westminster, 1978), 579.

13. It must be noted that, despite the subsequent discussion, Sarna (*Genesis*, 334), echoes most scholars by concluding, "Any translation of this unique word is guesswork."

an intriguing case for this term to be translated "circumcision knives," as in "their circumcision knives are weapons of violence" (cf. 34:24–26). It is argued that *mekera* is derived from the Hebrew *karat*, meaning "to cut," which appears in Exod 4:25 to denote circumcision.[14]

As it turned out, the tribes of Simeon and Levi were indeed scattered throughout the land of Israel, but in different ways and for very different reasons. At the first wilderness census, the tribe of Simeon numbered at 59,300, but sank to only 22,000 a generation later (cf. Num 1:23; 26:14). The tribe's involvement in the immorality at Peor is assumed to have been the reason (Num 25:1–14; cf. Ps 106:28–31). This may also explain why Moses did not mention the tribe in his farewell blessing (Deut 33). When it came time to portion out the land of Canaan, Simeon was given a small allotment within Judah's territory (Josh 19:1, 9). From that point on, the tribe's role in Israel's history was largely insignificant.

The tribe of Levi, on the other hand, redeemed itself. At Sinai, they sided with Moses in the golden calf episode and were in turn given the honor of the priesthood (Exod 32:28–29). The tribe did not receive a territorial allotment in Canaan (Num 18:20; Deut 10:9), but they were apportioned 48 cities throughout Israel (Num 35:7).

JUDAH

The lengthiest part of Jacob's last will and testament applies to Judah, the one who would eventually assume rule over all Israel, though Joseph was the leader of the tribe at the time. The imagery of this blessing is rich; Jacob alludes to a lion, a scepter, a staff, a donkey, a vine, wine, and milk. Originating here is the popular phrase "lion of Judah," considered to be "a metaphor of strength, daring, and unassailability."[15] Jacob specifically promises that Judah would triumph over fleeing enemies, that he would rule over the other tribes, and that such a position "shall not depart ... from between his feet" (49:10). "Feet" (Hebrew *regel*) can be a euphemism for genitals (Judg 3:24; 1 Sam 24:3), so the phrase probably means "someone from Judah['s seed] will always be on the throne" (49:10 NCV).

But while it is clear that Judah will reign supreme, the second half of 49:10 has proven controversial to translate, let alone interpret. Most agree that the statement is messianic in tone, but disagree as to how. Opinions abound: "until

---

14. Mitchell J. Dahood, "MKRTYHM in Genesis 49,5," *CBQ* 23 (1961): 55.

15. Sarna, *Genesis*, 336.

tribute comes to him" (ESV), "until he to whom it belongs shall come" (NIV), or "until Shiloh comes" (NKJV). The NIV may be the best option since it resembles the Hebrew text of Ezek 21:27. If this is so, "it" modifies "scepter" and "ruler's staff."[16]

It will help to know that the English word "until" leaves us with an impression the Hebrew term does not. In its other four occurrences elsewhere in the OT (26:13; 41:49; 2 Sam 23:10; 2 Chr 26:15), the term signifies a climax;[17] English speakers, however, often use "until" in the sense of cessation (e.g. "I won't stop until I drop"). This means we are left with Jacob prophesying that Judah would dominate the nation of Israel, a dominance that would climax in the coming of the one to whom the scepter belonged (i.e. Christ). For whatever reason, it would be through Judah, not Joseph, that God would bless the world with the gift of his Son.

Jacob envisioned for Judah both dominion and abundance. Prosperity in the OT was often portrayed in terms of a surplus harvest (cf. Lev 26:3–5). Jacob prophesied that Judah would prosper so much that his descendants could tether a donkey to a fruitful branch and not care if the animal ate of the produce;[18] so abundant would the grape harvest be that he could wash his clothes in wine! Incidentally, that latter image may be just as much one of terror for Judah's enemies (cf. Isa 63:2–3) as it is one of prosperity for Judah's descendants.

That Judah dominated the rest of Israel almost goes without saying. The tribe was the largest in both censuses in the wilderness (Num 1:27; 26:22), and they held the privileged position of being camped just to the east of the Tabernacle (Num 2:3). They were first to bring their gift to the Tabernacle (Num 7:12), and first in procession whenever Israel broke camp (Num 10:14). Beginning with David's ascendancy, one of his sons sat on the throne until Nebuchadnezzar deported the southern kingdom to Babylon (cf. 2 Sam 7:16). Another of David's descendants, Zerubbabel, led the Jews out of exile and served as their first governor (cf. Ezra 2:2; Hag 1:1; Matt 1:12).

But Judah's dominance and the establishment of David's throne "forever"

---

16. Mathews, *Genesis 11:27–50:26*, 895.

17. Walton, *Genesis*, 715.

18. Waltke (*Genesis*, 608) calls this "a hyperbole of tremendous prosperity. No one but an incredibly wealthy individual would tether a donkey to a choice vine, for the donkey would consume the valuable grapes." But the award for best comment on this verse goes to Hamilton, who compares tying a donkey to a rich vine to "lighting a cigarette with a dollar bill," (*The Book of Genesis: Chapters 18–50*, 662).

found their ultimate fulfillment in Christ (Heb 1:8), the son of Judah (Matt 1:2), who anticipated the reception of a glorious throne in the world to come (Matt 19:28). Even now, though he is the ascended Lord exalted to God's right hand, we anticipate with longing the day when the King of kings "will tread the winepress of the fury of the wrath of God the Almighty" (Rev 19:15), cause every knee to bow to him (Phil 2:10), and receive "the obedience of the peoples" (49:10). With a roar, the Lion of Judah "shall speak peace to the nations; his rule shall be ... to the ends of the earth" (Zech 9:10), "and he shall reign forever and ever" (Rev 11:15).

What a day, glorious day, that will be.

ZEBULUN

The blessing on the tribe of Zebulun is rather odd; their land-allotment in Canaan never bordered Galilee or the Mediterranean (cf. Josh 19:10–16). In fact, virtually the entire Mediterranean coast in Israel lacks a natural harbor—when Solomon built a fleet of ships, their port was at Ezion-geber on the Red Sea (1 Kgs 9:26). So why did Zebulun receive a maritime blessing?

One suggestion is that, though Zebulun never geographically touched the sea, the Philistines and Phoenicians (whose capital was Sidon) employed several men from the tribe in sea trade. The tribe certainly lived near enough to the coast to profit from maritime activity.[19] An international trade route leading to the coast passed through Zebulun's territory. Perhaps this is what Moses envisioned when he said Zebulun (and Issachar) would "feast on the abundance of the seas, on the treasures hidden in the sand" (Deut 33:19 NIV).

Further mention of Zebulun in the OT is positive. They readily answered Barak's call to oppose the Canaanite threat (Judg 4:10; 5:14, 18), as well as Gideon's summons to ambush the Midianites (Judg 6:35). They supplied David with 50,000 experienced, well-equipped, and deeply loyal troops (1 Chr 12:33). The tribe's greatest honor in Scripture, however, was foretold in her darkest hour. When Tiglath-pileser III deported the tribe of Zebulun (along with the rest of Israel) to Assyria, Isaiah prophesied that contempt would give way to glory, that light would shine in the darkness: the land of Zebulun and Naphtali would one day be home to the ministry of the Lord Jesus Christ (Isa 9:1–2; cf. Matt. 4:12–17).

---

19. This interpretation is strengthened by Waltke's note (*Genesis*, 609) that the Hebrew preposition rendered "by" (49:13) can also mean "near" (cf. NCV).

ISSACHAR

For the second time while blessing his sons, Jacob used animal imagery. Issachar is said to be "a strong donkey" (49:14) at rest between... And this is where it becomes confusing. English translations render the Hebrew *mishpetayim* variously as "sheepfolds" (ESV) and "saddlebags" (HCSB). Which is it? In the word's only other occurrence (Judg 5:16), the meaning is almost certainly "sheepfolds." But it's also possible for the word to mean saddlebags,[20] and that translation seems best here given the context. The Carmel and Gilboa mountain ranges did surround Issachar's land-allotment in Canaan like two saddlebags.[21]

The larger issue, however, is whether Jacob's prophecy was meant to praise or criticize Issachar. Scholars lean toward the latter;[22] "Issachar is supposedly castigated for exchanging independence for the self-satisfied serfdom of Canaanite domination."[23] The tribe was eventually granted the Jezreel Valley that separated Samaria from Galilee. A main highway connecting Babylon with Egypt passed through the Jezreel, but instead of exterminating the Canaanites in the region, Issachar settled down wherever it could and was thus subjected to "forced labor," at least until the revolt led by Deborah and Barak.

Not much else is mentioned about the tribe of Issachar in the rest of Scripture, though they did contribute a judge (Tola, Judg 10:1) and two kings (Baasha and Elah, 1 Kgs 15:27; 16:8). In David's day, the tribe was known for her "men who understood the times and knew what Israel should do" (1 Chr 12:32).

DAN

In the wilderness, the tribe of Dan was quite large, second only to Judah (Num 2:26; 26:43), and in Jacob's blessing, it enjoyed the favored place of seventh in line. But the tribe eventually dwindled in size. Only one son is attributed to Dan (46:23), and in his genealogies, the Chronicler gives the tribe no mention whatsoever. Whenever Israel traveled towards Canaan, Dan was at the end of the line (Num 10:25). What is more startling is Dan's absence from Revelation's list of the tribes of Israel (Rev 7:5–8). That the tribe would be essentially omitted from the commonwealth at some point in the future may

---

20. HALOT 2:652.

21. Walton, *Genesis*, 716.

22. Hamilton, *The Book of Genesis: Chapters 18–50*, 667; Waltke, *Genesis*, 610.

23. Joel D. Heck, "Issachar: Slave or Freeman? (Gen 49:14–15)," *JETS* 29 (1986): 386–95.

explain why Jacob prayed that Dan be "one of the tribes of Israel," i.e. that Dan would always be numbered among the tribes.

One has to wonder if the decline of Dan was due to its tendency to intermarry among the neighboring nations (Lev 24:10–11; Judg 14:1–2), which was clearly prohibited (Deut 7:3). If so, Dan's decline is a warning that we cannot expect to retain God's blessing while ignoring his will.

According to Jacob's imagery in 49:17, Dan would be like a small snake biting a large horse, "his strength will be greater than his size."[24] The tribe's most glorious moment was Samson's career as a judge, his guerilla tactics decimating the more powerful Philistines. But with these menacing neighbors on their southern border, the tribe failed to completely conquer their territory (Judg 1:34–35), and they eventually relocated to the northern region of Canaan (Josh 19:47; Judg 18).

It is therefore no wonder that Jacob's blessing of Dan is punctuated with an appeal to God's deliverance (49:18), an appeal that only a father could make on behalf of his son. With so many threats lying before Dan (and for that matter, all of Jacob's sons), how could he possibly survive without divine intervention?

GAD, ASHER, & NAPHTALI

The future allotment of Gad lay east of the Jordan, and the tribe was often raided by its neighbors, including the Ammonites (Judg 11:4–5; 1 Sam 11:1), Moabites,[25] Arameans, (1 Kgs 22:3; 2 Kgs 10:32–33), and Assyrians (2 Kgs 15:29). But Gad's military was a formidable threat (1 Chr 5:18; 12:8; cf. Deut 33:20). Jacob's blessing, then, warns that the tribe would have more than its fair share of skirmishes, but it would also experience more than its fair share of victories, though (like Dan) such victories would come by means of guerilla tactics.

Asher's descendants settled in a very fertile area west of Galilee and north of Mount Carmel (Josh 19:24–31), running all the way to Phoenicia, one that proved quite prosperous for the tribe (Deut 33:24). Their provision of "royal delicacies" is supposed by most scholars to indicate the tribe furnished food for early Canaanite rulers until these pagan kings were vanquished by Barak and Deborah (Judg 4–5).

Jacob's blessing of Naphtali has proven impossible to interpret. Not only

---

24. Hamilton, *The Book of Genesis: Chapters 18–50*, 670.

25. According to the Moabite Stone, the Moabite king Mesha boasted that he had ransacked the Gadite town of Ataroth (2 Kgs 3:4–5; cf. Num 32:34) and captured their tribal chief, Arel (ANET 320).

can scholars not agree on a proper translation of the Hebrew,[26] but even when a correct translation is determined, coherent interpretation appears elusive. Is Jacob's comment to be taken positively or negatively? At this point, we simply don't know for sure. One alternative pictures Naphtali as a free-roaming deer that eventually settles down to birth fawns in a fold, meaning the tribe would exchange "her original freedom for a later more sedentary domesticated lifestyle."[27] The other alternative follows the LXX translation of 49:21, opting for "oak" instead of "doe," and imagines Naphtali as a great tree that puts down deep roots and prospers (cf. Ps 1:3).

Those who take Jacob's words negatively speculate that they allude to the time when Naphtali would consent to co-existence with the Canaanites instead of expelling them (Judg 1:33). They were subsequently oppressed by the Canaanites until the tribe, led by native son Barak and prophetess Deborah, won a decisive victory.

For the record, if on his deathbed my father had compared me to "a doe … that bears beautiful fawns" (49:21), I would have required years of intense therapy to overcome it.

JOSEPH & BENJAMIN

This is, far and away, Jacob's most eloquent blessing. Judah was arguably promised the greatest of riches (i.e. Christ), but when he blessed Joseph, Jacob's affection for his favored son became very evident. Scholars and translators are torn between whether 49:22 should be understood as an animal or vegetable metaphor: "Joseph is a fruitful vine" (49:22 NIV) or "Joseph is the foal of a wild donkey" (NLT)? Most English translations render it as the latter, but scholars persuasively point to a couple of factors, including: a vegetable metaphor seems out-of-place in a chapter full of animal imagery, and in light of 49:23, an animal metaphor makes sense—why would archers be shooting at a plant? There are also linguistic and textual reasons for preferring this interpretation, but such are too technical and complicated to be discussed here.[28]

What is very clear, however, is that Jacob anticipated for his favorite son

---

26. Hamilton lists no less than six possibilities (*The Book of Genesis: Chapters 18–50*, 676).

27. Wenham, *Genesis 16–50*, 483.

28. Wenham calls the blessing of Joseph "an exegete's nightmare," (Ibid., 484). For an extended discussion of the issue, see Hamilton, *The Book of Genesis: Chapters 18–50*; 678–84; Wenham, *Genesis 16–50*, 484–85.

divine deliverance from all of Joseph's enemies. His brothers had tried "bitterly" to do away with Joseph, but Jacob knew they had not been successful due to God's power and provision. These two perceptions of God force their way into Jacob's blessing: God is "the Mighty One," "the Shepherd," and "the Stone of Israel" (49:24). Jacob boasts that this blessing on Joseph would be greater than the one given to Abraham and Isaac, and that nothing in heaven or below the earth could negate it as long as God showed Joseph such favor (cf. Rom 8:38–39). With this blessing, Joseph, "who was once separated from his brothers through spite is now separated from his brothers by blessing."[29] In his farewell address, Moses echoed this blessing (Deut 33:13–17).

Jacob cryptically called Benjamin "a ravenous wolf," a metaphor that is typically interpreted as predatory, and that description is spot-on for Benjamin's tribe since their territory "became an arena for wars."[30] It was a Benjamite, Ehud, who assassinated Eglon (Judg 3:15–30), and the tribe also joined Deborah and Barak against the Canaanites (Judg 5:14). Later in the Judges period, their army of 26,700 massacred 40,000 enemy troops in two days of bloody civil war (20:14–25). Men of Benjamin were known to be "mighty warriors" with bows and slingshots (1 Chr 8:40; 12:2), but their prowess in battle was due to God's favor and benevolent providence (cf. Deut 33:12), something they lost on the third day of civil war against their Israelite brothers (Judg 20:26–36).

GENESIS 49:29–50:26

His sons now blessed, Jacob made them swear they would bury him in the cave of Machpelah, the family cemetery. This dying wish reflects a major theme in Genesis—the Promised Land of Canaan belongs to Abraham's descendants. Anywhere else, including Egypt, is only a temporary stop. It had been a tremendous act of faith when Abraham had purchased a small plot of land in order to bury Sarah; Jacob maintained that faith with his dying request.

It is touching that, for his eternal resting place, Jacob specifically asked to be beside Leah (49:31), the wife he had loved less, and not Rachel. Had Jacob grown more affectionate for Laban's oldest daughter over the passing years? Was theirs always a loveless marriage?

This scene marks a remarkable consummation to Jacob's life. For much

---

29. Hamilton, *The Book of Genesis: Chapters 18–50*, 686.

30. Sarna, *Genesis*, 345.

of his early existence, Jacob had resorted too often to his own sufficiency and too little to God's providence. To scorn God's gracious providence is to scorn his great promises. But on his deathbed, Jacob declared his confidence in those promises. And because the God of his fathers had been faithful to him in death (46:4), Jacob responded in kind. The patriarch's redemption was complete.

For those that could afford it, mummification was a common practice in Egypt that held great religious significance. Temple priests would remove the body's internal organs and soak it in embalming fluid for forty days; the organs themselves were sealed in containers and buried with the body.[31] Concerning the afterlife, Egyptian theology maintained that the corpse was the repository of the soul.[32] Jacob's body was mummified per the custom of Egypt, but note that it was Joseph's personal physicians, not the priests, that performed the procedure, meaning the act held no religious significance to Jacob's family.[33] That the Egyptians mourned Jacob's passing for 70 days is significant; according to the Greek historian Diodorus, 72 days was the customary period of mourning for Pharaoh (*Histories* 1.72).

After receiving permission from Pharaoh[34] to bury Jacob in Canaan, Joseph led the funeral procession to the cave of Machpelah. As is still the case today, the amount of pomp and circumstance over a person's passing signified their importance (cf. 2 Chr 21:20), so the sight of so many Egyptian dignitaries and officials making this journey to pay their final respects had to have been an impressive one. It is remarkable to think that Abraham had been a wealthy, but comparatively unremarkable, nomad from Ur. The death of his grandson, however, was memorialized by a veritable Who's Who of Egypt. God was fulfilling

---

31. The forty-day mummification process was in stark contrast to the rest of the ANE, where burial typically took place within 24 hours (Arnold, *Genesis*, 385–86).

32. Walton, *Genesis*, 720.

33. Sarna, *Genesis*, 347.

34. McKeown (*Genesis*, 191) observes the oddity of Joseph having to make this request of Pharaoh's household rather than of Pharaoh personally (cf. 47:1). Is Joseph's influence diminishing? McKeown may be making much of little; Sarna argues that it's a simple case of a mourner being unclean to enter the king's presence (Gen Rab 100:4; cf. Esth 4:2). But it is widely known that there did come a time when Egypt's Pharaoh knew not Joseph (Exod 1:8), and Sarna ultimately acknowledges that Joseph's request "hints at something of a deterioration in the situation of the Israelites in Egypt," (*Genesis*, 348).

his promise to Abraham: "I will bless you and make your name great" (12:2).[35]

Waltke's summary of Jacob's legacy bears repeating in full:

> This scene concludes Jacob's finest hour. On his deathbed—a scene extending from 47:28 to 49:32—Jacob has assumed total and dynamic leadership of the family. Even Joseph bows down to him. Jacob gives the double blessing to the deserving firstborn son of the wife he loves, not to the detestable firstborn of Leah. With prophetic insight, he crosses his hands against even Joseph the traditionalist. Without wavering, he looks forward to Israel's divine destiny in the land of promise. Renouncing even his love for Rachel, his last words instruct his sons to bury him with his unloved wife so he can rest in faith with his fathers.
>
> At the beginning of the act he comes trepidly to Egypt, not for its riches, comforts, and security, but out of love for a son. While showing great respect and sensitivity to Pharaoh, he never bows his knee to the Egyptian but instead, as the greater, blesses the lesser. Isaac's old age shamed his youth, but Jacob's redeems his, just as Judah's heroic self-sacrifice redeems his tragic beginnings.
>
> All honor Jacob in his death. Joseph and his brothers mourn their father's death and faithfully carry out his instructions to bury him in the ancestral grave. The Egyptians mourn him for two and half months as they would mourn their king. The skilled physicians embalm him for forty days, and the most senior dignitaries both from Pharaoh's own court and from the whole empire bear Jacob's body homeward from Egypt to Canaan in a grand and grave funeral cortege. With these details the narrator asserts Jacob's true redemption and exaltation.[36]

Returning to Egypt, Joseph's brothers worried his forgiving spirit had been a ruse all along, and they sought his forgiveness for the first time. They acknowledged their betrayal as "sin," "evil," and a "transgression." The brothers likely put words in daddy's mouth in a self-serving manner (50:17), and

---

35. Walton, *Genesis*, 720.

36. Waltke, *Genesis*, 617.

sadly, that can happen in families when a loved one passes: "Daddy wouldn't have wanted you to…" or "Your mother would have wanted you to…"[37] But the brothers were carrying a lot of guilt because sin haunts the offender for a very long time—forgiving self is often the most difficult forgiveness to grant. Note that they dared not identify themselves to Joseph as his "brothers," but as "servants of the God of your father."

Joseph's response in 50:19–20 stands, not only as the perfect summary of Genesis, but also as a shadow of how the rest of human history would unfold with God at the helm. At the beginning of Genesis, Adam and Eve attempted to erase the line distinguishing God from man (3:5–6); here, Joseph refused to cross that line, acknowledging that some things belong to God alone[38] (cf. Deut 32:35; Rom 12:19). Joseph understood that life is not a series of unfortunate events, but rather events that unfold under the sovereign watch of God. At times, it requires tremendous faith to believe this truth, but God will never allow an event to occur that he cannot use to glorify himself and redeem our brokenness. "Through sinful men God works out his saving purposes."[39]

Exhibiting remarkable perspective, Joseph assured his brothers that he would use his position of influence to care for them and their families—the use of "I" in 50:21 is emphatic in the Hebrew, for "Joseph was promising something more personal than philanthropy."[40] Such a response on Joseph's part can only be borne within the heart of one absolutely confident that God is in control, that God is crafting a wondrous story of redemption and grace.

Joseph himself was able to see the births of his great-grandchildren, which in the ANE was considered proof of immense divine blessing (Job 42:16; Ps 128:6) or, secularly, great fortune.[41] Joseph lived to the age of 110, considered

---

37. Considering the close bond Jacob and Joseph had enjoyed, it is difficult to imagine that Jacob never broached this subject with him. But on the remote chance Jacob's words were authentic, the concern of Joseph's brothers is arguably legitimate; "the loss of an authoritative, restraining father might have threatened the cohesion of a family in which brothers had so wronged another," (Waltke, *Genesis*, 617).

38. Hamilton, *The Book of Genesis: Chapters 18–50*, 705.

39. Wenham, *Genesis 16–50*, 490.

40. Kidner, *Genesis*, 224. Sarna again notes that this may indicate a deteriorated relationship between Israel and Egypt since the famine had ceased twelve years prior (*Genesis*, 350).

41. The mother of Babylonian king Nabonidus claimed, "I saw my great-great-grandchildren, up to the fourth generation, in good health and (thus) had my fill of old age," (ANET 561).

by ancient Egyptians to be an ideal age, though most Egyptians did not live past forty or fifty.[42]

My dad was a preacher for my entire life, and I often heard him conclude his sermons in this way: "I don't know your family doctor, but if I were to ask him, I would probably be told that you will eventually die. What will happen? If you are lucky, the preacher will say a few nice things about you, but then they will take you to the cemetery, dig a six-foot hole in the ground, bury you, return to the church building or somebody's house, and eat potato salad and fried chicken. You will be gone, and the only thing that will matter is whether you died in a right relationship with God. Only you can decide whether you will die in Christ."

One of the final articles my dad penned before his death was a eulogy for a beloved friend who had passed away unexpectedly in July 2004. Steve Pope was a good man who loved children, loved his family, and loved the Lord. Steve was a teacher at the local middle school, and he served as an elder and preacher in the Lord's church.

In fact, Steve passed away while preaching the funeral of a man he had recently baptized into Christ. No sooner had he warned the audience that death could call our name at any moment than Steve collapsed from a blood clot and died. He had been speaking of how life is a vapor (Jas 4:14), and his own vanished in mid-sentence before he could complete the thought. A few days later, my father had a part in preaching Steve's funeral. And when, in the article, my dad talked about Steve and how much he would be missed by those who knew him, he concluded with this exhortation to the reader: "Let us all be reminded that death is certain for all of us and that we ought to live in such a way that we can 'die in the Lord' for our family's sake!"[43]

No one but God knew that my dad would also pass from this life unexpectedly less than a month after writing that article. Like Steve's family, mine was also grateful that dad had died in the Lord. That very fact enabled me to grieve as one with a great hope. We buried dad next to Steve under a Mississippi oak tree and returned to the place where the family was to be fed. As I walked in, I noticed potato salad and fried chicken awaiting us on the table.

---

42. ANET 414; Walton, *Genesis*, 721.

43. Daniel Whitworth, "Died Preaching a Funeral," *MM* 26, no. 4 (August/September 2004): 11.

I couldn't help but smile.

Yes, many fine things had been said about my father at his funeral. Yes, he had now been buried in a six-foot hole. And yes, he was gone. Everyone dies. But he had died in Christ. And in Christ, death has no victory. Side by side, my dad and Steve await the great resurrection promised to the people of God. And what a day, glorious day, that will be.

As I age, I pray that the last thing I forget is God's faithfulness and goodness to me as one so unworthy. I pray that, as did Jacob, I exhort my family to trust in the Lord with all their heart and commit their future to him, for God holds their future in his hand anyway. I pray my family will know beyond any doubt that my death does not mean the death of God's promises, of God's providence, of God's love for them. I pray that, when their time comes, my children will take their place among the tribes of spiritual Israel.

And I pray that I die in the Lord for my family's sake.

The Book of Beginnings closes on a note pregnant with expectation. "Joseph said to his brothers, 'I am about to die, but God will visit you and bring you up out of this land to the land that he swore to Abraham, to Isaac, and to Jacob.' Then Joseph made the sons of Israel swear, saying, 'God will surely visit you, and you shall carry up my bones from here'" (50:24–25). So confident was Joseph of Israel's eventual return to Canaan that he made his tribe swear to it.

In the intervening years, Israel's confidence in God would be severely tested by slavery. Yet their faith would be nurtured by generations of Hebrew parents who rocked their children to sleep with stories of God's faithfulness to Abraham, Isaac, and Jacob. In so doing, Israel looked forward to a time when God would choose a forgotten desert shepherd to resume an incredible story of redemption and grace—

A story known as the Epic of God.

TALKING POINTS

In Christ, death has no victory. But it is indeed a cruel master, and the OT portrays it in not so flattering terms. It is depicted as a fleeing shadow (Job 14:2), "the journey of no return" (Job 16:22 NCV), "the king of terrors" (Job 18:14), and a "return to the dust" (Ps 104:29 NIV). The Bible's most iconic and memorable image is John's depiction of death as a rider astride a pale horse (Rev 6:8). But even though the passing of a loved one causes immense grief as it did for Jacob's family, Christians have been promised that death is not the end. In light of the Resurrection, "Death has been swallowed up in victory" (1 Cor 15:54 NIV). There is no reason, therefore, why our family and friends should have to grieve so painfully when we pass from this life. As Jacob and Joseph exhorted their tribe to trust in God, encourage your family to do the same. Live a life of faith so that they are not forced to grieve as those who have no hope (1 Thess 4:13). Die in Christ for their sake, for in Christ, death has no victory.

Guilt can be as powerful a force as death. "Very often the barriers put up by those who have been most to blame are the hardest to remove."[44] More than seventeen years after coming to Egypt, Joseph's brothers still were haunted by their selling him into slavery. They were painfully aware of the suffering they had caused. Even in Gen 50, they could not bring themselves to be completely honest, preferring instead to hide behind the sacred cow of their dead father's moral authority. God does not want us to feel any more guilt than is necessary to drive us into his arms—"Godly sorrow brings repentance that leads to salvation and leaves no regret, but worldly sorrow brings death" (2 Cor 7:10 NIV). God is not in the guilt-business because guilt imprisons; his grace liberates (John 8:36). And the only way that grace can free us from the prison of guilt is for us to own up to our sins. Joseph's brothers finally did that in Gen 50, and as far as we can tell, healing finally took place in their hearts. Perhaps one of the promises of God you have yet to put your faith in is the one of 1 John 1:9. "If we confess our sins, he is faithful and just to forgive us our sins and to cleanse us from all unrighteousness." If God has forgiven us, how are we not also obligated to do the same?

---

44. Baldwin, *The Message of Genesis 12–50*, 219.

EPILOGUE

Joseph's life ends with Genesis' final words, but his story does not. He requested that he be buried in the land of his fathers instead of Egypt. "God will surely come to your aid and take you up out of this land to the land he promised on oath to Abraham, Isaac and Jacob" (50:24 NIV).

However, Israel languished in Egypt for four more centuries. Generations of Hebrews lived and died wondering if they would ever return to the land promised to father Abraham. How many mothers rocked their children to sleep with stories of the patriarchs? How often did fathers remind their families about God's past faithfulness? At what point did the Hebrews consider Joseph's coffin little more than a creepy, dusty relic of a bygone era?

How close did Israel come to abandoning hope?

We too are in the midst of our own sojourn in Egypt. Satan appears strong, for he is the prince of this world (John 16:11). Sin so often seems our master, and a tyrannical one at that. The burning sun of trial and trouble saps our spiritual strength. We comfort ourselves with tales of a bygone era; we remind ourselves (sometimes half-convincingly) that this world is not our home, that we are citizens of another country (Phil 3:20) destined for a Promised Land. We long for God to come to our aid, to deliver us from our suffering with a mighty hand and an outstretched arm, to lead us beyond the Jordan where faith shall become sight.

How close have you come to abandoning this common hope?

I suppose that's why, when I read Josh 24:32, my eyes tear up a bit. "Joseph's bones, which the Israelites had brought up from Egypt, were buried at Shechem in the parcel of land Jacob had purchased from the sons of Hamor, Shechem's father, for 100 qesitahs. It was an inheritance for Joseph's descendants" (HCSB).

After more than four centuries of oppression, exodus, wandering, and conquest, Israel made their home in the land sworn to father Abraham, and Joseph's dying wish was honored by his posterity. Faith had become sight (Heb 11:22). Hope had become reality.

God had been faithful.

And just as he was faithful to the patriarchs of Genesis, God will be faithful to us. He has sworn that he hears the cries of his people (Rev 6:10–11), that he will visit us and come to our aid (2 Thess 1:6–10). "Surely I am coming soon" (Rev 22:20). All of creation groans in expectation of the day when God's narrative is not ended, but gives way to another story of endless glory and praise. On a not-so-distant day, Jesus, the Seed of woman and Lion of Judah, will return with a roar. Satan, sin, and suffering will be banished forever, and "we will rest in the fair and happy land … with Jesus evermore."

What a day, glorious day, that will be.

ABBREVIATIONS

ABD   *The Anchor Bible Dictionary.* Ed. David Noel Freeman. 6 vols. New York: Doubleday, 1992.

ANE   Ancient Near East(ern)

ANET   *Ancient Near Eastern Texts Relating to the Old Testament.* Ed. James B. Pritchard. 3rd ed. Princeton, NJ: Princeton Univ. Press, 1969.

ASTI   *Annual of the Swedish Theological Institute*

BA   *Biblical Archaeologist*

BASOR   *Bulletin of the American Schools of Oriental Research*

BBR   *Bulletin for Biblical Research*

CBQ   *Catholic Biblical Quarterly*

CEV   *Contemporary English Version*

DOTP   *Dictionary of the Old Testament: Pentateuch.* Eds. T. Desmond Alexander and David W. Baker. Downers Grove, IL: InterVarsity Press, 2003.

EQ   *Evangelical Quarterly*

ESV   English Standard Version

ExpTim   *Expository Times*

Gen Rab   Genesis Rabbah, a rabbinical commentary on Genesis

GNT   Good News Translation

HALOT   *The Hebrew and Aramaic Lexicon of the Old Testament.*

	Ludwig Koehler, Walter Baumgartner. Trans. and ed. M. E. J. Richardson. 4 vols. Leiden: Brill, 1994–1999.
HCSB	Holman Christian Standard Bible
HTR	*Harvard Theological Review*
IEJ	*Israel Exploration Journal*
ILR	*Israel Law Review*
ISBE	*The International Standard Bible Encyclopedia*. Ed. G. W. Bromiley. 4 vols. Grand Rapids: Eerdmans, 1986.
JAOS	*Journal of the American Oriental Society*
JBL	*Journal of Biblical Literature*
JETS	*Journal of the Evangelical Theological Society*
JNES	*Journal of Near Eastern Studies*
JSOT	*Journal for the Study of the Old Testament*
JTS	*Journal of Theological Studies*
KJV	King James Version
LXX	Septuagint, the Greek translation of the Old Testament
MM	*Magnolia Messenger*
MSJ	*The Master's Seminary Journal*
Msg	The Message
NAB	New American Bible
NASU	New American Standard Bible — Updated Edition
NBD	*New Bible Dictionary*. 3rd ed. Downers Grove, IL: InterVarsity Press, 1996.
NCV	New Century Version
NIDOTTE	*New International Dictionary of Old Testament Theology and Exegesis*. Ed. Willem A. VanGemeren. 5 vols. Grand Rapids: Zondervan, 1997.
NIV	New International Version, © 2011
NJB	New Jerusalem Bible
NKJV	New King James Version

NLT	New Living Translation
NRSV	New Revised Standard Version
NT	New Testament
OT	Old Testament
ResQ	*Restoration Quarterly*
TDOT	*Theological Dictionary of the Old Testament.* Eds. G. J. Botterweck and H. Ringgren. Trans. J. T. Willis, G. W. Bromiley, and D. E. Green. 15 vols. Grand Rapids: Eerdmans, 1974–.
TynBul	*Tyndale Bulletin*
VT	*Vetus Testamentum*
WTJ	*Westminster Theological Journal*
ZAW	*Zeitschrift für die alttestamentliche Wissenschaft*
ZIBBCOT	*Zondervan Illustrated Bible Backgrounds Commentary: Old Testament.* Vol. 1. Ed. John Walton. Grand Rapids: Zondervan, 2009.

ACKNOWLEDGMENTS

Coffee will shave a few years off of my life, but this book would not have been written without it. So I want to express my sincere kudos to the fine staff at Starbucks in Franklin, TN, Tyler, TX, and Houston, TX for serving up the delectable nectar of the gods.

I also want to express my gratitude:

To countless friends and family who, over the course of four and a half years, prayed for the successful completion of this project. I truly felt the power of your faithful intercession.

To Billy and Gwen Alexander. Friends like you make easier the life of faith.

To Tim and Pam Ashley. Until I cross Jordan, I have every intention of honoring the many kindnesses done by your family for mine.

To Shirley Eaton and Wade Osburn of Freed-Hardeman University's Loden-Daniel Library. Shirley, you perform an invaluable service by fetching many an article for me. From a grateful Hittite, thanks for finding needles in haystacks. Wade, you always put your hands on exactly what I'm searching for, even when I have little idea of what it is I need.

To Dr. Ralph Gilmore. You answered my many questions with remarkable grace, patience, and wisdom. I have learned a great deal from your instruction and example. Thank you.

To Josh James, Rebecca Thompson, Pam Ashley, and Lindsay Kelly for superb editorial work.

To Jeff and Laura Jenkins. You both have taught me so much about what it means to live by faith. Jeff, you believed in this project when I did not. Thank you for penning such a fantastic *Foreword*. By far, it is the best part of this book.

To Dr. Jay Lockhart. Your counsel and encouragement came at a pivotal moment in the life of this project, and for that I am immensely grateful.

To Dr. Jesse Robertson. It was in your course "Survey of the Old Testament" where I realized that the church has too-often misunderstood or neglected three-fourths of her canon. For this, and many other lessons, thank you.

To Skippy DIL. You deserve so much better; I deserve so much worse. Forever and always, I love you with all my heart.

To my mom. Deep and strong has been your commitment to my spiritual education. May your name echo with those of all the righteous matriarchs of Israel.

To my dad. When I was a little boy, I first heard about these ancient heroes of faith from your lips. Today, though dead, you are my hero because of your faith. Thank you for such a rich heritage.

Finally, to יהוה, the God of my fathers—the Friend of Abraham, the Fear of Isaac, and the Mighty One of Jacob. Thank you for creating, blessing, and saving me. May this book and its human errors—typos, split infinitives, and rogue apostrophes—bring you much praise. S.D.G.

BIBLIOGRAPHY

Arnold, Bill T. *Genesis*. Cambridge: Cambridge Univ. Press, 2009.

Baldwin, Joyce G. *The Message of Genesis 12–50*. Downers Grove, IL: Inter-Varsity Press, 1986.

Brueggemann, Walter. *Genesis*. Louisville: John Knox, 1982.

Calvin, John. *Commentaries on the First Book of Moses Called Genesis*. 2 vols. Trans. John King. Grand Rapids: Eerdmans, 1948.

Coffman, James Burton. *Commentary on Genesis*. Abilene, TX: ACU Press, 1985.

Hamilton, Victor P. *The Book of Genesis: Chapters 1–17*. Grand Rapids: Eerdmans, 1990.

—. *The Book of Genesis: Chapters 18–50*. Grand Rapids: Eerdmans, 1995.

Henry, Matthew. *Commentary on the Whole Bible*. Vol. 1. New York: Revell, 1970.

Hughes, R. Kent. *Genesis*. Wheaton, IL: Crossway, 2004.

Kidner, Derek. *Genesis*. Downers Grove, IL: Inter-Varsity Press, 1967.

Maclaren, Alexander. *Expositions of Holy Scripture: Genesis*. Grand Rapids: Baker, 1978.

Mathews, Kenneth A. *Genesis 1–11:26*. Nashville: Broadman, 1996.

—. *Genesis 11:27–50:26*. Nashville: Broadman, 2005.

McKeown, James. *Genesis*. Grand Rapids: Eerdmans, 2008.

Roop, Eugene F. *Genesis*. Scottdale, PA: Herald, 1987.

Ross, Allen. "Genesis" in *Cornerstone Biblical Commentary: Genesis, Exodus*. Carol Stream, IL: Tyndale House, 2008.

Sarna, Nahum M. *Genesis.* Philadelphia: Jewish Publication Society, 1989.

Von Rad, Gerhard. *Genesis.* Philadelphia: Westminster, 1972.

Waltke, Bruce K., and Cathi J. Fredricks. *Genesis.* Grand Rapids: Zondervan, 2001.

Walton, John H. *Genesis.* Grand Rapids: Zondervan, 2001.

Wenham, Gordon J. *Genesis 1–15.* Dallas: Word, 1987.

—. *Genesis 16–50.* Dallas: Word, 1994.

Youngblood, Ronald F. *The Book of Genesis.* 2nd ed. Grand Rapids: Baker, 1991.

—, ed. *The Genesis Debate.* Grand Rapids: Baker, 1990.

ὥσπερ ξένοι χαίρουσι πατρίδα βλέπειν
οὕτως καὶ τοῖς κάμνουσι βιβλίου τέλος

www.ingramcontent.com/pod-product-compliance
Lightning Source LLC
Chambersburg PA
CBHW050232270326
41914CB00033BB/1881/J